MORE ADVANCE PRAISE FOR
KINGDOMS OF FAITH

"Mediterranean studies have been shaped in an informative and innovative way by Brian Catlos's contributions in the recent decades. His incursion now into the history of a specific region and polity—that of al-Andalus (Medieval Iberia under Muslim rule)—brings to the fore the same qualities that characterize his previous work: an inquisitive and incisive mind that homes in on perceptive questions, combined with the ability to recreate past events in an appealing manner for a wide audience."

—Maribel Fierro, research professor at the Institute of Languages and Cultures of the Mediterranean, CSIC (Madrid)

"*Kingdoms of Faith* constitutes a fresh and original contribution to the history of al-Andalus, rooted in the author's profound knowledge of medieval Iberian history. Brian Catlos has managed to produce a very well-written and lively narrative that provides an up-to-date synthesis of the most recent developments in this field of history."

—Alejandro García Sanjuán, University of Huelva

ALSO BY BRIAN A. CATLOS

Infidel Kings and Unholy Warriors:
Faith, Power, and Violence in the Age of Crusade and Jihad

The Muslims of Medieval Latin Christendom: c. 1050–1614

The Victors and the Vanquished:
Christians and Muslims of Catalonia and Aragon, 1050–1300

KINGDOMS
OF FAITH

A New History of Islamic Spain

BRIAN A. CATLOS

BASIC
BOOKS

New York

Basic Books
Hachette Book Group
1290 Avenue of the Americas, New York, NY 10104
www.basicbooks.com

Printed in the United States of America
First Edition: May 2018

Published by Basic Books, an imprint of Perseus Books, LLC,
a subsidiary of Hachette Book Group, Inc. The Basic Books name and logo
is a trademark of the Hachette Book Group.

The publisher is not responsible for websites
(or their content) that are not owned by the publisher.

Library of Congress Cataloging-in-Publication Data
Names: Catlos, Brian A., author.
Title: Kingdoms of faith : a new history of Islamic spain / Brian A. Catlos.
Description: 1 | New York, N.Y. : Basic Books, 2018. | Includes bibliographical references and index.
Identifiers: LCCN 2017045534 | ISBN 9780465055876 (hardback) | ISBN 9780465093168 (ebook)
Subjects: LCSH: Spain—History—711–1516. | Spain—Civilization—711–1516. | Muslims—Spain—History. | Spain—Civilization—Islamic influences. | BISAC: HISTORY / Europe / Western. | RELIGION / Islam / History. | HISTORY / Medieval. | HISTORY / Europe / Spain & Portugal.
Classification: LCC DP102 .C38 2018 | DDC 946/.02—dc23
LC record available at https://lccn.loc.gov/2017045534

ISBNs: 978-0-465-05587-6 (hardcover), 978-0-465-09316-8 (ebook)

LSC-C

10 9 8 7 6 5 4 3 2 1

For Peter Vladimir Catlos (1923–2013)

and

Dzintra Lia Catlos née *Liepinš (1928–2004)*

In seed time learn,
in harvest teach,
in winter enjoy.

—WILLIAM BLAKE

Contents

A Note on Names, Places, and Dates

Readers will have to contend with many strange and foreign-sounding names in this book. Arabic (and Hebrew) names consist of several elements, normally a first name and a series of patronymics (e.g., *ibn* for "son of" or *bint* for "daughter of," in Arabic), as well as titles, honorifics, and other components relating to place of origin or residence, profession, clan, tribe, or accomplishment. A given individual might be referred to by any of these. For example, the caliph 'Abd al-Rahman III was 'Abd al-Rahman ibn Muhammad ibn 'Abd Allah al-Nasir li-Din Allah. He is typically referred to as "'Abd al-Rahman" or "al-Nasir" (but never "'Abd" or "Rahman"). The "III" is a modern addition; rulers were not typically referred to numerically in this era. The patronymic can function like a surname, particularly if it relates to an ancestor regarded as illustrious or the founder of the family. For example, 'Ali ibn Ahmad ibn Sa'id ibn Hazm is usually referred to as "Ibn Hazm." His larger family might be known as the "Banu Hazm" (the sons, descendants, or clan of Hazm).

Latin Christian names can also be confusing, if only because of the propensity for certain ones to become popular at certain times, making for proliferations of Alfonsos, Pedros, and Sanchos that can drive even a seasoned medievalist to distraction. To alleviate some of the potential frustration, I have usually used the form of each name that corresponds to the individual's region of origin or identification. Hence, an Alfonso from Castile or León is "Alfonso," from Portugal, "Afonso," and from Catalonia, "Alfons." The names of the Arista family are given in Basque; as per convention, Castilian versions are used for their successors as rulers of Pamplona and Navarre. Exceptions are made for the names of popes, for individuals who have standard names in English, and for some minor characters. Thus, you will encounter Count Julian, Charlemagne, Pope Innocent III, Thomas Aquinas, and the emperor Charles V.

In order to help keep track of the myriad individuals, groups, and non-English terms, a table of Umayyad caliphs and a table of Nasrid sultans are provided at the end of the book, together with a glossary that lists the main dynasties, clans, and ethnic groups, as well as other foreign vocabulary.

A SIMPLIFIED FORM of Arabic transliteration has been used. Special characters have been avoided, and both *hamza* and *'ayn* are represented by a single quotation mark. The suffix -*un* or -*in* is a frequent plural form, while the suffix -*i* can turn a noun into an adjective (e.g., the Shi'a faith versus a Shi'i imam).

REGARDING PLACE-NAMES, the general rule I have followed is to refer to places by the name used by their modern inhabitants. So, you will read of Córdoba, Zaragoza (as opposed to Saragossa), and Lleida (as opposed to Lérida). Exceptions are made for some places that have a standard name in English, such as Seville (Sevilla), Fez (Fas), or Mecca (Makka). The Arabic names of places in al-Andalus are provided in parentheses, normally the first time they appear in the text.

ALL DATES IN the text are provided in the calendar of the "Common Era" (BCE/CE), an adaptation of the Christian Gregorian calendar (BC/AD) that superseded the Julian calendar in 1582. It is based on a solar year of 365.25 days that begins on January 1 and is counted from the notional birth year of Jesus (now reckoned at 4 BCE). In the Visigothic calendar, years were counted from 38 BCE, the beginning of formal Roman dominion over Hispania. Known as the "Spanish era," this was phased out between the twelfth and fourteenth centuries in favor of the Julian calendar, which reckoned from the time of Christ (AD or *Anno Domini*, "in the year of Our Lord"). In early Catalonia, dates sometimes used the old Roman reckoning of the indiction, or the regnal years, of Holy Roman Emperors. Using the Julian system, the new year was often counted from March 25, the presumed date of Jesus's conception, until January 1 eventually returned as the standard.

The *hijri*, or Islamic calendar AH, has a year of twelve lunar months counted from July 16, 622 CE, which is the date associated with Muhammad's departure for Medina (the *hijra*) and is held to mark the foundation of the Muslim *umma*. Because the *hijri* year is shorter than the solar year, they do not exactly coincide. Therefore, unless a definite, single date is referred to, one *hijri* year is usually indicated as spanning two Common Era years; for example, 720 AH is 1320/21 CE. It was not uncommon for Muslims in formerly Christian-ruled lands to also use the Christian calendar, particularly in contexts relating to agriculture, given that it consistently corresponded to the seasons.

INTRODUCTION

The front line of a "clash of civilizations"; a foreign incursion on European soil; the theater of *Reconquista*, crusade, and Holy War; or a land of multireligious tolerance and *convivencia*—the history of Islamic Spain has been recounted many times, in many ways. Typically, the narrative begins with the arrival of the commander Tariq ibn Ziyad on the shores of Christian Spain in the year 711 and his dramatic defeat of its Visigothic rulers. Under the rule of Arab Umayyads, al-Andalus—Islamic Spain—blossoms. In this period Muslims, Christians, and Jews live here in concord, turning al-Andalus into a cosmopolitan Arabo-Islamic society, and making Córdoba, "the ornament of the world," a magnet for scholars and scientists and a model of cosmopolitan enlightenment. Shortly after 1000, the empire collapses, and al-Andalus is fought over by crusading Christians seeking to "reconquer" Spain and by puritanical Berbers who persecute Christians and Jews. As the Christians triumph, the Muslims are corralled in the kingdom of Granada, the final enclave of Islam in Spain. This endures until 1492, when the "Catholic Kings," Fernando and Isabel, conquer it, sending its defeated king, Boabdil, into exile, bringing to a close the history of al-Andalus and ushering in an age of intolerant oppression.

What almost all these histories share is the presumption that religion was at the heart of this history—that the Muslim and Christian principalities engaged in a contest defined by their religious identity and ideology. Christianity, Judaism, and Islam are seen as

1

protagonists in an operatic history, battling it out on the stage of the centuries. Reinforcing their supposed civilizational differences, Christians and Jews are presented as "Europeans" and Muslims as foreign "Moors." It is a perspective that invites nostalgia and moralizing, and it is appealing precisely because of its melodramatic oversimplifications.

But as history, it has serious limitations. First, the roots of Islamic Spain must be sought not in 711, or even 622, when Muhammad struck out from Mecca, but in the broader world of the Mediterranean of Late Antiquity, of crumbling empires and encroaching "barbarians." This was an era when Christianity, Judaism, and Islam, each diverse and divided, were only beginning the gradual processes of self-definition, processes in which they remained very much entwined. Nor can the end of Islamic Spain be pegged to January 1, 1492, when Boabdil handed over the keys of the Alhambra to Fernando and Isabel. Hundreds of thousands of Muslims remained in Spain until 1614, suffering discrimination, forced conversion, and eventually, expulsion. As for the Muslim conquest of al-Andalus, it was not part of a deliberate campaign of world domination and holy war. Its causes were complex and spontaneous, and it was driven as much by opportunity as by ideology. Likewise, the ideas of reconquest and crusade were later developments and invoked only occasionally when it suited the agendas of Christian powers. The era from 711 to 1492 was not a time of unremitting religious conflict; the Muslims and Christians of the peninsula spent more time at peace than at war and as much time fighting among themselves as against each other. Christian rulers did not typically expel the Muslims from the lands they conquered but tried to entice them to remain. And for the most part they did, choosing to live in their ancestral lands as subjects of infidel kings.

As for the Moors: the word refers to the inhabitants of Mauritania, the old Roman name for the area the Arabs would call al-Maghrib ("the West"), and which includes most of what is now Morocco and Algeria. People of this region were called *Mauri* by early Latin chroniclers, and this word emerged in the Spanish vernacular as *moro*. Eventually, *moro* simply came to mean "Muslim" in Castilian Spanish, although in English the word took on the additional, racialized baggage of the Elizabethan-era "Blackamoor"—the dark-skinned, African outlaw. The problem with using "Moor" or "Moorish" to refer to Muslims of medieval Spain is that it implies they were foreigners and ethnically distinct from the native population. In fact, relatively few foreign Muslims came to the Iberian Peninsula. Al-Andalus became Islamic through conversion, and the overwhelming majority were of indigenous descent—they were no more foreign and no less European than the Christians of Spain.

Of course, "Spain" itself is a misnomer when applied to the medieval period. The nation of Spain and its culture of today are modern, not medieval, phenomena. If the unity Spanish national culture presumes is ephemeral even today, in the Middle Ages it simply did not exist. For this period, it is better to say "Spains" when referring to Christian-ruled principalities. When "Spain" is used in this book it refers simply to the Iberian Peninsula—what the Visigoths and their Roman predecessors called Hispania, and what the Arabs called al-Andalus (probably a corruption of the Visigothic *landahlauts*, or "inherited estate"). In other words, the very use of the term "Moorish Spain"—an anachronistic Anglo-American invention—invites a racialized, romanticized, Orientalized, and inaccurate view of the history of al-Andalus and of Islam on the peninsula, one that has fed misconceptions and nurtured misrepresentations of this chapter of European history. The concept of "Europe" is equally thorny. It too is a modern concept. Like Muslims, who defined their larger sphere as the *dar al-Islam* ("the realm of Islam"), European Christians thought of themselves as living in "Christendom," not "Europe," and certainly not as "Europeans."

Sorting fact from tendentious myths and conjecture is crucial, for Islamic Spain not only is an important element in the history of the Mediterranean world, of Europe, of Islam, and of the West, but also remains of great significance today. Many politicians and public figures—and not a few scholars—continue to view the history of the West as one of a conflict between two fundamentally incompatible civilizations: a Christian (or, very recently, Judeo-Christian) one, and an Islamic one. This view exercises tremendous appeal because of both its simplicity and its self-validating quality, and it is often invoked by pundits and demagogues of all stripes as a justification for aggression and repression. For others, al-Andalus presents an idealized vision of premodern enlightenment that we in today's supposedly less tolerant world should emulate. But this too is a mirage. In Spain itself, right-wing politicians continue to draw on the ethos of *La Reconquista*—a potent national myth that conveniently justifies the domination of Castile over the other regions of the peninsula, even as tourist boards promote a sanitized vision of Spain as "the land of the three religions" and of Christian-Muslim-Jewish harmony.

There are good reasons for emphasizing the importance of religious identity in this history, starting with the rather obvious fact that we refer to Islamic Spain as "Islamic Spain." Religious identity was, in many circumstances, the most important way in which people conceived of themselves. It dictated which legal regime they came under and—in theory—whom they could marry or have sex with, the professions they could practice, their social and economic status, what taxes they owed, what clothes they could wear, the foods they could eat, and all sorts of other details of daily life. There are many historical sources, both Christian and Muslim, that present this history as one of religiously fueled conflict, beginning with the earliest Latin and Arabic accounts of the conquest and continuing through the emergence of the tradition of Saint James "the Muslim Killer" (Santiago Matamoros), the *Reconquista*, the legend of the Cid, and the appeal to *jihad* by various Muslim rulers. Many of the wars were consecrated as Crusades by the papacy, and a half-dozen military orders, dedicated in principle to fighting the infidel, were founded here. Ordinary Muslims might serve as *mujahidun*, stationed in fortress-monasteries that dotted the frontier zone, whereas in Christian Spain, raiding became so much a way of life that historians have characterized it as a "society organized for war."

That said, people are far too complex to be reduced to living caricatures of their religious ideologies. Religious identity was only one means by which individuals imagined their place in the world. They saw themselves also as members of ethnic groups, subjects of kingdoms, inhabitants of towns and neighborhoods, members of professions and collectives, seekers of knowledge, customers and clients, men and women, lovers and friends. And more often than not, these bonds of association bridged or overcame affinities individuals shared on account of religious orientation. Moreover, in a society divided formally by religion, one's rivals and competitors, whether in personal, political, or financial matters, were typically members of the same faith community; consequently, one's natural allies were often members of other groups. Conflict was waged more within these faith communities than between them. Thus, this is also a history rife with episodes of cross-religious and cross-ethnic solidarity; of alliances and friendships, whether of kings or commoners, that were forged between the faiths; and of collaborations carried out among poets, musicians, artists, scholars, scientists, and theologians of different religions.

However, these cross-religious relationships rarely make it into the historical narrative. Part of the problem is the nature of our sources. Most of our written evidence was produced by rulers, bureaucrats, and men of religion—wealthy, privileged males, who were themselves extraordinarily invested in the notion that religious identity was the foundation of society, and who also had vested political and personal interests in portraying history as a moral struggle between the followers of the true religion (that is, their own) and everyone else. In formal terms, the authority of rulers rested on their ability to present themselves as the legitimate upholders of the divine order, and so they tended to express their agendas in the language of faith. In an era in which people generally attributed the workings of the world to the will of God, historical events were often explained in religious terms, as God's reward or punishment.

At the same time, the chronicles and histories that historians use as their data, and that constitute much of our surviving evidence, were written or compiled many years, often centuries, after the events they describe. As a result, they are distorted by hindsight, as well as by the prejudices, ideals, agendas, memories, aspirations, and convictions of their authors. Moreover, histories were not written as education or entertainment; they were political documents, intended to support the claims of the rulers, families, or individuals by glorifying

the memory of their predecessors and establishing historical prece-
dents for their policies. Exaggeration, distortion, and invention were
deployed both consciously and unconsciously by medieval writers as
they set out to describe the past to justify the present.

One of the jobs of the historian, then, is to assess the biases and
inaccuracies built into these sources and to attempt to uncover the
reality behind the proclamations, myths, legends, errors of fact, con-
tradictions, and carefully crafted historical fictions that make up the
record. The goal is to determine what really made people tick and
what forces truly shaped events—even when the details can never be
definitively established. The historian should not assess guilt, appor-
tion blame or virtue, or moralize; the aim is merely to understand.
Thus, no book can claim in good faith to be the "definitive," "true,"
or "real" history of Islamic Spain; there are simply too many factors
to account for and too many uncertainties clouding the past. As enlightened and self-critical as we may be, historians today are not that
much less vulnerable than our medieval counterparts to bias and presumption. Whether we realize it or not, we tend to write histories that
reflect and reinforce our own ideals or play to those whom we see as
our constituencies.

As for the present book, it represents a "new history" of Islamic
Spain in two senses. First, rather than following the well-worn sto-
ryline of the rise and fall of al-Andalus, I have set out to build a fresh
narrative from the ground up and have tried, as much as the economics of publication has permitted, to get behind the scenes and examine
dynamics that are often obscured but are crucial in the formation of
history: the stories of women, slaves, renegades, and functionaries.
Second, I have based this study largely on the tremendous amount of
innovative scholarship that has been carried out in recent years, particularly by scholars from Spain, North Africa, and Europe. Our understanding of al-Andalus has been transformed by new studies of
texts, archaeology, and art history, but much of this has not yet reached
English-speaking readers.

And finally, there is the question of faith. Both the Muslim and
Christian principalities of the medieval Spains were consciously defined by their religious orientation, and for their constituents, religious

community was the primary pole around which they constructed their social identity. But it was not the only one. And for much of this history, most of the rulers—and most of their subjects—often behaved in ways that defied the mandates of their religious ideologies. So, just how faithful were they? The answer, of course, is that they were no more or less faithful or idealistic than we are. They were people burdened by imperfections and plagued by self-contradiction, people capable of both great cruelty and tremendous generosity, of selfishness and of sacrifice, and of self-serving rationalization; ultimately, they were prisoners of their bodies, their ambitions, their vanities, and their appetites. In short, they were like us, and this is precisely what makes this history worth reading today.

PRELUDE

The Beginning of Islam and the End of Antiquity

Islam originated in the Arabian Peninsula of the early seventh century, a marginal and largely inhospitable desert region populated by tribes of nomadic herders and oasis dwellers. Yet the Arabs had long been a presence in the antique world of Rome and Persia. Traders and herders had journeyed north for centuries, settling in Syria and Mesopotamia on the margins of and within the Roman/Byzantine and Persian empires. Like other peripheral "barbarian" peoples, they were attracted to the wealth and culture of the great empires and were valued as warriors and traders. Both empires used Arab tribes as proxies in their struggle against each other, and Bedouin nomads had driven their herds throughout the Near East for centuries.

The traditional religion of the Arabs combined paganism and animism, but through contact with the imperial world, Christianity and Judaism penetrated the peninsula. Neighboring Axum, in Ethiopia, had been Christian since the fourth century; the Arab kings of Himyar, in Yemen, had converted to Judaism in the 400s; and some clans of the Arabian peninsula identified as either Christians or Jews. Within this environment, indigenous, monotheistic traditions began to develop, culminating in the emergence of Islam in the early 600s—

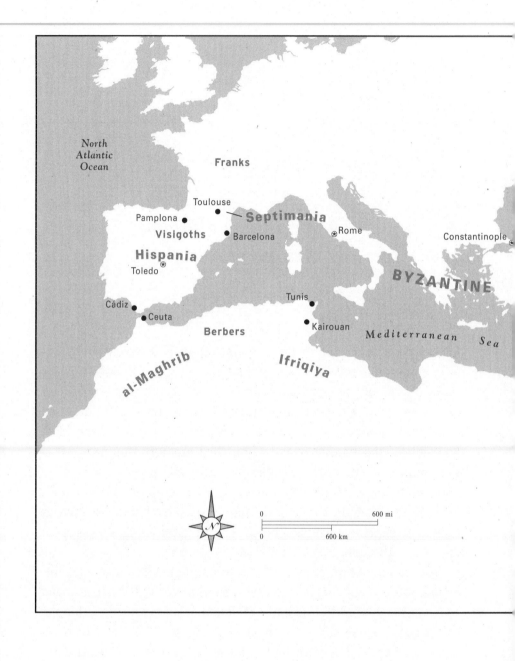

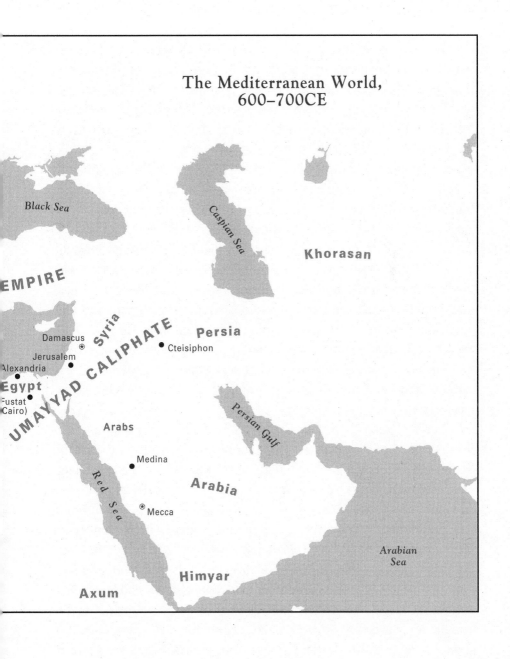

The Mediterranean World,
600–700CE

Black Sea

Caspian Sea

Khorasan

EMPIRE

Damascus

Jerusalem

Alexandria

Egypt

Fustat
(Cairo)

Syria

UMAYYAD CALIPHATE

Cteisiphon

Persia

Persian Gulf

Arabs

Medina

Arabia

Red Sea

Mecca

Arabian
Sea

Himyar

Axum

a consequence of the divine revelations received by Muhammad ibn 'Abd Allah ibn 'Abd al-Muttalib ibn Hashim, a merchant from Mecca. The *hijra*—Muhammad's departure from Mecca, where he was persecuted and under threat by the city's rulers, to Yathrib (or Medina) in June 622—marks the beginning of the Islamic era. In 629 he returned in triumph, purging the holy precinct, the Ka'aba, of its idols and accepting the conversion of the Quraysh, Mecca's leading tribe (and his own).

Muhammad saw himself not as starting a new religion but as the last in the line of prophets who worshipped the one true God, beginning with Adam and continuing through Abraham and Jesus. This accounts in part for the ambivalent relationship Islam had with its sister religions from the outset. The fact that Christians and Jews did not recognize Muhammad as a prophet provoked frustration; nevertheless, both Christianity and Judaism were regarded by Muslims as legitimate, if mistaken, interpretations of the worship of the One God, the God of Abraham—whether called Yahweh, Kyrios, Deus, or Allah. Under Islamic rule, these non-Muslim communities lived as *dhimmis* ("protected peoples"), secure in their property and free to follow their laws and religion as long as they acknowledged the superior authority of the Muslims.

On a religious level, Islam strove for a return to a pure monotheism, stripped of unnecessary ritual, and to create a just and peaceful society that reflected the will of God as revealed in Arabic to Muhammad in the Qur'an. The guiding principle was surrender of one's will to God; indeed, this is the meaning of "Islam." It was to be a religion with no hierarchy, no clergy, and no monks, and in which members of the *umma*, or "people," were each responsible for their own salvation. Its simplicity was summed up in the brevity of the *shahada*, or declaration of faith: "There is no god but God, and Muhammad is the messenger of God." To create this just world, Islam focused on the regulations needed to create a stable community. This was crucial in a society that had no formal government and in which a culture of vengeance contributed to disorder and anarchy. At the same time, Islam emphasized personal morality and the rewards and punishments of the afterlife. Arabs were in the grips of the same millenarian impulses as contemporaneous Jews and Christians in the Mediterranean world; there was widespread conviction that the end of the world was imminent and that a new age of postapocalyptic justice was nigh—a sentiment the military successes of the early Muslims seemed to confirm.

Islam also developed as an ethnic movement. Despite its universal claims, Arabic was understood to be the language chosen by God, and Arabs had a sense of themselves as a sort of "chosen people." Their folk beliefs, traditions, and mores strongly informed Islam in its earliest, formative period. Moreover, it was the warrior culture of the Bedouin that enabled Islam to pour forth from the peninsula and to quickly dominate the lands around it. Still, the Arabs were hardly a unified people; indeed, as is typical of nomads, individualism and independence were considered high virtues. The new Muslim society was meant to efface previous divisions of class, clan, and tribe, but instead the factionalism that characterized Arabic society, and even the family of the Prophet himself, came to be expressed in the language of religion.

Islam was thus at once a framework for unity and a platform for divisiveness and conflict. In contrast to Christianity, which developed as a secretive, persecuted cult, Islam was a social and political movement from the outset, and this shaped its internal development and its relations with other religions. The struggle to do good (*jihad*) could be expressed in improving both oneself and the larger world. The virtue of the warrior became a moral virtue, and in a self-justifying dynamic, the warfare meant to bring the world the opportunity to live under God's rule also drove the conquests that enriched and empowered the Arab clans and positioned them as the new earthly elite.

Had Muhammad lived a century earlier or later, Islam might never have developed as it did, or perhaps at all. The early seventh century happened to be a pivotal point in the history of the Mediterranean and Near Eastern world. The Roman Empire, disintegrating from within and beset by barbarian attacks from without, had crumbled in the west. In the east, the efforts of emperors to force religious and political unity on their subjects had left many of the empire's subjects embittered and resentful. In Persia, the unity of the empire was undermined by religious and class tensions, fueled by the resistance of provincial governors to the central authorities.

Arabia itself was in crisis. Popular satisfaction with the traditional animist and pagan religious traditions seems to have been slipping, and some tribes in the interior began to identify as Christian or Jewish. Thus, Muhammad's message—as the last Prophet of the God of Abraham—was a potentially attractive and not unfamiliar claim. Islam's emphasis on social justice also found a ready audience, as did its focus on the coming Day of Judgment. Crucially, once the rulers of the oases and the warriors of the nomadic tribes came to realize that Islam could empower and enrich them, they became enthusiastic adherents of the new faith. Thus, at the precise moment when Byzantium and Persia were most vulnerable, the Arabs were gaining strength. The centuries in which they had settled in and fought on behalf of the two empires laid the groundwork for their swift conquest of the Roman Near East and the whole Sassanian Empire. But this would not take place until after the death of Muhammad in 632.

The death of the Prophet provoked a crisis that foreshadowed later tensions—notably between leading clans of the Quraysh, who controlled Mecca and were intent on holding onto power, and the early supporters of Muhammad, based at Medina, who chose 'Ali ibn Abi Talib as his successor. 'Ali was not only an early convert and intimate of the Prophet; he was also Muhammad's cousin and the husband of his daughter Fatima. However, 'Ali was young and had a narrow base of support, and so the Meccan elite prevailed and established the leadership of the community under a caliph (from *khalifa*, or "successor"), initially chosen from among themselves. 'Ali did not resist, and the first three universally recognized, or "Rightly Guided," caliphs— Abu Bakr, 'Umar ibn al-Khattab, and 'Uthman ibn 'Affan—were all prominent members of the Quraysh and of Muhammad's inner circle, the Companions of the Prophet. Under their rule, Islamic dominion expanded quickly, extending over Syria and Palestine, Egypt, and eastern Ifriqiya (modern Libya), as well as most of the defeated Persian Empire and parts of Anatolia and the Caucasus. In this period Islamic law began to take shape: the Qur'an was standardized; the office of the *qadi*, or Islamic magistrate, was instituted; and the *hijri* (Islamic) calendar came into use.

When 'Uthman was assassinated in 656, 'Ali's supporters in Mecca quickly had him declared caliph, prompting the Umayyad family to accuse them of complicity in the murder and to claim the election was invalid. Mu'awiya, the senior member of the Umayyad clan and the governor of Syria, refused to submit. In response, 'Ali's supporters seized Iraq, and the stage was set for a war between the two sides: the Umayyad family and their sympathizers, who backed Mu'awiya, and 'Ali and his followers, who declared him the rightful caliph and *imam* ("prayer leader"). Thus began the first great *fitna*—"strife" or "civil war"—in Islamic history. Attempts at a negotiated settlement failed, and the armies of the two sides met in northern Syria at a site called Siffin on July 26, 657. After a bloody and inconclusive day of fighting, Mu'awiya proposed arbitration as a gambit to buy time and split his opponent's forces. It worked: some of 'Ali's troops left the field, rejecting the validity of any caliphate, claiming that they would recognize no authority but the words of the Qur'an alone, and not any human intermediary. 'Ali was forced now to battle also these Kharijites ("splitters"), one of whom would assassinate him in 661. The fight against Mu'awiya and the Umayyads was to be carried on by 'Ali and Fatima's two sons, Hasan and Husayn, but Hasan chose to abdicate and Husayn was defeated in Iraq by Umayyad forces in 680 at Karbala, where he and his army were massacred, beheaded, and left ignominiously to rot on the field. Husayn's followers recognized him as the true imam, and his martyrdom is a key event in the development of Shi'a Islam (from *shi'at 'Ali*, "the party of 'Ali") as distinct from Sunni ("traditionalist") Islam. With Husayn's death, the Umayyads were victorious, but only for the time being.

From their new capital in Damascus, the Umayyads would hold sway over the expanding *dar al-Islam*, but many Muslims were unhappy with their rule. Mu'awiya was criticized for contravening Arab custom and converting the caliphate into a form of hereditary kingship, and indeed, the Umayyads, who would endure until 750, represented a synthesis of an Arabic clan and a Byzantine dynasty. They tended to style themselves as down-to-earth warriors and men of the people and not get overly involved in matters of faith, even though technically they claimed to hold the highest religious authority. And, although their rule was not necessarily passed from father to son, it was closely guarded within a pool of eligible clan members. The family had strong roots in Syria and a deep affinity for Romano-Byzantine culture, and with the defeat of Persia, it was only Christian Constantinople that seemed to stand between them and world conquest, their destiny. However, their determination to limit power to their family members and clients, and to make Syria their center, exacerbated resentment toward them by Muslims in the former Persian empire and by the religious elite of Arabia.

Under the Umayyads, territorial expansion continued apace. The period saw regular incursions into Byzantine Anatolia and two major but unsuccessful attacks on Constantinople, the first in 674–678 and the second in 717–718. By the late 600s, Byzantium and Damascus had settled into a fragile détente, with periodic treaties and agreements on tribute (to the stronger party) alternating with outbreaks of war. The early Muslims did not set out from the Arabian Peninsula with the intention of conquering North Africa, much less Spain or Europe. According to Islamic historical tradition, the conquest of Egypt—Byzantium's most populous and wealthy province—was undertaken spontaneously in the 640s by 'Amr ibn al-'As with an army of only four thousand men. 'Amr carried out his campaign through a combination of force and coercion, aided by the chaos in the region. There were few pitched battles. Many towns submitted reluctantly when his army arrived at their gates, although in other cases he was forced to defeat meager but sometimes determined Byzantine garrisons.

The conquest of Egypt meant that the Arabs had both the opportunity and the obligation to move further westward. Mu'awiya and his early successors saw themselves in an existential struggle against Byzantium and were determined to conquer Constantinople. In their view, North Africa was an important theater of operations in this larger war. Their ambitions would be aided by the fact that late seventh-century Byzantine Africa, recently recovered from the

Germanic Vandals and under attack from Berbers, was in anarchy. Many of the Romanized citizenry were resentful of Byzantine rule, and within the Byzantine camp there were deep divisions. At one point, a desperate Emperor Heraclius accused Pope Martin I of being in league with the Arabs and had him arrested. In the 640s, a local official, Gregory the Patrician, declared himself emperor and rallied sympathetic Berber and Byzantine factions until his forces were smashed by a Muslim army in southern Tunisia in 647. The Berber tribes, who operated on the periphery of the urbanized coastal lands, were also divided. Some would come over quickly to the Arabs and convert to Islam, adding much needed manpower to the Muslim forces. Others resisted fiercely, such as those under the leadership of the possibly Jewish-identifying Berber "queen" Kahina ("the Sorceress"), who was not defeated until 702.

The Arab conquest of the region dragged out over some sixty years, as much in consequence of conflicts within the fledgling caliphate as of local resistance. After the Arab invasion of the 640s, which captured Tripoli, another was launched in 665. Pushing west into Tunisia under the command of 'Uqba ibn Nafi'—a Companion of the Prophet—the Arabs established the fortress-town of Kairouan as a forward operating base. It soon became the capital of the new province of Ifriqiya ("Africa"). In 698, the Arabs captured and razed the port of Carthage to deprive the Byzantines of a beachhead and established the city of Tunis just inland. Meanwhile, Arab forces, bolstered by Berber clients and converts, pushed westward across the highlands of northern Algeria and Morocco, reaching Tangier on the Atlantic. The fortified city of Septem (Ceuta; Sabta in Arabic) on the Mediterranean coast was Byzantium's last outpost in North Africa. However, the threat of the imperial navy remained, prompting the Muslims to launch an unsuccessful invasion of the Balearic Islands in 708—a naval campaign that must have depended on Byzantine captives, converts, and collaborators, given that the Muslims had little seafaring ability and no ships.

The fitful pace of the conquest of North Africa carried advantages despite the various setbacks. It allowed for gains to be consolidated and for indigenous people to become accustomed to Muslim rule and be gradually incorporated into the Arab military and administration. The divided Christian society of the region was undermined by the destruction of urban centers and isolation from the Byzantine world and went into rapid decline. Jews, who had been the subject of severe legal repressions under the empire, may have reacted with guarded relief now that they were granted legitimate status as *dhimmis* of the Muslims.

The situation of the Berbers was more complex. They did not comprise a united "people"; rather, like the Arabs, the large ethnolinguistic groupings—here, the Sanhaja and Zanata—included tribes and clans who pursued their own independent objectives and did not present a unified front. As they defeated the pagan Berbers, the Arabs incorporated them into the Arabo-Islamic religious and kin framework, and Arab leaders took captured Berber women as wives and concubines. Some or most of the Christian and Jewish tribes may also have converted, although they would not have been forced. For the Berbers, as for the Bedouin of Arabia, Islam provided a religious justification for political ambitions and a morally elevated outlet for the military energies of tribesmen. Religious fervor or ideology was not the motor behind the conquest; this was a process of political expansion little different than that which the Romans and their various barbarian nemeses had engaged in.

In the early 700s, Musa ibn Nusayr, a Syrian Arab and favorite of the caliph al-Walid, was appointed governor of Ifriqiya. Using forces composed almost entirely of Berber converts, he pushed westward and subdued much of Morocco before withdrawing to Kairouan, leaving his native freedman, Tariq ibn Ziyad, at the head of his troops. As his Muslim forces gathered at Ceuta, Tariq would have been able to see the distant peaks of Visigothic Hispania on a clear day. The thin strait, only nine miles across at one point, marked the Greek geographers' Pillars of Hercules. It separated Africa from Europe and provided a natural and well-traveled passage to the prosperous and fertile former Byzantine provinces of Hispania—now unified, but hardly united, under the rule of the Visigothic nobility and bishops of the Latin Church of Rome.

PART I

CONQUEST, 700–820

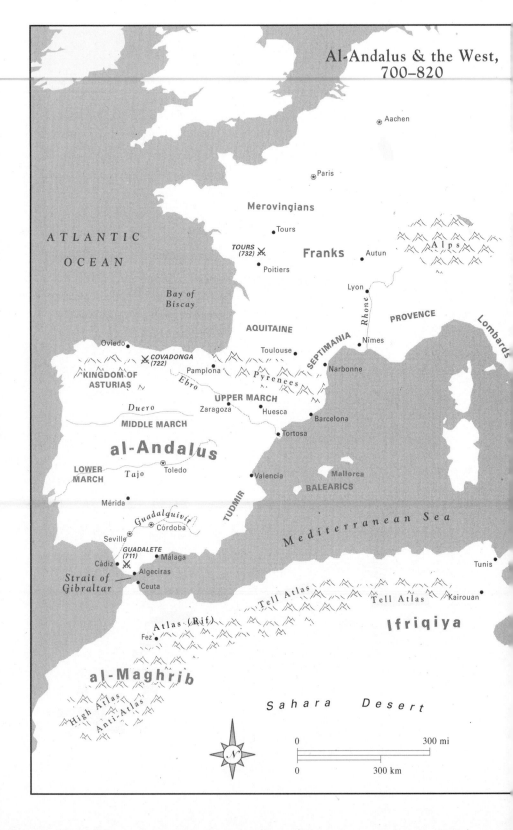

Al-Andalus & the West,
700–820

Aachen

Paris

Merovingians

Tours

TOURS
(732)

Franks

Autun

Alps

ATLANTIC

OCEAN

Poitiers

Bay of
Biscay

Lyon

Rhône

PROVENCE

Lombards

AQUITAINE

Toulouse

SEPTIMANIA

Nîmes

Oviedo

COVADONGA
(722)

Pamplona

Pyrenees

Narbonne

KINGDOM OF
ASTURIAS

Ebro

UPPER MARCH

Huesca

Barcelona

Duero

Zaragoza

Huesca

MIDDLE MARCH

Tortosa

al-Andalus

LOWER
MARCH

Tajo

Toledo

Valencia

Mallorca

TUDMIR

BALEARICS

Mérida

Guadalquivir

Córdoba

Mediterranean Sea

Seville

GUADALETE
(711)

Málaga

Tunis

Cádiz

Algeciras

Strait of
Gibraltar

Ceuta

Tell Atlas

Tell Atlas

Kairouan

Atlas (Rif)

Ifriqiya

Fez

al-Maghrib

Sahara   Desert

High Atlas

Anti-Atlas

N

0   300 mi

0   300 km

I

An Opening

On June 8, 1898, in the windswept desert east of Amman, Alois Musil, a Czech scholar and adventurer, stumbled upon Qusayr 'Amra, a long-forgotten hunting lodge and pleasure palace of the Umayyad caliphs built in the 740s. Inside, he found badly damaged but dazzling Byzantine-style frescoes: naked, cavorting dancers; prancing animals playing musical instruments; a zodiac and star map; and a mise-en-scène featuring six regal figures—the great kings of the world—rendering willing homage to a seated sovereign. Bilingual captions in Greek and Arabic identified the first three as Khosrau, Shah of Persia; the Byzantine "Caesar"; and the "Negus" of Ethiopia. Of the three remaining figures, the name of only one survived, spelled out as "Rodorik" in Greek and "Ludheriq" in Arabic. This was a portrait of the last Visigothic king of Hispania, who was killed in battle by the forces of Tariq ibn Ziyad in 711, but who had been resurrected here, a generation later, acknowledging the glory of the caliph of Islam.

Only thirty years after the Islamic conquest of Spain, the fall of Roderic had already taken on mythical proportions in the Arabic imagination. Al-Andalus was the furthest point west that Muslim forces had reached, in the Arab imagination a distant and exotic land, fertile and overflowing with wealth, and another step in the strangulation of the

Roman Empire. Roderic, the proud king, had become a figure of legend—both disdained and admired. In the various narratives of the conquest, he comes across as a haughty character whose undoing, and that of his people, was a consequence of the sins of pride and lust and of his reckless defiance of the magical powers that had vouchsafed the rule of the Visigoths.

THE CONQUEST OF Visigothic Spain—what the Arabs would call "al-Andalus"—commenced in earnest in April 711 when Musa ibn Nusayr's lieutenant, Tariq ibn Ziyad, gathered his forces and crossed the narrow gap that separated Ceuta and the southern coast of Spain, landing at the rock that would bear his name (Gibraltar, from *Jabal Tariq*, "Tariq's Mountain"). But, he was not taking a leap into the unknown; the previous year he had sent ahead an expeditionary force to conduct reconnaissance raids on the southern tip of the peninsula. Once Tariq's troops, who may have numbered a few thousand light cavalry and infantry, together with their families, had been ferried across, they began to move north toward the urban centers of the Baetis River, which the Arabs would call al-Wadi 'l-Kabir, "the Great River" (the Spanish "Guadalquivir"). At some point inland, they were met by Roderic's army, composed of his household and the men of his loyal magnates. The two armies clashed on the banks of the Wadi Lakku (later, "Guadalete," in Spanish), probably just east of Cádiz (Qadis). Here, in a single day, the fate of the Visigothic kingdom was settled. Roderic's forces were routed and put to the sword, including the king himself. The Arabic word for conquest is *fath* (pronounced "fat-hah"), which also means "an opening up," and after the defeat of the Visigothic army in this single battle, all of Hispania lay open to Tariq.

When word of these events reached Musa ibn Nusayr, the governor of Ifriqiya, he sent reinforcements, and the following year he came over himself, together with his sons 'Abd al-'Aziz and 'Abd Allah. Thus, the conquest of the Visigothic kingdom proceeded much as that of Syria and Egypt. With their defensive capacity all but destroyed, the natives had little choice but to acquiesce, and there were few significant episodes of resistance. As for the Muslims, the challenge was to move as quickly as possible to take advantage of the defenders' disarray, balancing speed with their capacity to maintain control over the territory they had conquered. By 714, Musa and his sons were moving into northern Spain and had overrun the cities on the great central plateau, subduing the towns along the southern slopes of the Pyrenees by 716.

Continuing along the Via Domitia, the ancient Roman highway that linked Cádiz to Rome, Muslim forces crossed the mountains in 717 into Visigothic Septimania—the "land of the seven cities" of Béziers, Elne, Agde, Narbonne, Lodève, Maguelonne, and Nîmes. Just to the west, another barbarian principality, the Duchy of Aquitaine, a dependency of the great Frankish kingdom of the Merovingians to the north, offered organized resistance. To avoid immediately confronting its ruler, Duke Odo (or Eudes), the Arab-led forces raided eastward, arriving at the Rhône River, the border with Provence, in 718. The great river valley was a highway leading north through a string of venerable towns built around cathedrals and monasteries. Following it upriver, the Muslim raiders sacked and temporarily occupied Lyon, and even Autun, far to the north in Burgundy. After, they withdrew to Narbonne (Arbuna), chosen as their local capital for its stout walls, its access to the sea, and its Jewish traders, who could offer logistical support.

The chaotic situation in Septimania aided the Muslims. The surviving Visigothic elite feared Frankish domination, thus the invaders were able to negotiate the submission of local communities. But the Muslims were stretched increasingly thin. Although their forces were augmented by local recruits, they could no longer count on large numbers of Berbers, almost all of whom had settled in Hispania. Nevertheless, they struck west toward Odo's capital of Toulouse, where in 721 they were decisively defeated by the duke.

These events were closely watched by Charles Martel, the mayor of the Merovingian palace and the force behind the Frankish throne. In 732, fate would favor Charles when the governor of al-Andalus, 'Abd al-Rahman al-Ghafiqi, assembled a huge force aimed at crushing Odo. Crossing the Pyrenees, al-Ghafiqi sacked Bordeaux and drove the duke northward before him into the arms of the palace mayor. He continued on, determined to loot the rich Abbey of Saint

Martin at Tours, two hundred miles further to the north and deep in Merovingian territory. But it ended in disaster. Charles, now aided by Odo, met al-Ghafiqi about fifty miles south of their objective (just north of Poitiers), and the Muslim army—overstretched, overburdened, and overconfident—was lured into battle. The result was a resounding victory for the Franks, and many Muslims were killed, including al-Ghafiqi himself. The prestige of this victory was such that Charles, known thereafter as "the Hammer," could have himself crowned king-regent of the Franks in 735. Over the next decades, Charles and his successors would slowly take control over Aquitaine and dislodge the Muslims from Septimania. Subsequently, the victory at the Battle of Poitiers (or Tours) was exaggerated by European historians and became the foundation of the French national myth, with Charles held up as the savior of Christian Europe from Islam. But the attack on Tours was no civilizational clash or campaign of conquest; it was only a raid. Despite their loss, the Muslims remained in the south of France until 736, with the help of Christian allies who opposed the growing power of the Merovingian Franks.

Even as the Muslims were slowly pushed out of Septimania, their hold on the land they called al-Andalus strengthened. It was clear they had come here to stay. For Musa, Tariq, and their troops—whether Arabs, Berbers, or Byzanto-Roman North Africans—al-Andalus, unlike the cool, wet lands north of the Pyrenees, was neither far nor foreign. It had been an integral part of the Mediterranean and Roman world, and the Strait of Gibraltar had always been a natural bridge between the southern and northern shores. Aside from the rainy, mountainous fringe along the northern Atlantic coast, its geography bears a strong resemblance to the Maghrib, Ifriqiya, Egypt, and Syria—a succession of arid plains punctuated by scrubby mountains and crossed by rivers whose waters, if harnessed, can awaken the sunbaked but fertile soil into shimmering, abundant green. Thus, to many newcomers it would have seemed not only familiar but idyllic—a paradise. And that is how al-Andalus quickly came to figure in the Arabo-Islamic imagination.

Yet, the invasion was not one prong of a grand campaign on the part of the caliphate to conquer "Europe," which was at that time a poor and underdeveloped backwater and did not figure at all in the Arabo-Islamic imagination. There may have indeed been vague ambitions to encircle Byzantium, but this would not have represented a tactical strategy for the caliphate. Rulers in this era were rarely positioned to execute complex or long-term operations on the strength of their authority, and the caliphs were no exception. Moreover, not everyone back in the Arabo-Islamic heartland was comfortable with the adventure in Spain. It is said that the caliph 'Umar II (717–720) had contemplated pulling out of al-Andalus altogether, fearing that the Muslims would be too isolated and vulnerable in the cold and distant lands of the far west.

A combination of forces propelled the Arabs and Berbers across the strait and into Spain. Certainly, religion was one. It lent the invaders coherence and determination and the sense that they were participating in a higher moral cause. If these warriors perished on campaign, at least they might die as martyrs. So, there was a feeling, albeit imprecise and inconstant, among both the invaders and the Christians of al-Andalus and Septimania that they were engaged in a religious struggle. This view would have been particularly strong among the Christian clergy, who saw the conquest in providential terms—a scourge of God—and evoked the language of the Old Testament tribulations of Israel to describe their defeat. Many priests, bishops, and monks fled the Muslim advance, taking their churches' treasures and relics with them and heading to the safety of the barbarian kingdoms. Leading the way was Archbishop Sindered of Toledo, who appeared in Rome in 721, having abandoned his flock to its fate.

But religion was not sufficient motivation for such an epic endeavor, and not all of those who crossed the strait were particularly pious. A prime motivation was undoubtedly the desire for treasure. The sparsely defended churches and monasteries of Latin Christendom were repositories for gold, silver, and bejeweled furnishings, all ripe for the picking. This was in addition to the crops, livestock, and people they could carry off. Slaves were a valuable resource, and foreign women were particularly sought-after. In short, many of the invaders, particularly the Arab elite, sought glory and power and the opportunity to turn themselves into the lords of the newly conquered land—ambitions that fit neatly with the moral imperative to extend the *dar al-Islam*.

On the other hand, most of the Berber warriors who provided the manpower of the conquest crossed the strait with their kin with the aim of colonizing the fertile expanses of the peninsula. Once in al-Andalus, however, they too were drawn forward into the vacuum left by the collapse of the Visigothic kingdom and by the allure of abundant and easy riches. So, although the conquest was often presented as a religious endeavor, the process was much more complex. Indeed, Arab chroniclers tended to ground the events in human factors, such as lust, pride, and greed, and even Christian historians acknowledged the conquest could not have taken place had it not been for the many non-Muslims who aided Tariq and Musa, not the least the many enemies Roderic had among the Visigothic nobility.

FIRST AMONG THE non-Muslims who helped the Muslims conquer al-Andalus was the legendary Count Julian. Julian (Yulyan, in Arabic) appears in later histories described as the lord of Septem—the last holdout against Tariq's forces in North Africa, or "the Green Island" (al-Jazira al-Khadra', either Algeciras or Cádiz). He is usually described as a Byzantine governor and is credited with providing Tariq with the ships and the intelligence necessary for his invasion. Certainly, it would be understandable that, in the face of the Muslim conquest of North Africa, the governor of such a lonely Byzantine outpost might cast his lot with the Muslims. But early medieval historians tended to see things in operatic terms and embellished a tale to account for Julian's collaboration and present Roderic as deserving of his fate. Hence, the fable of Florinda.

According to the tale, Roderic had requested that the count send his daughter to be educated in the royal court at Toledo, the Visigothic capital. This was a reasonable request, as this way she would grow up in courtly circles and Roderic would gain a hostage to vouchsafe Julian's loyalty. In any event, it was said that once Roderic laid eyes on the ravishing girl—who eventually came to be known as Florinda, or La Cava (from "fallen woman")—he was overcome by lust and raped her. Word of this outrage soon made its way back to Ceuta, and Julian swore to avenge the honor of his daughter. Thus, for him, Tariq ibn Ziyad's arrival was nothing short of a godsend, and the conquest became a vehicle for a very personal revenge.

But what facts lie behind the story? Julian has been described as a Byzantine official or perhaps a Christian Berber, but the sources are extremely vague. It is just as likely he was a Visigothic nobleman, the lord of Cádiz as well as Ceuta, which would have given him an interest in maintaining links between the peninsula and a North Africa that had come under Muslim control. It is said that as early as 710, Julian lent ships to Tariq to probe the Visigothic kingdom's defenses. The following year, Julian committed fully, putting his fleet at Tariq's disposal and providing intelligence and logistical support, a role he continued in 712 after Musa ibn Nusayr arrived. It was a daring, but astute, betrayal. Julian rose in the esteem of the new rulers and settled in Córdoba after the conquest. After his son converted to Islam, the family's future generations went on to enjoy status and prestige in the court circles of Muslim al-Andalus.

Although the tale of Florinda is almost certainly a complete invention, without Julian, his followers, and those like them, the conquest of al-Andalus would not have been possible. The Arabs of Syria had no tradition of the sea. They depended on the collaboration of conquered peoples to assist in their maritime adventures, as well as for intelligence and direction while on campaign. Just as in the Near East, Arab successes here were as much a consequence of the dissensions among the peoples they sought to dominate as of the Muslims' own unity of purpose. Indeed, further hints of divisions among the Christians and within the Visigothic kingdom can be found in another legend that centers on the figure of Roderic, this one involving a locked chamber and an ancient curse.

AS THE STORY goes, Roderic came to the throne in 710 as a young man with a fierce reputation and a noble pedigree: the grandson of the great king Chindasuinth. His coronation took place in Toledo, the kingdom's capital, where the new king was to be anointed by the archbishop, the head of the church in Hispania. But, for all his promise, his accession was overshadowed by dark omens when at his coronation the crown and scepter slipped from Roderic's grasp and fell to the floor. Not even the holy oil that was dabbed on his forehead by the archbishop of Toledo would save him.

The Catholic church had not always offered the Visigothic kings its magical protection. The Visigoths had long been Christians, but of the Arian creed, which held that Jesus was a lesser being than God the Father, a theological position that had been declared heretical by the imperial church at the Council of Nicaea in 325. Thereafter, Arius's followers had preached their faith to the Germanic barbarians, some of whom, like the Visigoths, were well-disposed to accept a Christianity that would not subordinate them to the religious authority of their enemy, the Roman emperor.

Not unlike the Arabs, the Visigoths were a seminomadic warrior folk who saw their kings as mere war leaders, temporarily elected on an as-needed basis. When they settled in Hispania in the early 400s, the Arian Visigoths ruled over the Romanized Christian population as a caste apart, maintaining their own language, laws, and religion. However, just like the Arab Muslims in the east, they could not ignore the church, which with the collapse of Roman civil society provided a crucial institutional framework for the administration of justice and the collection of taxes. Thus, the Arian Visigoths and the Catholic clergy lived in an uneasy equilibrium: hostile, but mutually indispensable.

By the late 500s, it was clear the church and the monarchy needed each other. Continuous feuding among the leading noble families for the title of king had put the kingdom in a state of intermittent civil war, and the Visigothic aristocracy was slowly becoming entangled with the remaining native Catholic elite. If brought on board, the church might provide some stability, giving Visigothic kingship a quasi-sacred character and working fully for the stability of the realm. Thus, in the aftermath of one of these succession struggles, a prince named Reccared came to the throne and converted to Catholicism in 587. And in the fashion of the time, his Arian subjects were obliged to follow their king's lead and also convert.

However, the factionalism within the Visigothic upper class was too deeply rooted to disappear.

In 672, when the long reign of Chindasuinth came to an end, a new king, Wamba, was elected by the magnates and bishops of the realm. Immediately, he was forced to contend with rebellions in Septimania and an attack by the Basques in the north. His death in 680 prompted a series of struggles for the throne, which ultimately saw an unpopular king, Egica, break with the practice of elective kingship and appoint his son Wittiza as heir. Wittiza reigned only ten years, and with his death in 710, several contenders, including, perhaps, Julian, vied for the throne. At that point, a faction of the Visigothic nobility chose the dashing and proud young warrior Roderic as king and imposed him by force on those who resisted. This was precisely the moment Musa ibn Nusayr's forces were reaching the Atlantic coast of Africa.

Now in power, Roderic had to contend not only with his rivals but with renewed Basque aggression in the north, and it was there he found himself when Tariq's forces landed in 711. Forced to march south at speed to counter the Muslim invasion, Roderic arrived with an army that was exhausted and riddled with disloyal elements who secretly supported other claimants to the throne. Tariq's troops, on the other hand, were fresh and well-motivated; most importantly, they had not only the assistance of Julian and his men, but also, it seems, the support of Wittiza's family, some of whom had agreed to desert Roderic once battle was joined. The details of the battle are lost in legend, but clearly, Roderic's forces suffered a complete defeat and the king himself was killed. Rightly or wrongly, blame for the fall of Hispania fell squarely on his shoulders. As chroniclers struggled to symbolically represent the tensions that had brought the kingdom down, they invented a legend to describe it.

One of the mythical heroes associated with Spain is the demigod Hercules, who, as one of his Seven Labors, was charged by the gods with rustling the cattle of the three-headed giant, Geryon, who lived in the far southwest of Spain. It was due to his time here that the two great mountains that gird the Strait of Gibraltar and mark the end of the "known world" came to be called the Pillars of Hercules. The story went that Hercules, who in this tradition was Spain's first king, founded the city of Toledo and constructed a tower there to hold his treasure, placing a lock on the door and protecting it with a curse. Each of the kingdom's subsequent twenty-four rulers added a lock to the door out of respect for Hercules's wishes—except the proud and impetuous Roderic, who had the locks struck off and entered the tower. However, instead of the treasure, he found carvings (or paintings) of mysterious turbaned horsemen and a written warning that opening the tower would unleash these invaders upon Spain. And so, it was fated that Tariq and Musa should arrive in al-Andalus.

THE VISIGOTHS WERE not the only people who suffered from pride and ambition, of course. Musa, the conqueror of al-Andalus, would fare little better than the king he vanquished. Musa ibn Nusayr owed his position to the fact that he was the son of a *mawla*, or freedman client, attached to the Umayyad family and had been appointed governor of Ifriqiya by the caliph 'Abd al-'Aziz in about 698. After the caliph died in 705 and was succeeded by his son al-Walid, Musa continued to be a royal favorite. It was Musa who directed the conquest of west North Africa, bringing the Berber peoples under Islam, including Tariq, who was evidently a prisoner of war before Musa freed him and appointed him his lieutenant. And it was Tariq who would, on his own initiative, invade the Visigothic kingdom with his Berber troops in 711.

Traditional Arabic society was based on relations of tribe, clan, family, and clientage, where the more powerful took the less powerful under their protection in exchange for loyalty. During the great age of Arabic expansion in the late 600s, *wala* (clientage) was crucial to the success of the venture. Converts—usually pagan captives or non-Muslim Arabs—were incorporated into the family networks of their captors; they took Arabo-Islamic names and sometimes appropriated the genealogy of their sponsors. If they began as household slaves, they were often manumitted once they had gained the confidence of their masters and then continued to serve their former owners' families. This does not mean they were necessarily subservient. As the complex relationship of Musa and Tariq shows, clients were all too ready to follow their own agendas, and patrons needed to keep a vigilant eye on ambitious underlings. Thus, the practice of *wala* provided a powerful mechanism for incorporating new peoples into Arab-dominated Muslim society. For Musa, someone like Tariq was particularly valuable because he could act as an intermediary with the new legions of Berber recruits—most of whom probably had little idea of what Islam was (even after converting) and few of whom would have spoken Arabic.

Tariq's success was stunning. After the defeat of Roderic's army, his forces fanned out across the south while he led a column to the kingdom's unprotected capital, Toledo, which would be known henceforth in Arabic as Tulaytula. However, Musa became incensed that his subordinate had marched ahead without permission, claiming a greater share of glory and of loot. So, Musa raised a force of trusted Arab soldiers and, together with his sons 'Abd al-'Aziz and 'Abd Allah, crossed the strait in 712 to take control of the situation. Alarmed by Tariq's successes, Musa removed him from command and finished the conquest himself. Within four years, almost the entire peninsula was under tenuous Muslim domination. The conquest made Musa, his sons, and their followers rich. Great quantities of slaves were rounded up and treasure stockpiled before the governor headed back to Kairouan in 714, leaving his son 'Abd al-'Aziz as his lieutenant in al-Andalus. Thus, the wealth of Hispania was packed off to Ifriqiya. And this, according to legend, is when the trouble started.

FROM IFRIQIYA, MUSA hurried to Damascus to render homage to al-Walid, to show off his booty and captives, and to present the caliph with his share of one-fifth of the profits of the conquest. Tariq was brought along lest he cause trouble in al-Andalus. But just after Musa's arrival, al-Walid died and was succeeded by his brother Sulayman, who was deeply unsympathetic to the governor of Ifriqiya. Sulayman believed Musa had been hiding some of the bounty of the conquest, a charge backed up by Musa's rivals and confirmed by his humiliated lieutenant, Tariq. The proof that Tariq brought forward related to the most impressive item of plunder that al-Andalus had yielded: the ancient Table of Solomon.

According to legend, when Tariq arrived in Toledo and entered the cathedral, he found a great gold and jewel-encrusted table, a relic of none other than the biblical king and prophet Solomon. In the most elaborate version of the story, Tariq discovered the table, but before handing it to Musa, he secretly replaced one of the legs with a mismatched copy. When Sulayman was presented with this prize as if it were Musa's own find, he asked why one of the legs looked different. Musa, of course, could not explain. Tariq then produced the matching fourth leg and denounced Musa as a liar who had taken undue credit for the conquest. As a consequence, Musa's wealth was confiscated and he was cast out of the royal court. As for Tariq, we learn nothing more. Some historians have suggested that the tale might contain some truth, and that the table may have indeed been a relic of the First Temple, carried to Toledo via the Roman sack of Jerusalem in 70 CE and the Visigothic sack of Rome in 410 CE. But it is clearly a later tale, a parable intended to explain the tensions and uncertainties associated with the Muslim conquest.

The conquest generated anxieties among both the conquerors and the conquered. However much they might be united by faith, Tariq was a Berber and Musa an Arab, embodying social and cultural division at odds with the egalitarian pretensions of Islam. The Arabs had the prestige, the Berbers had the numbers. The legend also reveals just how hard it was to control subordinates at a distance, whether Musa over Tariq or the caliph over Musa. And it reflects the dangers of extending the world of Islam so far into infidel territory. Sulayman had good reason to view Musa with suspicion; his successes in the west could be seen as signs of a larger ambition. By the time Musa made the journey back to Damascus, his hold on the Islamic West would have been troubling to the caliph. Not only had he taken the credit for the conquest from Tariq, but he had installed his three sons as governors: 'Abd Allah in Ifriqiya, 'Abd al-Malik in the Maghrib, and 'Abd al-'Aziz in al-Andalus. He was clearly building a dynasty.

2

Trouble in Paradise

Early Muslims had divided the world into the *dar al-Islam,* or "realm of Islam," and the *dar al-harb,* the "realm of war," the region in which Muslims were obliged to fight to impose God's peace. The *dar al-harb* was also the zone in which people and property could be captured and appropriated—so long as inhabitants did not surrender willingly to Islamic rule and become *dhimmis,* in which case their persons and property were to be respected. Muslims had a strong desire to denude the regions they conquered of their wealth in order to compensate their warriors and fund the Islamic community, but given their limited numbers and the challenges of imposing order by force, they had a strong interest in obtaining the consensual submission of native peoples. In al-Andalus, as elsewhere in the Islamic world, they also depended on the collaboration of the conquered peoples to administer new territory. They needed middlemen, tax collectors, and magistrates who understood the local laws and who could run these lands for the benefit of the Arabo-Islamic elite who were its new masters. And like the Visigoths before them, the conquerors needed the Church and its clergy to maintain order.

In the early 700s, Islam was only just developing a formal religious doctrine, and there is debate about the extent to which Muslims saw themselves as members of a discrete religion or as members of a broad "community of believers" that included Christians and Jews. But religion aside, it was clear that the invaders saw themselves as belonging to a distinct caste with distinct rights, and that *dhimmis* were subordinates and expected to pay the taxes, such as the *jizya* (poll tax), associated with their status. Early coins minted in al-Andalus featured the *shahada*, but written in Latin, perhaps to advertise this difference. By 716, bilingual coins were being issued, and by 720, Arabic-only coins.

The attitude of Christians at the time of the conquest seems even more ambiguous, and it is only later sources that make an issue of Muslims' religious identity. Latin chroniclers of the time tend to refer to the Muslims as "Ishmaelites" or "Hagarenes" rather than, for example, "Saracens" or "infidels." They distinguished between the Arabs and Berbers, presenting the invaders as "peoples" rather than as members of a religious community, and were aware of conflicts within the Muslim community. In the Latin *Chronicle of 754*, written within living memory of the conquest, Arab commanders are referred to in the same morally neutral terms as Christian rulers, praised if their actions were just and condemned if they were not. The near-contemporary *Chronicle of 741* even refers to Muhammad in respectful terms. Religious lines were blurred from the start, but even more so as the invaders integrated with the native elite. The collaboration of Count Julian and the followers of Wittiza with Tariq is just one example. The short career of Musa's son 'Abd al-'Aziz offers several more.

ACCOMPANYING HIS FATHER in the second wave of the invasion, 'Abd al-'Aziz landed on, and began moving up, the Mediterranean coast. North of the town of Murcia, he entered the territory of a Visigothic potentate named Theodimir (Tudmir, in Arabic), with whom 'Abd al-'Aziz made a peace settlement, promising protection for the inhabitants of his territory and their property, and assuring he would not attack their churches or interfere with their religious life. In return, Theodimir pledged loyalty and promised to pay a rather modest tribute in the form of cash and produce. Significantly, the agreement did not affect Theodimir's position as the local ruler; he was to remain in power but recognize the authority of his Muslim overlords.

The treaty reflects the pragmatic approach many among the elite of both the invaders and the natives took toward the Muslim occupation, marking a pattern followed across the peninsula, whether with local noblemen, bishops, or collectives of local citizenry.

'Abd al-'Aziz's policy in Toledo, the capital under the Visigoths and the center of the Spanish church, had the same tenor, but contrasted with that of his father. When Musa reached Toledo, he was determined to snuff out any potential resistance and allegedly rounded up and executed the remaining nobility. Next, he established Seville (Ishbiliya) as the new capital, further depriving Toledo of its influence. However, when 'Abd al-'Aziz arrived, he took a conciliatory approach and, following time-honored custom, sought to legitimize his new position by taking Egilón (known as Umm 'Asim after her conversion), the widow of the vanquished king, Roderic, as his wife. But if this sent a message of conciliation to the native nobility, it alarmed the Arab military elite. It was said that with Egilón's encouragement, 'Abd al-'Aziz began to style himself a king and took to wearing a crown in private. It was even rumored he had secretly converted to Christianity, making him an apostate and deserving of death. And so, the Arab commanders surprised him while he was praying in a former church and struck him dead, sending his head back to Damascus to the caliph. Among those who took part in the coup were members of the al-Fihri clan, an Arab family that would soon rule over both Ifriqiya and al-Andalus.

Marrying into local families was a strategy for establishing networks of power, and it would have been common among leading Muslims who were planning on staying in al-Andalus. Marriages were a political tool, and the fact that Muslim men were permitted up to four wives allowed them to simultaneously construct multiple networks based on kinship by marriage. Moreover, that women who were "People of the Book" were not obliged to convert to Islam made marriage to a Muslim a somewhat acceptable state of affairs in the eyes of their own extended families. But intermarriage was only one manifestation of the engagement of the conquerors and the conquered. The invaders found willing allies among the relatives, and later, the descendants, of Visigothic magnates, most of whom would convert to Islam. Members of the Muslim elite were also prepared to cultivate alliances with local Christian powers, even against their fellow Muslims. Indeed, the governor 'Abd al-Rahman al-Ghafiqi embarked on his ultimately fateful attack on Aquitaine in 731 because a Berber commander named 'Uthman was establishing a semi-independent principality in the Pyrenees with the support of Duke Odo of Aquitaine, whose daughter 'Uthman planned to marry. Realpolitik trumped religious identity, and political struggles would take place as much between Muslim and Muslim, and Christian and Christian, as across religious lines.

BY THE 720s, it was clear that Christian Hispania had been superseded by Islamic al-Andalus. The conquest did not, however, mark the end of Christian society here, but rather it was the beginning of a long process of political, social, and cultural creation involving Muslims, Christians, and Jews, including Arabs, Berbers, and descendants of the Visigoths and the Romanized indigenous peoples. The next decades would be characterized by resistance and revolt, not just in al-Andalus, but across North Africa and in the very heart of the caliphate itself. Yet the result, after an unlikely and unforeseen chain of circumstances, would be the stabilization of Muslim Spain under the Umayyad emirate of Córdoba.

BY 750 CE, with the fall of Musa's sons, the al-Fihris—the descendants of 'Uqba ibn Nafi'—were in tentative control of the Islamic West. 'Abd al-Rahman al-Fihri, or Ibn Habib, reigned in Kairouan, while in al-Andalus, his uncle Yusuf struggled to dominate the divided peninsula. In 750, their nominal overlords, the Umayyads of Damascus, were overthrown, and the center of the Islamic world shifted to Persia with the accession of a new caliphal family, the 'Abbasids. The rebels showed no quarter to the defeated dynasty. Those who were not killed in battle were assassinated under the pretext of an amnesty or hunted down as they fled Syria. The sole potential heir who survived was a young prince, 'Abd al-Rahman ibn Mu'awiya, who was only a teenager when the revolution broke out. 'Abd al-Rahman's father, Mu'awiya, had been named heir by his father, the caliph Hisham (d. 743), but he died prematurely in 737, after which a series of uncles held the caliphal title in quick succession.

Having barely escaped the uprising with his life, at one point swimming across the Euphrates River to shake his pursuers, 'Abd al-Rahman rallied faithful family members, clients, and servants and set out westward, secretly crossing Egypt before arriving in Ifriqiya and the court of Ibn Habib. But Ibn Habib could scarcely be expected to welcome the young prince. 'Abd al-Rahman was now an outlaw and constituted a threat to the power of the al-Fihri clan. Thus, the young prince took refuge among Nafza Berbers to the west: the people of his mother, Rah, a captive who had been sent back to Syria as a prize for his father. 'Abd al-Rahman's trusted freedman, Badr, contacted the Nafza who had settled in Spain, and together with members and clients of the Umayyad clan, prepared for his master's crossing. When word of these plans reached Yusuf al-Fihri, the aging governor of al-Andalus turned for advice to his scheming lieutenant, the Arab commander al-Sumayl ibn Hatim al-Kilabi. He had supported Yusuf al-Fihri because he felt the governor could be easily manipulated, and, thus, al-Sumayl was far from enthusiastic at the prospect of a new Umayyad overlord. He urged caution, noting dryly, "'Abd al-Rahman is from a family who, if one of them pissed in this land, it would drown us all."[1] These words would prove prophetic. But 'Abd al-Rahman would wait several years in the Maghrib, quietly biding his time and laying the groundwork until the opportune moment to escape the long arm of his enemies, the 'Abbasids, and establish himself as ruler of al-Andalus.

UNDER THE ROMANS, Hispania had been a wealthy and productive part of the empire, thoroughly Romanized with a bustling urban life; a highly developed network of roads, bridges, and ports; and a thriving economy based on agriculture and mineral resources. The integration of Spain into Roman networks can be seen in the early successes of Christianity here in the 300s and in the vigor of the

Spanish church and its intellectual culture. Whether Christianity penetrated the countryside is less easy to gauge, and it is likely that many
"rustics" continued to practice the pagan traditions of their ancestors
alongside whatever Christian rituals they had been exposed to.

The unraveling of Roman power in the early 400s resulted in
sweeping changes in the region. A cycle of decline quickly set in:
commerce collapsed, infrastructure decayed, and the economy moved
from cash to barter and from trade to subsistence. The common folk
took refuge in the countryside, gradually losing their freedoms to
wealthy landholders. In Roman cities, emptied of their populations,
the baths, fora, and temples were quarried for their stones. Ports silted
up and aqueducts fouled. Bridges collapsed and roads deteriorated.
Mines were abandoned and industry stagnated. Travel became uncertain and dangerous, and secular high culture all but disappeared. As
across the Latin Mediterranean, Roman villas devolved into "privat-
ized" strongholds surrounded by squalid, primitive hamlets and reoc-
cupied pre-Roman hill-forts. Historians today may rightly eschew the
term "the Dark Ages," but there was not much light in late Visigothic
Spain.

The church and the upper clergy provided whatever glue held the
former provinces together, but some of the old elite persevered too.
The large country estates of the wealthiest senatorial families enabled
them to support private bands of warriors and to resist the barbarian
invaders. And with the conversion of the Visigoths to Catholicism,
the two elites merged. By the early 600s, the people of the peninsula
(with the exception of the Jews) came to be seen as constituting a
single "Gothic people." City life may have recuperated modestly, at
least in larger centers, such as Toledo, Zaragoza, Tarragona, Barcelona, and Seville, thanks to the church and the monarchy, but in the
countryside, regional warlords consolidated their power, contributing
to the political instability that characterized Visigothic rule.

One group that the conversion of the Visigoths had a profound
effect on was the Jews. There had been Jewish communities scattered
across the Roman world since Antiquity, and in Hispania, Mérida was
the most important site of Jewish settlement, but Toledo and Tarragona also had substantial communities. Reccared's conversion in 586

empowered elements in the church who were determined to curtail the status of Jews, whom they vilified for their role in the crucifixion and who were seen as traitors and a dangerous contagion within Christendom. A series of repressive laws were promulgated, some going as far as to call for either forced conversion or mass enslavement, although it is not clear how many Jews were actually in Visigothic territories or if these laws were ever enforced.

Sources suggest that there were Jewish revolts in North Africa in the decades leading up to the Islamic conquest, and that these may have been coordinated with communities in Hispania. Historians have postulated that Jewish merchants provided the ships that carried Muslim troops to the European shore, and later Muslim chroniclers credited Jews as collaborating in the Islamic conquest, volunteering to serve in the garrisons of conquered Visigothic towns. Intriguing as these accounts may be—and they were taken at face value by many historians until recently—they date from two centuries after the fact, an era of profound Muslim-Jewish integration, and are likely nothing more than a trope: a literary formula that both Muslim and Jewish writers for their own reasons found appealing and incorporated into their historical narratives. The Jews of Hispania may well have welcomed the conquest, but we have no idea what role, if any, they played or how many they were.

NOR CAN WE be sure of the numerical strength of the invaders and the settlers themselves. The core of the invasion force comprised a small number of Arabs from high-prestige clans associated with the early figures of Islam, and with them, clients, converts, and slaves, as well as members of clans from Syria and Iraq. Together, these groups claimed the lion's share of the wealth and power. Gravitating toward the centers of power, they displaced the Visigothic aristocracy. These early settlers, or *baladiyyun* (from *baladi*, meaning "of the land"), settled around the peninsula, the new lords of the land, jealously guarding their prestige and power. Clan members tended to stick together for strength and protection and were allotted their own territories scattered around the peninsula, but especially in the south.

The extended family or clan was the political unit of prime importance, and Arabian society was dominated by two larger tribal collectives: the southern Yamanis and the northern Qaysis. Within the
family, authority resided with a senior clan member; power and title
were not transmitted father to son, but laterally among uncles. Typical of nomadic peoples, influence was conceived of in terms of the
people and livestock one controlled rather than land. Women were
considered part of a clan's wealth and were to be conserved; hence,
the ideal was for men to marry their female cousins, and it was the
husband who pledged the bride-price in compensation for a valuable
asset rather than the bride's family paying a dowry.

The bulk of the Muslim forces, however, were made up of Amazigh, or "Berbers," who had a similar social structure. To group the
Berbers together as a people, however, is deceiving; the term, which
essentially means "barbarians," originated as a disparaging reference
to indigenous North Africans on the part of the ancient Greeks and
was eventually assumed by the Arabs. They were a diverse group,
divided into several nations—tribal affiliations with their own languages and traditions, each of which was further divided into clans.
Although all the invaders were united as members of the Islamic
umma, there was a tremendous amount of ethnic prejudice aimed at
Berbers by the Arabs, and their common cultural and religious orientation provided opportunities for competition and conflict as much as
for collaboration and common purpose.

THUS, 'ABD AL-RAHMAN did not arrive to a unified al-Andalus.
There were deep divisions among and between the Arab and Berber
invaders, and the surviving Visigoth lords continued to be a source
of intrigue and outright resistance. Their capacity to rebel was limited, but the situation of the conquerors was also tenuous, hence
Musa ibn Nusayr's uncompromising approach at Toledo and the
subsequent move of the Andalusi capital first to Seville and then to
Córdoba—each an attempt to reset the influence of potentially rebellious members of the elite. Native opposition was more entrenched in the northeast and in the isolated and less accessible
mountains of the north coast. The most famous Christian rebel was
Pelagius (Pelayo, in Spanish), whose successful defiance of the

conquerors eventually became the seed of the Castilian national myth of *La Reconquista*, or "the Reconquest."

Pelagius was a warrior of some sort—either a local strongman or a refugee from the south—who had become a client of the conquerors (not unlike Theodimir), but who, sensing their debility, refused to render tribute. In response, a punitive expedition was mounted, consisting of a modest detachment of troops together with some native collaborators. In the event, at an isolated mountain valley in Asturias called Covadonga, Pelagius's band defeated the Muslim force, and thereafter he was left to his own devices, becoming the ruler of a small independent principality, the germ of what would become the late ninth-century kingdom of Asturias.

Centuries later, monk-chroniclers, in an effort to link the kings of Asturias to the preinvasion kingdom of the Visigoths, inflated the skirmish at Covadonga into an epic encounter in which Pelagius's small band defeated "an army of almost 187,000" infidels—a landmark victory of Christianity over Islam made possible by the miraculous intervention of the Virgin Mary.[2] In reality, it was nothing of the sort, and whatever notion there was of a "reconquest" in the aftermath of 711, it would have faded within a few short years with the destruction of the Visigothic order and the establishment of the new status quo. By the time the tale was first told, over a century later, Balay (Arabic for "Pelagius") was presented as a poor desperado whom the Muslims simply could not be bothered to root out. He can be seen as an archetype, representing the assorted Christian montagnards who managed to break away during the first decades of Arab rule in what was merely one of several acts of resistance by local players.

Some were successful, others not. Uprisings in Mérida and Seville were suppressed. But the leaders of Pamplona (Banbluna), another distant mountain town, managed to break free, only to be conquered in turn by the Franks in 778. Seven years later, the inhabitants of Girona (Jarunda) overthrew their governor and welcomed in the Franks. In fact, the Muslims held little territory in the Pyrenees for very long; they did not have the capacity or will to occupy areas that were so difficult to control, offered so little by way of tribute, and posed so little threat.

AS IT WAS, the real threat to the power of the Umayyad caliphate here came not from unreformed Visigoths, but from fellow Muslims. Tensions appeared from the outset, and the friction between Tariq, the Berber, and Musa, the Arab, only heralded greater conflicts. Entitlement to land and booty was a major source of discontent, particularly among the Berbers, who had provided the muscle of the conquest but were apportioned less of the profits and were considered of secondary status to the Arabs. The previous half century had seen a mass conversion of Berbers, and many must have felt disappointed when the promise of equality in an egalitarian Islamic *umma* did not bear out. But there were also tensions among the Arabs. Yamanis, the bulk of the Arab settlers, complained of abuse by Qaysi governors. Such vexations were even more acute in North Africa, where Arabs continued to treat the Berber majority as infidels even after they had converted, taxing them relentlessly and seizing their women as slaves. In 740, tensions in North Africa boiled over into open revolt.

The ideological justification for the uprising was provided by 'Ibadi Islam, an offshoot of Kharijism, the creed that recognized no authority except the Qur'an. 'Ibadism originated in southern Iraq but found willing acolytes among discontents across the *dar al-Islam*. Berber clans took to it eagerly after missionaries arrived in Kairouan in the early 700s, and in 740 they rose up and seized Ifriqiya from its Arab rulers. Revolts followed in the Maghrib and al-Andalus, where tensions had been simmering for two decades as both Berbers and *baladiyyun* smarted under the heavy hand of Syrian officials. In 740, the pro-*baladi* governor 'Abd al-Malik ibn Qatan al-Fihri adopted more conciliatory policies, but by this time, the discontent was too acute, and uprisings flared up both in the south and across the north of the peninsula, where Berber settlement was heaviest, as well as in North Africa.

The caliphate reacted quickly to the uprising in Ifriqiya, sending a huge army of trusted Syrian soldiers under the able general Kulthum ibn 'Iyad in 741. But this force was nearly annihilated near Fez, thanks largely to the arrogant behavior of Kulthum's nephew Balj ibn Bishr. Balj survived the battle and fled west to Ceuta with several thousand survivors, pursued by hostile Berbers. Trapped in the city and surrounded by rebels, he sent word to 'Abd al-Malik ibn Qatan al-Fihri, who was struggling to contain the revolt in al-Andalus. A reluctant Ibn Qatan agreed to rescue Balj and ferry his men across the strait if Balj would use his Syrian soldiers to suppress the Berber uprising in al-Andalus and promise that once this was accomplished, he and his troops would then return to North Africa. Balj agreed, on the condition he and his men be conveyed from al-Andalus back to an area of Ifriqiya that remained safely under Arab control. However, once Balj's contingents had crushed the uprising in al-Andalus at great cost, Ibn Qatan reneged and tried to send them back to Ceuta, where their Berber enemies and certain death awaited them.

At once trapped in al-Andalus and attracted to the riches of the country, the Syrians determined to stay and seize the land for themselves. In the ensuing struggle, Ibn Qatan was captured and crucified outside the mosque at Córdoba in 741. Balj's coup brought him to power as governor, but he was killed the following year in a battle against *baladi* forces. Being of different clans and kin networks, Balj's *jundis* (from *jund*, "army" in Arabic) had little affinity for the Arabs who had settled a generation earlier, and the two groups squared off. At this point many Berber clans joined the *baladis* against the Syrians. Three years later, a compromise was reached on the initiative of Ardabast, a son of Wittiza who served as the ruler of the Christian community of al-Andalus on behalf of the Muslims. Under his plan, contingents of Balj's army were scattered throughout the peninsula—away from the capital, so they would not cause trouble—and granted stipends with the understanding they could be called up for service as needed. Even so, soon enough al-Andalus spiraled deeper into civil war.

Historians have described this as a "tribal" war between Yamanis and Qaysis, but by this point, tribal identity had become largely abstract and Arab and Berber clans formed alliances based on their particular networks, which did not necessarily coincide with larger tribal loyalties. In many respects, al-Andalus in 750 was a microcosm of the larger Muslim world. Islamic religion and Arabic culture provided a common frame of identity, but the *dar al-Islam* remained fractured by ethnic, family, and ideological cleavages, while regional differences unleashed centrifugal forces that became too powerful for the caliphate to contain.

In the decade that followed, both Islamic Spain and the *dar al-Islam* as a whole would be transformed as a consequence of the same chain of events that would bring the young Umayyad prince 'Abd al-Rahman ibn Mu'awiya to Kairouan as a refugee in 751.

3

The Falcon of the Quraysh

In the aftermath of the victory over 'Ali in the 660s, the Umayyad caliphate had transformed, or striven to transform, itself into a unified monarchy on the model of Rome or Persia, in which authority was held by a single family supported by a privileged elite (here, Arab Muslims), who enjoyed political and economic advantages and ruled over an array of subject peoples. The center of this empire was Syria-Palestine, and although Arabs as a whole held high prestige, it was the Syrian clans closest to the Umayyads who wielded disproportionate power.

The first centuries of Islam, like those of Christianity, witnessed immense creativity, innovation, and variety as many different groups brought their own expectations, anxieties, and cultural contributions to the grand, amorphous project of the new religion. However, as the eighth century progressed, the true centers of economic power, religious innovation, and demographic strength emerged in the former heartland of the Persian Empire: southern Iraq and Iran, and eventually in Khurasan, the vast and populous province of northeast Iran that extends into Central Asia. The conversion of local peoples was a crucial component of this development; Islam became less an Arab phenomenon, and the notion of Arab privilege, whether financial (through the *diwan*, the dole system for ethnic Arabs), social, or religious, came to be seen as incongruent with Islam's universal message and grated on non-Arab Muslims, who did not receive a share.

Many pious Muslims, who focused on the element of personal responsibility essential to the message of Muhammad, were uncomfortable with any authoritarian regime, while others were drawn to Christian- and Zoroastrian-inflected interpretations of Islam that emphasized an esotericism that sat uneasily with the legalism of many Sunni *'ulama'*. At the same time, there was an increasing expectation that the caliphs should be religious figures and that Islam should develop a systematic theology and law characterized by an egalitarian Islamic *umma* positioned above clearly subordinated non-Muslim communities. Meanwhile, rival Arab clans, even those within the Umayyad circle, continued to battle for power. Together, all these developments fed tensions that could not be contained by the Umayyads and finally boiled over in 750 in a general uprising that destroyed the caliphate.

THE UMAYYAD FAILURE to vanquish the Roman Empire was also problematic, from both an ideological and a political viewpoint. The last siege of Constantinople, from 717 to 718, was an expensive failure, and when the caliphs became occasional tributaries of the empire, this not only signaled the military resurgence of the Byzantine Empire, but also cast doubt on the notion of Umayyad manifest destiny. The dynasty itself became increasingly unstable as the 700s wore on, as evidenced by the intrigues and volatility that came to characterize the family. In the 740s, no fewer than six individuals ruled as caliph.

That decade saw uprisings both by Kharijites and by Shi'a, the latter of whom followed the tradition of 'Ali and believed the caliph should serve as imam and be of the Prophet's bloodline. When a powerful former slave named Abu Muslim rallied discontented army factions in Khurasan and rose up in rebellion in 747, he found common cause with the al-'Abbas clan, which was seeking to overthrow the Umayyads. Descended from the Prophet's uncle 'Abbas ibn al-Muttalib, they claimed a closer family link to Muhammad than the Umayyad, thus appealing to the Shi'i emphasis on lineage. As the uprising gathered steam, 'Abd Allah ibn Muhammad al-Saffah, a leading figure in the clan, was proclaimed caliph in October 749 in defiance of the Umayyads in Damascus.

It would take more than a decade of violent struggle for the new 'Abbasid dynasty to assert itself. First came the defeat of the Umayyad army at the Battle of the Upper Zab River in northern Mesopotamia in January 750, and then the pursuit and extermination of the ruling family and their most important clients. In the most notorious episode, eighty of the clan's grandees were massacred and their bodies literally thrown to the dogs. The caliph, Marwan II, was pursued to Egypt and killed. Soon, Shi'a groups, realizing they had been manipulated by the 'Abbasids, began to resist the new regime and were also crushed. In 754, al-Saffah was succeeded by his brother Abu Jafar 'Abd Allah, who ruled under the name al-Mansur bi-'Llah ("Victorious by God") and would lay the foundations of the 'Abbasid caliphate. It was al-Mansur who founded the caliphate's new capital at Baghdad and paved the way for the "Golden Age of Islam" of the ninth and tenth centuries. After the revolution, Shi'ism was repressed, but many Shi'a, particularly Persian converts, were incorporated into the power structure of the caliphate.

THUS, WHEN THE young 'Abd al-Rahman ibn Mu'awiya arrived in Kairouan, his position was anything but secure. He was an outlaw whose clan had been decimated by its enemies and abandoned by its allies. It was only the disorder in al-Andalus and Ifriqiya that would save the young fugitive. Once among his mother's people, the Nafza Berbers in Morocco, and out of the reach of Ibn Habib, the governor of Ifriqiya, he began to reach out to the many Syrian *jundis* in al-Andalus who still had Umayyad sympathies. Later histories presented 'Abd al-Rahman's crossing to al-Andalus as the manifest destiny of the resurgence of the Umayyad dynasty, and modern historians have found it hard to resist the romanticized versions of the tale of his unlikely escape and rise to power. In reality, 'Abd al-Rahman's preoccupation would have been mere survival. Wearing out his welcome among the Nafza, al-Andalus was the only place he could run to next. He would have been aware of the disarray there: the tension between Yusuf al-Fihri and al-Sumayl and among the various Arab clans, plus the dissatisfaction of the Berbers—all compounded by six years of poor harvests and widespread famine.

Thus, in 754 he sent his freedman Badr across the strait to make contact with Umayyad clients among the Syrians and the *baladis*. Badr found considerable support in the very southern tip of the peninsula, and in late 755, the prince landed there with a handful of supporters. His sympathizers gave him shelter and allowed him to reach out to the other Qaysi elements of the *jund*, al-Sumayl in particular. But al-Sumayl and his Qaysi troops closed ranks with Yusuf al-Fihri to oppose the prince, leading 'Abd al-Rahman to appeal instead to the Berbers and Yamani Arabs. The two sides met in battle just outside Córdoba on May 14, 756; it was a Friday, the day of communal prayer, and after defeating his rivals, 'Abd al-Rahman was proclaimed *amir* ("prince" or "commander") of al-Andalus in the city's mosque. He would be known popularly as al-Dakhil: "He Who Came In."

In fact, al-Andalus had been functionally independent of the caliphate since the era of Musa ibn Nusayr four decades earlier. Now, the caliphate was anchored farther east than Damascus, in Baghdad, and its power in the west was further diminished. But, pedigree notwithstanding, 'Abd al-Rahman was only the latest strongman to try his hand at bringing al-Andalus under his control. The title of *amir* he claimed may have endowed him with a certain theoretical legitimacy, but in real terms, his authority beyond the capital would depend entirely on his ability to convince, threaten, or force the various local Muslim potentates and communities across this territory to recognize him and cede a portion of their own power.

And he proved himself up to the task. 'Abd al-Rahman was possessed of an innate political genius, and this, together with his good fortune and longevity, allowed him to consolidate his rule. He combined an outward caution and flexibility with an instinct for turning rival factions against each other, and—no surprise, given his own traumatic experiences—a complete readiness to deal with any resistance with swift and unflinching brutality, whether against allies, clients, or members of his own family.

IN THE IMMEDIATE aftermath of his victory, 'Abd al-Rahman pardoned al-Sumayl and Yusuf al-Fihri. But when Yusuf fled to Mérida and raised an army in 759, Umayyad forces vanquished his army in battle and then hunted him down in Toledo. Al-Sumayl was then arrested and died soon afterward in custody. The al-Fihri family, based in Toledo, enjoyed strong Berber support and put up a spirited fight. It took 'Abd al-Rahman twenty-six years to crush them. In the meantime, the surviving remnants of the Umayyad family network had been heading to al-Andalus from across the Islamic world, buttressing the new prince's power. As they arrived, he assigned them generous incomes and positions, which reinforced his political base but alienated many of his early supporters.

Some of these discontents soon allied with the 'Abbasids in the latter's attempts to destabilize the renegade regime. This took the form of a certificate of investiture as governor of al-Andalus sent by al-Mansur, the caliph in Baghdad, to al-Yahsubi, a *jund* leader whose powerbase was in what is now southern Portugal. The gambit nearly worked, and 'Abd al-Rahman was forced to gather his troops and march on the rebel. Outnumbered and in hostile territory with his camp under siege by his enemies, the amir ordered his trusted Umayyad loyalists to burn the scabbards of their swords, so that they might not resheath them, and led them out in a desperate sally against the enemy. In the aftermath of the resulting victory, the amir had the embalmed head of al-Yahsubi sent back to Kairouan as a riposte to the caliph. Five years later, a Berber uprising flared up in the hills of central al-Andalus. It would take nearly a decade of warfare to suppress the rebels. And twice 'Abd al-Rahman faced serious uprisings in Seville, where renegade *jundis* led by members of al-Yahsubi's clan attempted to establish a breakaway emirate in 766 and in the early 770s. Both uprisings were crushed with exemplary violence.

Whatever ideological or ethnic dimensions historians have attributed to these rebellions, at bottom, they were about local power. Because the conquest of the peninsula had been so unorganized, Arab and Berber clans had been able to preserve their autonomy, and through collaboration and intermarriage with locals, had laid down strong roots in the locales under their control. Thus, locals and occupiers together resisted centralized control as a matter of course. Larger cities, such as Toledo and Zaragoza, and the other towns north of the Duero and Ebro Rivers, which were not under the direct control of Córdoba, were constantly rebelling, and zones far from the center of power, such as Septimania, the Pyrenees, Cantabria, and Galicia, would prove impossible for ʿAbd al-Rahman to hold.

SUCH WAS THEIR determination to resist that local rulers in Zaragoza did not hesitate to seek allies among their Christian neighbors and famously sent envoys to Charles the Great, king of the Franks (Charlemagne), in 777, inviting him to invade the peninsula, which he did in 778. That same year, ʿAbd al-Rahman's forces laid waste to the city of Valencia (Balansiya), another enclave of regional resistance. To free up resources to attend to these internal matters, the amir made a peace treaty as early as 759 with Fruela, the king of Asturias in the northwest. Within his territories ʿAbd al-Rahman is recorded as wrecking churches and destroying the relics of saints, likely in order to weaken the fabric of Christian society and undermine its potential for resistance. Meanwhile, he began to systematically replace local Muslim commanders with handpicked loyalists, mostly family members or Umayyad clients. *Jund* leaders, like the Visigothic nobility before them, saw themselves as essentially independent and under only a discretionary obligation to support the amir, so it was crucial for ʿAbd al-Rahman to put trusted dependents in power, even at the cost of alienating and provoking his early supporters.

THROUGH ALL THESE challenges, ʿAbd al-Rahman prevailed, and in doing so, laid the foundation for the next centuries of united Islamic rule in Spain, without which al-Andalus may have disintegrated. Along with his escape from the hands of his ʿAbbasid enemies, this was an altogether singular accomplishment. Even the ʿAbbasid caliph, al-Mansur, with whom ʿAbd al-Rahman traded an acid correspondence and who despised the Umayyad family, could not help but grudgingly acknowledge his enemy's acumen. Al-Mansur honored him with the nickname Saqr al-Quraysh, "the Falcon of the Quraysh," for having escaped the revolution: "He who by his own cleverness escaped the spear-heads and sword-blades, crossed the desert and the ocean until he landed on a foreign shore; who repopulated cities, revived armies; and set up a kingdom after its collapse by the force of his own ability and determination." And unlike any caliph since the era of the Rashidun, himself included, 'Abd al-Rahman had done it, al-Mansur noted, "alone, aided only by his intelligence and without any aid except his own determination."[3] Perhaps unsurprisingly, this echoed 'Abd al-Rahman's own assessment, as expressed at the beginning of one of the many poems he composed:

> No one can accuse me and no one can claim,
> "Thanks to me is the success of the One Who Came."
> It was my good fortune, resolve, and sharp blade,
> my lance, and my destiny that these things made.[4]

'ABD AL-RAHMAN IBN MU'AWIYA, "the Falcon of the Quraysh," reigned for twenty-six years, dying at Córdoba in September 788 in his fifty-ninth year and leaving behind the foundation of an Arabo-Syrian style monarchy that would endure for generations. He was clearly an imposing individual with a tremendous force of will and was known as a powerful orator and an accomplished poet. Physically, he was said to be tall, thin, and fair, and he styled his long bangs parted in the middle so that they hung in two bunches along his temples—a fashion meant to evoke Alexander the Great: Dhu'l-Qarnayn, or "He of the Two Horns," of Qur'anic lore. Blind in one eye, he dressed in white and wore the turban of a man of religion, a presentation of piety and populism reinforced by his ostentatious acts of charity and faith. Most important was his longevity, which afforded him time to consolidate his kingdom and prepare his succession.

ONE THING 'ABD AL-RAHMAN did not do was take the title "caliph." This would have been too presumptuous and provocative in an Islamic world whose members believed in the ideal of a single caliph and accepted the 'Abbasids as the legitimate dynasty. Moreover, there was no need; Baghdad was distant and held little authority in the west. The Maghrib had been effectively lost and was now ruled by various amorphous, indigenous clan-based "kingdoms" that were Muslim but did not recognize the 'Abbasids. In Ifriqiya, the Banu Aghlab (or Aghlabids), an Arab dynasty of governors, had established what was effectively an independent kingdom.

BY THE TIME of 'Abd al-Rahman's death Septimania had been all but lost, leaving his emirate of Córdoba in control of most, but not all, of the Iberian Peninsula. The Pyrenees and the Cantabrian Mountains of the north had slipped out of Arab control, coming under the power of various local strongmen and the breakaway kingdom of Asturias. The population of al-Andalus remained overwhelmingly Christian, and although there was certainly a Jewish minority, it is all but invisible to historians. Arab settlement was thickest in the south, with important nodes in the larger towns across the peninsula. Some of the Berber population, disillusioned with Arab rule, had evidently left al-Andalus after the revolts of the 740s, but significant populations remained around Toledo, along the northeastern coast (*Sharq al-Andalus*, or "the East"), and in the central and southern highlands.

'Abd al-Rahman's reign was one of consolidation. His agenda was not some abstract impulse to expand the *dar al-Islam* or wage war against "the infidel," but to forge a coherent kingdom out of this ad hoc society of tribute-taking warlords. Prior to his reign, there had been little new construction by the conquerors—even of mosques—and there is little evidence of the establishment of judicial institutions or regularization of taxation. Tribute was collected and kept haphazardly and locally, largely under the supervision of indigenous Christian officers. Among the Arabs, Berbers, and natives, there was little recognition of central authority. Thus, the amir and his successors set out to reorganize the army, create a bureaucracy, rebuild infrastructure, found mosques, and Islamize the administration by setting up a Muslim judiciary. All this required money and therefore made fiscal reform necessary. Islamic taxes were to be paid by Muslims, and non-Muslim taxes were to be collected by representatives of the amir, with as much as possible going to the central treasury of the emirate. Large *baladi* estates were broken up, and the territories of the surviving indigenous Christian elite were encroached on, treaties notwithstanding, to endow loyal commanders and Umayyad clan affiliates. Naturally, such changes would provoke resistance, and this resistance would outlast 'Abd al-Rahman's reign.

ONE OF THE AMIR'S priorities was to make his base at Córdoba into a royal capital. As Umayyad kin and clients and other members of the elite and their households arrived, and as builders, artisans, craftsmen, and merchants came to service them, the former Roman city of Corduba morphed into Arabo-Islamic Qurtuba. The consequent increase in commerce required the construction of a *suq*, or large central market, which itself became an engine of growth. New suburbs sprouted up outside the limits of the ancient walls, and within, what had been the grid of Roman streets became a tangled mass of narrow, winding alleyways. A Visigothic-era fort was reconfigured by 'Abd al-Rahman as a castle worthy of the new king. His preferred residence, however, was outside the city. Two miles to the northwest, where the foothills of the Sierra Morena rise out of the broad river plain, he constructed the first garden-palace in al-Andalus. Named after his childhood home, Rusafa, set on the banks of the Euphrates in northern Syria, it was a magnificent villa surrounded by gardens stocked with exotic plants, the pride of which was a pomegranate tree seeded from fruit sent to the prince from Syria by one of his sisters. It is said that on encountering a lone palm tree in the grounds, 'Abd al-Rahman extemporized a short poem that concluded poignantly:

> You grow in a land to which you are a stranger,
>   we are alike in our distance [from home];
> May the rain clouds water you and nourish you in your exile.[5]

But the most significant project the amir undertook in the capital was the foundation of a congregational mosque, which would be the center of religious and legal administration and the gathering site of the prince and the Muslims of the city for Friday prayer. Tradition has it that previously the Muslims had shared the Byzantine basilica of Saint Vincent with the Christian population, and that in 784 CE 'Abd al-Rahman purchased it from them for a generous sum in order to raze it and build his grand mosque. But this story bears a resemblance a little too close to the foundation legend of the Umayyad mosque of Damascus. In any event, by 787 a new building was constructed, oriented toward the *qibla*: the direction of prayer, which is to say, in principle, toward Mecca. It was modeled on the mosque constructed at the house of the Prophet in Medina, providing a conceptual bridge to the Arabian homeland and subtly reinforcing the dynasty's legitimacy.

The temple consisted of a single space, approximately fifty by eighty yards, decorated in a stunning fusion of indigenous, Eastern Mediterranean, and Arabo-Islamic styles. The prayer hall was divided into eleven aisles separated by rows of columns crowned by a double row of alternating white- and red-striped arches in evocation of the Roman *opus mixtum* (brick and stone) building technique. The 110 mismatched stone columns, and the fine marble capitals perched upon them, were *spolia*, recycled from ruined Roman temples from around the peninsula. Other elements were borrowed from the Visigoths, notably the nearly circular horseshoe-style arches set in doorways and windows. An adaptation of a Roman-era sun symbol, this arch was a common feature of Visigothic churches and went on to become emblematic of western Islamic architecture. One of the most striking features of the mosque—the double arches that bridged the pillars—was probably inspired by surviving Roman aqueducts, like that of Segovia. The interior evoked a thicket of palm trees, resonating with the Arabs' desert origins and recalling the trees of the Rusafa palace in northern Syria whose gardens 'Abd al-Rahman missed so much. Even today, the subtle geometry of the hall, and the interplay of light and shadow, draws the viewer's eyes upward, and walking through the forest of columns, one senses the beauty and design of an ordered universe. The mosque hints at the presence of higher being or truth, ineffable and beyond human comprehension, without resorting to decadent luxury, ostentation, or imagery of any kind.

The prayer hall in the Great Mosque, Córdoba. *Timor Espallargas, 2004 (Creative Commons)*

In a period when Christians remained the overwhelming numerical majority, as well as an important segment of the elite in al-Andalus, demonstrating both the distinctiveness and superiority of Islam would have been a crucial means of reinforcing the faith of the conquerors and reaffirming their higher status. But the design of the mosque also reflected the traditional Arabic ethos of the Umayyad monarchy. The main hall was an open space for communal prayer, homogenous in design and plain of decoration, reflecting the rejection of a hierarchy among believers and reinforcing the notion that the amir was a member of the *umma*—a first among equals and a man of the people, whether at prayer or in war. It was a political as well as a religious monument, signaling Córdoba as a new Damascus.

Typical of early mosques, attached to the building was a large, walled-in patio. This served as a precinct that could accommodate an overflow of worshippers and a place to ritually wash before entering the prayer hall. It also was one of the few open public spaces in a densely packed Islamic city: a compact urban park for socializing and relaxing. Together with the city market, it was a place to encounter nonfamily members, to see and be seen, and to perform public acts, such as declarations and oaths. In these ways, it was analogous to a Roman forum or Greek *agora*. The patio was also the main seat of justice in the emirate. It was here, near the door to the prayer hall, that the religious magistrate, or *qadi*, would have heard the disputes among Muslims, whether criminal or civil, that were brought before him.

This function was related to another important facet of 'Abd al-Rahman's state building. Given the 'Abbasid propaganda that painted the Umayyads as impious decadents and the need to establish institutions to unite his fragmented Muslim populace, 'Abd al-Rahman courted the *'ulama'*, the pious intellectuals of North Africa and al-Andalus, and particularly the *fuqaha'*, those who were experts in Islamic jurisprudence. Deriving the laws of the world from the word of scripture and *hadith* (the sayings of the Prophet) had preoccupied pious Muslims since the inception of Islam. The first to lay the foundations for a systematic Islamic law was Malik ibn Anas (d. 795) of Medina. His Maliki school of law would eventually dominate both the Maghrib and al-Andalus—here, thanks to the emphatic support of Hisham I, who succeeded 'Abd al-Rahman. Usually described as conservative, the Maliki school is characterized by a strong rejection of "innovation"—any distortion of the Prophet's original and perfect Islam. By supporting the *fuqaha'* and incorporating them formally into his administration as magistrates, 'Abd al-Rahman gained their support for his dynastic project. They provided the religious glue that held the kingdom together and served as a bridge between the amir and his Muslim subjects. As in other parts of the Islamic world, they became politically powerful, thanks to their capacity to shape public opinion and declare rulers to be legitimately acting in the spirit of Islam, or not.

Just as important for the prince, and, therefore, his dynastic project, were the people he trusted as his agents and representatives. First and foremost, this meant family, particularly his sons Sulayman,

Hisham, 'Abd Allah, Umayya, al-Mundhir, and Maslama, who became governors of key cities and military commanders. Next came *mawlas* (clan members and clients), many of whom had been associated with his family for generations, and several of whom had established their own little bureaucratic dynasties within the emirate. These included former slaves (Badr, the youthful prince's confidant, was an ex-slave of Byzantine origin), Berbers, indigenous converts, and Arabs. Once ensconced in this network of privilege, these families dominated the cultural and political landscape in the centuries that followed, producing poets, scholars, government officials, and men of religion. And, like other rulers of his age, 'Abd al-Rahman also depended heavily on household slaves, who served as domestics, managers, officials, and military commanders. In fact, as a consequence of the violent opposition he faced and in direct response to the Arab-led uprising in Seville, 'Abd al-Rahman assembled a military unit independent of the *junds*, a royal bodyguard that was composed entirely of slaves—the only individuals of whose loyalty he could be absolutely assured.

4

A New Emirate

One of the many Arabic traditions carried into Islamic law concerned inheritance. Each son was entitled to an equal share of a parent's estate, with daughters receiving a half share. In terms of the succession of leadership of the family, this would go to any senior relative (as often a brother as a son) whom the father saw as the most appropriate, and whom his wider circle of family and clients would accept. Thus, the notion of an inherited caliphate was an innovation that grated against Arabic tradition. Because of the practice of polygamy and unlimited concubinage, Muslim aristocrats had the capacity to generate many potential heirs and thereby avoid the political crises that so often occurred in the Christian world when a ruler failed to produce a son old enough to govern by the time the ruler died.

Yet, because inevitably a number of potential heirs were sidelined, there was always the risk of a power struggle in which factions within the elite might encourage one of the noninheriting family members to revolt. In the best of circumstances, an heir would be chosen in advance and afforded the opportunity to consolidate bonds of clientage prior to the moment of succession. Then, on assuming the title, the new ruler would be presented to the powerful parties of the kingdom, who would be expected to publicly acclaim the ruler and pledge their allegiance in an act of acclamation and consent known as the *bay'a*.

In the case of Umayyad al-Andalus, 'Abd al-Rahman favored his second son, Hisham. By reputation a pious, sober, and capable individual, he came to the throne in 788 at age thirty with considerable experience and the support of the religious elite. However, he was immediately opposed by his elder brother Sulayman, who ruled in Toledo and who quickly recruited another brother, 'Abd Allah, to his cause. Sulayman was a seasoned fighter who enjoyed the loyalty of the Syrian troops, but after losing Toledo to Hisham and failing to regain the initiative, the two rebellious brothers agreed to accept permanent exile in the Maghrib together with a huge cash settlement. But this was not Hisham's only challenge. Zaragoza and the north were gripped by upheaval when the governor, Husayn ibn Yahya, declared independence in 788/89, and two years after he had been defeated, a warlord of Berber descent seized the city. In these cases, two indigenous magnates came to the aid of the Umayyads: Musa ibn Fortun ibn Qasi ("the son of Fortunatus, son of Cassius") and 'Amrus (Ambrose) ibn Yusuf, a member of another line of local *muwallads* (indigenous converts). This reflected powerful changes within the elite of Muslim Spain: many of the old Arab lineages were losing power and being replaced by Visigothic and Hispano-Roman families who had hung on and were now converting to Islam.

These episodes aside, the reign of Hisham was one of comparative stability, allowing him the opportunity to reinforce his position at home and reassert the emirate's power against its neighbors to the north. In terms of domestic policy, Hisham continued his father's initiatives, completing the mosque of Córdoba and making improvements to the city, including repairing the great Roman bridge, which had partially collapsed over the preceding centuries. He depended heavily on Umayyad family clients to govern and entrenched the emerging Maliki school of *'ulama'* in the emirate's power structure. They repaid him with gratitude. Malik ibn Anas himself was said to have praised Hisham as an example of piety and justice.

His aggressive turn against the infidel kingdoms was also lauded. In the decades previous, the Christian powers had taken advantage of the emirate's weaknesses, expelling vulnerable Muslim governors and seizing territory. In Asturias, Pelagius's son-in-law had come to the throne as Alfonso I in 739. Once he had subdued his Christian neighbors, he began to encroach on territory north of the Duero River. The Franks had been on the march too, presenting themselves as allies to discontented communities and rebellious Muslim governors along the length of the Pyrenees. In response, Hisham's generals carried out raids, including a spectacular attack on Narbonne and Carcassonne in 793, which garnered many prisoners and enough loot to satisfy both his army and the populace, and to pay for the work on the great mosque at Córdoba. It was the prospect of plunder, rather than religious duty, that was behind campaigns like this, and even as the Umayyads and Franks chipped away at each other's territory, they became increasingly engaged diplomatically. One of the fruits of this Umayyad-Frankish thaw was Hisham's son al-Hakam, who was the amir's offspring by a wife named Zukhruf ("Golden Ornament"), a Frankish girl, possibly a noblewoman, who had been presented to him by Charlemagne on the occasion of the truce the Frankish king signed with 'Abd al-Rahman.

Hisham died in 796 after less than eight years on the throne, but he had laid the groundwork for a smooth succession. Having imprisoned his elder son, 'Abd al-Malik, Hisham named his twenty-six-year-old son al-Hakam as heir. In complete contrast to his father, al-Hakam evoked the brash, masculine Arab ideal of the pre-Islamic era. A striking physical figure said to be tall, dark, and slim, he would personally lead his troops into battle. He enjoyed both wine and women in quantity, cultivated his talents as a poet and orator, and promoted learning and high culture. Cunning and shrewd, he did not hesitate to unleash his violent fury to intimidate his subjects; his moves were calculated and he was determined to strengthen the kingdom, stopping at nothing to do so. This did little, however, to endear him to the religious elite, who preferred the pious near-asceticism of his father.

Al-Hakam's first test came when his uncles Sulayman and 'Abd Allah returned from exile, bent on overthrowing him. After a four-year struggle, Sulayman was captured in an engagement with al-Hakam's forces, handed over to the amir, and executed. His head was paraded on a pike around the streets of Córdoba before his remains were interred in the royal mausoleum alongside those of his father,

'Abd al-Rahman I. He may have been a traitor, but he was an Umay-yad. The younger brother, 'Abd Allah, fared rather better. After his attempts to raise support in Valencia and Zaragoza failed, he jour-neyed with his sons to the court of Charlemagne in Aachen to propose an alliance. Although this came to nothing, he reconciled with his nephew, who granted him lordship and a free hand over Valencia and the east coast of al-Andalus, together with a rich pension, on the con-dition he not leave that territory. To seal the arrangement, al-Hakam gave two of his sisters in marriage to his uncle's sons, thus reconcil-ing the family split according to Arab tradition. One of the sons, 'Ubayd Allah, went on to become a faithful general for al-Hakam.

In the meantime, there was more trouble in the provinces. In 796, the people of Toledo, mostly native converts to Islam with little affin-ity for foreigners, perennially discontented and still smarting at the decline of their city, expelled their governor, the haughty Bahlul ibn Marzuk. A descendant of Basque converts, Ibn Marzuk then headed for Zaragoza and the northern borderlands of al-Andalus. There he declared his independence and began to wage war on the local Umay-yad faithful, the Arab Banu Salama, and the indigenous Banu Qasi. Al-Hakam, busy with his brothers, called on a loyal muwallad, 'Amrus ibn Yusuf, who restored order through quick and decisive military action and fortified key points in the territory to brace against future unrest. Having decided once and for all to deal with the people of Toledo, al-Hakam turned once again to 'Amrus. It was here, the chroniclers claim, that the amir would demonstrate his ruthless calcu-lation as never before.

As the story is told, 'Amrus arrived in Toledo in 797 and assem-bled the notables of the city, informing them that he, a fellow native, despised the amir just as they did. Having thus won their confidence, he announced he would be holding a banquet to honor the visit of al-Hakam's fourteen-year-old heir, 'Abd al-Rahman, to the city. On the appointed day, the prince arrived, a feast was laid out, and the aristoc-racy assembled outside the governor's palace where they were in-structed to enter separately in small groups. It was a trap. As each group entered the palace, they were directed through a narrow corri-dor, emerging from which they were ambushed by executioners and put to the sword in front of the young crown prince, their bodies then dumped unceremoniously into the moat. As the story goes, the sound of the musicians who were playing masked the screams, as seven hundred leading citizens marched unwittingly to their deaths. Although the story of the "Day of the Moat" is certainly a fiction (the banquet/massacre is a common literary trope), it reflects the amir's determination to terrorize the local elite into acquiescence. With Toledo pacified, by 806 'Amrus was sent back to the Upper March, where the Banu Qasi had now risen in alliance with the petty Christian rulers of neighboring Pamplona, Álava, and the Cerdanya.

BUT DISCONTENT ALSO brewed closer to home, a sign of general resistance on the part of city folk to the centralizing policies of the amir. In 800, a group of leading officials and jurists in Córdoba secretly approached al-Hakam's cousin Muhammad ibn Qasim, offering to install him as amir. But Muhammad was loyal and betrayed the conspirators, seventy-two of whom, many of high rank and prestige, were placed under arrest and executed, their crucifixes lining the banks of the Guadalquivir as a mute warning to would-be conspirators. Al-Hakam showed no mercy; among the *'ulama'* caught up in his vengeance was Yahya ibn Mudar, a venerable figure who had studied law under Malik ibn Anas himself.

This act of revenge did little to calm the populace, and fearing another coup, al-Hakam strengthened the city's fortifications and had his uncles Maslama and Umayya, who had been held in prison since the reign of Hisham, killed. He also reconstituted his personal bodyguard, assembling a troop of Frankish warriors, including prisoners who had been captured on the 793 raid against Narbonne and mercenaries from the Christian North. Known as al-Hurs, "the Silent Ones," because they could speak no Arabic, these foreign Christians were hated by the Muslim populace, hence al-Hakam could count on their absolute loyalty.

This was one example of the amir's general strategy of promoting powerful natives, whether muwallads or Christians, in his administration. One of his most trusted officials was Rabi' ibn Teodolfo, a Christian of Visigothic descent who served as "count" of his Christian

subjects, chief of the palatine guard, and commander of the mercenary regiments. Endowed with his own palace and bureaucracy, he
became a shadow-amir for the Christian population. Over the course
of the following years, his influence grew, and the ostentatiousness of
this *dhimmi* offended the sensibilities of the *'ulama'*. As his responsibilities extended to include the Muslim population of the capital, he
became a focus for popular dissatisfaction, particularly in relation to
taxation. To finance his military operations, the amir imposed new
taxes, a policy decried as un-Islamic, given that according to the
Qur'an, Muslims were to be subject to only two taxes: the *'ushr*, or
"tenth," on income, and the *sadaqa*, a mandatory alms tax. The clerics were particularly indignant because the amir tolerated public vice,
notably the sale of wine, to generate income. In the years that followed, Córdoba simmered as al-Hakam, frequently absent to squelch
other local rebellions, left the capital in the hands of overly proud
agents and his increasingly hated palace guard.

The breaking point came in the spring of 818, when the city folk
rose in a rebellion sparked by the killing of a townsman by a member
of the palace guard, and the amir's tone-deaf and violent response to
the protests that followed. The epicenter was the neighborhood known
as Shaqunda (from the Latin "Secunda"), across the Roman bridge on
the southern bank of the Guadalquivir. Populated mainly by recent
converts, it was home to workers and craftsmen and was fertile ground
for religious agitation. With the encouragement of a leading *faqih*, a
general strike was called. Finally, the townsfolk took up their weapons
and poured across the bridge to storm the city. Disaster was averted
only by the swift action of al-Hakam's cousin 'Ubayd Allah ibn 'Abd
Allah, who led a body of troops out of a side gate and surprised the
rebels from behind. The slaughter lasted for three days as al-Hakam
turned Shaqunda over to his troops for looting, swearing he would
raze the suburb and sow wheat fields where it had stood. Houses were
sacked, women were seized as slaves, and boys were taken and castrated. On the fourth day, the amir ordered a halt and issued his verdict:
three hundred leading citizens were to be publicly crucified, and
the entire surviving population of Shaqunda—thousands of Muslims,
as well as Christians and Jews—were given four days to leave

al-Andalus. Some made their way to Fez, where a local prince, Idris II, welcomed them, and others went as far as Egypt. One group conquered Byzantine Crete, where they set up an independent emirate.

Al-Hakam's remaining years were quieter, and he sought to restore his reputation among the *'ulama'* and the common folk. He shrewdly pardoned the leading *faqihs* who had been involved in the uprising and, as a gesture to them, allowed his heir-designate, 'Abd al-Rahman, to put on trial and execute his Christian familiar, Rabi' ibn Teodolfo, who had played a leading role in the repression of the revolt. With the amir ailing, his son saw an opportunity to rid himself of a wealthy and much-hated courtier and to mark a new era of collaboration with the religious elite. And so, a few days before al-Hakam died, the once-powerful Christian count was publicly crucified to the great delight of the populace. The famous Córdoban poet, Ibn al-Shamir, celebrated the execution of this "infidel who empowered his own people, and thereby provoked the vengeance of God" in verse, celebrating a death that "filled the people with happiness" and praising the new amir as generous, great, and faithful to God.[6] It was no exaggeration; the accession of 'Abd al-Rahman II to the throne of al-Andalus would signal a new era in the history of Islamic Spain.

THE EMIRATE THAT 'Abd al-Rahman II inherited was very different than the one his great-grandfather had founded some six decades earlier. Al-Andalus had been transformed as a consequence of the policy of the Umayyad rulers and of subtle but powerful forces at work deep within its society and culture. No longer a patchwork of local power-sharing arrangements, al-Andalus had the aspect of an organized kingdom. Much of the territory was divided into *kuras* (provinces), most of which were centered on a city or large town—the urban centers where most Arabs had settled. Each *kura* was ruled by a *wali* (governor) appointed by the amir and who did not enjoy any hereditary rights but often enjoyed considerable independence. Military command in each province was held by a prefect or *qa'id*. Several frontier zones—"Marches," or *thugur* (in singular, *thaghr*)—based at Badajoz/Mérida, Toledo, Zaragoza, and, early on, at Huesca (Washqa), remained semi-independent. In the Marches, the military and civil authority was not separated, and there was a tendency for local military dynasties to coalesce and take control, a state of affairs the amirs tolerated as long as these governors remained loyal.

Córdoba was now clearly the capital: the residence of the amir and the center of administration. Justice was overseen by the *qadi al-jama'a* ("chief judge") appointed by the prince. Taxes were collected to a significant extent in cash, and the economy began to gather momentum due to a greater availability of precious metal (some of which had been stripped from churches) for coinage and the growing craft and commercial market that was emerging in Córdoba and provincial capitals, such as Seville, Zaragoza, Toledo, and Valencia. The local currency of al-Andalus of this period speaks to the expanding tax base and Islamization of the administration. The first three amirs minted coins not only in gold but also in silver, and even circulated copper *fulus* (pennies; singular: *fals*). The relative abundance and variety of this currency enabled al-Andalus to move toward a cash-driven, commercialized economy of the type that had all but disappeared in Latin Europe even prior to the collapse of the Roman Empire.

In an effort to prevent regional rebellions, the Arab military aristocracy was gradually sidelined as the amirs recruited mercenaries, slaves, and captives, and cultivated other groups to counterbalance the strength of the clans. However, if the Syrian elite was on the wane, Arabic culture only became more entrenched, as the conquerors married native women and absorbed local families into their lineages and culture. However, while these muwallad families converted to Islam, learned Arabic, and immersed themselves in Arabo-Islamic culture, they did not necessarily lose their local connections. The petty noble families of the frontier maintained their bonds with their former co-religionists outside of the emirate, intermarrying and allying with them to pursue shared agendas. Among those who identified as Arabs, clan and tribal identity came to serve as a sign of social prestige rather than a framework for political action.

The situation of those Christians who did not convert was also in flux. After the conquest, some of the bishops who did not flee found employment with the new rulers and became local proxies: *amins* ("trusted agents"), administering and taxing the Christians, either independently or alongside a *qumis* ("count") drawn from the old aristocracy. But by 800, bishops had all but disappeared from the Islamic administration; as urban dwellers converted, their flocks and influence were diminishing. The Christian landed nobility were also outliving their worth. For example, Wittiza's son Ardabast, the first *qumis*, who had initially managed to maintain his considerable land holdings, was reduced to poverty after 'Abd al-Rahman I confiscated his estates and gave them to Umayyad clients.

By 800, urban life in al-Andalus began to revive in areas where the administration had made inroads. The towns themselves, however, would have been unrecognizable to earlier inhabitants. Surviving Roman buildings were dismantled, and what remained of the grids of straight streets and open public spaces was built over in Arabo-Islamic styles. Members of clans settled together in dense neighborhoods, which grew into warrens of windowless alleys concealing the self-contained, cloistered household typical of the Islamic East. The abandonment of cart traffic, eschewed in favor of the pack mule and camel, meant that streets no longer needed to be broad and straight; instead they tended to reflect the natural physical geography of the town, meandering around rises to mirror the flow of the seasonal but torrential rainstorms so common to much of the peninsula. As rural folk, for the most part new converts to Islam, were drawn to the cities, they constructed suburbs and took up trades now in demand thanks to the newly invigorated economy of patronage.

Conversion had not been encouraged, but a religious transformation of the population was also well under way by the second quarter of the 800s. Among the earliest converts had been the upper classes, who could thereby protect their wealth and status, as well as slaves, who were numerous in Visigothic Spain. Because non-Muslims were not to own Muslim slaves, conversion could be seen as a path to manumission; however, there was no sudden flood of slave conversions. One needed a Muslim patron to convert, and in any event, for a poor slave it was often better to be a slave of a wealthy Muslim than a freedman who was poor. In Visigothic Spain, the local church had been controlled by the landed nobility, who built and staffed churches for their dependents. Once they converted to Islam, it would have been ever more difficult to find pastoral clergy, and chapels and churches would have been neglected or abandoned. With rural Christianity set adrift, many peasants would have found their way toward Islam with or without the encouragement of their lords.

Those who emigrated to the suburbs and towns encountered a vigorous Islamic culture, and in this Muslim-dominated world, conversion held out the prospect of full legal rights, greater prestige (at least relative to non-Muslims), and opportunities of employment and patronage. Islam, although still only developing, may have seemed attractive with its egalitarian promises, participatory rituals, such as communal prayer and fasting, and its quality as a new and vibrant religion, which promised betterment not only in the hereafter, but also in the here and now. Private rural monasteries, founded by the remaining better-to-do Christian families and established away from the surveillance of Muslim religious authorities and converts, represented a rare exception to the decline of organized Christianity.

As for the countryside, in some areas peasants and slaves continued to labor on large, Roman-style agriculture estates, which passed into Muslim hands. Little would have changed in areas where hamlet-dwelling free peasants farmed their own small plots. However, areas settled by Berber clans changed dramatically. Although those Berbers who stayed in al-Andalus soon lost their language, they seem to have maintained their habits of social organization over many generations. They established traditional, egalitarian settlements and agricultural arrangements, and transplanted irrigation and land-distribution practices from North Africa that helped lay the foundation for the tremendous expansion of agricultural productivity that would come.

Across al-Andalus, Islamic consciousness was growing even as Islam itself was becoming more complex and regimented. In the 'Abbasid East, new schools of legal interpretation were emerging, the study of scripture was advancing, and the critical analysis of *hadith* was refined. A sense of normative Islamic practice was emerging, which filtered back to the far west by the medium of exiles, pilgrims, and traveling scholars. In al-Andalus more mosques were built, as sharing places of worship with Christians came to be seen as inappropriate. Separate Muslim cemeteries were established. Local centers of pilgrimage appeared, such as in Córdoba, where a copy of a Qur'an said to have been held by 'Uthman when he was assassinated held pride of place in the Great Mosque, and at Zaragoza, where the graves of two *Tabi'un* (Companions of the Companions of the Prophet) attracted worshippers. Rural sites, long venerated by Christians and pagans, were incorporated into the popular observance of the new faith. Across the peninsula, common folk paused to wash and pray in unison—five times per day if they were very pious, at Friday noon if they were less so—turning together in the direction of the *qibla* along with countless worshippers from the Atlantic to the Indus in a communal choreography of worship. Islamic law and Arabic custom began to shape social and gender relations, domestic politics, public behavior, manners of dress, notions of purity and propriety, and choices of diet and entertainment. Except in isolated hamlets, the corrupted spoken Latin of the Visigothic era was making way for Arabic as the language of administration and daily speech, leaving those Christians who had hoped decades earlier that the Arabic occupation would be a passing scourge not only figuratively but literally speechless.

IN SUM, BY the time 'Abd al-Rahman II came to the throne in 822, Islamic Spain was truly Islamic and, despite the challenges it faced, well-poised for prosperity. The dynasty was apparently stable, geographic isolation provided security from enemies, and as its economy gained strength, the population continued to grow, going from the perhaps three or four million inhabitants of the Visigothic era to upward of seven million by 800. But success would bring challenges, both from outside powers and in the form of new factions within Andalusi political culture. Over the next century, Islamic al-Andalus would step on the world stage and evolve from a provincial emirate into an international power. Through all of this, however, disaster often seemed only one wrong-footed step away.

PART II

Transformation, 820–929

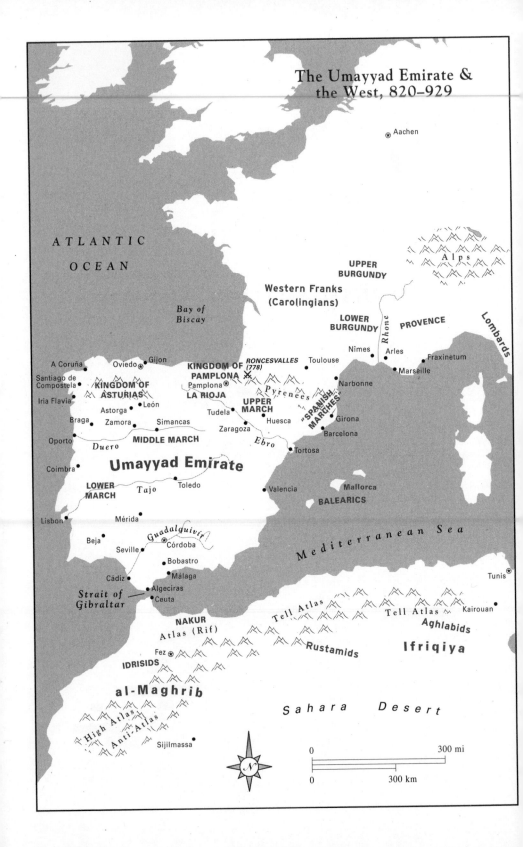

The Umayyad Emirate & the West, 820–929

⊕ Aachen

ATLANTIC

OCEAN

Bay of
Biscay

UPPER
BURGUNDY

Western Franks
(Carolingians)

LOWER
BURGUNDY

PROVENCE

Alps

Rhône

Lombards

Nîmes

Arles

Fraxinetum

Marseille

A Coruña ⊛
Santiago de
Compostela •
Iria Flavia •

Oviedo ⊛

Gijon •

**KINGDOM OF
ASTURIAS**

Astorga •

León •

Braga •
Zamora •
Simancas •

Oporto •

Duero

MIDDLE MARCH

Coimbra •

**LOWER
MARCH**

Tajo

Toledo •

**KINGDOM OF
PAMPLONA**

Pamplona ⊛

LA RIOJA

**UPPER
MARCH**

Tudela •

Huesca •

Zaragoza •

Ebro

RONCESVALLES
(778)

✕

Pyrenees

"SPANISH
MARCHES"

Girona •

Barcelona •

Toulouse •

Narbonne •

Tortosa •

Umayyad Emirate

Valencia •

Mallorca

BALEARICS

Lisbon •

Mérida •

Beja •

Guadalquivir

Seville •

Córdoba ⊛

Bobastro •

Málaga •

Cádiz •

Algeciras •
Ceuta •

*Strait of
Gibraltar*

NAKUR
Atlas (Rif)

Fez ⊛

IDRISIDS

al-Maghrib

High Atlas

Anti-Atlas

Sijilmassa •

Mediterranean Sea

Tunis ⊛

Tell Atlas

Tell Atlas

Kairouan •

Aghlabids

Ifriqiya

Rustamids

Sahara   Desert

0 _____ 300 mi

0 _____ 300 km

N

5

The Emirate on the Edge

High in a mountain pass in the western Pyrenees, brave Roland, count of Brittany and champion of the emperor Charlemagne, was fighting without quarter. Surrounded by treacherous, pagan Saracens, he had been betrayed by his false ally, the Muslim king Marsile, and the traitorous knight Ganelon. As the troops of the imperial rearguard fell dead around him, he knew his time was drawing near. Finally, realizing there was no alternative and content to die in the name of Christianity, he raised his mighty horn, Olifant, and blew it with all his might to summon Charlemagne's main force to avenge them on the infidel. In doing so, he burst his temples and collapsed dead, "his brain . . . coming out through his ears."[7] So recounts *The Song of Roland*, perhaps the most famous of the medieval *chansons de geste* and one that went on to become the French national epic. Although the hero's death recounted here is pure late-medieval fantasy, it hints at an engagement between European Christendom and Islamic al-Andalus that was complex and driven by both ideology and pragmatism.

Perceptions of Islam held by Europeans beyond Spain were shaped by medieval chivalric poems like *The Song of Roland*. It purports to recount Charlemagne's campaign of 778 to conquer al-Andalus, which was to be accomplished thanks to the offer of Marsile, king of

Zaragoza, to convert to Christianity and submit to the emperor. But the *Song* was only set down three centuries later, as the Crusade movement coalesced and Frankish knights were seeking their fortunes battling Muslims in Spain. In fact, Charlemagne was not yet emperor in 778, and his military efforts were focused on the pagan Saxons to his northeast and the Christian Lombards of Italy. For him, al-Andalus—wracked by rebellions—merely presented another opportunity. Thus, after pacifying Septimania, Charlemagne's forces crossed the Pyrenees in 785 and, with the support of locals, took the city of Girona, north of Barcelona, thereby establishing the frontier zone that would be known as the Spanish Marches and, later, Catalonia.

Charlemagne had come because the governors of Barcelona (Barshaluna) and Zaragoza—proud Arabs who had no intention of submitting to a refugee Umayyad prince—had sent envoys to his court, far north on the Saxon frontier, to request support for a rebellion against 'Abd al-Rahman I. Better to owe loyalty to a distant Frankish king than be forced to serve a Muslim prince so close to home, they thought. Their plan fit well with Charlemagne's agenda here, which was to secure his southern frontier and pacify the ever-rebellious Gascons (Basques, or Bashkunish). The center of Basque resistance was Pamplona, a strongly fortified redoubt nestled in the western Pyrenees. Charlemagne and his army arrived at Zaragoza, a metropolis founded seven centuries earlier by the emperor Augustus but attributed by Arab geographers to the Biblical Solomon. Girded by stout and gleaming Roman walls, it lay at the heart of a broad and fertile plain, spreading out from the banks of the wide and tranquil Ebro and flanked by arid, rust-red cliffs—in the words of a tenth-century Andalusi geographer, "a white stain surrounded by the vast emerald green of its countryside."[8]

To Charlemagne's dismay, however, the governor, Husayn ibn Yahya, refused to open the gates; the Frankish king's recent conquests had caused him to reconsider his proposition. Taking Zaragoza by force would be impossible, so the king gave up and led his army northwest, toward Pamplona, where the townsfolk submitted immediately and paid him willing homage—or so it seemed. Charlemagne was not aware that the leading families of Pamplona—Christians who had thrown off Muslim rule a half century earlier—were kinsmen through generations of intermarriage with the neighboring muwallad clans. By the time the proud king confidently departed, having taken down Pamplona's gates in a gesture of domination, the trap had been set.

The way back to Aquitaine would take Charlemagne over the Pass of Roncesvalles, where his army would be forced to move in a drawn-out defile within the confines of a thick wood. Hidden from view, the forces of Pamplona and their Muslim kinsmen lay in wait. Once the bulk of the Frankish army had passed and the royal baggage train followed by the rearguard—commanded, according to legend, by the heroic Roland—had entered the ravine, the ambush was sprung. Rocks and missiles rained down on the vulnerable Frankish line, whose powerful cavalry was hemmed in, unable to charge. Finally, the attackers swept in, massacring the panicked enemy and capturing the king's treasure and supplies. Although the episode would eventually take shape as an anti-Muslim legend, contemporaries were clear on who was to blame. In the words of Einhard, Charlemagne's biographer, it was at Roncesvalles that the future emperor "had a brief taste of Basque treachery."[9]

Indeed, rather than provoking a war with al-Andalus, the debacle of Roncesvalles prompted a series of embassies, and later sources even claim a marriage alliance between the two royal houses was proposed. For all his posturing as a Christian king and champion of the church, Charlemagne approached Muslim rulers no differently than Christian ones—and as a result, pragmatism and opportunity came to shape relations between the Umayyads and Charlemagne's Carolingian dynasty.

Distant as their realms might have been, the rulers of the lands in and around the Mediterranean were keenly aware of each other. Diplomats crisscrossed the region regularly, bearing exotic gifts as tokens of their lords' power, concluding treaties, and bringing back valuable intelligence. The storied embassy sent by the 'Abbasid caliph Harun al-Rashid to Charlemagne in 801 included "an elephant, balsam, nard (an aromatic plant), and various ointments, spices, perfumes and different medicines," as well as a mechanical clock, while ambassadors from Aghlabid Africa brought "a North African lion and a Numidian bear, red dye from Spain and purple from Tyre"—gifts fit for an emperor.[10] And by 801, this was precisely what Charles claimed to be, having been crowned "Emperor of Rome" by Pope Leo III the previous Christmas. Assuming that mantle was part of his larger program to defeat Byzantium and establish a new Roman Empire under Frankish control—thus, the 'Abbasid caliphate, Byzantium's enemy, was a natural ally. For their part, the 'Abbasids' Aghlabid allies in Ifriqiya shared a common interest with Charlemagne in undermining Umayyad al-Andalus.

So, the peace between the Franks and the Umayyads was a hot one, as each side took advantage of the other's weaknesses. In 801, for example, Charles's son, Louis the Pious, took Muslim Barcelona after a short siege. Subsequently, Frankish incursions deep into Andalusi territory temporarily captured Tarragona (Tarrakuna) and repeatedly besieged Tortosa (Turtusha), the main Mediterranean port in the northeast. The amirs responded in kind, supporting anti-Carolingian uprisings in Catalonia in the 820s, besieging Narbonne in 840, and briefly retaking Barcelona and sacking Girona in 856. In 824, history would repeat when a Frankish army that had subdued Pamplona was once again ambushed in the Pass of Roncesvalles, this time by local Basque warriors and their kinfolk, the Banu Qasi. None of these campaigns were decisive, and a stable frontier coalesced in a line stretching from just south of Barcelona westward along the foothills of the Pyrenees. The Muslims controlled the plains and the lowlands, while the remote high mountain valleys were held by local Christian strongmen. The situation was a stalemate.

CHARLEMAGNE'S CAMPAIGN, HOWEVER, was not without consequences for al-Andalus, as it exacerbated problems the Umayyads faced in Zaragoza and the Ebro Valley—a region that had rarely been effectively governed from the south, even under the Visigoths. It was now known as the Upper March (*Thaghr al-'Ala*) or Furthest March (*Thaghr al-'Aqsa*), a frontier province and one of three Marches established in the 800s, including the Middle March (*Thaghr al-Awsat*), ruled from Toledo, and the Lower March (*Thaghr al-Adna*), centered on Mérida. As for Pamplona, occasional punitive campaigns were launched against it, but the city proved too distant to be dominated by Córdoba. For safety, it pledged submission to the fledgling Christian kingdom of Asturias, although it remained an intermittent tributary of Córdoba and ties remained strong with Zaragoza. Eneko (Iñigo, in Spanish) Arista (Yannaqu ibn Wanniku, in Arabic), the first "King of Pamplona," was obliged to send his son Garsea (García) to be raised at the emiral in Córdoba, and Garsea's daughter, Oneka (Íñiga), would marry the Umayyad amir 'Abd Allah in the late 800s.

In Zaragoza, meanwhile, al-Husayn ibn Yahya's repeated rebellions hastened the end of Arab rule and paved the way for the rise of the muwallad Banu Qasi. This clan of Spanish-Roman origin, whose patriarch, Cassius (whence came "Qasi" and "Banu Qasi," or "the clan of Cassius"), converted to Islam at the time of the conquest, had entrenched themselves by intermarrying with Muslim and Christian clans in the Ebro Valley and the Pyrenees. In 839, a great-grandson of Cassius, Musa ibn Musa, set out to establish an independent kingdom based in Zaragoza, with the help of his uncle Eneko Arista. The amir, 'Abd al-Rahman II, could not afford to lose Musa, so he brought a combination of coercion and compromise to bear, launching a series of raids against Pamplona, which he qualified as jihad. This obliged Musa to participate, effectively forcing him to attack his ally Eneko.

In 852, when both 'Abd al-Rahman II and Eneko Arista died, Musa turned his energies against his former allies in Pamplona and attacked the Frankish-allied lords of Catalonia and Christians of Asturias. Musa was now styling himself the "third king of Spain," but the new amir, Muhammad I, distracted by rebellions in the south, had little choice but to give Musa a free hand in the north, on the condition he nominally recognize Córdoban authority. In exchange, the amir could take some credit for Musa's campaigns, including the 856 sack of Barcelona. Musa died in 862, but ten years later, the clan—now known as the Banu Musa in his honor, and led by his four sons, Lubb (Lope), Fortun, Mutarrif, and Isma'il—seized the Upper March once again. In response, Muhammad I launched expeditions against the family and cultivated rival clans, including the muwallad Banu 'Amrus and the Arab Banu Tujib. However, the Banu Qasi proved simply impossible to dislodge from the region. The city of Zaragoza's walls made it almost unconquerable, and the March was dotted by castles and fortified towns, such as Tudela (Tutila) and Huesca, that could easily resist the expeditions that the amirs were able to muster.

Time, however, was ultimately on the side of the Umayyads. By the 880s, Musa's various sons and their offspring were fighting each other, a rivalry the Umayyads stoked by skillfully offering and withholding support and encouraging family members to turn against each other. For their part, the Banu Qasi took up or broke their vows to the Umayyads as opportunity suited. This cycle of reconciliation and betrayal was continued through the end of the century by Musa's grandson Muhammad ibn Lubb, and then by his son Lubb ibn Muhammad. Like his great-grandfather Musa ibn Musa, Lubb ibn Muhammad combined a strategy of aggressive military action and intensive diplomacy, including marital alliances with local Muslim and Christian clans. But in 907, after Lubb ibn Muhammad met his death on campaign outside Pamplona, the Banu Qasi's power quickly waned. Leading members fled as refugees to Christian lands, where they converted and were absorbed into local aristocracies, or skulked back as supplicants to Córdoba, where they finally came to serve the Umayyad dynasty. Lubb's son Muhammad, the last of the Banu Qasi, was treacherously executed by his kinsman Count Ramon of Pallars, with whom he had taken refuge in 929, the same year the triumphant Umayyad amir 'Abd al-Rahman III took the title "caliph of Islam."

BUT THERE WAS more for the amirs to contend with than rebellious governors and Frankish armies, and trouble could come in the most unexpected form. For example, by the mid-ninth century, Seville, the second city of al-Andalus, had enjoyed over 150 years of peace. The amirs of Córdoba, ninety miles to the east, had quashed the rebellious Yamani Arabs who had risen up in the 770s. 'Abd al-Rahman II had just completed the construction of a monumental congregational mosque in Seville. And now the city, set amid lush agricultural lands, was enjoying growing prosperity. It served as a marketplace for the surrounding region, rich in olives, figs, livestock, and grain, and had a commercial port, thanks to the Guadalquivir, the "Great River" that connected it to the royal capital to the east and the Atlantic Ocean to the west. However, its privileged location would prove its undoing, when in October 844, fifty-four dragon-headed longboats lurched ashore on the city's grassy riverbank. Roaring their battle cries, hundreds of towering, bearded Norsemen leapt from their ships and rushed into the unfortified city, swinging their axes as the inhabitants scattered in panic. The Vikings had arrived in al-Andalus.

After looting Seville, the Norse raiders gathered their booty and captives and withdrew, rowing back into the marshy, mazelike delta of the Guadalquivir, where they established their camp. Soon reinforcements arrived, and they returned to Seville for a week of looting, while 'Abd al-Rahman II sent desperate calls to the governors of the south and gathered forces to repulse the invaders. The Vikings' arrival was not entirely unexpected; in the previous months, a squadron of longships had cruised along the Bay of Biscay and been repulsed at Gijón and A Coruña by Ramiro I of Asturias. They had better luck at Muslim Lisbon (al-Ushbuna), which they looted for thirteen days before continuing to Cádiz. From there, they fanned out inland, raiding with impunity. As Seville burned and its garrison hunkered down in the fortress, the citizenry took refuge in nearby Carmona (Qarmuna) while the amir gathered an army.

It was then that the importance of the fickle frontier lords was made clear. Among those who brought troops was none other than Musa ibn Musa of the Banu Qasi. The Viking raid served to reconcile the amir and the rebellious frontier lord. Musa formally affirmed his status as a client in good faith and thereby received the amir's confirmation as lord of the Upper March. For his part, 'Abd al-Rahman reinforced his own role as sovereign and harnessed the military might of the Banu Qasi. Thus, on November 11, 844, the Vikings were beaten back, having been ambushed by the Umayyad cavalry and seen their ships attacked with "Greek Fire," a napalm-like substance launched from shipborne flamethrowers. They suffered heavy losses, and after 'Abd al-Rahman had the prisoners slaughtered on the battlefield before their countrymen's eyes, the survivors retreated in panic. Following a series of ineffective raids on the southern coast, and perhaps on North Africa, the Vikings set sail once again for the northlands. For the amir, the battle at Seville was a triumph, and he sent heralds as far afield as the Maghrib to trumpet his victory.

Some fourteen years later, the Vikings would return. This time the emirate was ready. A Muslim fleet intercepted them off the Portuguese coast in 858, and their plans to ravage the Guadalquivir valley were aborted when they learned that the amir, Muhammad I, had marshalled an army to meet them. The ever-mobile Norsemen broke off and, threading the Strait of Gibraltar, sailed eastward, sacking Algeciras, burning its mosque (the first founded in al-Andalus) and taking the port town as a base. From there, they crossed over to the Maghrib, landing near the capital of Nakur, an independent Muslim kingdom, which they sacked, carrying off prisoners, including women of the royal household. By this time, the Umayyad fleet had been called up, and the Vikings again struck eastward, raiding along the Andalusi seaboard. They attacked Frankish Septimania and finally settled for the winter in the swampy and isolated Camargue delta at the mouth of the Rhône River.

In the Mediterranean, as elsewhere, the Vikings' success depended largely on the element of surprise, particularly when they attacked areas that had not had to contend with serious threats from the sea in generations, like the coasts of al-Andalus. Undoubtedly, they came to trade too, or at least to convert less portable booty and locally valuable assets, like important captives, into cash, jewelry, or whatever supplies they needed. Prisoners they seized would have been forced to serve as guides to take them to their next targets. After their experience in Britain and Frankish lands, the Vikings may have spoken some Latin or brought captive clerics from the north to use as interpreters. Indeed, the sources relate that the Umayyads managed to ransom the royal women of Nakur, so some sort of negotiations must have taken place. Although to Muslim chroniclers the Norse were anonymous barbarians, or *Majus*, as they called them, Norse tradition identifies their leaders as Björn Ironsides and Hastein, two sons of the legendary Ragnar Lothbrok.

When the winter of 859 broke, the Norsemen sailed back toward al-Andalus, attacking the Balearic Islands, where Muhammad I's fleet caught up with them. Unable to risk further losses, they resolved to return home and, with characteristic ingenuity, outfoxed their pursuers by heading inland. The broad and gentle Ebro was precisely the type of waterway their longships were made for. Sailing to Tortosa, at the river's mouth, the Vikings switched to oars and powered upstream, leaving the wind-borne Umayyad fleet behind. Except for a short portage at the rapids near Flix, they faced an easy paddle through the lands of the Banu Qasi, under the Roman bridge at Zaragoza, and onward to the territory of the Basques. Here, they disembarked and, marching their loot and prisoners forward, descended on Pamplona, capturing its king, Garsea (the son of Eneko Arista), whom they held hostage for an enormous cash ransom. Thus, the Vikings were able to reach the Bay of Biscay, reconstitute a fleet, and sail home with their prisoners and booty. The entire adventure had lasted just over a year.

In the end, while the Viking raids on Islamic Spain captured the imagination of Muslim and Christian chroniclers, they did not result in sustained contact, and the lasting consequences were few. There is a tradition that some of the prisoners from the first raid were spared execution and settled near Seville, where they became cheesemakers(!), but this is a misreading of an Arabic chronicle. Another source records a diplomatic mission to the Norse led by one of al-Hakam's favorite poets, Yahya ibn al-Hakam al-Ghazal, but this was mere legend. Nor did the Norsemen develop a consistent trading presence in al-Andalus as they did in the 'Abbasid East. All they could offer to Andalusis were slaves, and although slaves were in great demand here, there was already an abundant supply—namely, captives taken in raids against the Christian North, or pagans captured in Eastern Europe and imported by Frankish and Jewish merchants.

EXCEPT FOR THE flow of slaves to al-Andalus, transcontinental trade, such as it existed in the first half of the eighth century, would not have been robust here. Al-Andalus remained a relatively poor and isolated corner of the world, its era of wealth and glory still a century away. In the meantime, small-scale Muslim and Christian merchants undoubtedly carried slaves and merchandise between the emirate and its neighbors. Trade over longer distances was apparently dominated by a mysterious group of Jewish traders, referred to as al-Rahdaniyya (or Radhanites), whose routes stretched across the Mediterranean, through the Near East, up into northern and eastern Europe, and as far east as China and India. The tenth-century Persian traveler and geographer, Ibn Khurradadhbih, pointed to their importance to al-Andalus being in "the girls and handsome boys they bring from France and *Jilliqiyya* (the northwest), as well as Slavic slaves."[11]

THE VIKING ATTACK of 844 demonstrated just how vulnerable al-Andalus was to invasion by sea, and the amir immediately commissioned the construction of a war fleet. Coastal defenses were also strengthened, and it is perhaps during this period that an Andalusi civil defense network was developed in the form of watchtowers along both the coastal and the land frontiers. Communicating via optical signals such as fire and smoke, watchmen could relay information rapidly over great distances and warn of enemy movements or impending attack.

Such preparations proved of crucial importance in fending off the second Viking attack, which for all its violence, inflicted little damage. Yet the Norsemen were not the only seaborne threat the Umayyads faced. In Ifriqiya, the Aghlabid rulers had faced a revolt of their Arab subjects, and to divert their military energies, the amir Ziyadat Allah launched a naval invasion of Byzantine Sicily in 824 under the banner of jihad. Even before the island had been subdued, their forces continued northward to the Italian mainland, sacking Rome in 847, taking Taranto, establishing an emirate at Bari, and raiding the port towns up and down the Italian coasts. By the mid-800s, Muslims were being recruited by local Christian lords as mercenaries. Malta was conquered in 870. Although these attacks did not constitute a direct threat to al-Andalus, the Aghlabids were enemies of the Umayyads to whom they could not afford to relinquish control of the sea.

The Umayyad fleet doubled as a vehicle for foreign policy. It allowed for closer contact with the Maghrib. Here, 'Abd al-Rahman II was working to establish himself as the powerbroker and protector of the small but increasingly important principalities coalescing there, including Nakur; Fez, which was ruled by the Banu Idris; the Rustamid kingdom of central Algeria; and Sijilmassa, ruled by the

Banu Midrar. These volatile, little states, populated by Berbers and ruled over by Berber, Arab, or Persian families, were drawn to the more radical fringes of Islamic doctrine, whether Kharijism or 'Ibadism, and were thus opposed to the 'Abbasids and their Aghlabid clients.

The kingdom of Sijilmassa was of particular importance. Set on the eastern flank of the Atlas Mountains and the fringe of the western Sahara, it was emerging as the northern terminus for the caravan routes that led south to the Sahel and the grassy southern fringe of the great desert. Beyond this lay the lands of Niger and Ghana, rich in gold, ivory, slaves, and other exotica. The fleet first established by 'Abd al-Rahman II in response to the attacks of the Vikings would become the means by which the destinies of al-Andalus and the Maghrib would once again become joined—politically, religiously, commercially, and demographically. This renewed relationship would launch Umayyad al-Andalus as a superpower in the tenth century, but it would also plant the seeds for its collapse only a century later.

The emirate's transition to naval power also enabled it to impose its will on Mallorca (Mayurqa) and Menorca (Minurqa), two strategically located islands that served as commercial and military links to Ifriqiya, Italy, and Provence. Until the late ninth century, the islands were only intermittently controlled by Córdoba, and the population remained overwhelmingly Christian, with Islam only a tenuous presence. It was under Muhammad I, 'Abd al-Rahman's successor, that a concerted campaign was launched to bring the islands under control. This was accomplished only a half century later, under Muhammad I's son 'Abd Allah, who authorized a privateer, 'Issam al-Khawlani, to lead a fleet against Mallorca. The natives resisted doggedly, but after eight years, al-Khawlani subdued them. Once recognized as governor by both the amir and his new subjects, he embarked on a concerted policy of Islamization and infrastructure development, constructing mosques, baths, inns for traders, and other utilities. Mallorca thus became a launching point for incursions into Frankish territory, notably the raid on Saint Tropez, which led to the establishment of a permanent base at Fraxinetum (Fréjus, or La-Garde-Freinet) in 887.

From as early as the 840s, Andalusi ships had been harassing the ports of Septimania and Provence, including Arles and Marseille, and the towns of the Rhône valley, but the nature of these campaigns continues to be debated. Were they piratical? Or part of a deliberate Umayyad policy to control the Western Mediterranean? Were they religiously motivated? Or were they merely the same opportunistic plundering the Norsemen engaged in? In fact, these campaigns probably combined all these elements. For all its efforts, the Umayyad "state" did not have a centralized, regimented military. Power resided with local strongmen, who were happy to enjoy the sanction of the emirate and the moral legitimacy Islam provided for their campaigns, but at bottom, the raids were a natural response to the vulnerabilities of Frankish Provence. These vulnerabilities were made patent by the success of the enclave at Fraxinetum, an all but impregnable fortress that became the tributary power over neighboring Provençal towns and served as a base for raids deep into Frankish territory in the 900s, the most dramatic of which would be the storied plundering in 954 of the great monastery of Saint Gallen in Switzerland.

As for the Norsemen, they would return to al-Andalus, but not until the second half of the tenth century, when in 966 and 971 they raided the Atlantic coast south of Lisbon. In each case, the caliphal fleet repulsed them. By then the Viking age was drawing to a close; within a century, the pagan religion of the Norse would be eclipsed by Christianity and the seminomadic ways of their forefathers abandoned. The Vikings were domesticated. Some served in the imperial Varangian Guard at Byzantine Constantinople, while others joined the chieftain, Rollo, who submitted to the Frankish kings in 913, taking the title Duke of Normandy. In this latter guise, the Norseman, now Normans (*al-'Ardmaniyyun*, to the Arabs) would continue to play a crucial role in the transformation of the Islamic Mediterranean and of al-Andalus, figuring in the later conquests of Muslim lands carried out by Christian princes that came to be known misleadingly as the "Spanish Reconquest."

6

The Invention of al-Andalus

By the time al-Hakam died after twenty-six tumultuous years on the throne, he had sired no less than twenty-one sons and seventeen daughters. With no shortage of heirs, he had dozens of children he could marry into prominent and up-and-coming families to strengthen the network of Umayyad in-laws and clients. The son he eventually chose to succeed him—the same son who as a young man was said to have witnessed the massacre of the "Day of the Moat"—turned out to be a wise choice. When he came to power in 822, 'Abd al-Rahman II was thirty years of age and very much his own man: experienced in battle, having observed his father's uncompromising approach to rule, and adept at navigating the complex politics that undergirded (and constantly challenged) the Umayyad power structure. He was also physically robust, and if later accounts can be trusted, notable for his tall stature, aquiline nose, and blue eyes. To create an even more striking impression, he lined his already penetrating eyes with *kohl* and dyed his abundant beard with red and black henna, in emulation of the Prophet.

He not only reigned for thirty years, but managed to pass the throne to his son Muhammad I, who would rule over al-Andalus for thirty-four years, from 852 to 886. Such longevity was crucial, providing for constancy in an era of more or less continuous rebellion.

85

This was also the period during which Islamic Spain truly became Islamic, both as a consequence of conversion and through 'Abd al-Rahman's deliberate creation of al-Andalus as a distant mirror of the 'Abbasid caliphate and his determination to build the emirate into a cultural and economic powerhouse.

WHEREAS HIS FATHER, al-Hakam, met threats head-on, 'Abd al-Rahman II learned to use the religious elite to his advantage and turn rebellious subordinates into allies through compromise. Hence, rather than punish Yahya ibn Yahya al-Layti, the Maliki *faqih* of Berber origin who had been the voice behind the 807 rebellion in Córdoba, the amir made him his close confidant and religious advisor. This approach was also used with the ever-restive provincial governors, like those of the Banu Qasi of the Upper March, and in Toledo, where he appointed governors from among the leading Umayyad clients, changing them frequently to prevent them from establishing roots. To the west, in Beja (Baja), he marched out in person against a rebellious governor, but when the rebel sued for peace, he invested him with additional autonomy in exchange for his loyalty. And in Tudmir, where rival Arab clans battled for control, 'Abd al-Rahman pulled the rug out from under them by reorganizing the province and founding a new capital city, Murcia (Mursiya), which he placed under the rule of loyal family members. He could be vicious too. When the people of the Balearics rose up in the 820s, he ordered the islands sacked, claiming his one-fifth share of the loot as ruler.

To restructure the administration, 'Abd al-Rahman II drew directly on the model of the 'Abbasid caliphate. He expanded his household, transforming the "Silent Ones"—the foreign-born palatine guard—into a permanent army of cavalry and purchasing large quantities of castrated slaves to work in the palace and provincial administrations. These eunuchs, most of whom were *Saqaliba*, or Slavic pagans by origin, had no family and would have no loyalties or community beyond the amir and his court. The most promising among these were raised to high positions in the royal household.

He also cultivated a clutch of *mawali* families, including Arabs, natives, and Berbers, none of whom would be allowed to become too powerful, and all of whom saw their fortunes as tied to that of the Umayyads. Official positions, such as *hajib*, or royal chamberlain, that had been largely ceremonial, were now assigned concrete powers. In imitation of the 'Abbasids, he created a civil service comprising branches and departments, including finance, interior, defense, and economic development, each under the control of a *wazir* (minister), all of whom were required to report regularly to the amir. The formalization of the chancery and the appointment of trained *kuttab* (secretaries; singular: *katib*) enabled orderly recordkeeping and increased the amir's control over the day-to-day function of the emirate. He also established a postal service to facilitate communication and relay intelligence to the capital.

Instead of resisting the growing power of the religious elite, 'Abd al-Rahman II harnessed it, appointing Maliki jurists as magistrates and recruiting many into the civil service. If the people saw the amir as the foundation of the greater worldly order, it was the *'ulama'* they looked to for guidance in daily affairs. And because it was their consensus that determined whether a ruler was legitimate and should be obeyed, religious scholars held tremendous power, particularly in relation to the common folk. By contrast, the amir embodied *sultan*, or executive political authority. He could wage war, appoint officials, and manage the kingdom, but with few exceptions, he did not make laws. His natural constituency was the *khassa*, or aristocracy, a loose and porous upper class composed of *mawali* families, members of old Arab and muwallad high society; the cultural and intellectual elite; and those entrepreneurs and adventurers who rose to fortune through commerce or warfare. It also included leading figures of the Christian and Jewish communities—a minority elite who identified increasingly with Arabic culture and social mores, and with the emerging Umayyad state.

Incorporating the *'ulama'* into the power structure had other advantages too. Because authority within the scholarly community was based on knowledge, it became a natural meritocracy, in which birth was no guarantee of prestige and even the humblest slave or convert could rise to fame and influence. There was no formal distinction, as in Christianity, between clergy and layfolk; a religious scholar could be a tradesman, landowner, merchant, warrior, or any combination thereof. Indeed, many came out of the swelling urban population and were artisans, craftsmen, or merchants by trade. Consequently, what was previously a tributary system dominated by the Umayyad clan began to evolve into a system in which urban folk gained a voice and stake in the running of the emirate.

As al-Andalus became increasingly Arabic culturally, and more Islamic in terms of demography and religion, the amir promoted an Andalusi identity to reinforce his own authority. Hence, 'Abd al-Rahman continued to invest in the monumental aspects of his capital, Córdoba, notably the great mosque. A new minaret was added, and the floor space of the prayer hall was doubled. By this time, the population of Córdoba was about 75,000—triple that of the time of 'Abd al-Rahman I. It was also during 'Abd al-Rahman II's reign that new congregational mosques were built in other cities, such as Seville and Zaragoza, reflecting the growing size of the Muslim community and the political role played by these buildings, which advertised the prestige not only of Islam, but also of the amirs and governors who financed their construction.

IN THE FIRST half of the ninth century, commerce began to play an important role, providing wealth to the emirate and its people. Although silver supply was limited, 'Abd al-Rahman II minted immense quantities of *dirhams* of consistent weight and purity, as well as nonprecious *fulus*. Thus, currency was widely available and trusted. This sound monetary policy was continued by Muhammad I, who would be faced with a silver shortage. He resisted the urge to debase the currency, which would have led to inflation and a crisis of confidence, and instead minted fewer coins of the same purity. Most importantly, 'Abd al-Rahman II's political engagement with the Maghrib would lay the groundwork for Andalusi domination of northwest Africa, which would in turn provide direct access to the gold routes of the Sahara. In the meantime, some manufactured goods, notably silk from southern al-Andalus and fine leather from Córdoba, were exported to Italy and the Frankish North in exchange for slaves—mostly young girls and eunuchs—and other luxury goods, notably furs. In this era, cotton, hemp, and saffron (for dying) were brought to al-Andalus for the first time, further fueling a growing textile industry.

The emerging cash economy of al-Andalus contrasted with the subsistence economies of Frankish Europe and Christian Iberia, where rural servility remained the norm, social mobility was low, and there was little by way of urban culture, infrastructure, or currency. Christian rulers collected revenue through the direct consumption of food surpluses, forcing them to continuously circulate through their lands with their households in tow. This itinerant lifestyle prevented them from accumulating easily transferrable wealth, and from developing secular institutions and bureaucracies. In al-Andalus, as the economic and, therefore, political weight of the urban common folk grew, that of the old rural aristocracy was declining. As this reversal became more acute over the course of the century, it would help spark the revolts of the muwallad elite that would nearly tear the emirate apart in the later 800s.

AND WHAT WAS this 'Abbasid East 'Abd al-Rahman looked to as a model for al-Andalus? By 800 Baghdad was in the midst of the Islamic "Golden Age" of Harun al-Rashid, *The One Thousand and One Nights*, and Sinbad the Sailor. Ascendant on the world stage, its formal primacy and prestige within the Islamic world went unchallenged. Not only was Islam coalescing as a religious and legal culture in the 'Abbasid lands, but the caliphate was creating an institutional framework for empire. Meanwhile, Arabo-Islamic culture, heavily infused with Persian, Byzantine, Syriac, Hebrew, and South Asian influences, was reaching new heights of sophistication and innovation in virtually every field of science and art, not to mention philosophy and theology. As 'Abd al-Rahman II eagerly appropriated these advances, al-Andalus would become "Orientalized."

The essence of the cosmopolitan turn in Islam is epitomized by the upper-class emphasis on sophistication and refinement (referred to generically as *adab*) as a measure of prestige. Language—the ability to engage in repartee and to recite and compose complex verse (preferably extemporaneously)—was all-important. Also crucial were knowing how to dress well and behave with courtesy and appreciating, if not personally engaging in, music and song and the discourse of the sciences, arts, and philosophy. It is difficult today to appreciate the economy of wisdom that developed in the Islamic and Byzantine Mediterranean and Near East during this time. Books were like treasure chests and knowledge was like gold. As well as having an intrinsic value, it served as a currency that could purchase favor and position and be exchanged for wealth. Men strove to possess it or surround themselves with it, not only for the practical advantages it bestowed, but also as both an ornament and a signal of status and power. And for men of the aristocracy, there were additional virtues to cultivate: learning and wit were obligatory, but members of the *khassa* were also to exhibit more traditionally masculine Arab qualities. They were to be fearless warriors, dogged hunters, accomplished riders, tireless lovers, and insatiable drinkers, as well as proud (but not vulgar), jealous (but not envious), quick both to anger and to forgiveness, hospitable to strangers, loyal to friends, and generous to excess. The emerging Arabo-Islamic masculine ideal was like chivalry on steroids, and key to ‘Abd al-Rahman II's success was his ability to embody this new standard.

The amir's father had planted the seed. Al-Hakam had a keen interest in poetry and appreciated high culture. He was known for patronizing poets and astrologers, and he established a coterie of learned courtiers who helped educate his sons. Under their influence, ‘Abd al-Rahman II set out to become a model of *adab*, showering gifts and cash on the literati who attended him, surrounding himself with men of learning, and cultivating a persona that epitomized the notions of prestige emerging in the cosmopolitan Islamic East.

He modeled himself as an ideal king: a fierce and indomitable lion, but magnanimous and generous to those who showed the same masculine spirit, even if they dared defy him. Both his fits of rage and his gestures of gentleness had a deliberately unpredictable quality that served to keep his subordinates, attendants, and suppliants on solicitous edge. No armchair general, he rode out onto campaign at the head of his troops—neither foolhardy nor brash, but as a man secure in the armor of destiny. As a man of learning and faith, he had

A hunter with two lions. From an ivory box made for Hisham II
by the workshop of Faraj (1004/5 CE). *Museo de Navarra/
Comunidad Foral de Navarra*

memorized the Qur'an by heart, composed poetry, and studied astrology. Proof of his virility and sexual potency was found in the scores
of concubines he maintained and the legion of children he sired by
them and his wives. Despite there being no stigma attached to nonvir-
ginity, the amir made a specific point of taking no woman to bed who
had lain with another. What was his, was his and his alone.

As was the custom in the east, he established a *tiraz*, or royal silk
workshop, which turned out royal regalia, gifts for his favorites and
for foreign dignitaries, and decorations for his palaces. Finally, if
there was any doubt as to his majesty, this was confirmed by life in his
court, which turned ever more on the choreographed ritual of public
spectacle.

Among his most treasured resources and valued adornments were the individuals with whom he surrounded himself—his entourage of advisors, aides, sycophants, supporters, and friends. First among these was Abu 'l-Fath Nasr. Nasr was the son of a Christian from Carmona who had converted to Islam and somehow been caught up in the rebellion of Córdoba of 818. In the aftermath of the uprising, a furious al-Hakam carried out reprisals against the inhabitants of the suburb and members of the aristocracy who supported them by seizing and castrating some of their sons (Nasr included)—Islamic prohibitions of such mutilation notwithstanding—and forcing them into service in the palace.

As a young man in the palace of al-Hakam, Nasr distinguished himself and became a confidant of the young 'Abd al-Rahman, rising with him when he came to the throne. During the first Viking raid, Nasr helped command the emirate's forces to victory, which gained him the honorific Abu 'l-Fath ("the Father of Conquest"). Climbing further in 'Abd al-Rahman's estimation, he acquired enough wealth to build a great palace outside the capital on the banks of the Guadalquivir. To establish a broad political base, he curried favor among the common folk and the aristocracy and with the powerful *faqih* Yahya ibn Yahya. As a eunuch entrusted with the prince's harem, Nasr formed alliances and cultivated agents within the royal household.

Here, the wives and concubines with whom he mixed were important players at the court: wealthy, ambitious, and fierce promotors of their own children among the prince's sprawling brood. Having a son inherit the throne could transform a concubine into an *umm walad*, or queen mother, while a son who did not inherit would be in danger of death or imprisonment at the hands of his more fortunate half sibling. These women also had tremendous influence with the amir, who was famous for driving his accountants to despair by presenting sacks of gold to whatever woman was the present object of his sexual or emotional obsession (and who, of course, would rebuke and rebuff him and demand ever more lavish tokens of his love). With this wealth, concubines and wives built estates and palaces, founded mosques, and established their own political networks.

Nasr's moment seemed to have come when 'Abd al-Rahman suffered a serious illness in the late 840s that obliged him to all but retire from public life. Appointed as regent, Nasr began to dismiss the amir's trusted officials and plotted with the favorite wife, Tarub, to make her son, 'Abd Allah, the heir, rather than Muhammad, who had been chosen by the amir. But as 'Abd al-Rahman's illness dragged on, and then showed signs of improvement, an impatient Nasr resolved to kill him, bribing the royal physician, al-Harrani, to prepare a poison, which the eunuch would present to his lord as if it were medicine. Fortunately, another wife, Fajr, was a student of pharmacopeia and friend of al-Harrani. He confessed the plot to her, and she informed the prince. And so, when Nasr presented 'Abd al-Rahman with his morning "medicine," he first feigned an upset stomach before turning to Nasr and ordering him to drink it himself. Nasr had no choice, and after quaffing the potion, he ran off in search of al-Harrani and the antidote, but dropped dead in agony before he could get it.

This death was met with some relief by 'Abd al-Rahman's other confidants. Poems were recited in celebration. The ambitious Nasr, like the puritanical Yahya ibn Yahya, had been an odd duck in the prince's circle. The worldly amir preferred his entourage of dashing and witty aristocrats: well-read and sophisticated men of the world, equally at home drinking, fighting, composing poetry, or dabbling in astrology. Indeed, poetry and astrology pervaded the court, much to the offense of some clerics. The study of the stars was crucial to Islam, marking as they did the religious events of the year, but many *'ulama'* were less than comfortable with the cultivation of Hellenistic and Persian astronomical sciences. These were used to read portents and glean news of faraway events—activities that encroached on the divine prerogative.

A typical figure of the time was Ibn al-Shamir. This aristocrat and astrologer, who had served al-Hakam I and known 'Abd al-Rahman II in his youth, left al-Andalus as a young man and journeyed to the east, having already cast a horoscope that predicted the rise of the young prince to the throne. When he returned to Córdoba years later, he brought with him a penchant for the latest Iraqi fashion, a healthy drinking habit, some talent as a poet, and the latest astrological techniques. After he presented himself at the amir's palace requesting an audience, the two became inseparable and intimate companions.

In one episode that captures the masculine high culture of the time, 'Abd al-Rahman and Ibn al-Shamir rode out on campaign in 839/40 against the Christians of the north. They had not yet reached the frontier when one morning the amir—who was at this point absolutely obsessed with Tarub—confessed to Ibn al-Shamir, in verse, that he had had a wet dream about her. To this, Ibn al-Shamir replied,

> The dusky night was where she greeted you from;
> Welcome to her who in the darkness does *come*.[12]

The verse so inflamed 'Abd al-Rahman that he abandoned the campaign and galloped straight back to Córdoba to have sex with Tarub, leaving command in the hands of his son al-Hakam. The masculine culture of the Andalusi elite was ninth-century "gangsta"— a testosterone-driven, wine-fueled culture revolving around bling, bros, and biyatches, of biting freestyle wordplay and conspicuous consumption.

Ibn al-Shamir enjoyed a dangerous intimacy with the prince, pushing the limits of his familiarity and confidence and never holding his tongue, even to the point of insolence. Together with his uncanny astrological abilities, this earned him rewards in the form of wealth and official positions, but also at least once enraged the ruler so much that he threw him in jail. After a brief stay, Ibn al-Shamir sent the amir a clever and solicitous poem, which resulted in his release.

While many aristocrats, like Ibn al-Shamir, went east on their own account, some were sent deliberately by 'Abd al-Rahman II to bring back the culture of the Byzantine and 'Abbasid East, in the form of either knowledge or books. Many books were carried back, including works on science, medicine, astrology, religion, Arabic grammar, history, literature, and poetry, and the travelers themselves were imbued with 'Abbasid culture. The most famous individual among the new Orientalized cultural elite was undoubtedly 'Abbas ibn al-Firnas, an Umayyad courtier of Berber descent. 'Abbas returned from a voyage to Baghdad and Egypt with an array of technical skills. Famed as a poet, musician, philosopher, astrologer, and practitioner of white magic, he dabbled in alchemy and brought to al-Andalus the art of cutting rock crystal lenses. He constructed a clock, as well as a mechanical model of the Ptolemaic universe, but he is best known for his attempt at flight using a pair of bird-like wings of his own design. This experiment very nearly killed him when he jumped off the roof of the caliphal palace to test his invention—his apparatus had no tail and so after a fleeting Wile E. Coyote moment of apparent success, he tumbled to earth.

Many women went, or were sent, east as well, particularly slave girls. Qalam, a captive Basque woman of noble birth whom 'Abd al-Rahman acquired and later married, was sent to Medina in Arabia to learn music and song and be instructed in *adab*. The best and most valuable slave girls were not merely sex objects but witty, cultured, and sophisticated companions, so sending them off to be educated was an investment.

Once the scale of 'Abd al-Rahman's patronage became known, easterners began to trickle over to al-Andalus, spurred in part by political upheavals that made Baghdad a less lucrative and more dangerous environment for artists, musicians, and intellectuals. One of these was al-Harrani, the physician and repentant would-be regicide, who was among the first to bring "modern" Islamic medicine to Córdoba. But the most famous was an enigmatic individual known as Blackbird, who would single-handedly transform the culture of al-Andalus.

ABU 'L-HASAN 'ALI IBN NAFI, or Ziryab ("Blackbird"), was an accomplished player of the *'ud* (an ancestor of the guitar) in the court of the 'Abbasid caliph, Harun al-Rashid. Little is known of his origin, but repeated references to his dark skin suggest a sub-Saharan African origin. The traditional story is that he was such a brilliant instrumentalist that his teacher, the famous Ishaq al-Mawsili, the senior musician of the caliphal court, was driven to jealousy and plotted his pupil's death, thus forcing him to flee Baghdad. But it is more likely he left simply in response to the caliphate's descent into civil war in the early 800s. In any case, Ziryab made his way west to the court of the Aghlabids in Kairouan, but finding himself involved in intrigues there, set out for Córdoba, arriving in 822 at the invitation of al-Hakam sent via Abu 'l-Nasr al-Mansur, a Jewish musician of his employ.

Although al-Hakam died just before his arrival, Ziryab's virtuoso musicianship and his knowledge of poetry, science, and history ensured him a place in the palace, where he was welcomed into the inner circle of 'Abd al-Rahman II, who provided him with a luxurious residence and a generous stipend. His good looks, charm, and wit ensured him a favored place in the amir's entourage. As a musician, he dazzled the court with his playing and singing, and with the technical improvements he made to the instrument. He introduced an entire body of new song and music to al-Andalus: the latest Baghdadi styles, drawing on Greek, Persian, and South Asian traditions. Through the musical academy he founded in Córdoba together with his sons, these new styles were soon taught to musicians from across al-Andalus and the Islamic West.

But his impact went far beyond music. Ziryab popularized Islamo-Persian styles of dress, hair, and manners in al-Andalus. He revolutionized Andalusi cuisine, introducing unknown foods, such as asparagus and other garden crops, and a whole range of hot and cold soups and stews, combining meats, legumes, and herbs and spices, such as cilantro leaves, coriander seeds, tamarind, and saffron. At the time, food was not merely a matter of the table, but was regarded as crucial for the regulation of bodily humors, for the maintenance of physical and psychological health, and for counteracting disease in accordance with Greco-Islamic medical theory. Owing to Ziryab, ceramic dishes replaced plates of gold and silver, and the use of tablecloths (usually made of hide) became fashionable. He is also credited with introducing the honeyed, nut-filled desserts that have become a standard of Spanish cuisine today. The custom of eating meals in a series of set courses, beginning with soup and ending with nuts, which he also brought from the east, eventually spread all over Europe.

Prior to his arrival, many of the old styles of dress and coiffure dating back from the Visigothic period had survived among the upper classes. Ziryab changed that. Men and women would no longer part their hair in the middle and let it fall over their temples; instead, in imitation of him, they trimmed their bangs and the hair above their ears, and wore it mullet-like, long in the back (a style originating with the slaves of the 'Abbasid court). He also established the notion of seasonal wear. After the summer solstice, the fashionable now dressed in white, and only in autumn did they return to their colorful clothes, favoring a layered look that could adapt easily to changing temperatures.

The clothes themselves became more elaborate too, with brighter and more varied dyes, better-fitting cuts, and the use of hybrid materials like silk and wool blends and elaborate silk brocades woven with metallic (particularly gold and silver) thread. The wealthy maintained their valuable wardrobes by applying the antiperspirant Ziryab brought from the east—*litargirio*, a lead monoxide compound that counteracts sweat and odor and does not stain clothes. Ziryab's innovations quickly filtered through urbane Andalusi society, reaching even the humbler classes. His children would continue his work, and the academy he founded for music, style, and aesthetics survived in Córdoba for several generations. All of this may seem incredible, but what Ziryab did was merely bring to al-Andalus the entire package of 'Abbasid high culture and fashion, which had been perfected over the preceding half century.

IT IS LITTLE WONDER, then, that chroniclers looked on the reign of 'Abd al-Rahman as (in their words) a "honeymoon" era.[13] That said, such drastic change was only possible because al-Andalus had been so provincial. Ziryab had a lot to work with. Through the rest of the ninth century and into the tenth, the inhabitants of the Islamic east continued to regard Andalusis as uncultured and gullible bumpkins and crude copycats. This is reflected in the original works produced in Spain at the time, which had their focus fixed firmly on the east. For example, 'Abd al-Malik ibn Habib, a famous Maliki jurist and rival of Yahya ibn Yahya, produced a history of the world that incorporated all sorts of mythical and legendary material that he had gathered in the east—tales of genies, spirits, and magic, all taken at face value. At the turn of the tenth century, the Umayyad court poet Ibn

'Abbasid slave girls (*qiyan*). From a fresco in the Jawsaq
al-Khaqani, the caliphal palace in Samarra, Iraq (ca. 860 CE).
Robert Delord

'Abd Rabbih produced a massive, twenty-five-volume encyclopedia
of *adab*, in which al-Andalus went virtually unmentioned and no local works were cited, except for the author's own mediocre poetry.
When it arrived at the 'Abbasid court, it was roundly mocked.

Nor was everyone back in Córdoba enamored of this budding, secular cosmopolitanism and the effete sensuality it promoted. Conservative imams, of whom the powerful Yahya ibn Yahya was in the
vanguard, tended toward intellectual puritanism. For them, only
Qur'anic scripture and law were worthy of study; of everything else,
it was better to be ignorant. Yahya too had gone east, but to Medina

to learn religion, not to Baghdad for *adab*. He too was famous for predictions, but his came from God, not the stars. And through the multitude of students he educated over the course of his long career, and the fact that he controlled the appointment of magistrates, his conservative, ascetic, antisecular Islam took strong root. He was suspicious not only of the scientific learning of Baghdad, but also of the dangerous religious ideologies that incubated there—he was behind the first capital charge of *zandaqa* (heresy) lodged in al-Andalus. The teachings of Yahya were echoed by the growing masses of new Muslims, the common folk with little access to the growing wealth and luxury of the *khassa*, and many of whom had converted to Islam in the trust that their worldly prestige and position would immediately be improved. When this failed to happen, they became anxious and frustrated, and their discontent would play out dramatically in the 840s when certain reactionary members of the Christian community made a dramatic stand against what they saw as the looming triumph of Islam.

7

Saints and Sinners

It was a day like any other in the bustling market of Córdoba in March of 850 when a priest named Perfectus was drawn into an apparently good-natured debate on the nature of his faith with some passersby— the type of conversation that often took place in the diverse capital. But conscious of his lesser status as a Christian, Perfectus asked his Muslim interlocutors to give their word they would not hold anything he said about their faith against him. They agreed, and so in Arabic he told them in no uncertain terms why he felt Jesus was the true prophet, making reference to an episode in Muhammad's life that was a source of embarrassment and confusion for many Muslims. Such was their offense at his insolence, when they bumped into him again the next day they turned him in to the authorities on a charge of blasphemy against Islam. Because it was the month of Ramadan (which likely made his fasting accusers' tempers all the shorter), Perfectus was imprisoned to await judgment. His bad luck was compounded by the fact that the eunuch Nasr was ruling for the ill 'Abd al-Rahman II at the time. The ex-Christian wazir, a ruthless opportunist at the best of times, was trying to gain favor among the hard-line *'ulama'* and bolster his standing among the common people. He was not about to show clemency. And so, after protesting innocence for some weeks, Perfectus embraced his fate and chose to stand as a martyr to his faith.

This ambition was realized when, to mark the end of the Holy Month, Nasr had the unfortunate priest beheaded.

A year or so of relative quiet followed. Then, apparently out of the blue, a Christian named Isaac, who had served many years as a functionary of the emirate before retiring and taking the habit of a monk, appeared in person at the palace and began to repeatedly insult the Prophet Muhammad before the city's Islamic magistrate. Nonplussed, 'Abd al-Rahman II and his courtiers (who had been friends of Isaac) sought for a way to avoid prosecuting him. Had he been drunk? Was he mad? Would he convert to Islam to escape condemnation? But Isaac would have none of it and repeated his fulminations until with much regret they sentenced him to death in accordance with the law. After his decapitated body had been hung on display at the end of the Roman bridge, it was burned and his ashes scattered in the river. Then, within the following thirty-six hours, seven more Christians stepped forward (including a soldier) to publicly insult Islam and provoke their own executions. Over the next six years, twenty-eight more Christians would die in Córdoba for the same reason, while a further thirteen would be condemned for apostasy, charged with living as Christians when by law they were Muslims.

This was not some spontaneous wave of religious hysteria. Most of the martyrs had carefully considered their fates and had conscientiously made the necessary spiritual and personal preparations for death. Their acts of blasphemy were theatrically staged in Arabic to provoke the most visceral reaction from both the administration and the public, and once they were arrested, they endured imprisonment, resisted offers of clemency, and marched proudly to their executions. Traditionally, historians have painted this movement as an instance of Christian or "Spanish" resistance or fanaticism, or of Islamic intransigence or restraint. And while there may have been elements of all of these at play, the story of the "Voluntary Martyrs of Córdoba" reflects tensions as much within as between the transforming Islamic and Christian societies of al-Andalus.

CHRISTIANITY IN AL-ANDALUS was in crisis, abandoned by the nobility that had once sustained it and short on clergy to provide

instruction in the faith. As Christians converted, the church's income
and its influence in the amirs' court declined, and the clerical career
became less attractive. Within al-Andalus, the See of Toledo, officially the head of the Spanish church, was being sidelined by Córdoba, a lesser diocese now at the center of Umayyad power. And
although the amirs appointed the bishops, heterodox beliefs and her-
esies began to creep in because the Muslims had no concern for en-
forcing Christian orthodoxy. The connections between the church in
the peninsula and Christendom beyond became tenuous, while the
clergy of Asturias condemned their Andalusi counterparts as turncoats. The bishops themselves were increasingly divided between
those who chose to protect their flocks (and their fortunes) by collaborating and those who came to feel that it was Christian duty to resist
the infidel at any cost.

Pressure on Christians from the Muslim population was also increasing, with the beginning of the conversion of large numbers of
ordinary city folk to Islam. Perhaps a third had converted by 840, and
undoubtedly a higher proportion did so in Córdoba and other major
cities. Fired by the zeal of the convert and a wave of apocalypticism
sweeping the Islamic West, these new Muslims had high expectations
for what their faith would provide in this world and the next. However, as more people converted, the relative advantage diminished—
the club of the conquerors was no longer an exclusive minority.

That said, if conversion did not bring instant prestige, Islam did
instill converts with the conviction they should be regarded as morally, legally, and socioeconomically superior to their Christian neighbors. Populist dissatisfaction among new Muslims, exacerbated by
the lavish lifestyle of the Umayyad elite and the economic and social
advantages enjoyed by "old Muslim" families, could not be directed
toward the ruling classes, so Christians were sometimes scapegoated.
Hence the widespread celebration at Rabi' ibn Teodolfo's gruesome
fall from power in 822 and the bitter betrayal of Perfectus twenty-
eight years later.

Moreover, this was precisely the era when Muslim jurists in the
east were elaborating stricter rules for the behavior of *dhimmis*—
innovations falsely attributed to the "Pact of 'Umar," the surrender

agreement purportedly made by the second caliph with the Christians of Jerusalem in 637. Public observations of Christian faith, including bell-ringing and religious processions, and the building of churches were to be curtailed. Social interaction among the faiths was to be discouraged, and a series of restrictions on what non-Muslims could wear, the arms they could carry, and what animals they could ride were intended to humiliate them and reinforce their secondary status. If such decrees were rarely enforced or observed, they nevertheless provided a moral justification for discrimination. Some reactionary jurists went further, portraying non-Muslims as a dirty, polluting influence to be avoided.

Paradoxically, to the alarm of both stalwart Christians and overly zealous Muslims, the lines between the three faith communities in al-Andalus were blurring. "Romance" (the Latinate vernacular that was gradually evolving into modern Spanish) was spoken by the rural lower classes and Arabic by the middle and upper classes, regardless of faith community. Arabic became so common among Christians that by the late 800s, clergy were forced to translate religious texts. Ambitious Christians who wanted to work as civil servants (and this included clergy) had to speak Arabic but also write it very well, indeed. The best way to learn high Arabic was to read the Qur'an, which opened the door to sympathy and possible conversion on the part of these functionaries. Moreover, whereas after the conquest the Arab and Berber elite had adopted some native styles and customs, with the Orientalization of al-Andalus under the rule of al-Hakam and 'Abd al-Rahman II, the indigenous Christians were now taking up Arabo-Islamic clothing, habits, and social mores.

So thorough was this acculturation that when Andalusi Christians began to arrive in northern Spain in the eleventh century, they would be called *Mozarabs* (from the Arabic *must'arab*, "would-be Arab"). The mixing of traditions and cultures spread into social and religious life, and Christians and Muslims (including members of the *'ulama'*) took part together in public ceremonies, such as the processions for rain held in Córdoba in times of drought and popular religious festivals, including 'Id al-Fitr (marking the end of Ramadan), Christmas, Easter, and Saint John's Day (summer solstice). Such religiously tinged social fraternization was viewed with alarm by many members of the religious elite of both faiths, who feared it would undermine the divinely ordained social order or lead to apostasy. As late as the early 1100s, for example, the jurist al-Turtushi complained of Muslim children happily partaking of the sweets baked by Christians at Lent. *Manteca*, or pork lard, was a common ingredient in Christian cuisine.

Nowhere was the impact of fraternization more profound and problematic than in the family environment, where mixed marriages and conversion brought the murky frontier between Christianity and Islam right into the home. The church had forbidden all intermarriage at the Council of Córdoba of 839, and under Islamic law, only Muslim men were free to marry Christians, but neither edict was consistently observed. The Christian wives of Muslim men were not required to convert, but any children would be considered Muslim. This created problems because it was women who raised children, meaning that such offspring were often steeped in Christian beliefs and practices as children, only to be forced to reject these as adults. For some, this was too much to handle. Of those executed in Córdoba for apostasy or abetting apostates, five were women who had been born of mixed marriages, and two were the daughters of Muslim women who had illegally converted to the faith of their Christian husbands. All had been given the opportunity to return to Islam and be forgiven, and all had refused. Such were tensions that could tear families apart, leading kinfolk to denounce each other, whether out of genuine outrage or out of fear that a charge of apostasy might stain them and the larger family with guilt by association.

ONE OF THE last Christians to be executed in Córdoba was a priest named Eulogius, a vocal supporter of the martyrs, who together with his enigmatic collaborator, Paul Alvar, was at the center of the movement. The two had been boyhood friends and disciples of a local priest named Speraindeo ("Hope in God"), who had dedicated his life to combating heresy and Islam. Both were members of the old Christian aristocracy, many of whom (including Eulogius's own brother) pursued careers in the administration, which Eulogius and his ilk saw as an act of treason. To counter the influence of Islam, pious Christian resisters advocated disengagement from the Umayyad regime and strove to reaffirm the discipline of the clergy, put a brake on their adoption of eastern styles, and put a halt to the decline of Latin letters, which they saw as the pillar of Christian culture and devotion. They also founded private rural monasteries that served as nodes of spiritual and political resistance. Tabanos, for example, on the outskirts of the capital—where Isaac had taken up his vocation—sheltered and inculcated several of the martyrs with a militant Christianity that would inspire them to sacrifice their lives as an act of faith and of inspiration to their coreligionists.

Christianity had a long history of venerating martyrs, and both Alvar and Eulogius hoped that their movement would inspire the faithful to throw off the shackles of Islamic domination. But Eulogius's reactionary stance did not gain him many supporters, whether among the collaborationist Christian elite or a populace largely content under Umayyad rule. The martyrs were seen as troublemakers who made their community look disloyal and put it in danger of reprisal. But 'Abd al-Rahman II reacted carefully and did not fall into the trap of punishing the Christian community as a whole or advertising the movement. First, he convened a church council in 852, which ruled that to provoke one's own death amounted to suicide—a mortal sin. Next, reactionary priests, including Eulogius, were arrested and placed in preventative detention. Finally, the physical remains of executed martyrs were disposed of to prevent the veneration of their relics. When Eulogius himself was beheaded in 857, it was not for a dramatic and defiant act of public blasphemy. He had been released from jail previously and was captured on the lam, on a warrant for having helped to hide a woman named Leocritia. She was one of those unfortunate casualties of circumstance who was by conviction a Christian but by the law of the conquerors a Muslim, and who went to her death willingly rather than betray her beliefs.

Far from provoking an uprising, the movement fizzled and was largely forgotten, both in al-Andalus and in the north. Muslim historical sources do not even record it, and the only surviving accounts are works penned by Eulogius and Alvar themselves, which can hardly be regarded as objective. Eventually, the remains of Eulogius, together with his writings and those of Alvar, were discovered by two Frankish monks who had come to al-Andalus hoping to find relics of early Christian martyrs to take home. Instead, the remains were taken north to Oviedo, the capital of Asturias, in 883, by a priest from Toledo named Dulcidius who came to Córdoba to negotiate a peace treaty on behalf of Alfonso III. In Asturias, the idea of Christian resistance resonated with the political agenda of its kings, and here Eulogius and the others were venerated as saints. But rather than Alvar and Eulogius, those who truly epitomized the struggles of Christians in al-Andalus in this era were people like Leocritia, a victim of her convictions, and Isaac, the powerful and successful functionary whose conscience was torn apart by his collaboration with the Muslim regime. In any event, the phenomenon of the voluntary martyrs was more a symptom than a cause of the changing situation of Christians here, and of the emergence of a new Mozarabic society and culture that would gel during the reign of 'Abd al-Rahman's son and successor, the amir Muhammad I.

THE EPISODE OF the martyrs marked an ominous close to 'Abd al-Rahman II's otherwise gilded reign. During the amir's long illness, which prevented him from conducting audiences in his final three years, various factions led by court eunuchs maneuvered in favor of one or another of his forty-plus sons. His favorite, Muhammad I, successfully took the throne and quickly put these intrigues to rest. Even so, according to one chronicler, 'Abd al-Rahman's death had been kept secret, and once they convinced Muhammad it was not a trap, the clique who supported the prince smuggled him into the palace dressed as a woman, enabling him to take control before his rivals could act.

Under his rule, Christian-Muslim relations restabilized. The more intransigent Christian resisters emigrated, and those elite Christians who remained were largely complacent collaborators who embraced the new culture. Their children were instructed in Arabic and *adab*, and Arabo-Islamic customs, such as circumcision and cousin-marriage, seem to have come into fashion. The integration of the church into the Umayyad state was laid bare at the Council of Córdoba of 862, a synod called by Muhammad I more as a political exercise than a religious conclave. It was led by Bishop Hostegesis of Málaga (Malaqa), who served the amir as a tax collector, and the *qumis* Servandus, and was attended by both Jewish and Muslim functionaries. Samson, a well-respected abbot who had been sympathetic to the martyrs, was accused of heresy. He fled Córdoba for the refuge of a monastery, and in a last ripple of resistance, composed a polemical tract, *The Defense Against the Perfidious Ones*, decrying Hostegesis as a faithless mercenary and puppet of the regime, and Servandus and company as low-class, sexually deviant parvenus.

But collaborators faced their own challenges, even when they chose to convert, including resistance from the established Muslim elite, who saw newcomers as a threat to their monopoly on power. The careers of Qumis ibn Antunyan and 'Amr ibn 'Abd Allah are illustrative. Qumis was a highly educated Christian with great facility in Latin and Arabic who served 'Abd al-Rahman II as a scribe, translator, and advisor. In fact, it was Qumis who convinced the amir not to take reprisals against the Christian community in response to the martyrs and in exchange secured their condemnation by the bishops. Soon after the ascent of Muhammad I, he was tapped for promotion to the position of chief scribe but was told that the amir could not consent to placing a Christian in such a high position. Taking the hint, Qumis converted, but then he found himself persecuted by his fellow Muslim courtiers, who accused him repeatedly of being a false convert and a secret Christian. Hounding him out of office, they pressured the amir to confiscate his property so it could not be passed down to his children.

'Amr ibn 'Abd Allah faced a similar experience, although he was not a convert to Islam. However, he did come from an indigenous family, and this was apparently enough to stir up the Arab aristocracy against him. With a reputation for deep knowledge of Islam and the law, unimpeachable moral probity, and staunch conservatism, 'Amr was appointed by Muhammad I as chief magistrate in Córdoba. This alone was an affront to the power of the Arab elite, who openly expressed their displeasure at being put in the position where they would be judged by an upstart native. But the *qadi* made the fatal error of prosecuting an influential courtier and general, Hashim ibn 'Abd al-Aziz. Hashim, who had been one of the agitators against Ibn Antunyan, then made it his mission to undermine 'Amr, inciting his fellow Arabs to boycott 'Amr until Muhammad I reluctantly retired him. Hashim himself, who rose to become Muhammad I's confidant, was something of a poster boy for the overly entitled, corrupt, and self-interested Arab elite. He was an energetic military commander, but his record was uneven; captured by Alfonso III in 876, he spent two years as a prisoner before he was freed. The heavy taxes the amir placed on the people of the rural south to raise Hashim's ransom are said to have helped spark the revolt of Ibn Hafsun, which would nearly bring down the emirate in the late 800s.

Relations between Muslims and Jews in this period, by contrast, do not seem to have been problematic, but we have very little to go on. Ironically, the best known Andalusi Jew of the period is Eleazar of Zaragoza, by origin a well-connected, Christian-born Frank named Bodo, who had served as a deacon in the royal court of Louis the Pious and who in 838 converted to Judaism. Apostasy was a capital crime, but whatever the cause, he kept his epiphany a secret and determined to reach the safety of the *dar al-Islam* where he could live openly as a Jew. To do so, he recruited a band of Frankish faithful, ostensibly to take them to Rome as pilgrims, but traveled instead to al-Andalus, where he sold them as slaves and used the proceeds to set himself up under his new name and faith in Muslim Zaragoza. There, he garnered some renown as a polemicist against his former faith and as an advocate of Judaism. By 840 he was carrying on a correspondence with none other than Paul Alvar, the future chronicler of the martyr movement, in a series of letters that began cordially but soon descended into bitter, mutual insults as they argued about the identity of the Messiah, the validity of Mosaic Law, and the paradoxes of Christian doctrine. Bodo's defection greatly affected the Frankish court, and allegations that Eleazar was lobbying 'Abd al-Rahman II to forcibly convert the Christians of al-Andalus reached the emperor in a letter written in 847 by certain Christians in Córdoba. However improbable this claim may have been, it reflects the desperation and hysteria brewing in certain Christian quarters in the years prior to the explosion of the martyr movement.

But, both Bodo and Alvar each represented only a small extremist minority in their communities, and in any event, the Muslim authorities were quite indifferent to clashes between representatives of the two subject religious communities. However, Alvar and Eleazar were not just arguing as Christian and Jew, but as Visigoth and Frank, members of rival ethnic groups that had been subjugated in al-Andalus by the Muslim Arabs. Identity was not merely religious in nature; ethnic community (Gothic, Frankish, Arab, Slav, muwallad, and Berber), clan affiliation, networks of patronage, and social class also played important roles.

In any event, each religious group was fractured ideologically: Christians by heretics and collaborators; Jews by the conflict between Rabbinates and Karaites; and Muslims by a whole array of heterodox trends, including rationalist Mu'tazilism and esoteric Shi'ism. Dissent even existed within the "conservative" Maliki 'ulama'. The all-powerful Berber *faqih*, Yahya ibn Yahya, whose knowledge of Islamic law was unparalleled, clashed with his rival 'Abd al-Malik ibn Habib, a millenarian-obsessed populist who prophesied an imminent and catastrophic End Time. The amirs, for their part, understood that ethnic and religious divisions could be manipulated, and rulers like 'Abd al-Rahman II and Muhammad I played the various parties against each other with skill. But the amirs also had more pressing concerns—not only the threat from foreign Vikings or the Christians of the north, but also a series of major rebellions that broke out across al-Andalus in the mid-ninth century.

IN THE END, it was Muslim revolts, and not the episode of the martyrs, that defined Muhammad I's reign. In Toledo, the muwallad families, some of whom were descendants of the Visigothic elite, chafed at the supremacy of Córdoba and the rule of the Umayyads and their privileged, Arab-identifying supporters. In 852 they rose up, expelling their governor and launching raids against territory to the south. Their discontent resonated with local Berber clans, who were also discriminated against, and with other muwallad families of neighboring areas, notably the Banu Qasi of the Upper March, who joined them as allies. They also established an alliance with Christian Asturias in the north, where King Ordoño I, eager to capitalize on any Umayyad weakness, sent forces south to attack the emirate.

It would be a mistake, however, to see the uprisings as some sort of "Spanish" or crypto-Christian response to Islamic rule, or to see these alliances as durable coalitions rooted in ethnocultural solidarity. They were alliances of opportunity based on the politics of the moment, and loyalties among these clans, cliques, and kingdoms coalesced and disintegrated according to how those politics changed. The rebels of Toledo were not Spanish protonationalists, as some historians have maintained, but were driven by their commitment to establish a religiously Islamic and culturally Arabic al-Andalus, in which their contributions and role as indigenous Muslims would be recognized and valued, and in which they would be given what they saw as their due of power and prestige.

In response, Muhammad I had no choice but to raise forces to counterattack, drawing on his faithful network of *mawali* families and cultivating new clients among Berber clans who were enemies of the Berbers who supported the Toledo uprising. Among these rivals were the Banu Dhi 'l-Nun, a family of Zanata Berbers who had come to al-Andalus at the time of the conquest. With the support of the Umayyads, they would rise to preeminence in the region, although their loyalty was hardly dependable and they too would rebel when they saw the opportunity. In the eleventh century the Banu Dhi 'l-Nun would take control of Toledo itself and declare it a separate kingdom. In the meantime, the city would remain only intermittently and tenuously under the control of the amirs, as they struggled to contain the rebellions that erupted across the peninsula.

Conditions were no less unstable in the Lower March, the territory to the northwest of Córdoba, which had as its capital the ancient Roman city of Mérida (Emerita Augusta; Marida, in Arabic). In the 800s, the city was home to a volatile mix of restless Berber and muwallad clans whose ceaseless internecine warfare had kept the region on the brink of chaos, together with Christians, who had broadcast their disloyalty in 828 by appealing for help to the Frankish emperor, Louis the Pious. In 868, the governor, 'Abd al-Rahman ibn Marwan, whose muwallad roots were reflected in his nickname, al-Jilliqi (or Ibn al-Jilliqi, "the son of the Northerner"), threw off his loyalty to the Umayyads. The reaction was swift; the governor was captured and taken back to Córdoba, where he could be better monitored. However, after clashing with the haughty Umayyad courtiers and other royal favorites, he fled with his family and supporters to a fortress in his home territory. A bitter but inconclusive three-month siege by Muhammad I in 875 led to a compromise: al-Jilliqi would be reinstated as governor and allowed to reside in the town of Batalyaws (modern Badajoz) in his family's ancestral lands.

Al-Jilliqi presented the same conundrum to the amirs as did the Banu Qasi; inconstant as he might be, he could not simply be disposed of. The amirs needed governors and local military commanders who could rally locally levied warriors to fight for the cause of Córdoba. But once al-Jilliqi was home, he began to test Muhammad's authority, until the amir finally sent a force under Hashim ibn ʿAbd al-ʿAziz to subdue him. However, this general's heavy-handed tactics, which included the massacre of Christian and Muslim townsfolk and the arbitrary enslavement of their women, only galvanized resistance. With the help of neighboring muwallad lords and Alfonso III of Asturias, al-Jilliqi not only defeated Hashim but took him prisoner and sent him as a gift to the Christian king, whose demand for a 150,000-*dinar* ransom forced the amir to tax his subjects in the south to the point of rebellion. Al-Jilliqi himself took refuge in Asturias, where he stayed for eight years before reconciling with Muhammad in 884.

By this point, the amir needed whatever support he could get. Uprisings against the Umayyads were raging across the peninsula, and so, in exchange for his loyalty, Muhammad allowed al-Jilliqi to establish a nominally loyal but functionally independent client state in the west of the peninsula, with Badajoz as its capital. The new state would enjoy its status during the reigns of the following two amirs, al-Mundhir and ʿAbd Allah. With this reprieve, the muwallad warlord set about transforming the city into a metropolis, constructing an immense fortress, a congregational mosque, baths, inns, and all the other accoutrements of a prestigious Islamic city. His descendants would rule it for three generations, laying the groundwork for the independent kingdom that would emerge here after Umayyad authority collapsed only a century or so later.

8

Kingdoms of Faith

In the summer of 928, a macabre spectacle played out in front of the royal palace of Córdoba. Three corpses, one ten years dead but patched together for the occasion, were hoisted onto crosses in a grisly scene that mockingly evoked the New Testament execution of Jesus and the two thieves. Crucifixion was commonly used as an exemplary punishment in al-Andalus and the rest of the Islamic world, particularly against rebels, who were sometimes hung together with a dog and pig crucified on either side, unclean animals added for symbolic effect as a burlesque of the scene of Christ's passion. But the exhumation of an offender who had been dead for a decade was remarkable even by the standards of the day.

This individual at the center of the tableau was 'Umar ibn Hafsun, a muwallad potentate and adventurer who had led a rebellion against the Umayyad regime in the hills above Málaga in southern al-Andalus that lasted nearly forty years. His crucifixion carried a special significance, given that it was held that in 899/900 he had converted to the Christian faith of his ancestors. At one side hung his son Sulayman, who had been captured in battle and beheaded in 927, and on the other, another son, al-Hakam. Although Ibn Hafsun's rebellion had long since petered out, the posthumous execution marked the end of the long and nearly fatal tenth century in al-Andalus.

The three crosses would stand until 942, long after their grisly cargo had rotted off. By this time, the rebellions that had threatened to destroy Umayyad power through the second half of the ninth century had finally been quashed. The Christian princes of the north were effectively being held at bay, the dynasty was wealthier and more powerful than ever, and 'Abd al-Rahman III—the sovereign who oversaw Ibn Hafsun's defeat and "execution"—was about to leave behind the simple title of amir of al-Andalus and become, by his own estimation and that of his followers, the "caliph of Islam."

THE UPRISING OF Ibn Hafsun had its origin in the late 870s, the final years of the long reign of Muhammad I, when, in addition to the ceaseless rebellions of the frontier provinces and the ever-more confident incursions of Alfonso III of Asturias, the amir suddenly had to contend with a flurry of uprisings across his southern heartlands. First, rebellions in both Málaga and Algeciras in 878 menaced what was left of the emirate's shaky fiscal foundations. In response, Muhammad sent his son al-Mundhir, a far more reliable general than the amir's feckless favorite, Hashim ibn 'Abd al-Aziz, at the head of military expeditions to suppress them. But there were limits to what al-Mundhir could accomplish on the field of battle when the roots of the unrest stemmed from processes that were much more profound and elusive than the mere opportunism of a few disloyal magnates.

And the causes of these rebellions have remained a subject of debate up to today. The established narrative recounts that the ninth century marked the end of muwallad power, the end of those descendants of the converted, collaborating Visigothic elite. In this view, the rebellions represented their concerted attempt to retain or regain control of the peninsula. Some historians have incorrectly imagined the revolts, such as the martyr movement, as part of a Spanish proto-national struggle against foreign Berbers and Arabs. But, this is not borne out by the politics of the era, which featured many well-integrated and staunchly loyal muwallad families. Nor was Ibn Hafsun, as some would have it, a populist "Robin Hood" figure, defending the peasants from a grasping monarchy. Whatever muwallad "movement" there might have been was certainly not nationalist, not populist, not anti-Islamic, and not anti-Arabic, at least not on a cultural or linguistic level. With the possible exception of Ibn Hafsun, the muwallad rebels were committed to Islam: what they objected to primarily was their political marginalization. Ibn Hafsun had no moral objection to grasping oppression; he just wanted to be the one doing the grasping.

Accounts of 'Umar ibn Hafsun's origins are varied and unreliable. Claiming to be the descendant of a preconquest "count," he was certainly of muwallad origin, and likely from the hills southwest of present-day Granada. This zone was still inhabited largely by Christians, although there were also significant Jewish populations, as well as indigenous converts to Islam, many of whom continued to dabble in Christian belief and ritual. Ibn Hafsun was a member of a loose class of rural strongmen who enjoyed local, quasi-feudal power and extracted wealth directly from the peasantry, some of which went to providing patronage to local religious institutions and hiring soldiers to reinforce their own power.

Ibn Hafsun's revolt had a tellingly prosaic beginning. Apparently, he had fled into exile after murdering a member of a rival family and took refuge in North Africa in the domains of the Rustamids, an 'Ibadi dynasty of Persian origin that ruled over part of present-day Algeria. Once the heat died down, Ibn Hafsun returned home and began to build a fortune and plot his rise. His family's base at Bobastro, a hilltop redoubt north of Málaga, would be the epicenter of the rebellion and capital of his would-be kingdom. Taking advantage of the discontent of the largely Christian populace of the region, he raised an armed band and declared his independence. One of the local grievances that fed his movement was the tax levied on the region to ransom Muhammad's general and favorite, Hashim ibn 'Abd al-'Aziz, from captivity in Oviedo, which added to an already heavy state burden.

Muhammad I reacted to Ibn Hafsun's uprising swiftly, sending a force under al-Mundhir to bring the rebel to heel. Once Ibn Hafsun had been subdued in 883, his family was forced to relocate to Córdoba, per the amir's strategy for provincial upstarts. At this point, he seems to have been content to throw in his lot with the regime, and he and his men served the amir loyally on campaign against both his fellow muwallad rebels, the Banu Qasi, and Alfonso III of Asturias. But as in the case of al-Jilliqi, the antagonistic behavior of Muhammad I's favorite, Hashim ibn 'Abd al-'Aziz, toward non-Arabs aggravated the situation; fed up with his abuse at the hands of the general, Ibn Hafsun escaped from the capital and reestablished himself in Bobastro, reigniting his rebellion. Perhaps Hashim was attempting to sabotage and discredit al-Mundhir, whom he was coming to see as a rival. Regardless, emboldened by the struggles at the Umayyad court and by the death of Muhammad I in 886, Ibn Hafsun began allying with other local malcontents, both Berber and muwallad, and came to control an ever-larger swath of territory.

Once on the throne, al-Mundhir made it his mission to stamp out the rebellion. He launched another campaign, combining retaliatory violence with overtures of reconciliation, leading Ibn Hafsun to submit in return for being appointed governor of the region. Tiring of Hashim's machinations, al-Mundhir tried first to mollify the general by appointing him as *hajib*, but when this failed, he had him arrested and executed and confiscated his family fortune. Soon after, Ibn Hafsun, sensing the amir's vulnerability, attacked Córdoban territory in violation of the oath of allegiance he had only just sworn. Infuriated, al-Mundhir returned personally to besiege Bobastro in 888, but after six weeks he fell dead in his camp, ostensibly of an illness, but likely the victim of poisoning on the part of his own brother 'Abd Allah, who, keeping his brother's death secret for three days, quickly moved to secure his own acclamation as amir. 'Abd Allah would be remembered by sympathetic chroniclers for his piety and dedicated patronage of Islamic culture, but his twenty-five-year reign would be characterized by violent court intrigue, the execution of family members, and more rebellions.

Taking advantage of these upheavals, Ibn Hafsun declared his total independence, claiming to be sovereign of the people of the south, vaunting himself as their "supreme leader" and positioning himself as the one who would liberate them from the oppression of the Arabs, who burdened them with taxes, humiliated them, and treated them as "slaves." The claim aimed to stir up the rural elite, both Christian and

Muslim, as well as Berber clans, who, like the muwallads, had been pushed to the margins by the clients of the Umayyad family, of whom Hashim ibn 'Abd al-'Aziz was merely the most obnoxious representative. More through skillful coalition building than force, 'Umar ibn Hafsun won the loyalties of those who felt left out of the Umayyad power structure.

As Ibn Hafsun's realm expanded across the mountains north of Algeciras and Málaga and nudged up toward the south bank of the Guadalquivir, he became ever more bold and ambitious. To build support among local Christians, for example, he patronized the construction of churches and established a bishopric at Bobastro—an exercise in Umayyad-style state building. He sent envoys to the amir's other enemies, including al-Jilliqi, the Banu Qasi, and Alfonso III of Asturias, and by 891, he was confident enough to move his base out of the highlands and down to present-day Aguilar de la Frontera, a mere thirty miles south of Córdoba. Turning his sights on the capital, he attacked it repeatedly but without success—a failure that marked the highpoint of Ibn Hafsun's insurgency.

To consolidate his rule, Ibn Hafsun needed to establish some basis for legitimacy, and in al-Andalus this could only be articulated within an Islamic context. Hence, in addition to the deals he struck with local Muslims, he sent representatives to the 'Abbasids, proposing to convert al-Andalus into a client state of the caliphate with himself as governor. He also dabbled in Kharijism, and even welcomed missionary envoys from the 'Abbasids' archenemies, the heretical Shi'a Fatimids, who had recently seized Ifriqiya and declared their own rival caliphate. It would later be claimed by his enemies—and this is what Ibn Hafsun is perhaps most famous for—that he went so far as to convert to Christianity as a means of raising local support. Of this we cannot be sure. The allegation was certainly raised by Umayyad chroniclers to disgrace his memory and his movement, and it would have certainly alienated his Muslim allies. However, it is clear that some of his children converted, and it may be that, in different contexts, Ibn Hafsun presented himself ambiguously as either Christian or Muslim, depending on his audience and agenda. At bottom, what he truly worshipped was power.

As SENSATIONAL AS his early successes were, and his religious pro-paganda notwithstanding, Ibn Hafsun's revolt was all but doomed to fail. His coalition of rural strongmen was tenuous, vulnerable, and lacking a coherent ideological or institutional base. But most impor-tantly, it was out of sync with the times. In al-Andalus, cities and commerce were becoming the engines of prosperity and power, and it was only cities that could successfully anchor political move-ments. The more successful rebellions of the era were in and around urban centers, such as Seville, which was taken over by the Arab Banu'l-Hajjaj, and Murcia, where an uprising was led by the mu-wallad Daysam ibn Ishaq. Among city folk, Ibn Hafsun's rustic re-volt held little appeal, especially in comparison to the sophisticated political culture of Umayyad al-Andalus. But, as it stood in the late 800s, al-Andalus was on the verge of another major transformation, and Ibn Hafsun and his ilk, whether muwallad, Christian, Arab, or Berber, would be left behind.

CHANGE CAME MOST forcefully in the form of the new amir, 'Abd Allah's grandson 'Abd al-Rahman III, who ascended to the throne in 912 at the age of twenty-one on the death of his grandfather. What-ever he lacked in experience, the new prince made up for in will-power and instinct. Relying on the combination of brute force and conciliatory diplomacy characteristic of his predecessors, 'Abd al-Rahman deprived Ibn Hafsun of his most important allies and then organized a naval blockade of his ports. In 916, the aging rebel sued for peace and was granted exceedingly generous terms by 'Abd al-Rahman. The agreement contained Ibn Hafsun and his family in Bobastro, and after Ibn Hafsun's death in 918, his sons jockeyed for power and for the favor of the amir—fighting among each other, serv-ing in the Umayyad army, and occasionally launching short-lived and futile rebellions. Finally, in 928, once the family had outlived its use-fulness and 'Abd al-Rahman had dealt with more pressing threats, the amir conquered Bobastro, disinterred and abused Ibn Hafsun's rotting body, razed the churches the rebel had constructed, condemned his lineage to ignominy, and consigned Ibn Hafsun's former capital to oblivion.

The proliferation of rebellions against Córdoban rule in the late-ninth century can be seen as a consequence not of Umayyad weakness, but of its strengths. It was the ruling dynasty that was engaged in a revolutionary process, not the rebels. Centralized Umayyad power was a novelty that took shape only gradually, as amirs since the time of 'Abd al-Rahman I had struggled to impose their political will on a broad array of powerful local interests, who had little incentive to acknowledge this authority. It was the Umayyads, not their opponents, who were overturning the established order by moving toward a formalized state based on institutionalized citizenship and public, religiously based law. However, until the Umayyads could establish their authority, they would continue to face uprisings by opportunists who either ignored religious ideology altogether or cloaked their insurgencies in Islamic terms. The exception to this would be the kingdom of Asturias in the north, which instead constructed its legitimacy on its opposition to Islam and its role as the instrument of Christian faith in the peninsula.

IT WAS THE year 844, as the story goes, and the army of 'Abd al-Rahman II was arrayed on the south bank of the Ebro River at a place called Clavijo, in the region of northern Spain near Pamplona, now known as La Rioja. On the opposite bank, and much fewer in number, stood the ragtag forces of Ramiro, king of Asturias. The cruel Muslim prince, as the legend fancifully claimed, had marched north to punish the Christian king for his refusal to render the annual tribute of one hundred virgin girls. Although outnumbered, Ramiro was confident. His victory had been presaged in a dream. God was on his side. And as the Muslim host swept into his line, a heavenly figure appeared in the skies—a knight on a white horse who, together with a celestial army, turned the tide of the battle and led Ramiro's forces to victory and the massacre of his foe. That figure was none other than Saint James the Greater, who would eventually be called *Matamoros*, "the Muslim Killer," and would take on the role of patron saint in what would later be referred to as *La Reconquista*, the Spanish "Reconquest." Thus, the Battle of Clavijo passed from legend into history. But why Saint James? And why in Spain?

Around the same time, another miraculous event was said to have occurred, when in the very far northwest of Spain, guided by a prodigious star, Bishop Theodemir of the town of Iria Flavia came upon the tomb of James the Apostle—the remains of whom were eventually reinterred nearby at a site that would be known as Santiago ("Saint James") de Compostela ("the little burial ground"). According to legend, Saint James the Greater had evangelized Roman Hispania before his martyrdom in Judea in the year 44 CE, after which his body was miraculously conveyed by boat to Iria Flavia and laid to rest. By the late ninth century, the site was the focus of veneration for Christians in northwestern Spain and would eventually become the most popular site of pilgrimage in medieval Christendom. Santiago Matamoros—Saint James "the Muslim Killer"—would be adopted as the protector of the "Emperors of León," as the kings of Asturias would come to style themselves, propping up their claim that they were the heirs of the defeated Visigothic kings and therefore the rightful rulers over the entire peninsula. The narrative they crafted—one of an eternally united Spain, defeated by foreign Muslims, but then gloriously reclaimed through a process of crusade and reconquest—is no less false than the legends of Clavijo, Santiago, and Pelagius. But, in its dramatic simplicity and self-affirming moralization, it has exercised an incredible appeal both in Spain and elsewhere.

IF PELAGIUS HAD meant for his victory at Covadonga in 722 to herald the reconquest of al-Andalus, it got off to a rather rocky start. At his death in 737 he managed to pass his authority on to his only son, Favila. When the new ruler was eaten by a bear just two years later, the throne passed to Pelagius's son-in-law, Alfonso I, who was explicitly presented by his propagandists as a descendant of Visigothic royalty. However, little about this protokingdom resembled its Visigothic antecedent, except that over the course of the next century Alfonso's descendants and kin, together with the clans of other local strongmen, would squabble and intrigue against each other either to maintain their own autonomy or for control over this poor, isolated, mountainous region and all but ignore the Muslim power to the south.

Saint James "the Muslim Killer." From the *Liber Sancti Jacobi*, or *Codex Calixtanus* (early twelfth century), f. 120r. *Certo Xornal (Wikicommons)*

If the kingdom embodied some special, historical destiny, this was not evident at that time. From the point of view of the amirs, Jilli-qiyya (Galicia), as the Arabs called the peninsula's Atlantic North, was merely another troublesome frontier zone. The Banu Alfunsh ("the clan of Alfonso") was little different from other contemporary indigenous clans of the frontier, such as the Banu Wannaqu ("the clan of Eneko," or the Aristas of Pamplona), led by Eneko Enneconis, who claimed the title King of Pamplona in the early ninth century, or the Banu Qasi, whose realm consolidated in the early 800s under Musa ibn Musa, "the third king of Spain." Alfonso II, who took the throne in 791, established his capital at Oviedo and, having been recognized as king by both Charles the Great and the papacy, began to cultivate the trappings of formal kingship.

The harsh reality that belied Alfonso and Pelagius's grand ambitions and put their affectations of imperial glory in almost comic light was the fact that Asturias was a poor and weak backwater. The same characteristics that insulated it from the Arab conquest—its lack of resources, its challenging terrain, and its isolation—acted as a brake on its own prosperity. Its gold mines had been exhausted by the Romans, it did not sit on any commercial routes, and aside from whatever could be raised from timber and hides, its meager subsistence economy was based on agriculture, herding, fishing, and hunting. Even the kings had little purchasing power; foreign luxuries were all but unobtainable. Its population of poor farmers and rural slaves supported a class of uncouth warriors who were fiercely committed to preserving their own meager prosperity against the claims of their own rulers. Its few ramshackle towns were small and rough-edged, clustered around churches or sheltered within the vestiges of Roman-era walls. Economic opportunity, such as it was, was largely provided by raiding and rustling, whether against rival Christians of the highlands or, more temptingly, the wealthier, Muslim-dominated lands to the south.

That al-Andalus formally identified as Islamic and these lands were all but homogenously Christian helped to encourage the notion that Asturias was engaged in a religious struggle. This endowed the local dynastic project with an outsized moral mandate and bolstered its claims of supremacy over all the Christians of the peninsula. And it was attractive, too, to members of the clergy here, who aimed to impose their authority over the church in the rest of the peninsula; to enforce orthodoxy; and to challenge the claims of the Archdiocese of Toledo, which, although it was under Islamic rule, officially remained the metropolitan diocese of Hispania. One impulse behind the myth of Santiago's evangelization was precisely to undermine Toledo's claims of primacy.

Alfonso II's fifty-two-year reign was crucial to the future of the realm, providing a long respite from succession battles and a foundation for territorial expansion. On his death in 842, family in-fighting led to a series of coups that eventually put Ramiro I (he of the legend of Clavijo and Santiago) on the throne. Ramiro, who con-tended with Viking attacks and internal resistance from the magnates of Galicia, was able to pass the crown on to his son, Ordoño I, in 850. As Ordoño came to power during the era of rebellion in al-Andalus, he had ample opportunity to gain some advantage over the Aristas of Pamplona and the Banu Qasi, who continued to oscillate between loyalty and resistance to the Umayyad regime. But on his death, the nobility of the realm once again embarked on a bloody struggle for the throne, in which Ordoño's teenage son Alfonso emerged victori-ous in 866. Alfonso III, who would be known as "the Great," ruled for forty-four years, coinciding with the period of greatest disarray in al-Andalus, when the Umayyad regime, beset by rebellions throughout the peninsula, appeared to be on the brink of collapse.

It was likely during Alfonso's reign that both the cult of Santiago as warrior saint and the veneration of his relics at Compostela were formally established, and that the legend of Pelagius and Covadonga began to be promoted as a dynastic myth. It was also under Alfonso III that Asturian control expanded over the whole Atlantic North. But most significant was the expansion of the kingdom southward. Astur-ias was ideally positioned to take advantage of the weaknesses of the emirate, moving into the rolling plains on the northern banks of the Duero River—a thinly inhabited area that was impossible for Cór-doba to control.

The Umayyads' vulnerabilities here were compounded by the re-belliousness of the Middle March of Toledo and the Lower March, which stretched north and west from Mérida. In 854, the aristocracy of Toledo and their allies, the Banu Qasi and the Aristas, called on Ordoño I for support against the Umayyads, but the rebels and their Asturian allies were defeated by the forces of Muhammad I, who had the heads of the vanquished—8,000, according to the chroniclers—sent back to Córdoba and to other towns of al-Andalus and the Maghrib, where they were hung in the streets as trophies. Asturias was constantly sending troops to the rebels in the Lower March or giving shelter to fugitive insurgents. In 828, after a failed uprising in

Mérida, the Berber warlord Mahmud ibn al-Jabbar took his men north, where he was granted a fortress and territory in Galicia by Alfonso II. Later on, after his revolt in Mérida in 868, al-Jilliqi would be welcomed as an honored exile in the court of Alfonso III. And once back in Mérida, he again allied with Alfonso III, who launched an attack deep into al-Andalus in 877.

With their limited resources, the Umayyads had to choose carefully which threats to face. So, although Muhammad and al-Mundhir launched regular military expeditions, these tended to be directed at the Banu Qasi or other rebels of the Upper March, or toward the Christians of Pamplona or Catalonia. Asturias itself was rarely attacked. Seldom conclusive, these campaigns served to keep the military productively occupied; to oblige local warlords to contribute men and supplies; to disrupt regional alliances among potentially rebellious frontier clans; to acquire loot, livestock, and slaves; and to weaken the enemy by destroying infrastructure. They also had a symbolic dimension, evoking the traditional annual summer raids of the pagan Arabs and the early Muslims and acquiring an air of moral or religious struggle (that is, *jihad*). By leading or participating in these missions, the amirs gained prestige and younger princes gained valuable command experience.

Thus, by the third quarter of the ninth century a loose frontier between Asturias and the emirate had been established in the rambling plains north of the Duero River. A number of important towns had been conquered or resettled and fortified by the Asturians, including Oporto, Braga, Zamora, Astorga, Simancas, and León. The thick walls of the latter, a former Roman military colony, would prove too sturdy for the amir's artillery to breach in 845/46, 878, and 882. On the Atlantic coast, Alfonso III's invasions had resulted in a salient that reached as far south as Coímbra (Qulumbriyya). The new frontier was a land of risk, but also of reward, with the danger of attack balanced by the prospect of plunder. And so, with the encouragement of the Asturian kings, settlers began to move south into these new territories, joined by Arabized Christians who were fleeing the increasingly reactionary Islamic culture of the emirate.

Despite the conflict, Asturias and the emirate remained diplomatically and politically engaged. Treaties were concluded and embassies exchanged from the time of 'Abd al-Rahman I forward, and the Umayyads did their best to capitalize on crises within the kingdom. In the 820s, 'Abd al-Rahman II leveraged a very favorable ten-year truce, and in the 870s, Muhammad I tried to undermine the power of Alfonso III by supporting the Christian king's rebellious brother, Bermudo, who declared himself king in Astorga. Military engagements and diplomacy fostered a certain integration among the ruling classes that crossed the religious divide, as captives and fugitives took refuge in infidel courts or were sent as hostages in order to guarantee treaties. Just as Garsea Enneconis and other rulers of Pamplona sent their sons off to be raised at Córdoba, Alfonso III sent his son Ordoño, who became the first king of León, to the court of the Banu Qasi. These young aristocrats were treated as honored guests, and during their stay they were exposed to the culture and mores of their religious and political rivals.

Such exchanges helped to establish an aristocratic culture that bridged the formal divide between Christian and Muslim Spain. Intermarriage among the elites continued, and marriages were now sought from among the aristocracy as well as from among captives. In 862, for example, the future amir 'Abd Allah married Onneca, the daughter of Fortún Garcés, the heir to Pamplona, a union likely intended by both parties to block Asturia's attempts to dominate the northern Pyrenees. Although Onneca and 'Abd Allah's son, Muhammad, was assassinated before he could take the throne, his son was none other than 'Abd al-Rahman III, the first Umayyad of al-Andalus to claim the caliphal title.

AS FOR ALFONSO III, his confidence was such that he was said to have purchased an "imperial crown" from the Franks in 909, and with it the right to call himself "Emperor of León." But his imperial project, which seemed so secure at the time, could not be saved even by saintly intervention. In his last years, his ever-restless nobility sowed discord among the king and his sons, García, Ordoño, and Fruela.

They rose up against their father in 910, forcing him to abdicate and break up his realm into three independent kingdoms: León, Galicia, and Asturias. But, by 925 the three brothers were dead and the region once more plunged into a struggle for succession, and for the next century it would come under the effective domination of the caliphate of Córdoba.

The legend of Christian unity and continuity has endured, despite the fact that we have almost no dependable sources from the era, and those that we do have support it only in the most limited and qualified manner. The histories from the era of Alfonso III, and those composed in the eleventh century and later, were written by foreign clergymen who had an explicit commitment to supporting the political supremacy of the Leonese monarchy and endowing it with a providential, divine character. They happily invented histories, forged documents, and concocted genealogies in order to frame the history of Spain in terms of a grand Christian-Muslim conflict that has served as the rationale for the eventual domination of Castile and León in the peninsula from the later Middle Ages until today. The monks and priests who wrote these histories conceived of the world in terms of celestial struggle; their language was biblical and their rhetoric apocalyptic. For them, the Christians of Spain were the "true Israel"—a people chosen by God but cast down for their disobedience and sin, and who were now called on to reclaim their rightful place through inner piety and earthly battle against the infidel.

While they probably did not believe this themselves (or at least did not act as though they did), Alfonso III and his successors understood both the power of myth and the compelling force of faith. In the same way that the rebellions of the 800s demonstrated to the Umayyads that they needed a religious ideology to legitimize their claims of superiority over Islamic Spain, the kings of Asturias realized they needed religion to legitimize their own claims over Christian Spain. Any Christian ambitions, however, would need to be put on hold. In 929, Córdoba, now ruling over a united al-Andalus, was about to enter its greatest era of glory, one that would make the Ummayad caliphate the uncontested superpower of Western Europe and the Western Mediterranean and its capital city "the ornament of the world."[14]

PART III

TRIUMPH, 929–1030

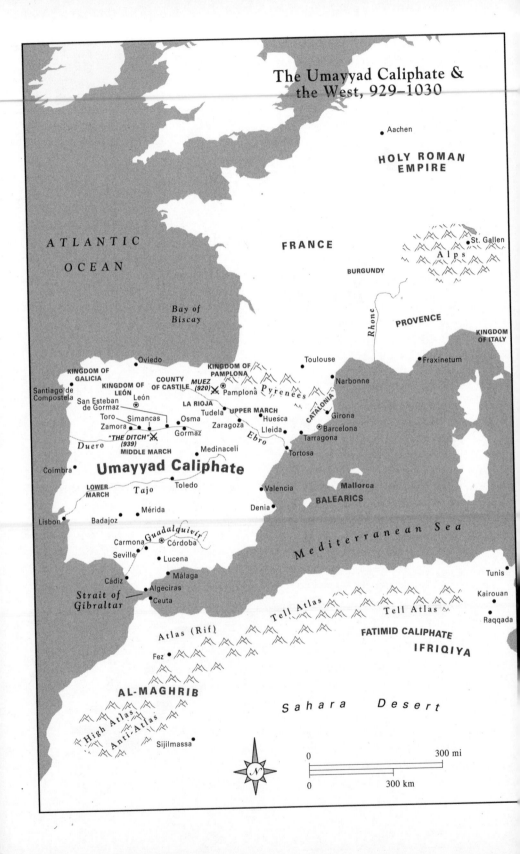

The Umayyad Caliphate &
the West, 929–1030

• Aachen

HOLY ROMAN
EMPIRE

ATLANTIC

OCEAN

FRANCE

• St. Gallen

Alps

BURGUNDY

Bay of
Biscay

Rhone

PROVENCE

KINGDOM
OF ITALY

• Oviedo

KINGDOM OF
GALICIA

KINGDOM OF
PAMPLONA

• Toulouse

• Fraxinetum

Santiago de
Compostela

KINGDOM OF
LEÓN

COUNTY
OF CASTILE

MUEZ
(920)

Pamplona

Pyrenees

Narbonne

San Esteban
de Gormaz

León

LA RIOJA

Tudela

UPPER MARCH

CATALONIA

Girona

Toro

Simancas

Osma

Huesca

Lleida

Barcelona

Zamora

Gormaz

Zaragoza

Tarragona

"THE DITCH"
(939)

Duero

Medinaceli

Tortosa

MIDDLE MARCH

Coimbra •

Umayyad Caliphate

LOWER
MARCH

Tajo

Toledo

Valencia

Mallorca

Denia •

BALEARICS

Mérida

Mediterranean   Sea

Lisbon •

Badajoz

Guadalquivir

Carmona

Córdoba

Tunis

Seville

• Lucena

Kairouan

Cádiz

• Málaga

Algeciras

Strait of
Gibraltar

Ceuta

Tell Atlas

Tell Atlas

Raqqada

Atlas (Rif)

FATIMID CALIPHATE

IFRIQIYA

Fez •

AL-MAGHRIB

Sahara   Desert

High Atlas

Anti-Atlas

Sijilmassa •

N

0   300 mi

0   300 km

9

A Sun Rising in the West

It was noon on January 17, 929, and the throngs of Muslim faithful had gathered for Friday prayer, jamming the aisles of the congregational mosque in Córdoba. For the first time, when the imam gave the traditional opening dedication for the *khutba* (or sermon) after the conclusion of the call to prayer, he did not acknowledge the title of the 'Abbasid ruler in Baghdad as was customary across the Sunni world, but instead hailed 'Abd al-Rahman III as "Prince of the Faithful." The amir, who now went by the honorific al-Nasir al-Din Allah ("God's Victor in the Regime of God"), had claimed for himself the position of caliph of Islam.

This was an extraordinary and shocking event by any standard. Never had the Umayyad princes, their caliphal pedigree notwithstanding, explicitly denied the authority of the 'Abbasid rulers, nor had any Sunni prince challenged their title. It was particularly extraordinary considering the state of al-Andalus when 'Abd al-Rahman III had come to the throne seventeen years earlier—nearly bankrupt, shredded by rebellions, and under attack from the north. In the 890s, the reign of his grandfather 'Abd Allah had descended into bloody intrigue, the amir's paranoia such that he constructed a covered passageway to protect him against assassination as he scurried between his palace and the great mosque. He took severe reprisals against any who appeared to cross his path, even members of his own family. Just after 'Abd al-Rahman's birth, his father, Muhammad, 'Abd Allah's heir-apparent, had been murdered by his own half brother, al-Mutarrif—a crime that went unpunished by the amir, who was evidently complicit, although he later also had al-Mutarrif put to death on unrelated suspicions of disloyalty.

So it was that when 'Abd Allah passed over his surviving sons and designated his twenty-one-year-old grandson 'Abd al-Rahman as heir, the decision was greeted with relief. A young man, beholden to none, his name resonated with the dynasty's founder, 'Abd al-Rahman I al-Dakhil, and many believed he would usher in an age of glory, triumph, and unity. Others may have imagined it to their advantage to have an inexperienced man on the throne. Certainly, he did not cut an imposing figure; his legs were so short his stirrups had to be raised until they hung just under the saddle. But, he was handsome, even if the dark dye he put in his beard to evoke his Arab lineage could not disguise the fair features he inherited from his grandmother, Princess Onneca of Pamplona, and his mother, the Christian slave girl Muzna.

He was, however, endowed with a keen and curious intellect that had been nurtured by the best education the palace could provide, as well as sharp political instincts, a cosmopolitan view of culture, and a force of will that would manifest itself in both steadfast determination and the cruelest violence. Those who betrayed him were subject to gruesome and exemplary punishment: menaced by his fierce lions or tortured, beheaded, or crucified alive, sometimes with their tongue cut out. Surrendering garrisons, Christian or Muslim, might be put to the sword, and the heads of vanquished enemies were displayed in public around his realm to advertise his power. Concubines who flinched at his advances could be dispatched on the spot or cruelly disfigured, and in 950 or 951 he executed his son 'Abd Allah, who was accused of plotting rebellion. It was said 'Abd al-Rahman put him to death by his own hand in front of the crowds gathered in Córdoba for the public celebration of the 'Id al-Adha, the "Feast of Sacrifice," which commemorates Abraham's willingness to kill his own son.

Violence of this sort was typical of the age, and it is likely that without such ferociousness 'Abd al-Rahman III could never have accomplished the task at which his predecessors had failed: unifying al-Andalus and converting it into the greatest and most prosperous kingdom in contemporary Europe. But, he balanced his fury with largesse and mercy, as when, for example, he forgave betrayals by family members or welcomed former rebels into the inner circles of the court. Although some called 'Abd al-Rahman III a tyrant, his strength earned the acclaim of many of his subjects, Muslims, Christians, and Jews alike, who hailed him as a hero and praised him in messianic tones as a "sun . . . risen in the West, which will shine with splendor on the two Easts."[15]

SUCH OPTIMISM BELIED the situation when 'Abd al-Rahman III came to power. Even the territory around Córdoba was teeming with rebels, such that the city's southern gate had been barricaded permanently shut. Hence, his first task was to subdue his enemies closest to home—Ibn Hafsun, in particular. This would not be accomplished until 928, when the victorious prince had the long-dead rebel's remains symbolically crucified in Córdoba. Meanwhile, other nodes of resistance fell: Carmona, Seville, Mérida, Badajoz, and Valencia, as well as the perennially rebellious Toledo in 932, and, finally, Zaragoza in 933. The process took twenty-five years of warfare, threats, and conciliations. 'Abd al-Rahman took the rebels on one by one, frequently leading the military expeditions himself, plundering the countryside to spread terror and hardship before setting up a siege to contain the enemy, while he rode off to the next operation. Those who proved incorrigible were put to death, but he preferred to obtain the submission of rebels. In irredeemably troublesome cities, like Toledo, he simply deposed the local elites and dispatched his own trusted governor, either a *mawla* or a slave, to rule over the subdued territory.

'Abd al-Rahman III approached the task systematically. By first securing the south, he consolidated his revenue base and military capacity. Then he turned to the frontier zones: Badajoz in the Lower March, Toledo in the Middle March, and Zaragoza in the Upper

March. He kept his armies continually in the field and circulating through his territory, thereby preventing further uprisings by forcing local lords to provide troops and supplies, and by maintaining a state of alert across the land. The result was that Córdoba would finally be in a position to effectively govern virtually the whole of al-Andalus. Entrenched muwallad families were removed from governorships and replaced by Arab and Berber clans, such as the Banu Tujib and the Banu Dhi 'l-Nun, while indigenous families and Berbers were incorporated into the bureaucracy and the religious elite, undermining the monopoly enjoyed by ethnic Arabs. Together with other *mawali* clans of local, North African, or Arab descent, as well as members of the Christian and Jewish elite and the thousands of slaves owned by the royal family, these new clients came to constitute the fiercely loyal core of the Umayyad administration.

The army was also progressively de-Arabized as the power of the tribal militias, or *junds*, was deliberately reduced. To take their place, 'Abd al-Rahman purchased large quantities of slaves and began to recruit Berber mercenaries from North Africa. The ubiquity of slaves and their influence within the regime is difficult to overstate. The royal court employed them by the thousands, as did the estates of Umayyad princes and princesses and other members of the aristocracy. Many slaves acquired great influence. Early in his reign, the then-amir's right-hand man was Badr al-Siqlabi, a foundling who had served as *hajib* to the amir 'Abd Allah and whom 'Abd al-Rahman invested as administrator and military commander. Although many slaves were eunuchs, some of those who were not managed to make the jump from slave to grandee. In his later years, the caliph's most trusted general was the ex-slave Ghalib al-Nasrani, who was honored with the *nasab* (or patronymic) "ibn 'Abd al-Rahman." Freed by the amir, he married into the *khassa* and rose to the highest echelons of power.

Although historians have long thought of 'Abd al-Rahman III as a great patron of culture, it was warfare that defined his reign. As he slowly brought al-Andalus under his control, he began also to mount regular campaigns against the Christian North, beginning in 916.

The princes here had always been ready to capitalize on Córdoba's weakness, and Alfonso III's son Ordoño II, king of León and Galicia, launched a series of campaigns in the second decade of the tenth century. His inconstant ally, Sancho I of Navarre, was a local strongman who with the help of Alfonso III had risen up against and deposed Fortún Garcés, the last king of the Arista dynasty of Pamplona. Sancho, Fortún, and 'Abd al-Rahman were, of course, all related by marriage.

For his part, 'Abd al-Rahman's attacks against the Christian North were not campaigns of conquest, and his military policy abroad was reactive. He responded to the threats on the frontier, aiming to destabilize the Christian kingdoms, not to destroy them. This kept his army occupied and provincial governors on their toes, while these campaigns of jihad reinforced his claim to be "Commander of the Faithful." Some of his campaigns were successful, others less so. A victory against León and Navarre at Muez in 920 brought a windfall, which he apportioned among his soldiers, and it also brought a harvest of Christian heads, which he had sent as trophies as far afield as North Africa. Soon after, his army attacked Christian strongholds along the Duero and even sacked Pamplona. But the campaign was primarily a response to a less successful raid three years earlier, which saw an Andalusi force wiped out by the enemy at San Esteban de Gormaz.

To further bolster his image as a *mujahid* and impose his authority on his reluctant governors, 'Abd al-Rahman led these campaigns in person. But after narrowly escaping death at the Battle of the Ditch in 939, when he was betrayed by leaders from among the provincial nobility, he left the army in the hands of trusted commanders, such as Ghalib al-Nasrani. That August, the caliph had raised a massive army at Toledo and set out to strike at Simancas, a forward operating base for Leonese expansion into the Duero region. But after falling into a lethal ambush as his troops approached the city, the caliph escaped with his life but little more. His baggage train was captured, and his personal effects, including his copy of the Qur'an, became trophies for his enemies. The defeat, however, did not undermine 'Abd al-Rahman's status in al-Andalus. If anything, it ushered in a new period of stability, particularly in the frontier zones, where thereafter the governors remained loyal to the Umayyad regime in exchange for greater autonomy, a place in the caliphal aristocracy, and the right to pass on their titles to their children.

In addition to his incursions into the Christian North, 'Abd al-Rahman established a fortified frontier along the southern bank of the Duero and the foothills of the Pyrenees, where the many new forts he constructed tightened the caliphate's grip on the borderlands. Existing fortifications were also enlarged, such as the castle at Gormaz, along the eastern section of the Duero. One of Europe's largest fortifications, the impressive redoubt became a platform for future raids into León and Navarre, and into the emerging county known as Castile (al-Qila', or "the Castles"). These forts served as an advertisement of Umayyad strength, both to foreigners and his own subjects. Regional potentates and local communities also built and maintained fortifications, and the landscape of al-Andalus—particularly in the *thughur*, the vast swath of frontier territory that ran from the Atlantic to the Mediterranean—came to be characterized by what historians have called the *hisn-qarya*, or "fortress-village" pattern. Taking advantage of the small but steep plateaus that dot the Spanish landscape, walled enclosures were raised adjacent to villages so as to provide shelter for people and livestock in the event of a raid—a practice that would become important in the coming centuries as Christian cross-border raiding intensified.

'Abd al-Rahman was also obliged to expand the navy and to strengthen defenses along the Mediterranean seaboard in response to Aghlabid raiding. Mallorca and Menorca were finally fully subjugated in 935 and 943, respectively, and 'Abd al-Rahman dispatched fleets to harass the coasts from Catalonia to northern Italy. Each time they returned with considerable booty, as well as treaties establishing favorable commercial relations with the Christians. During 'Abd al-Rahman's reign, Muslim privateers, including disenfranchised muwallads, increased their activity at their fortified base at Fraxinetum in Provence and began to raid far up the Rhône, reaching even the Swiss Alps, where they sacked the monastery of Saint Gallen and exacted tolls from Christian pilgrims who crossed their territory en route to Rome. These "pirates," as the Christians saw them, were interested in raiding, not conquest, and Córdoba likely had limited control over their activities. Nevertheless, their raiding provoked a diplomatic incident when in 953 Otto I, king of the Germans and soon-to-be Holy Roman Emperor, dispatched an embassy to Córdoba angrily demanding the caliph put a stop to the attacks—a request that reflected the prestige the caliph had achieved by that point.

BUT IF THE ire of a distant Christian king was of little concern to 'Abd al-Rahman, the events then unfolding in North Africa, by contrast, did concern him. The Aghlabid dynasty was collapsing and a new power, the Fatimids—a Shi'a sect whose imams claimed direct descent from Muhammad's daughter Fatima and his cousin and brother-in-law, 'Ali ibn Abi Talib—had risen. Driven underground and fleeing persecution in the 'Abbasid caliphate, the eleventh Fatimid imam had taken refuge in Sijilmassa, on the edge of the western Sahara, and began to gather support among the indigenous Kutama, who felt marginalized in Arab-ruled Ifriqiya. These Berbers were drawn to the esoteric, millenarian theology of the Fatimids, which promised the imminent arrival of the Mahdi (the "Rightly Guided One"), a messianic figure who, alongside Jesus, would usher in the End Times.

The Fatimids envisioned nothing less than the transformation of the Islamic world by overturning what they saw as illegitimate Sunni Islamic regimes. Their strategy combined diplomacy, espionage, and infiltration, and once they controlled a state, military action. In al-Andalus, an opening was provided by none other than the struggling and desperate Ibn Hafsun, who, as his other options failed, reached out to these Shi'a revolutionaries to support his rebellion. Just after 910, he welcomed two Fatimid envoys to Bobastro and soon after ordered that the name of the Fatimid imam, 'Ubayd Allah, be called out at the beginning of Friday prayers. It was this act, as much as his supposed conversion to Christianity, that sealed Ibn Hafsun's reputation as an apostate. The previous year, the Fatimids had seized the Aghlabid capital of Raqqada, where late in 909 or early in 910, 'Ubayd Allah revealed himself as al-Mahdi and claimed the titles of

"Commander of the Faithful" and caliph in defiance of his archen-
emy, the 'Abbasid caliph, al-Muqtadir.

It was a bold move, particularly because the Fatimids remained a
small clique of foreigners in North Africa, where an ever-shifting ka-
leidoscope of Berber nations, tribes, and clans clashed continuously
with each other and with the Arabs, who had now lived there for over
two centuries. Fatimid ideology would meet opposition not only from
a multitude of Sunni and Kharijite adherents, but also from an array
of local, would-be prophets. Hampered by internal rivalries and tensions with their Kutama supporters, the Fatimids nevertheless consolidated their hold on Ifriqiya, made inroads into Sicily, and then struck
westward into the Maghrib. Local dynasties fell before them one by
one, including the Idrisids of Fez in 917 and the Umayyad protectorate of Nakur that same year. By 927 they would be at Tetuan, and
Fatimid ships began to raid the Andalusi coast.

In response, 'Abd al-Rahman established new shipyards and
continued to build up his navy. Going on the offensive, he sent his
armies across the strait to North Africa, where they established a
cluster of beachheads. Chief among these was Ceuta, which he took
in 931. This strongly fortified citadel would provide a base for the
expansion of Umayyad power into North Africa over the course of
the tenth century—a long campaign that would launch the legendary prosperity of the Umayyad al-Andalus but also sow the seeds of
its destruction.

'ABD AL-RAHMAN III'S decision to take the caliphal title may have
been bold, but it was also obvious, necessary, and all but inevitable.
By 900, the Islamic world had outgrown the pious fiction of a universally acknowledged Sunni caliph in Baghdad. 'Abbasid authority was
collapsing and the caliphate had lost control of virtually all of its
territory beyond the environs of the capital, either to rebellious governors or to radical esoteric groups from the fringes of the Islamic
world. In 908, palace officials in Baghdad had orchestrated the succession of the boy, al-Muqtadir, to the throne as caliph, ushering in a
period of palatine intrigue, and the following year 'Ubayd Allah declared himself caliph in Ifriqiya.

The Fatimids' claim to the caliphal title undermined 'Abd al-Rahman's authority and effectively obliged him to present himself as the successor to Muhammad as head of the Muslim *umma*. Like the Fatimid caliphs, he would now cultivate a messianic, almost semi-divine, public persona. Claiming imperial status also put him on the same level of prestige as the other great sovereigns of the west: the Byzantine Roman emperors in Constantinople and the self-proclaimed Frankish "Roman emperors" of post-Carolingian Europe (not to mention the petty "emperors" of León).

The prestige and legitimacy that came with the title would also help him at home. No longer could he be conceived of merely as "first among equals" by the grandees of al-Andalus. Unable to challenge his new, elevated authority, members of the territorial elite would channel their ambitions elsewhere by working to rise within the Umayyad power structure rather than by plotting to undermine it. Military campaigns, whether within al-Andalus, against the Christian kingdoms, or in North Africa, could now be characterized as holy wars against "polytheists," providing a religious rationale that would quell Muslim resistance and galvanize the resolve of the caliph's subordinates and troops. The *sikka*, the minting of gold coinage, was the prerogative of caliphs, and now that he had greater access to African gold, 'Abd al-Rahman could mint the abundant, high-quality gold *dinars* that would become the standard coinage of the Western Mediterranean and an emblem of the tremendous prosperity of his caliphate—the "greenbacks" of their day. The internal peace he brought to al-Andalus came as a relief to his war-weary common subjects and yielded economic dividends as commerce began to thrive.

All these benefits were presented as tangible manifestations of his messianic character. And, even if 'Abd al-Rahman showed little personal interest in theology, his caliphal title acted as a brake on the ever-growing power of the Maliki *'ulama'*, who had claimed to be the highest religious authorities in the land. By placing himself above them, 'Abd al-Rahman opened a space for other Sunni legal traditions, as well as mystical and esoteric approaches to Islam—all of which were gaining traction among his subjects but also aggressively persecuted by some Malikis. Finally, his new title allowed him to more clearly claim legitimate authority over, and extend protection to, the Christians and Jews of the peninsula, as Peoples of the Book.

The ethnoreligious diversity of al-Andalus was a fact, not an ideal, and one that 'Abd al-Rahman was obliged to respond to. Indeed, he cultivated it, thereby reinforcing his sovereignty and laying the groundwork for the era of integration that would follow. The caliph was the son and grandson of Christian women, and the domestic environment he grew up in was strongly infused with Spanish Christian language and culture, including the songs and poems that were sung, the festivals that were celebrated, and the religious rituals practiced by the concubines and slaves he was surrounded by as a child and youth.

IO

The Resplendent City

Once he had become caliph and claimed the title "Commander of the Faithful," 'Abd al-Rahman was obliged to create a home for his court that would reflect his magnificence and that emulated and challenged the palace-cities of the 'Abbasid and Fatimid caliphs. Sometime around 936, after the center of Córdoba had been devastated by a great fire, construction began on an immense complex five miles west of the city. In 941, the great mosque at Madinat al-Zahra', "the Resplendent City," would be inaugurated, and six years later the caliph would take up residence and move the apparatus of state to the palace, including the chancery, the caliphal guard, the mint, the treasury, and the *tiraz,* or royal silk workshop.

The scale of the endeavor boggles the imagination. The caliph raised three adjoining palaces on the terraced slopes of the Sierra Morena, descending, one lower than the next, onto the broad floor of the valley of the Guadalquivir, each with extensive gardens. The uppermost palace, looking out over the nearby metropolis of Córdoba, was the caliph's private residence, the harem: home to his wives, his hundreds of concubines, and his household staff. In 961, the year 'Abd al-Rahman died, these were said to have amounted to 3,750 male and 6,750 female slaves. Below this was the administrative palace, where audiences and ceremonies were held, embassies received, and the business of state carried out. Here, courtiers and high functionaries, Muslims, Christians, and Jews, lived together with their families, alongside the aristocratic hostages and envoys sent from around the Mediterranean and beyond. And, finally, at the bottom was the public palace, where thousands of workers, craftsmen, and ancillary staff lived. The entire complex—a self-contained city—was surrounded by a tower-studded defensive wall nearly one mile long and a half mile wide.

Madinat al-Zahra' was a showcase for the power and wealth of the caliph, built of the finest materials, including the thousands of tons of multicolored marble that covered the palace walls and were inlaid in its floors. Inside, light played through the elaborate wooden screens of the windows, illuminating elaborately painted stucco walls and ceilings and great, carved roof beams. Many of its 4,300 columns had been mined from Roman ruins in al-Andalus, while others were sent as gifts from foreign sovereigns: some from Rome, a score from the court of the Franks, and over a hundred each from Ifriqiya and Byzantium. The lush gardens, where the sound of rippling water mixed with the throaty grousing of peacocks and the occasional roars of the caliph's lions, were meant to evoke the gardens of Paradise. The gardens were presided over by plundered pagan statues, while richly carved ancient sarcophagi were built into the palace walls, serving as lintels over doorways or basins for fountains, thus also calling to mind the past glories of Rome and the richness of Hellenistic culture.

The walls of the upper two palaces were festooned with rich silk brocade, while at the center of the audience hall, or *majlis*, sat a large basin filled with liquid mercury, which when prodded would send off shimmering waves of light to dazzle visitors. Foreign envoys could admire the caliph's trophies, including prizes won in battle, relics and curiosities, and elaborate and luxurious gifts that had been sent by far-off rulers, such as the two marble fountains and the great pearl he received from the Byzantine emperor Constantine VII.

The gilded and bejeweled throne on which the ruler sat as visitors prostrated before him was intended as a re-creation of that of the Biblical Solomon. The furnishings and fixtures of the palace were no less sumptuous and included the finest ironwork vessels and lamps, fashioned in the shapes of exotic and mythical animals; furniture of rare woods; and boxes of delicately carved African ivory. The palace also held an immense library said to contain hundreds of thousands of volumes representing the knowledge of the Islamic, Byzantine, and Latin worlds, a testament to the worldliness of the caliph. Sponsorship of the caliphal library would become a special passion of his son al-Hakam II.

In the upper palace, the caliph, his wives, concubines, young children, and other family members were attended to by regiments of eunuch slaves, predominantly of northern Spanish or Eastern European origin. Three of 'Abd al-Rahman's wives stand out. One, known as Umm Quraysh ("the mother of the Qurayshis"), was a local woman of humble origins whom the caliph had encountered as she worked bleaching clothes on a riverbank. Their meeting was a boon for her family, particularly her brother, whom 'Abd al-Rahman promoted to a number of positions in the administration and who served eventually as a military commander. Following Arabic tradition, 'Abd al-Rahman also married within his own clan. His wife Fatima was a distant cousin, who despite her pedigree and having borne him a son, fell out of favor with the caliph, thanks to the machinations of an ambitious concubine.

Early in his reign, Marjan, a Christian woman of renowned beauty, approached Fatima to ask if she could purchase one of the wife's designated nights with the amir, and after Fatima agreed and the slave had passed an evening of sexual abandon with her owner, Marjan showed 'Abd al-Rahman the bill of sale. The amir's pique was such that he sidelined Fatima and made the concubine his favorite. 'Abd al-Rahman became so enthralled with Marjan that he made her his intimate confidant and the administrator of his household, endowing her with a tremendous fortune. It was she who bore him the son al-Hakam, who would inherit the caliphate.

From infancy, al-Hakam was groomed for the succession, serving as his father's deputy when the caliph was away on campaign as early as age six. Given the best education available, the boy demonstrated a considerable aptitude for intellectual pursuits. He was also trained in the affairs of state and granted his first military command when he was only twelve. Conscious of the importance of dynastic continuity,

'Abd al-Rahman III micromanaged his son's affairs and image, forbidding him from marrying even after he was well into adulthood, thus fueling rumors that the crown prince was homosexual. Such reports circulated regarding 'Abd al-Rahman too, particularly in the Christian North.

The caliph was said to have executed an adolescent captive named Pelagius after the young aristocrat rebuffed his sexual advances and refused to convert to Islam. The relics of this Saint Pelagius were eventually taken to León, while his legend traveled far north to the lands of the Franks. There, the Saxon canoness Hrotsvit of Gandersheim, in the course of a lurid denunciation in verse of the caliph's supposed depravity, acknowledged Muslim Córdoba as "an ornament bright" in "the Western part of the world."[16] Whatever the circumstances of Pelagius's death, the tale may have reflected the ephebophilism—the sexual idealization of adolescent boys—that had long been a feature of cultures in the Mediterranean, the Near East, and beyond. Decried as vice by the pious-minded, it was nevertheless practiced openly by Christians, Muslims, and Jews among the Andalusi elite, who composed poetry to celebrate their wine-fueled erotic encounters with their fair, downy-faced slave boys.

To prevent intrigues, the caliph's other children were installed in lavish country estates in the surrounding area and provided with stipends so that they might live a life of semi-isolated privilege under the tutelage and control of their mothers. Favored wives, concubines, and daughters were also given endowments, which enabled them to establish their own informal networks of patronage, but ultimately, their fortunes were dependent on the whims of the caliph, whose legendary volatility was a further line of defense against the ambitions of his household. Leading statesmen and courtiers, including slaves, Umayyad clansmen and clients, and members of the Arab and indigenous *khassa*, also constructed palaces and gardens in Córdoba and up and down the length of the Guadalquivir Valley in emulation of the royals. These were the scenes of celebration: of weddings and circumcisions, of banquets and drinking parties, of hunting trips and entertainments. One of the greatest of these villas, al-Rummaniyya, situated close by Madinat al-Zahra', was founded by the slave Durri ibn al-Hakam al-Saghir, who served as treasurer for al-Hakam II, and who astutely handed over the estate together with its rich pleasure and market gardens, and all its livestock and slaves, to his employer in 973.

The construction of these great manors was but one facet of the transformation of Córdoba, which had been expanding even before the founding of Madinat al-Zahra'. Córdoba remained the public and commercial capital, its great mosque and fortress-palace potent monuments to Umayyad power, the latter serving as the dynasty's pantheon. 'Abd al-Rahman III's public appearances were strictly choreographed affairs designed to communicate the magnificence of the ruler to his subjects. Religious celebrations were held in the city's two open-air prayer areas, where representatives of the city's various groups were arrayed carefully according to their place in the caliphal hierarchy as an expression of their submission and a reflection of their integration into the structure of Andalusi society. Likewise, displays marking the arrival of foreign dignitaries reinforced the Umayyad notion of order, power, and authority, and the princes of neighboring territories in Europe and Africa were presented as the caliph's subordinates and he as their patron. In times of drought, the ruler led processions held to invoke rain. The departure of armies on campaign were marked by parades, as were their triumphant returns, during which they displayed their loot and captives along with the corpses or severed heads of vanquished enemies. When the caliph and his household processed from Madinat al-Zahra' to Córdoba, this journey of only a few miles could take several days, as the royal entourage with its hundreds of attendants, mounts, and guards moved at a stately pace toward the capital over brocade-covered roads framed by great silk banners, stopping to rest, eat, and sleep at the stately villas that lay along its path.

As Córdoba's population grew to over 100,000 inhabitants, it was necessary to expand the great mosque. Al-Hakam II would double the size of its prayer hall and add decorative elements featuring mosaics by Byzantine artisans and rare woods from Africa and India. The mosque and fortress complexes, together with the great market of Córdoba, formed the heart of the city, which was girded by a roughly circular wall punctuated by seven stout iron gates, each decorated

Cast bronze incense burner (eleventh century). *Metropolitan Museum of Art (Purchase, Joseph Pulitzer Bequest, 1967)*

with recycled classical-era statues and meant to embody the seven gates of Heaven in Islamic lore. Other infrastructure projects included a large aqueduct to improve the city's water supply. As Córdoba expanded, so did its facilities: public ovens, baths, schools, hospitals, mosques, and inns—all sponsored by members of the elite, founded as investments or operated as charitable foundations. The elites emulated the caliph and founded their own salons, libraries, and academies, while more discreetly, the city's Jewish and Christian inhabitants continued to build synagogues and churches.

The megapolis of Córdoba–Madinat al-Zahra' comprised an immense market for luxury products, ordinary manufactured goods, and food staples and became the economic engine of al-Andalus. It is estimated that Madinat al-Zahra' alone absorbed a third of the caliphate's budget. The building and rebuilding of palaces and estates required thousands of workers, both skilled and unskilled. Every conceivable tool and implement needed to be manufactured, as did clothes, shoes, household articles, and furnishings, for both the elite and the common folk. High-end crafts like gold- and silversmithing, iron- and woodworking, glassmaking, sericulture, tailoring, and ivory carving reached new levels of refinement owing to the insatiable demands of the status-hungry elite and the growing population. Manufactured goods, including ceramic and leather, were produced both for local consumption and for export at home and abroad. Food poured in from the countryside to feed the masses and was re-exported as "night soil"—human waste collected from the city and sold as fertilizer.

The population was augmented by a continual ingress of slaves and free settlers. Order was maintained by the *sahib al-madina* ("master of the city") with support of a police force and aided by inspectors, agents, and the market master, who supervised not only commerce but public morality in general. Beggars, peddlers, and traveling salesmen were all strictly regulated. Littering was prohibited, and workshops and businesses were forbidden from polluting. Chimneys were introduced and made mandatory to cut down on the smog from domestic and commercial ovens. In sum, Córdoba was transformed over the course of the half century of 'Abd al-Rahman III's rule from a struggling provincial city into a bustling, cosmopolitan capital—a place of encounter and exchange for merchants, travelers, scholars, officials, immigrants, visitors, captives, and seekers of fortune from every corner of the caliphate and across the Mediterranean, as well as Europe, Africa, and the Near East. It was in this era that the reputation of al-Andalus as an earthy paradise was established by the poets and panegyrists who sang the praises of the caliph and characterized the land as prodigiously fertile, a land of unprecedented richness and bounty. For all of this, the caliph himself was somewhat more circumspect, claiming in his later years to have enjoyed only "fourteen days of happiness."[17]

ALTHOUGH THE CALIPHATE itself would endure for less than a century, the administrative framework 'Abd al-Rahman III established, the tremendous rise in agricultural and craft output his reign saw, and the investments in infrastructure he made fed a boom of urbanization across al-Andalus. Together these factors endowed it with a stability and cohesiveness that would enable Islamic Spain to endure the fragmentation of the caliphate that would occur in the early eleventh century. But such unprecedented prosperity obscured the tensions that were brewing as a consequence of these transformations, as the multiethnic, religiously plural reality of Andalusi society continued to grate against the emerging Islamic consciousness of the majority of the population.

In a scenario familiar today from Iran to Iowa, there was a growing estrangement of the liberal, cosmopolitan, and diverse aristocracy, whose fortunes lay with the dynasty and the state, from the more religiously and socially conservative common classes, whose advocates were members of the *'ulama'*. Influential *'ulama'*, many of whom were piously sober members of the business class of merchants and artisans, regarded the palatine elite as effete decadents and would tolerate their dominance only as long as the caliphate remained prosperous. Such problems were not unique to Umayyad al-Andalus, and similar tensions arose in contemporary Byzantium, as well as in the Fatimid and 'Abbasid caliphates, in each place with similarly catastrophic consequences. For the time being, however, the center would hold, and on his death in 961, 'Abd al-Rahman would be succeeded by his son al-Hakam II, the second—and last—caliph to hold real power in al-Andalus.

II

All the Caliph's Men

As singular an individual as 'Abd al-Rahman III may have been, he did not rule alone, and his success depended in great part on the officials and advisors who worked for him. His reign saw a tremendous elaboration of the apparatus of state and a diversification of his court and bureaucracy. As they strove to reduce the power of the great Arab families of the *jund* and the old muwallad territorial elite, the caliph and his successor, al-Hakam II, turned to newcomers and outsiders to maintain a balance of power within the administration. These included new *mawali* families; slaves, whether of Spanish or "Slavic" origin; Arabized Christians and Jews; and eventually, Zanata and Sanhaja Berbers and sub-Saharan Africans. This openness endowed the administration with a streak of meritocracy that provided opportunities for the best and brightest, no matter how lowborn, but also increased the power of the bureaucracy. As long as the caliph was able to exert his personality and take a firm hand in the running of the state, the institution would be secure; otherwise the state apparatus could take on a life of its own.

Conscious of the dangers that his own glorious isolation entailed, 'Abd al-Rahman III had carefully chosen his courtiers from among slaves, *mawali* families, regional aristocracies, and new dependents, rotating them through different offices and casting them down if found to be corrupt. In the same spirit, he suspended the office of chamberlain—the all-powerful caliphal deputy—soon after the death of his trusted *hajib*, the eunuch Badr, in order to rule directly. The office would not be revived until the reign of al-Hakam II, who appointed his slave Ja'far al-Siqlabi to the post, and subsequently—with fatal consequences—Ja'far al-Mushafi, a member of a long-settled, well-established, and integrated Berber family that had gained influence under Umayyad patronage. Al-Mushafi was, thus, different from the Berber mercenaries who were beginning to flood into al-Andalus as a consequence of the increasing Umayyad involvement in the Maghrib and of that region's growing importance, most of all as a source of African gold, slaves, and soldiers.

The caliphate's North African turn can be seen also in religious policy, particularly the appointment of magistrates, or *qadis*. Initially, 'Abd al-Rahman appointed chief *qadis* drawn from long-loyal families of distinguished Arabic origin, but by the end of his reign, individuals of North African origin were serving in these positions. Several factors contributed to this trend. The Maghrib was the front line in the struggle against Shi'ism and heterodoxy, and it consequently produced able and experienced Maliki preachers, which the Umayyads needed. Moreover, the better-established *'ulama'* of al-Andalus adopted a posture of reluctance to serve the caliphate, which, on principle, they looked down on as a corrupting "Mammon."

But, however much 'Abd al-Rahman may have wished to loosen the grip of the conservative Maliki religious party, he was locked in a relationship of codependence with them, wherein he guaranteed their preeminent authority and they vouchsafed his legitimacy as caliph in exchange. Judaism and Christianity were not seen as a threat to the regime, but Islamic heterodoxy was—in the form of not only unsanctioned messianic movements promoted by unofficial preachers but even rival Sunni legal schools. Religious and political discourse were inseparable; thus, 'Abd Allah, the son who rebelled against and was put to death by 'Abd al-Rahman III, identified with the Shafi'i legal school, and this fact alone was perceived as a sign of disloyalty.

Alongside North Africans, the most influential element in the caliphal administration was the Saqaliba, or "Slavs"—slaves and

freedmen of European origin—who were held to be trustworthy because of their sociocultural isolation; their dependence on the Umayyad family; and, in the case of eunuchs, their lack of offspring.
Whether castrated or whole, Saqaliba increasingly provided the back-
bone of the bureaucracy, serving as *hajib*s, wazirs, governors, diplomats, and military commanders. Castrated slaves were valued for
service in the harem not only because they could be trusted in intimate surroundings with a family's womenfolk, but also because of
their symbolic role. As was the case in contemporary Byzantium, eunuchs, with their distinctive features and mannerisms, were viewed
as liminal and otherworldly, almost angelic, and therefore as suitable
intermediaries for a near-divine ruler and the women of his household. Yet, as isolated as they may have been from the general population of al-Andalus, by the end of the tenth century a certain solidarity
was evident among the court slaves, and they would briefly become a
political force not only within the palace but across al-Andalus.

Of 'Abd al-Rahman's several favorites, the most famous was his
freedman Ghalib ibn 'Abd al-Rahman al-Siqlabi al-Nasrani, an un-
castrated former slave who rose to the pinnacle of the caliphal aristocracy. In the decades after the caliph had retired from active military
duty following the 939 debacle at Simancas, Ghalib would rise to
become his greatest general. In the 940s, as governor he consolidated
the caliph's hold over Toledo and the Middle March, and in the 950s
he led raids against the lands to the north that brought home plunder
and prisoners, cowing the Christian princes and raising the prestige of
his sovereign. In the same decade, in response to Fatimid attacks, he
raised a fleet and ravaged the coast of Ifriqiya. With the succession of
al-Hakam II, who retreated increasingly into isolation to pursue his
passion for high culture, Ghalib's star continued to rise. In the 960s
and 970s, he led successful raids against the Christian North and a
campaign of conquest in North Africa, and in 971 and 972 the caliph
charged him with personally leading the counterattack in response to
what would be the last Viking raids on al-Andalus. Soon after, he
would be awarded two gilded swords, together with the title "He of
the Two Swords" and an elevated seat in the council house of the
ministers of state. Now that the caliph was withdrawing into the

palace, Ghalib provided a much-needed public face for the regime. He was regarded as a hero across the land, and the departure and return of the caliphal armies from Córdoba under his command were occasions of great pomp.

The most significant of his accomplishments were his campaigns in North Africa. The Idrisid rulers of northern Morocco, who claimed descent from the Prophet Muhammad's cousin and son-in-law 'Ali, had been caught between the ambitions of the Umayyads and the Fatimids. With the help of Zanata Berber forces from Ifriqiya, the Fatimids had subdued the Idrisids and obliged them to turn against Córdoba in 958, so Ghalib was sent over with an army in 972 to reduce them. After a bitterly fought campaign, he forced the princes of the Banu Idris to return with him to Córdoba, where they were obliged to publicly swear allegiance to al-Hakam II and Maliki Islam. Morocco was now under Umayyad control. Although the Fatimids would strike back, by this time they were disengaging from the politics of North Africa, their center of gravity having shifted eastward to Egypt, where they had founded their new capital, Cairo, in 969. Over the nine years following his victory in the Maghrib, Ghalib, now in his seventies, would continue to lead raids against Christian Spain and work for the continuity of the Umayyad dynasty. But it was all in vain. The death of al-Hakam and the succession of his young son, Hisham, would unleash forces within the court that would bring about the downfall of the caliphate. In an irony typical of the history of al-Andalus, Ghalib would find himself striking an alliance in 981 with his old enemies, Christian Castile and Navarre, in a desperate effort to preserve the dynasty against the ambitions of Hisham's power-hungry *hajib*, Muhammad ibn Abi 'Amir.

THE ERA OF 'Abd al-Rahman III also saw the incorporation of Jews into the caliphal court and the stirrings of what would eventually become Sephardic culture. We know very little of the Jewish society in Spain prior to the era of the caliphate. The fact that Eleazar, the apostate Frank, chose to settle in Zaragoza in the 830s suggests that there was a significant Jewish presence in al-Andalus. Some of the Berber clans who settled in the peninsula at the time of the conquest probably identified as Jews, although they would not have practiced "normative" Rabbinical Judaism, which was only just coalescing in that era. Jewish culture clearly did thrive in the 'Abbasid lands in the 800s. Here, the exilarch functioned as a subordinate, shadow caliph for the Jews of the Islamic world. This was the Jewish king-in-exile, an office that dated back to the Babylonian Captivity and was recognized officially under the 'Abbasid caliphs. Jewish *dhimmis* became highly integrated and acculturated in the east and in Egypt, from where they served in high administrative offices and their trading networks radiated outward across the Mediterranean Sea and into the Indian Ocean and beyond.

Given this, there is no doubt that just as learned Muslims began to emigrate westward to al-Andalus beginning in the ninth century, learned Jews did as well. Like Muslim immigrants and travelers, they brought new ideas with them. Some, such as innovations in Arabic language—the spoken language of Jews—and Islamic medicine and science were welcomed by Andalusi Jews; others, like the Karaite Judaism considered heretical by Rabbinical authorities, less so. Karaism—which seems to have coalesced in eighth-century Baghdad—is somewhat analogous to Kharijism in Islam, in that Karaites did not recognize any authority other than the Talmud and therefore rejected the scriptural interpretations of Rabbinical Judaism. And just as in the 900s when the fragmentation of the 'Abbasid caliphate would give rise to independent, regional Islamic regimes, a parallel process would occur with the exilarchy and its Jews. After the early 900s, the pretense of the universal authority of the exilarch was abandoned.

In al-Andalus, the figure who marks the turning point in Jewish history is Hasdai ibn Shaprut. Born to a wealthy family from Jaén (Jayyan) and raised in Córdoba, Hasdai—known as Abu Yusuf in court circles—received the finest religious training, as well as an education in medicine and letters. He mastered Hebrew, Arabic, and likely Latin, as well as the corrupted spoken Latin vernacular that would eventually become Spanish. Family connections provided him with an entrée into the court of 'Abd al-Rahman III, where he rose to become the personal physician and trusted confidant of the caliph. He was discreetly awarded a series of important positions, including secretary of Latin correspondence. The most lucrative of these was chief customs officer, for which he collected a commission on all merchandise that came into the caliphate. Most significantly, he served the caliph as a diplomat and played a central role in negotiations with both the Byzantine and the Holy Roman Empires, as well as in keeping the kingdoms of Navarre and León and the counties of Barcelona and Castile in check. Hasdai inaugurated the Andalusi practice of employing Jews as diplomats, and it was likely this that prompted Christian rulers in Spain and the Frankish lands to do the same.

Hasdai set off on the first of his diplomatic missions in the 940s, when he was only in his twenties. Although set at opposite ends of the Mediterranean, the Byzantium empire under Constantine VII Porphyrogennetos and 'Abd al-Rahman's caliphate shared common enemies in the Holy Roman Empire and the 'Abbasid caliphate. A meaningful alliance may have been impossible in practical terms given the distance that separated them, but each saw an advantage in recognizing the authority of the other, and in transmitting evidence of their own majesty through envoys bearing exotic and valuable gifts. Due to the travels of Hasdai and his like, for example, the fundamental Greek pharmaceutical encyclopedia, *Peri hules iatrikēs* (*De materia medica*, in Latin), written by the first-century physician Pedanius Dioscorides, made its way to al-Andalus as a gift from the emperor, where it was translated into both Latin and Arabic. Because no one in al-Andalus could translate the Greek, the caliph asked the emperor for a translator and the latter obliged, sending a Greek monk by the name of Nicholas to Córdoba. Thus, this broad cultural exchange included translators and artisans (many of whom would work on the Córdoba mosque), as well as gems, silks, and other objects of beauty, not to mention new plants for the caliphal gardens, some of which were introduced as important agricultural products in the peninsula.

Thanks to his official incomes and his influence at court, Hasdai's wealth and prestige grew, enabling him to embark on a program of patronage of Jewish culture in Córdoba. Consequently, he came to be recognized as *Nasi*, or "prince," of the Jews of al-Andalus, a title meant to refer to a descendant of the House of David who served as the ruler of the Jewish community on behalf of the caliphs. It was a position he took to with messianic dedication, conceiving of himself effectively as a universal Jewish monarch, analogous to the caliph of Islam.

In this guise, he embarked on an independent foreign policy program, reaching out to, receiving petitions from, and advocating for Jewish communities around the Mediterranean. He once sent a petition to the empress Helena inveighing on her to ensure that the Jews of the Byzantine empire were not mistreated, holding up the model of the Christians of al-Andalus as an example to follow. When Hasdai heard rumors of a Jewish kingdom—that of the Khazars, a Turkic people of Central Asia whose rulers were said to have converted to Judaism in the eighth or ninth century—he had his secretary draft letters and sent envoys to make contact. The correspondence reveals Hasdai's great confidence in the caliphate vis-à-vis the Jewish community, as well as its immense prosperity.

We, indeed, who are of the remnant of the captive Israelites, servants of my lord the King, are dwelling peacefully in the land of our sojourning, for our God has not forsaken us, nor has His shadow departed from us. . . .

The land is rich, abounding in rivers, springs and aqueducts; a land of corn, oil and wine, of fruits and all manner of delicacies; it has pleasure-gardens and orchards, fruitful trees of every kind, including the leaves of the tree upon which the silkworm feeds, of which we have great abundance. . . .

There are also found among us mountains . . . with veins of silver, gold, copper, iron, tin, lead, sulfur, porphyry, marble, and crystal. Merchants congregate in it, and traffickers from the ends of the earth, from Egypt and adjacent countries, bringing spices, precious stones, splendid wares for kings and princes, and all the desirable things of Egypt. Our king has collected very large treasures of silver, gold, precious things and valuables such as no king has ever collected.[18]

More crucial to the political situation of the caliphate were Hasdai's interventions in the peninsula. In the 940s, in the aftermath of the defeat at Simancas, it was Hasdai who was dispatched to the court of León, where he befriended King Ramiro I. He was thus able to ransom the Tujibid governor of Zaragoza, who had been captured at Simancas, and conclude a peace treaty with the help of a delegation of bishops from al-Andalus. At this time, 'Abd al-Rahman had also sent his fleet to raid the Catalan coasts mercilessly, forcing the local counts into submission; this was accomplished after Hasdai was sent north and returned to Córdoba with the bishop of Girona. The terms negotiated by Hasdai were harsh. Not only was Count Sunyer of Barcelona obliged to formally submit and pay tribute, he was forced to bring about the annulment of his daughter's political marriage to 'Abd al-Rahman's upstart tributary, King García Sanchéz of Pamplona.

García Sanchéz and 'Abd al-Rahman were cousins through the king's mother, Queen Toda, the daughter of the Navarrese princess Onneca, who had once been married to the amir 'Abd Allah. After the death of her husband, Sancho I of Navarre, in 925, Toda became the most powerful figure in the Christian North, serving as regent for her son, García, as well as ruling over her own lands. Her connection to the Umayyads was a foundation of her influence. For example, on the death of her husband, she sought a personal audience with 'Abd al-Rahman to secure his support for the six-year-old García's succession to the throne. But once he came of age, the young king conspired with local Muslim leaders to rebel against the caliph and sided against him at Simancas, provoking 'Abd al-Rahman to launch a series of punitive raids against Pamplona until García submitted. García's marriage alliance with the count of Barcelona was seen from Córdoba as an attempt to establish a coalition against 'Abd al-Rahman, and so Hasdai put a stop to it.

Toda was also the grandmother of Sancho "the Fat," king of León, who came to the throne in 956. His succession was put in danger by his obesity, which was so great that it prevented him from even mounting a horse, and in 958 he was deposed by his cousin Ordoño, also Toda's grandson. After his cousin's death, Sancho recovered the throne but was deposed two years later by an upstart nobleman, Count Fernán González, the first independent ruler of Castile. Fearing her family would lose León, Toda appealed again to

'Abd al-Rahman III for help. This came not only in the form of military support but also from the intervention of Hasdai ibn Shaprut. This time it was Hasdai's medical skills that were of service, and under the envoy's care, Sancho slimmed down and recovered his throne. In return for saving Sancho's kingdom, 'Abd al-Rahman was acknowledged as overlord of Pamplona and León, and Toda, Sancho, and García Sanchéz were obliged to come personally to Córdoba. Here, the caliph received his Christian kinfolk with great pomp and honor, confirming both their submission to him and his status as effective ruler of the entire peninsula.

BUT, THE INTERVENTION of Hasdai that has attracted the most interest from European historians is his role in the controversy between the future Holy Roman Emperor Otto I and the caliph. The German king was furious at the depredations of the Muslim "pirates" of Fraxinetum, whose territories constituted a wedge between Otto's lands and Italy, which he hoped to take control of so that he could claim the imperial title. In 950 'Abd al-Rahman had sent envoys to Otto's court, and three years later a mission under the leadership of the monk John of Vandières (later known as John of Gorze) arrived in Córdoba, bearing gifts and a letter of demands. A prudent Hasdai was determined to find out the contents of the confidential letter before John met the caliph, but the monk was sworn to not divulge its contents to anyone but the addressee. However, Hasdai would not relent and alternated between endeavoring to charm John and concocting a series of excuses as to why the interview could not yet take place.

Effectively a prisoner in Córdoba and unable to complete his mission, John eventually yielded and disclosed the letter, which as Hasdai suspected, contained language 'Abd al-Rahman would have taken as blasphemous and insulting. Consequently, Hasdai would not allow the letter to be presented to the caliph and suggested John give only the gifts he had brought. But the Frankish envoy, undoubtedly inspired by the anti-Muslim rhetoric circulating in Frankish lands and perhaps by reports of the Córdoban martyrs of the 850s, was implacable. He remained set on delivering the letter, even in the face of assurances by the local bishop, John of Córdoba, that the

Christians of the caliphate lived in peace and security, and of the threat of his own martyrdom should he bear the offensive letter to the caliph.

Eventually, Hasdai engineered a compromise: a mission would be sent north to Otto's court to obtain either a new letter or permission for John not to deliver the original. The envoy chosen was Reccemund, a prominent Christian courtier known by the Arabic name Rabi' ibn Ziyad. Reccemund journeyed north to the Abbey of Gorze, about one hundred miles south of the old Frankish capital of Aachen. There he met with leading clerics and courtiers of the Frankish realm, sharing with them books and news he brought from Spain. The meetings were successful, a new letter was drafted, and a direct line of contact was established between the isolated Andalusi church and that of the Latin imperium. In 956, three years after his arrival in Córdoba, John was thus finally able to meet with 'Abd al-Rahman and complete his mission. So impressed was the monk by the physician-courtier, he was led to comment that he had "never seen a man of such subtle intellect as the Jew Hasdeu."[19] But the impact was negligible. Neither 'Abd al-Rahman III nor al-Hakam II, later, had the power or the will to rein in the Muslim raiders of Provence. Eventually, following a string of victories in the 950s and 960s provoked by the raiders' abduction and ransom of the prominent churchman Abbot Maiolus of Cluny the previous year, Otto finally eradicated the Muslim base at Fraxinetum in 972.

For his role in the diplomatic exchange, Reccemund was rewarded by the caliph with an appointment as bishop of Elvira (near present-day Granada). But we know little of his life other than that, like Hasdai, he was a member of the non-Muslim upper class who evidently had been raised with a career in government service in mind, serving first in the caliphal chancery. After the conclusion of his trip to the Frankish court, he was sent on a mission to Byzantium and Syria to obtain works of classical pagan art for the adornment of Madinat al-Zahra'. Educated in both Latin and Arabic, his proficiency in the latter was such that he coauthored a book dedicated to al-Hakam II. The work, known today as the *Calendar of Córdoba*, combines a traditional Arabic seasonal almanac incorporating geographical, climatic, astrological, and medical information, as well as agricultural advice, with a Christian liturgical calendar. The fact that Reccemund, who does not seem to have been a clergyman, would be rewarded for his service to the dynasty with an appointment as a bishop reveals the extent to which the Andalusi church and clergy had been incorporated into the Umayyad regime. Although many may have indeed been dedicated to their flocks, bishops were essentially civil servants, appointed at the will of the caliph and expected to work as administrators, translators, mediators, and envoys.

FIGURES LIKE GHALIB, Hasdai, and Reccemund show just how cosmopolitan the caliphal court had become. Certainly, the regime was still dominated by the Umayyad dynasty, its clients, and its dependents, and those among the population who could claim distinguished Arab or Islamic pedigree enjoyed the greatest prestige. But others, if they had the right connections and displayed significant merits, could get ahead too. This was a by-product of the principle of "divide and rule" that underlay Umayyad ethnoreligious diversity. But it was not unique to al-Andalus. This new Andalusi society was very similar to those of the contemporary Fatimid and 'Abbasid caliphates and the Byzantine empire, which were also diverse, cosmopolitan, and culturally sophisticated. Although it can hardly be said that interfaith toleration was deliberately advocated as an ideal, it certainly became the norm in all of these imperial societies, at least among educated courtly and intellectual elites. Toleration had its limits, of course. Non-Muslims, however powerful and influential, were not appointed to official positions in the Islamic administration of al-Andalus. Moreover, diversity generated tensions, although under 'Abd al-Rahman III and al-Hakam II, it was the introduction of new Muslim groups—particularly Zanata and Sanhaja Berbers—into the power structure of the caliphate, not the integration of Christians and Jews, that would prove most problematic.

12

"An Ornament Bright"

The seeds of high culture planted in Córdoba by the amir al-Hakam in the early ninth century would burst into blossom nearly two hundred years later under his distant descendant, the caliph al-Hakam II. Driven by his personal intellectual passions, the caliph assembled an immense library integrating the culture of the Visigoths with that of the 'Abbasid East, including the learning of ancient Greece and Rome, Persia, and even far-flung India. The over 400,000 works that it allegedly contained were recorded in an index said to have comprised forty-four twenty-page volumes. Its collection included philosophy, religion, medicine, astronomy, engineering, botany, geography, history, literature—no subject was omitted.

To hold the knowledge of the world had been treated as a signal of universal sovereignty since Ptolemy I Soter founded the great library at Alexandria in the third century BCE. Al-Hakam II's library, likely modeled on the 'Abbasid *Dar al-Hikma* ("House of Wisdom") and its Sassanian predecessors, augmented his stature as a ruler while helping shape a distinctly Andalusi cultural identity. In the time of the caliph's youth, the Córdoban scholar Ibn 'Abd Rabbih had compiled an immense encyclopedia of culture and knowledge, *Al-'Iqd al-Farid* ("The Unique Necklace"). When a copy arrived at the court in Baghdad with great fanfare, the Persian wazir Sahib ibn 'Abbad is said to have sniffed with scorn, "this is nothing but our own merchandise sent back to us"—a cheap imitation of 'Abbasid erudition.[20] A century later, however, the culture of Córdoba would begin producing original contributions to a range of fields. Aristocrats and scholars imitated the caliph by establishing their own private libraries, both in Córdoba and across the peninsula, unwittingly laying the foundations for the brilliance of the *taifa* (from *tawa'if*, or "sectarian") kingdoms of eleventh-century al-Andalus—an intellectual culture that would in turn revolutionize Latin Christian thought.

Al-Hakam II sent agents abroad to Byzantium and the east in search of books to add to his collection and poured immense resources into supporting scholars, who carried out research and trained disciples, and he hired (or acquired as slaves) legions of scribes and translators. His library was not merely a place to hold books, but an immense royal academy where virtually every subject could be studied and that attracted scholars from across the Islamic world and even Christian Europe.

ASTRONOMY (INCLUDING ASTROLOGY) was a foundational science in al-Andalus, necessary for properly calculating the months and days of the Islamic lunar calendar, including the beginning and end of religious feasts, as well as determining the authentic *qibla* (the direction of Mecca) so that prayer could be properly conducted. One can see the effect of the study of astronomy on the orientation of mosques in al-Andalus. The Syrians who constructed the Great Mosque of Córdoba in the eighth century, for example, did not account for the fact that the earth is spherical and therefore assumed that Mecca was to the south, as it was from Damascus, and thus oriented the mosque in that direction. By the time the mosque of Madinat al-Zahra' was founded, however, the builders were able to better calculate the direction of the Holy City and oriented the prayer hall toward the east. To calculate global position, Islamic thinkers had improved on the ancient astrolabe, an instrument for calculating latitude, and therefore the position of the moon, stars, and planets, for the purposes of reading horoscopes. The instrument would be perfected in al-Andalus with the invention of a more accurate "universal astrolabe," as well as mechanical models of the Ptolemaic universe that better enabled the calculation of planetary latitude and longitude, which made casting horoscopes much more efficient.

Learned Andalusis, whether Muslim, Christian, or Jew, lived and breathed the zodiac, even though it was morally problematic from the perspective of religious doctrine. Rulers were particularly concerned with having the best astrologers advising them. In 968, for example, al-Hakam II welcomed the renowned Egyptian Ahmad ibn Faris to his court and appointed him as his personal advisor. As they translated ancient astronomical texts, Islamic scholars—conscious of the suspicions of rigorously pious Muslims, who distrusted and wished to discredit sciences that were the legacy of pagan cultures—carefully corrected them and produced improved treatises based on empirical observation of the sun and stars. In Córdoba, the astronomer and alchemist Maslama al-Majriti improved the astronomical tables that had been produced by the Persian Muhammad ibn Musa al-Khawarzmi in the early 800s. Al-Majriti is sometimes confused with a contemporary, also named Maslama, who wrote two works on magic, the *Rutbat al-hakim* and the *Ghayat al-hakim*, the latter of which was later translated into Latin under the title *Picatrix* and became the standard reference work on the occult sciences in Europe for the next four hundred years.

Mathematics, including Euclidian geometry, was also intensively studied, but it was viewed as of secondary importance and largely a practical exercise. Scholars like Maslama al-Majriti, who was known as the "Euclid of al-Andalus," produced treatises on commercial math, including arithmetic and algebra, complete with appendices of everyday problems of the sort merchants faced. Engineering and instrument making were geared toward both practical and esoteric ends. Following in the tradition of the inventor and would-be aviator 'Abbas ibn Firnas, scholars tinkered away at clocks, automata, and perpetual motion machines, as well as on more quotidian innovations in irrigation and artisanal production. Chemistry, or rather alchemy, was as much an esoteric as a practical endeavor, with the actual creation of gold from base metal regarded as secondary to the existential transformation the process was believed to bring about in the alche-mist himself. Other forms of magic and divination, drawing on an-cient, indigenous, and Berber traditions, were also practiced, including geomancy (the casting of sand), ornithomancy (reading the flight pat-terns of birds), and the use of magic squares (diagrams incorporating letters and numbers) and talismans.

Medicine was another important discipline, one steeped in astrol-ogy and in which the influence of the Greeks, such as Galen, Hippo-crates, and Aristotle, was coupled with pharmacological knowledge from Persia and India. In Córdoba, scholars worked to absorb and synthesize both ancient texts and the latest medical advances emanat-ing from the 'Abbasid East. Within this atmosphere of dynamic inno-vation, a few flashes of originality could be discerned. Sulayman ibn Juljul, for example, who studied medicine under Hasdai ibn Shaprut and served as al-Hakam II's personal physician, produced not only an encyclopedic history of medicine and physicians but also a work on pharmacology that would circulate widely in medieval Europe under the name Gilgil. 'Arib ibn Sa'd wrote a text on obstetrics and pediat-rics that combined astrology with Greek medicine. Abu 'l-Qasim Khalaf al-Zahrawi, who served as the official physician of the usurp-ing hajib, al-Mansur, in the late 900s, gained international renown as a surgeon. His only surviving work, a lengthy treatise on the medical arts, included a number of breakthroughs in surgical techniques and instrument making and outlined complex procedures, such as dental and eye surgery, and the treatment of a range of wounds and condi-tions. It too would be translated into Latin centuries later and become one of the standard medical texts in European universities, where its author would be known as Abulcasis.

In terms of applied science, there was a particular focus on agron-omy, the practice of horticulture, and the study of nutrition (which was considered part of medicine and related to astrology). The trans-lation of Dioscorides' Materia medica launched a revolution in phar-maceutical botany in al-Andalus, with scholars including Ibn Juljul and Hamid ibn Samajun producing treatises on "simples," or medici-nal ingredients. The gardens of the great aristocratic estates were not merely built for pleasure; they were also the proving grounds for new

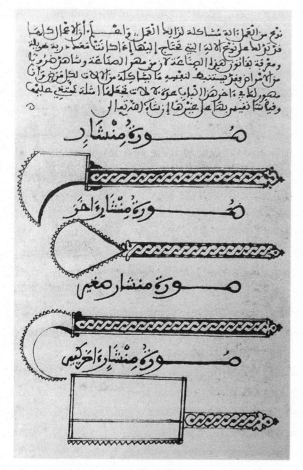

From Al-Tasrif,
the book of medicine
and surgery by
Abu 'l-Qasim Khalaf
al-Zahrawi (Abulcasis).
*Arkwatem, 2007
(Wikicommons)*

plants, fruits, medicinal herbs, and crops brought from the Greek and
'Abbasid East and beyond—often surreptitiously and at no small risk
to the smugglers. The Donegal fig is said to have originated in Byzantium, which had forbidden its export. According to legend it was
none other than a ninth-century envoy to the imperial court, the poet
al-Ghazal, who sneaked out a handful of figs hidden among his books;
he presented them to 'Abd al-Rahman II, who had them successfully
planted in his gardens. "Donegal" is a corruption of the Arabic *Dun-
aqal*, from "Dunahu qawli" ("Oh, lord, look!"), which al-Ghazal
claimed people were wont to exclaim in delight when they picked the
fruit. Reccemund and 'Arib ibn Sa'd's *Calendar of Córdoba*, written

for al-Hakam II, is an early example of the agricultural manuals that would be produced widely in eleventh-century al-Andalus.

Al-Andalus under 'Abd al-Rahman III became an agricultural powerhouse, owing to a combination of dry cereal farming, herding, and intensive irrigated market-gardening. Staples including durum wheat, sorghum, and rice were supplemented by a whole variety of high-calorie, high-yield fruits, vegetables, and nuts: lemons, limes, almonds, mango, sugarcane, eggplant, and artichoke, as well as legumes and high-value spices and aromatics, such as cloves, pepper, turmeric, and saffron (for color). Alongside flax and hemp, the production of cotton drove a textile industry that clothed the burgeoning population and, through the generation of rags, provided the raw material to make paper for the deluge of books that was suddenly being produced. Local silk production, along with the harvesting of natural dyes from plants, insects, and mollusks, provided the raw material for the luxurious robes and tapestries of the caliphal court.

The same travelers, diplomats, scholars, and merchants who brought new plants and products from across the Islamic world to al-Andalus also carried with them the latest trends in literature, poetry, and music. It was in this era that the tales of the *One Thousand and One Nights*, the legends of Alexander the Great, the parables of the "Seven Sages," and the Indian fables of the *Kalila wa-Dimna* were disseminated in al-Andalus. The content and style of these works would profoundly impact the vernacular literary traditions of Europe in the coming centuries. Thanks to the legacy of Ziryab, Córdoba had become a training center for *qiyan*—slave girls groomed as musicians and poets. The physician and philosopher Muhammad al-Kattani made such a fortune reselling girls he had trained in *adab* that he opened branch schools in the provinces. Particularly Andalusi lyrical styles, such as the *muwashshah*, which combined the vernacular Arabic of the street with Romance vernacular, were popularized. In search of fame and fortune, poets like Ibn Darraj al-Qastali composed works in high Arabic, praising 'Abd al-Rahman III, al-Hakam II, and eventually the usurper al-Mansur. Others, like Yusuf al-Ramadi, wrote on nature, love, and the emotions. Homoeroticism, whether chaste or

Pyxis of al-Mughira ibn 'Abd al-Rahman III showing a throne scene, 968 CE. Possibly from Madinat al-Zahra', Córdoba, Spain. Ivory. Al-Mughira was put to death by al-Mansur in 976 CE. © *Musée du Louvre, Dist. RMN-Grand Palais/Art Resource NY*

consummated, was a popular theme, religious and legal proscriptions on illicit sex notwithstanding.

Scholars also began to consciously construct the history of Umayyad al-Andalus. The most notable of the chroniclers was Ahmad al-Razi, who in the time of 'Abd al-Rahman III wrote the voluminous *History of the Rulers of al-Andalus*, which spanned the time of the Biblical Flood to his own age. Now lost, and known to us only through a later Portuguese translation and echoes in Latin and Castilian chronicles, it is a history not merely of the Arabs of al-Andalus, but of the land and its people as a whole—a reflection of Umayyad confidence and a sense of universal sovereignty. In contrast, Abu Bakr ibn al-Qutiyya ("son of the Gothic woman"), a descendant of Visigothic royalty who gained renown as a philologist and *qadi*, composed a history that emphasized the collaboration of members of the native Christian elite in establishing Islamic dominion over al-Andalus. Other important historical ideas appear for the first time in this era, including the supposed collaboration of the Jews of Visigothic Spain with the Arabo-Islamic conquerors. This was a notion that served to legitimize the integration of Jews in Andalusi society that had become a fact in the tenth century, one that both Jewish and many Muslim writers would want to reinforce.

The high culture of al-Andalus was remarkably inclusive, although it presumed that participants would conform to and respect the superiority of Arabo-Islamic culture and Islam as a religion. Diversity was possible because, leaving aside narrowly theological disciplines, fields such as medicine, astronomy, mathematics, and other sciences constituted a realm of discourse in which scholars of different religious persuasions could see themselves as engaged in a common intellectual project. Muslim intellectuals recognized that non-Muslims were making unique contributions to the Andalusi culture of knowledge; in other words, their cultural capital made them valuable to the dynastic project.

The active roles Jews and Christians played in the intellectual culture of Córdoba are clear, but the extant sources also reveal that women played roles not only as copyists and translators but as scholars and authors. Upper-class women had the resources and freedom to pursue intellectual passions, while under al-Hakam II, promising slave girls were educated according to their aptitudes in calligraphy, astronomy and astrology, medicine, mathematics, and other sciences. A slave named Lubna served as his scribe and librarian and was famous for her knowledge of poetry, calligraphy, and grammar. She was not unique. Highborn women, like 'Aisha ibn Ahmad, wrote poetry, copied out the Qur'an, edited legal texts, and founded important libraries. They studied *adab*, science, and religion, although given the pressure for women to limit their public interaction with men, opportunity was greater for those whose fathers were scholars and who could therefore study at home. Some women, like Fatima bint Yahya al-Maghami, were even renowned as *faqihs*, or experts on religious law. Not surprisingly, given the monopoly men exercised over the practice of formal theology, women were also drawn to less-easy-to-control asceticism and to the mysticism that was gaining ground in both popular and learned circles. And despite all we do know, given that historians in the masculine-dominated society were likely only to record the accomplishments of truly exceptional women who were known publicly, women's role in, and their contribution to, Andalusi culture was undoubtedly far greater than the sources reflect.

FOR INTELLECTUALS OF different religions, scholarship provided a framework for interaction in which religious hierarchies could be set aside. Muslims not only engaged in collaborations with *dhimmis* but studied under them. Similar integration was evident in other areas of society, and many Muslims, Christians, and Jews enjoyed relationships of affection and confidence, even if the tensions generated by the imbalance of prestige between Muslims and *dhimmis* were never far from the surface. These divisions are reflected in the inconsistency of the *fatwas*, or legal opinions, that survive from the era: while one *mufti* might rule that Christians should not be able to construct new churches or ring their church bells, another assured his petitioner that it was permitted for a Muslim to accompany his (Christian) mother to church.

The integration of non-Muslims in Andalusi culture and society is clearest in the case of the Jews of al-Andalus, for obvious reasons. Jewish and Islamic culture had enjoyed centuries of synergy in the east, in many ways continuing the intermixing of Persian and Hebrew culture that went back to the time of the Babylonian Captivity. Linguistically, Arabic and Hebrew are very similar; both are based on a three-consonant root system (the "Semitic" language structure) and share many common features. Judaism enjoyed the cachet of being the original Abrahamic religion, although some Muslim religious and folk traditions denied or downplayed this claim. And unlike Christianity, with the Trinity and the notion of

Jesus as God incarnate, Judaism did not appear to be polytheistic or anthropomorphizing.

Hasdai ibn Shaprut was the most famous Jew of the caliphal court; many others, however, were employed in the various branches of the administration or engaged in intellectual inquiry. The twelfth-century Jewish chronicler Ibn Daud would claim that in Hasdai's time, "everyday there used to go out of Córdoba to Madinat al-Zahra' seven hundred Jews in seven hundred carriages, each of them attired in the royal garb and wearing the headdress of Muslim officials, all of them escorting the Rabbi [Hanokh]. A second faction would escort [his rival] Ibn Shatnash."[21] Because of the importance of classical Arabic and the fact that Jews spoke vernacular Arabic on a daily basis, Jews contributed to a renaissance in popular and learned Arabic literature, as well as in Hebrew poetry and letters.

Yet it was Hasdai's determination to establish Andalusi Jewry as independent from the Babylonian academies of the east that set the course for Hebrew letters and Jewish thought in Spain and lay the foundation for the Jewish "Golden Age" of the eleventh and twelfth centuries. It was a project that met the approval of the Umayyad caliphs, given that raising the status of "their" Jews would augment their own prestige. Thus, just as Muslim poets lauded 'Abd al-Rahman III, Jewish poets composed songs of praise for the *Nasi*, Hasdai ibn Shaprut. Like al-Hakam II, Hasdai recruited foreign luminaries to al-Andalus. He appointed Moses ben Hanokh, from the great Babylonian Talmudic Academy at Sura, as *dayyan* (Jewish magistrate) in Córdoba. Another of Hasdai's recruits was the grammarian Dunash ben Labrat. A native of Fez trained in the east and a student of the great scholar Sa'adya Gaon, Dunash revolutionized Jewish letters in al-Andalus by adapting the meter of the Arabic ode to both Hebrew profane and devotional poetry. He would also bring about the disgrace of Hasdai's secretary Menahem ibn Saruq, who had authored a pioneering treatise on Hebrew philology but was denounced by his rival for his supposed Karaite leanings. Both Dunash and Menahem had disciples who carried on their work, and subsequent scholars and poets would labor to reconcile their positions. In any event, the controversies within the Jewish scholarly community were a symptom of the tremendous intellectual dynamism that resulted from 'Abd al-Rahman III and al-Hakam II's promotion of a culture of knowledge.

The high culture of the native Christians of al-Andalus, on the other hand, was a casualty of the Umayyad renaissance. By the tenth century, Latin letters had been all but subsumed by Arabic, and the Gospels, the Psalms, and the Epistles needed to be translated into Arabic for the benefit of the faithful. Culture cannot survive without patronage, and there were no wealthy people in al-Andalus who were interested in supporting the production of Latin literature—Arabic was the language of the Christian elite. The last redoubt of the language was in the liturgy. Church services continued to be conducted in Latin, although in al-Andalus, which had been cut off from the rest of the Roman church since the eighth century, distinct prayers and rituals had developed, a liturgy that became known as the Mozarabic rite.

The impact of Arabized Christians was felt most strongly outside of al-Andalus, mostly in the Christian kingdoms in the north of Spain, but also in Italy and the Frankish lands. Migrant clergy who journeyed to Latin lands brought with them the knowledge of al-Andalus, often in the shape of books and manuscripts that were lost or unknown in western Christendom. Christian envoys helped to disseminate the knowledge of al-Andalus and contributed to Córdoba's reputation as a center of learning and power. On his mission to the Ottonian court, Reccemund met Liutprand, the future bishop of Cremona, a diplomat, courtier, and scholar who was so taken with his Andalusi counterpart that he eventually dedicated his autobiography to him. Diplomatic relations between Córdoba and Barcelona were particularly close after 941, when Hasdai negotiated the submission of Count Sunyer while 'Abd al-Rahman III's admiral al-Rumahis sat with his fleet off the Catalan coast poised to ravage the county. Through the 970s, a series of embassies were exchanged, and it seems that a conduit for the conveyance of Arabo-Islamic learning was established, with Barcelona together with nearby Vic serving as a faint satellite in Córdoba's intellectual orbit.

Dramatic evidence of this reality can be found in the case of Gerbert of Aurillac, a monk from the highlands of central France who was invited by Sunyer's successor, Count Borrell II, to journey to Catalonia. Over the course of several years, he acquired considerable knowledge of mathematics, astronomy, and astrology that was unknown in Latin Christendom. Returning to a teaching position at the cathedral school in Rheims, he was credited with helping to establish the *quadrivium*, a new curriculum centered on math, geometry, music, and astronomy, and introducing Arabic decimal numbers to the Latin world, as well as a series of technical innovations, such as an improved abacus and instruments for observing and analyzing the heavens. As word of his erudition spread, Gerbert was commissioned as tutor to the young emperor Otto III and appointed bishop of Reims, and then archbishop of Ravenna. In 999, Otto would use his influence to have Gerbert crowned pope; he took the name Sylvester II.

But because of Gerbert's time in Spain, he was a controversial figure, and legends swirled around him. It was said that he had, in fact, lived in Córdoba, where he studied magic under a Muslim sorcerer and escaped by using a book of spells he had purloined from his master. Others claimed he was in league with a female demon, that he possessed a speaking robotic head that had the power of prophecy, or that the Devil had sworn to carry him down to Hell. Fantastic as such stories were, they reveal the awe and anxiety that al-Andalus provoked among the inhabitants of the far less developed Christian Europe. Such tales may have been "fake news" disseminated by Gerbert's opponents, but it reflected the looming presence of al-Andalus in the Christian imagination.

Nor were scholars the only ones fascinated by the prosperity of Muslim Spain. While Sunyer had been forced to submit to a truce with the caliphate, other commercially oriented Christian powers actively sought treaties with the Umayyads. Hugh, count of Arles and king of Italy, established diplomatic and commercial relations with al-Andalus, and merchants from the emerging Italian entrepôt of Amalfi could be found in the streets of Córdoba. Madinat al-Zahra' had become a showcase for the wealth and sophistication of the caliphate—a dazzling catalog warehouse of Andalusi luxuries for visiting dignitaries. Papal envoys paid their respects in the 940s, and beginning in the 970s there was a regular parade of royal and aristocratic visitors from the Christian North and beyond.

IT WAS NOT only foreign Christians who were concerned about the cosmopolitan climate of al-Andalus. Some members of the conservative Maliki *'ulama'* were also increasingly alarmed by the sophistication of the Umayyad court. Whereas the amirs of the eighth century had promoted Malikism as unchallenged orthodoxy and 'Abd al-Rahman III had officially supported the Maliki monopoly, al-Hakam II quietly encouraged other interpretations of Islamic law, both out of intellectual curiosity and in order to weaken the grip of this juridical-religious elite.

A challenge to the Malikis was inevitable, due in part to the particularly conservative and narrow interpretation of Maliki law current among Berber and indigenous Spanish Muslim thinkers, who, among other things, fetishized the writings of Malik ibn Anas and downplayed the importance of *hadith*. Their legal interpretations were increasingly seen as inflexible and dated. Nevertheless, any reformers in their midst were tarred with accusations of "innovation," impurity, and heresy, as well as "faithlessness" and immorality. The hard-liners were not above taking justice into their own hands, sometimes ransacking the libraries of opponents when they could not bring formal criminal charges against them.

And for all the scientific and literary activity surrounding the Córdoban court, it was the religious sciences that remained the most important and vibrant field of study in al-Andalus. Despite his intellectual openness and discreet encouragement of heterodoxy, al-Hakam II, who was known publicly as a dedicated patron of orthodox theology, took a sincerely pious turn as he fell ill late in life. But a challenge was brewing within Maliki Islam, as unsanctioned mystics and self-proclaimed prophets began cropping up all over al-Andalus and the

Maghrib. Although 'Abd al-Rahman III and al-Hakam II both publicly reinforced orthodox theology, the Maliki elite were not satisfied.
With the death of al-Hakam in 976 and the rise of the usurper, Muhammad ibn Abi 'Amir, or al-Mansur, they would see a chance to put
the genie of mysticism and Islamic heterodoxy back in its bottle.

13

The General, the Caliph, His Wife, and Her Lover

The efficiency and order established by 'Abd al-Rahman III would prove in the end to be the undoing of the caliphate he founded. With the day-to-day affairs of state in the hands of capable and loyal servants of the Umayyad state, and the elevation of the caliph as a distant, almost semi-divine figurehead, his successor, al-Hakam II, was left free to indulge his intellectual passions. The servants of the state saw an opportunity to move into the resulting vacuum and plotted to expand their own authority and influence, not only at each other's expense but at that of the ruling family, ultimately precipitating the implosion of the dynasty. A similar process would play out in the contemporary Fatimid and 'Abbasid caliphates, in Byzantium, and even within the Ottonian dynasty. Soon after the year 1000, the entire tenth-century imperial order would be swept away and replaced by new rulers drawn from the periphery of the world of the empires.

Al-Hakam II indulged the temptation to loosen the reins of power in no small part owing to the confidence he placed in his staff—most of all, his indefatigable general Ghalib ibn 'Abd al-Rahman and his trusted *hajib*, Ja'far al-Mushafi. Both remained loyal to the caliph. The crisis would result from al-Hakam's designation of his young son, Hisham, as heir, and the arrival in the palace of a brilliant and ambitious young man from the provinces named Muhammad ibn Abi 'Amir. Ibn Abi 'Amir—who would eventually be known as al-Mansur to the Muslims of al-Andalus and Almanzor to the Christians of northern Spain and beyond. He would usurp the caliphate in a whirl of intrigue and betrayal, leading it to its greatest triumphs while unintentionally precipitating its bloody dissolution.

BORN AROUND 938 to a Yamani family that traced its arrival in al-Andalus to the conquest of 711, Muhammad ibn Abi 'Amir was considered a member of the Andalusi elite by virtue of a pedigree that included generations of middle-level functionaries. An ambitious young man, he left his home village of Torrox, near Algeciras, to seek his fortune in Córdoba. There he studied *fiqh* (Islamic jurisprudence) with Maliki masters and *adab* and literature with some of the greatest teachers of the age, before aiming to find work in the burgeoning Umayyad bureaucracy. Whether through his connections, chutzpah, or good fortune, he ended up in the palace and, more specifically, the harem, where he caught the attention of al-Hakam II's *umm walad*, Subh, who recruited him as secretary. By 967 he was serving as her *wakil*, or administrative and financial trustee; as the masculine public face of her affairs; and as steward of her eldest son.

Subh was of Basque origin and had been well-trained in Arabo-Islamic high culture and *adab*, including singing, a fact that undoubtedly led to her being acquired by the caliph and finding a special place in his affections. The details of her background are unknown, but the fact that she had a brother, Fa'iq (or Ra'iq), who was also in the good graces of the caliph, suggests she was no ordinary captive ex-Christian. Al-Hakam, who was not known to be overly passionate as regards women, was evidently very attached to her; he had apparently manumitted her early in their relationship, and as a sign of his esteem gave her the masculine nickname Ja'far. She, in turn, bore him two sons: 'Abd al-Rahman, who died aged seven in 969/70, and Hisham, born in 965, whom al-Hakam would formally invest as his heir in 974 at age eight. For her part, she too had ambitions—namely, to ensure the succession of her son, although she was evidently also drawn to the considerable charms of Ibn Abi 'Amir.

Ibn Abi 'Amir was a keen judge of human character, and once he had his foot in the palace door, he wasted no time in trying to win over Subh and the other women of the harem by showering them with gifts and attention to a degree that provoked gossip. In 967, he had also been appointed master of the mint, and when allegations began to circulate that he had been embezzling, rather than counter them, he commissioned an intricate silver model of the palace, which he presented as a gift to Subh. Both the *umm walad* and the caliph were delighted by its ingenious design, and the allegations of misappropriation were quietly forgotten or forgiven. But, Ibn Abi 'Amir and the royal wife became so close that rumors of an affair began to circulate. Some claimed that he had suckled from her breast when she was nursing her second son, thereby becoming "Zir Hisham," the heir's "adoptive father." True or not, the story reflected growing suspicions regarding their relationship, and in the years that followed, ribald popular verses lampooning Subh's supposedly unbridled passion for him were whispered openly in the capital.

Whatever personal attraction she might have felt for her employee, Subh would have been looking for allies who would be personally invested in the survival and success of her young son against competing factions in the palace, so taking Ibn Abi 'Amir as a lover may have been strategic. For his part, Ibn Abi 'Amir was able to finance his courtly largesse thanks to Subh's support and the trust this inspired in al-Hakam, who appointed him in rapid succession to a series of lucrative and influential administrative posts, including executor of intestate estates, *qadi* of Seville and of Niebla, and chief of police and intelligence. Al-Mushafi was appointed *wakil* of the heir, Hisham, but seems to have delegated these financial responsibilities in practice to Ibn Abi 'Amir. These posts not only provided Ibn Abi 'Amir with considerable financial resources, they enabled him to develop his own networks of patronage outside of the palace through the appointment of subordinates, the granting of favors, and the distribution of gifts. And he became famous for his generosity. When a fellow officer of the palace complained to Ibn Abi 'Amir, who was then in charge of the mint, that his daughter's wedding was going to leave him broke, Ibn Abi 'Amir presented him with a heap of silver coins equal to the girl's weight.

Once ensconced in the harem and confidence of the caliph, Ibn Abi 'Amir set his sights on winning over Ghalib and al-Mushafi, the two powers behind the throne. Ghalib was something of a national hero— the trusted *mawla* of the great 'Abd al-Rahman III and a bulwark of the caliphate, famed for his military exploits. But by the time Ibn Abi 'Amir arrived in the palace, the general must have been in his sixties, a graying wolf. Al-Mushafi had also been a trusted retainer of 'Abd al-Rahman III: his personal scribe, governor of Mallorca, and other positions. He had the absolute trust of al-Hakam, whom he had also served as tutor and, later, *hajib*, but he was not a popular figure. He was the son of a literary scholar, and although his family had lived in al-Andalus for generations and he had been educated to the highest standards, his Berber origins were a stain in the view of the broad clique of Arab and *mawali* families who controlled the council of ministers.

The caliphate may have been a monarchy, but Umayyad power depended on the support of the great lineages of the *khassa*, whose members served as wazirs and in other key posts. Identifying ethnically as Arabs, they felt a bond of kinship and a common sense of entitlement with the dynasty. As a group, they were jealous of their power and were alarmed that a Berber could hold such influence, all the more so because al-Mushafi was promoting his own family within the palace. Their concern would have only increased in the early 970s as al-Hakam II began to actively recruit Berber mercenaries in large numbers. That many of these newcomers harbored Kharijite or Shi'a beliefs apparently did not worry the caliph. The new troops, drawn primarily from Zanata tribes in Morocco, would have felt little or no solidarity with Arabized Berbers, such as the family of al-Mushafi, but to the eye of the Arab elite, there was little difference. Both al-Mushafi's rise and that of the Zanata newcomers each comprised worrying signs of their declining influence at the expense of people they viewed as barbarians and arrivistes. Indeed, disdain for Berbers was widespread among both Arabs and the convert population. Ibn Abi 'Amir, however, although not highborn, was an Arab with a solid lineage, and he played on this, ultimately with fatal consequences for the chamberlain, al-Mushafi.

In the meantime, Ibn Abi 'Amir set his sights on the Maghrib, the arena for expansion under the caliphate. At stake were domination over the powerful Idrisid dynasty of Fez and the region's constellation of ever-mutating Berber statelets—and, ultimately, control of the trans-Saharan gold and slave trade. The Fatimids' transfer to Egypt in 969 had left a vacuum in North Africa, and the Idrisids re-emerged, ruling an emirate under their protection. Meanwhile, the Fatimids' Sanhaja Berber dependents in Ifriqiya began to attack the Zanata clans of Morocco. Al-Hakam's strategy was to use a combination of subornation and force to bring the region under his hand. He played the various warlords against each other and allowed none to become so powerful that he might challenge the Umayyad order. Once the Idrisids had been subdued, the various Zanata clans fell in line. All were made to submit to the authority of the Umayyad dynasty and to publicly acknowledge the family's mandate in all of their mosques at Friday prayer.

As was established Umayyad practice, important regional clans were obliged to relocate or send family members to Córdoba, while others were incorporated into the caliphal army, serving to integrate them into the Andalusi power structure and dilute the power of the Arab lineages. Conversely, the conflict in Africa provided a pretext for obliging Andalusi frontier lords, like the Tujibids of the Upper March, to send troops to Africa and drew them into the upper ranks of the army and administration.

Ibn Abi 'Amir was sent to the Maghrib alongside Ghalib to crush the Idrisids as a sort of viceroy for al-Hakam, serving as *qadi* and quartermaster—an ideal position for engaging in graft and networking. He returned to Córdoba in 974, flush with success; the Idrisids had been defeated and their leading family members obliged to return to the capital to pledge allegiance to the caliph in a grand public ceremony. Ibn Abi 'Amir had earned the trust of Ghalib and the respect of the Berber chieftains and was ever closer to al-Hakam. As a reward for his service, he was appointed chief inspector of the mercenary divisions (which is to say, the Berbers) of the caliph's standing army in al-Andalus.

As it happened, Idrisid resistance was not quite extinguished. The head of the family, Hasan ibn Qannun, escaped to Egypt, and in 979 when the Fatimid-backed Sanhaja warlord Bulughghin ibn Ziri overran the Maghrib, Ibn Qannun was sent back to rule on the Fatimids' behalf. This time the Umayyads would offer no quarter. In 985, when Ibn Qannun was captured by an army sent from al-Andalus, Ibn Abi 'Amir ordered the Idrisid prince put to death. Even this would not spell the end of the Idrisids. The family would spend the next four decades regrouping and plotting their revenge before returning to al-Andalus to claim the caliphal title as their own. But for the moment, Umayyad control over northwest Africa was firmly established. However, it would not be al-Hakam who would wield this control, nor his successor, Hisham II. By 985, Ibn Abi 'Amir—by then known as al-Mansur—would be the true ruler of al-Andalus.

THE FIRST SIGN of the crisis that would see al-Mansur seize the caliphate appeared in 974, when al-Hakam II suffered a stroke that resulted in partial paralysis. Although not fatal, it reflected his fragile constitution and heralded his imminent demise. Sensing this, he turned affairs of state almost entirely over to al-Mushafi and prepared for the formal investiture of his ten-year-old son, Hisham, as successor. The impending transfer of power brought Ghalib and al-Mushafi closer together, the mistrust the general felt for the *hajib* notwithstanding. Indeed, some suspected they had made an agreement to divide power after the succession, with al-Mushafi running the palace and Ghalib the army and provinces.

Perhaps to seal the deal, al-Mushafi had asked the general to betroth his daughter 'Asma to the *hajib*'s son 'Uthman. Ghalib agreed, and a contract was duly drawn up and signed. Once Ibn Abi 'Amir got wind of this, however, he went to work, seeding doubt in the general's mind and convincing him to break the agreement and engage 'Asma to him instead. To al-Mushafi's outrage, the marriage would indeed be called off. In August 977 a new betrothal contract was signed, and in 978, on the auspicious occasion of the spring equinox, Ibn Abi 'Amir and 'Asma were married in a lavish ceremony. Even had he wanted to, al-Mushafi could not have attended, for by then he was in prison on the orders of Ghalib and Ibn Abi 'Amir, locked in a cell in the royal dungeons from which he would never emerge alive.

Before his fortunes suddenly changed, however, al-Mushafi saw little reason to be concerned with Ibn Abi 'Amir's ambitions. The *hajib* was serving as regent and preparing for the transition of the caliphal title to al-Hakam's infirm and immature son, Hisham II. He was confident that he and Ghalib would take control of the state, with Subh and Ibn Abi 'Amir serving subordinate roles. Al-Hakam died aged sixty-one on October 1, 976, the day before Hisham's formal recognition as heir was to take place. The four co-conspirators, faithful to the deceased caliph's wishes, went ahead with the ceremony and presented the boy-heir to the notables and chief officials of the realm, insisting they acclaim him as the new caliph. But there were murmurs of discontent among the Arab grandees, who mistrusted al-Mushafi and suspected that he and Subh, or Subh and Ibn Abi 'Amir, were plotting to take power. The chief *qadi* also voiced his concern that a boy of ten might not legitimately serve as caliph, a worry shared by others of the religious elite. This aside, there would have been considerable concern whether the stability of the dynasty could be maintained should a child take the throne. The people of al-Andalus were well aware of how the 'Abbasid caliphate had been torn asunder in the previous century in just such circumstances.

The general uncertainty of the moment provided an opening for the other political force in the palace: the Saqaliba eunuchs, who in the time since Subh's dependence on Ibn Abi 'Amir had been increasingly marginalized. The faction was led by Fa'iq al-Nizami and Jawdhar al-Hakami, each of whom had been intimate confidants of al-Hakam II and had borne the titles "greatly favored servant" and "favored servant," respectively. They were rich and powerful in their own rights. Fa'iq had served as postmaster, head of the royal silk workshop, and commander of the royal guard, while Jawdhar was head falconer and chief of the royal gold- and silversmiths and also served as a military commander and in other ceremonial roles. Both had been deeply loyal to al-Hakam and personally held vigil at his deathbed, but both stood to be totally disempowered under the new regime. Hence, before word of their master's death got out, Fa'iq and Jawdhar discreetly approached al-Mushafi, told him the news, and inveighed on him to put aside Hisham and instead put forward al-Hakam's twenty-seven-year-old brother al-Mughira as the successor. Fa'iq insisted that Hisham should be assassinated. Al-Mushafi pretended to agree but summoned Ghalib, Ibn Abi 'Amir, and other Umayyad clients and disclosed the plot to them.

Ibn Abi 'Amir volunteered to dispose of al-Mughira, whom they all decided was too dangerous to be left alive. Gathering a detachment of troops, he headed to the prince's palace. When they arrived, al-Mughira was so distraught at the news of his brother's death that Ibn Abi 'Amir was moved to spare him. Yet word was sent to him from the loyalists insisting that al-Mughira must die, and thus, the prince was strangled to death in his own house in front of his own family, assuring Hisham's succession. Ibn Abi 'Amir ordered the corpse to be hung from a roof beam so it could be claimed al-Mughira had committed suicide out of grief at the news of his brother's death and he himself would not be stained with the taint of having killed a prince of the blood.

The next day, when al-Mushafi presided over Hisham's ceremony of investiture, Fa'iq and Jawdhar stood in positions of honor at his right and left side. But once the transition of power was complete, they and other leading eunuchs were arrested and had their property confiscated. Fa'iq was sent into exile to Mallorca, and Jawdhar was eventually executed. Taking advantage of the confusion, Ibn Abi 'Amir had other leading eunuchs who may not have participated in the plot killed. The power of the Saqaliba had been broken. Or almost—Jawdhar would turn out to have one last intrigue left in him.

Of course, it was never the intention of al-Mushafi and his confederates that Hisham should actually rule, and the young caliph, who had inherited his father's frail constitution, was immediately sequestered away in the palace, cut off from all communication and trapped in a life of impotent luxury. Al-Mushafi took the office of *hajib*, while Ibn Abi 'Amir was rewarded with a position as wazir and given

command of the palatine guard. Ghalib remained in principle the leading general, but al-Mushafi began to stack the chief of staff positions with his own appointees, imprisoning on thin pretexts anyone he saw as a threat to his ambitions. This further alarmed the Arabs who dominated the council of wazirs, as well as Ghalib, and Ibn Abi 'Amir gently stoked their fears. Subh, for her part, was left in a delicate situation, with no official or public standing, and now under the effective control of the *hajib*. It was then that Ibn Abi 'Amir made his next move.

By this point, Ibn Abi 'Amir had developed strong networks of patronage in the palace, the financial administration, some of the provinces, and the Maghrib, as well as among the religious elite and the Berbers of the army. What he lacked was the experience of a military field command. The occasion arrived soon after the death of al-Hakam, as trouble brewed on the northern frontier. A half century earlier, as the young 'Abd al-Rahman III struggled to bring the provinces under control, Ordoño II of León had struck deep into al-Andalus and pushed the boundaries of his kingdom into the lands south of the Duero River. As a reflection of his confidence, he left Oviedo and established a new capital, León, within the ancient walls of the old Roman city of Legio on the northern edge of the great central plains.

Meanwhile, a new power was emerging between León and Pamplona: the county of Castile, which broke away from León in 931 under Fernán González. Once 'Abd al-Rahman III consolidated his hold on al-Andalus, he was able to bring the various Christian princes under his thumb, and they regularly appeared as suppliants and tributaries, either in person or through the medium of envoys, in the caliphal court at Madinat al-Zahra'. They were well aware, however, of the vulnerabilities of the dynasty. With the rebellion of Hasan ibn Qannun in the Maghrib, the illness of al-Hakam, and Hisham's troubled succession, they began to probe the defenses of the caliphate, launching ever-bolder incursions in violation of the treaties they had been forced to sign.

By 977, the Christian princes appeared to constitute a real threat, alarming the *khassa* and striking fear in the heart of the palace. Subh began to worry for the future of the dynasty. Having weakened

the army through his shuffling of command positions, al-Mushafi
felt paralyzed and failed to react. Ghalib, thoroughly disillusioned
by al-Mushafi's duplicity and, by now, prepared to leave the *hajib*
dangling, was on campaign in North Africa. It was then that Ibn Abi
'Amir stepped forward, rallied the forces at his disposal, and after
gallantly promising the queen mother he would defend the caliphate, marched north to meet the Christian threat.

14

The Chamberlain, Victorious

Ibn Abi 'Amir marched out of Córdoba at the head of his army in mid-February 977. His destination was nearly three hundred miles due north, a fortified town known as al-Hamma, or Los Baños, on the frontier of the kingdom of León. He would return about two months later, to the elation of the people of Córdoba, loaded with booty and captives ("one thousand," according to a later chronicle) to be given away or sold as slaves. The campaign was the first of over fifty Ibn Abi 'Amir would lead against the Christian princes of the peninsula (including two more in 977). His ferocious and destructive raids would propel his rise as a popular and pious hero in al-Andalus, and as the demonic terror "Almanzor" to the Christians of Europe.

In the meantime, the triumph at al-Hamma won him the respect of Ghalib and the gratitude of Subh and positioned him to eliminate or neutralize both his enemies and his allies, including the old general and the impassioned queen mother. Muhammad ibn Abi 'Amir was a paradoxical figure. He was, at bottom, a usurper—a ruthless and ambitious seeker of power who hijacked the caliphate, played to the populist impulses of the *'amma*, pandered to the religious elite, and reduced Hisham II to a puppet in order to establish his own parasitical shadow dynasty, the 'Amirids, behind the façade of Umayyad authority. Devout Sunnis and Umayyad loyalists could hardly forgive this act. But, at the same time, he delivered: pulling al-Andalus back from the brink of catastrophe, saving it from a potential succession crisis, and establishing it, to all appearances, as the undisputed power in both the Iberian Peninsula and the Maghrib, a pole of order and faith and the scourge of infidels. Critics were disarmed by the fact that his rule reinforced the pride, prosperity, security, and stability of al-Andalus. They would have never guessed how fleeting it would prove to be.

THE MOST NOTEWORTHY casualty of the raids of 977 was not a Christian prince but Ibn Abi 'Amir's erstwhile co-conspirator, al-Mushafi. By 977, the *hajib* was isolated, with few supporters beyond his own family. Gathering allies from among the *khassa* and with the support of Subh and Ghalib, Ibn Abi 'Amir had him deposed and arrested, taking up the office of chamberlain of Hisham II. At about this time Ibn Abi 'Amir also had himself appointed *sahib al-madina*, the highest authority in the city of Córdoba, further entrenching his power. By this point, Ghalib was already in his new son-in-law's debt. Ibn Abi 'Amir had enjoined the twelve-year-old caliph to bestow the title *dhu 'l-wizaratayn*, "he of the two wizarates," on his father-in-law, thus placing the ex-slave in a position of honor above the other wazirs of the court. With al-Mushafi out of the way, however, Ghalib's days were also numbered. As a sign of things to come, Ibn Abi 'Amir, now *hajib*, began construction on his own palace complex located just east of the capital city. He would call it Madinat al-Zahira, or "the Radiant City"—an audacious affront to the great caliphal palace, Madinat al-Zahra'.

This was a clear signal of his intentions, and it provoked an immediate reaction within the palace and among the religious elite. In 978/9, leading members of the *'ulama'* together with members of the Saqaliba determined to assassinate Hisham II and place a cousin, 'Abd al-Rahman ibn 'Ubayd Allah, on the throne instead, thus ridding themselves of Ibn Abi 'Amir. The eunuch Jawdhar was to carry out the crime, but as he approached the caliph, drew his knife, and went to stab him, an 'Amirid loyalist, 'Ahmad ibn 'Amrus, who was standing at Hisham's side, intercepted the blade and saved the caliph's life. The *hajib* reacted with fury. Jawdhar and 'Abd al-Rahman were put to death immediately, 'Abd al-Malik al-Balluti (a leading plotter and respected judicial official) was publicly crucified, and other high-status conspirators were thrown in prison, where they would die in the following years.

Now determined to stamp out any potential rivals, Ibn Abi 'Amir fixed his attention on 'Abd al-Rahman al-Rumahis, the storied admiral who ruled over Pechina and Almería, the latter being the site of the caliphate's main shipyards and home port to the main Umayyad fleet. Al-Rumahis had led the fleets that raided Catalonia, Provence, and northern Italy, as well as Ifriqiya. When Ghalib fought off the Vikings in 971 and 972, he had been the naval commander. In short, the admiral was a formidable figure whose powerbase was far from the capital and who owed no allegiance or debt to Ibn Abi 'Amir. Like Ghalib and the rest of the Arab Andalusi political elite, he had little affection for the Berber troops with whom the chamberlain had been filling the ranks of the army.

Such a figure would have to be removed delicately. In late 979/early 980, Ibn Abi 'Amir had journeyed south to Algeciras, accompanying an army that was sent to Morocco to quell an uprising. Feigning a desire to pay his respects, he invited the admiral to his camp and then suggested they dine together. The sugared chicken—an Andalusi delicacy—prepared for the occasion was flavorful enough to disguise the taste of the poison that had been placed within it. Al-Rumahis barely managed to make it home before he succumbed to a slow and agonizing death. The *hajib* immediately stripped the dead admiral's family of its wealth and property, and the governorship of Almería was awarded to Ibn Abi 'Amir's own creature, 'Ahmad ibn 'Amrus.

From his own base near Toledo, Ghalib watched these events with growing alarm and was finally stirred to action. According to the chroniclers, in 980 he summoned Ibn Abi 'Amir for a parley in the general's stronghold at Medinaceli (Madinat Salim) in the Middle March, but during the course of the conversation lost his temper and struck the *hajib* with his sword, hacking off part of his fingers and slashing his face. Wounded, Ibn Abi 'Amir fled, leaping to his escape from the castle wall to the ground below.

Now there would be no compromise. Gathering the Córdoban army—consisting of Berber recruits, Christian mercenaries, Muslim troops from the Upper March, slaves, and Andalusis loyal to Hisham and his own family, the 'Amirids—Ibn Abi 'Amir marched north in late 980. The *hajib* mounted a series of raids against the Muslim lands that were loyal to Ghalib, striking at the towns of the Middle March— attacks that he qualified as jihad on the rationale that so many Christians were fighting in Ghalib's army—and making incursions into the county of Castile. Now in his eighties, Ghalib was no longer the imposing fig- ure of his youth, and his record as a war hero of the caliphate would not have inspired loyalty to him among the Berbers, many of whom had been his enemies in the Maghrib and who now dominated Ibn Abi 'Amir's army. He could count only on his own modest forces in the Middle March and thus appealed for help to the Christian rulers Ramiro Garcés, king in the Rioja, and Count García Fernández of Castile.

In anticipation of the coming fight, the *hajib* launched an attack on Ghalib's lands in early spring 981, but he was badly defeated, suffer- ing the capture of several loyal wazirs. A few months later, the two commanders met in what would be the decisive battle. Their two armies clashed near Atienza, a fortress about fifteen miles west of Medinaceli. Ghalib led two charges against the enemy lines and broke the right and left flanks of the *hajib*'s army, such that only the column held by Ibn Abi 'Amir remained. But to the misfortune of his allies and subordinates, the aged Ghalib fell dead on the brink of victory, either of exhaustion or old age, after which his ranks wavered and crumbled. The result was a rout, and Ibn Abi 'Amir ordered his troops to pursue and slaughter the fleeing enemy without mercy.

The casualties of the defeated army were immense, and number- ing among the many grandees who fell was King Ramiro Garcés him- self. Ghalib's body was recovered, after which Ibn Abi 'Amir ordered his deceased father-in-law to be skinned, the skin stuffed with cotton, and the taxidermal general hung on a crucifix at the gate of the palace of Córdoba for all to see. As for his head, some sources claim it was impaled on a cross and hung above the gate of Ibn Abi 'Amir's pal- ace, Madinat al-Zahira; another, that the *hajib* had it sent as a grisly token to Ghalib's daughter and his own wife 'Asma, who lovingly washed it in perfume and rose water and sent it on to the caliph. For Ibn Abi 'Amir, the defeat of Ghalib marked his ascent to total power, and in honor of the victory, he took the throne name al-Mansur bi-Llah—"Victorious by God."

NOW UNCHALLENGED, AL-MANSUR began to consolidate his power and transform the institutions of the state to serve himself and his own family. He resided now at Madinat al-Zahira, which had been completed in 982, and the palace started to displace Madinat al-Zahra' as the true seat of government. The state-focused civil service and bureaucracy that had developed over the previous half century were reoriented toward al-Mansur and his dynasty. He gave greater authority to the governors of the major cities on the condition that they remain faithful, unintentionally paving the way for the political fragmentation of al-Andalus. The network of Umayyad *mawali* that had provided a cohesive framework for the dynasty's power was marginalized. The native elements in the caliphal army were progressively disempowered in favor of slaves and mercenaries, particularly those drawn from North Africa, and Berbers took on ever-greater roles in the running of the state. The *burnus* and turban, previously scoffed at as the crude and uncivilized garb of semi-barbarians, came into fashion in palace circles, alarming both the Umayyad elite and the common people of al-Andalus, who together feared and loathed their North African neighbors and coreligionists.

Though Machiavellian in his political and personal life, al-Mansur also seems to have been a man of faith. He had trained as a Maliki jurist, served as a *qadi*, and was noted for such pious exercises as writing out his own personal copy of the Qur'an. Yet, his relationship with the religious elite remained complicated. As a whole, the Maliki *'ulama'* prided themselves on their independence, integrity, and loyalty to the caliphal dynasty, an allegiance the *hajib* attempted to counteract by appointing relatives and dependents to key judicial positions, including a maternal uncle as *qadi* of Córdoba. Although after the failed coup of 978/79 the religious elite would not dare attempt to overthrow him, their determination to resist was evident. For example, when al-Mansur sought to have the mosque at Madinat al-Zahira declared a *masjid al-jami'*—a congregational mosque, where the faithful could gather for Friday prayer—he was stopped by a series of near-unanimous *fatwas* declaring that his palace was merely a suburb or satellite of the capital and as such did not merit such an honor. Furious, he pressured the judicial elite into backing down but found that no prestigious *'alim* would agree to serve as the imam at his mosque and that few members of the Umayyad elite would venture there for Friday services.

Whether fighting Christians or fellow Muslims, al-Mansur wrapped his military campaigns in the sanctified aura of jihad, and he now set out to win over the religious elite with similarly grandiose gestures. One was to expand the great mosque of Córdoba, and under his sponsorship the size of the prayer hall and patio was effectively doubled by the addition of eight naves. But as with his palace, there was an ersatz quality to his construction, evident in the cheap materials and techniques he used. He also worked hand-in-glove with the Maliki elite in supporting the judicial persecution of members of the *'ulama'*, scholars, and literati who ran afoul of their orthodoxy. Another of his pious gestures aimed at currying favor with the conservative jurists was to purge al-Hakam II's famous library of the books that they found offensive. Countless works relating to the era of Christian rule, astrology, pagan-inspired philosophy, "non-Islamic sciences," and other subjects deemed immoral were seized and publicly burned. But this took place only in the last years of his reign.

In fact, al-Mansur appreciated culture and understood its political significance. He continued to patronize scholarship and the arts within the bounds of his own orthodoxy and made Madinat al-Zahira the locus of literary and scholarly salons like Madinat al-Zahra' had been. He welcomed the Iraqi poet and grammarian Sa'id al-Baghdadi to his court and showered him with favor and money, and appointed the Andalusi poet al-Husayn ibn al-'Arif, fresh from a long sojourn in Egypt, as the tutor to his sons. Thus, despite his attack on the library and his persecution of certain scholars, culture in al-Andalus continued to thrive. Cannily, the *hajib* never openly challenged or undermined the prestige of Hisham II and the institution of the Umayyad caliphate, nor did he aspire to the caliphal title himself. By 980, the power of the caliph may have been nothing more than a fiction, and widely recognized as so, but everyone knew that maintaining the illusion of Umayyad authority was crucial to the stability of al-Andalus.

Even as al-Mansur propped up the façade of the caliphal dynasty's stability, he faced internal resistance to his rule. Subh had become increasingly alarmed by his rise. During the triumvirate of Ghalib, al-Mushafi, and Ibn Abi 'Amir, which ruled in the period after Hisham's accession, she had been able to exercise considerable power through her position as *umm walad*, as her proud ostentation of the title Sayyida ("Lord") had shown. But now, with the center of power no longer at Madinat al-Zahra', she found herself almost as isolated and powerless as her son. In 996, with the aid of her brother, Fa'iq, she reached out to al-Mansur's increasingly restive governor of the Maghrib, Ziri ibn 'Atiyya, and hatched a scheme in which they would eliminate Ibn Abi 'Amir by publicly disavowing allegiance to him, while swearing their fealty to the boy caliph, Hisham, thereby cutting the *hajib* out of the equation. The revolution would be funded by the royal treasury.

But Ibn Abi 'Amir's spies in the palace caught wind of the plot, and he hastily convened the council of wazirs, who authorized him to transfer the royal treasury, the one thing of value still in possession of the ruling family, to Madinat al-Zahira. The *hajib*'s troops descended on the Madinat al-Zahra' and caught Fa'iq and the Saqaliba in the act as they tried to smuggle out gold and silver coins in huge jars disguised with layers of honey and other foods. It was all confiscated. The loss of the treasury deprived Subh of her already meager influence; she was now powerless. As for Ziri ibn 'Atiyya, the following year al-Mansur sent his armies to the Maghrib to rally the support of the weaker Zanata warlords and subdue this upstart. They dealt him a series of defeats and pushed him east toward the Sahara. In 998, Ibn 'Abi Amir's twenty-three-year-old son and heir-designate, 'Abd al-Malik, was given command of the mission to crush the rebel, who retreated into what is now Algeria. There he carved out a new principality centered on Tihert and Tlemcen before once again formally submitting to the authority of al-Mansur.

Subh and Ziri's open declaration of loyalty to Hisham II highlighted the fact that the caliph had not been seen in public for years, and with rumors still circulating regarding the queen mother's infatuation with the *hajib*, Ibn Abi 'Amir felt he needed to act. He did so with another grand gesture. In 996, a spectacular public ceremony of reconciliation and reaffirmation was staged in which Hisham II, decked out in caliphal glory, was conveyed on horseback from Madinat al-Zahra' to Córdoba through crowds of faithful subjects, with al-Mansur and his son 'Abd al-Malik on either side, and followed closely by Subh and the grandees of the court. The caliph's subjects were undoubtedly relieved to know he was still alive. Reaching Madinat al-Zahira, those present, including the 'Amirid family, renewed the *bay'a*, or pledge of allegiance to the caliph, while the caliph publicly conferred upon the *hajib* all of the powers of state, which al-Mansur was to wield in Hisham's name. The coup was complete. As a sign of his new confidence, al-Mansur took the titles Sayyid and al-Malik al-Karim ("the Noble King"). Subh, now thoroughly defeated, died two years later. Whether for the sake of appearances or out of genuine affection, al-Mansur led her cortege barefoot and recited poetry he had written himself in what was to outward appearances a deeply heartfelt eulogy.

Like the Umayyad princes before him, al-Mansur used marriage as a political tool, joining his family to those of powerful local lineages, including the Tujibids, and taking wives from among the Christian royalty of the peninsula. One of these, who evidently kept her faith, was Teresa, who historians have suggested was a daughter of Bermudo II of León. We know little about her, but after al-Mansur's death she apparently returned to her home kingdom, where she took up the life of a nun. Another, 'Abda, whose Christian name had been Urraca, was a daughter of Sancho II Garcés. She would bear al-Mansur a son, 'Abd al-Rahman, popularly known as Shanjul ("Little Sancho," in Arabic) due to his resemblance to his grandfather, the king of Pamplona. But it was al-Mansur's favorite son, 'Abd al-Malik, born of a former slave named al-Dhalfa', who was being groomed to succeed him through appointments to military command and incorporation into ceremonies of power. This sparked the jealousy of al-Mansur's oldest child, 'Abd Allah. In 989/90 he joined forces with his in-law, the ambitious governor of Zaragoza,

'Abd al-Rahman al-Tujibi, and with the governor of Toledo, 'Abd Allah al-Marwani (a distant member of the Umayyad clan, nicknamed "Dry Stone" for his fame as a cheapskate), to launch a rebellion against his own father.

Again, al-Mansur's spies uncovered the plot. Without revealing all that he knew, the *hajib* summoned 'Abd Allah home to Madinat al-Zahira and gently tried to convince him to remain loyal. But 'Abd Allah would not be moved. Next, the *hajib* announced he would mount a great raid against Castile and ordered his governors to muster their troops and rendezvous at the castle of Gormaz on the Duero River. Here, at the camp, Ibn Abi 'Amir arranged for 'Abd al-Rahman al-Tujibi to be publicly denounced as a traitor in front of the troops by one of his subordinates, after which he was arrested and taken to prison in Córdoba. Months later, he would be executed in al-Mansur's presence. As for "Dry Stone" and 'Abd Allah, realizing the conspiracy had been exposed, they fled the military camp and rode north, the former taking refuge with the king of León and the latter with the count of Castile. But the arm of al-Mansur was long. A punitive raid against León was enough to secure the return of "Dry Stone" by Bermudo II. He was sent back to Córdoba as a prisoner, although, perhaps because he was of royal blood, he escaped decapitation. As for 'Abd Allah, al-Mansur had only to send a letter to Count García Fernández requesting the fugitive be returned. And so it was that a detachment of Castilian knights escorted 'Abd Allah to the bridge over the Duero at San Estaban de Gormaz, where he was received by members of al-Mansur's army and immediately executed on the orders of the *hajib*. His body was buried near where it fell, and his head was sent back in a sack to the grief-stricken but unrepentant father.

García Fernández had good reason to comply with Ibn Abi 'Amir's request. Since he first commanded the raid against al-Hamma in 977, the *hajib* had made it his custom to personally lead two campaigns every year into Christian territory, in addition to those carried out by his generals and governors. The goal was not conquest, but to generate plunder, prevent the Christian kings from taking the political initiative, and cripple their rural economies. Churches and monasteries were looted and destroyed and fortresses demolished. On occasion, there were massacres, either in reprisal for Christian resistance or simply because it was too inconvenient to take prisoners, and after each campaign, the heads of the fallen enemy were displayed throughout al-Andalus. The raids kept the Christian principalities in a near-permanent state of disarray. Al-Mansur struck the Christian North at will and with impunity, thus obliging their princes to regularly journey to Córdoba as supplicants and to pay their respects. Christians were terrified of al-Mansur and came to see the Muslims of al-Andalus as brutal predators, notwithstanding the fact that there were many Christians serving as soldiers and guides in the caliphal army.

These successes, and his resulting reputation for invincibility, made al-Mansur a popular hero, an image he took an active role in cultivating through his patronage of poets. His official panegyrist, Abu 'Umar ibn Darraj al-Qastalli, was one of many poets who accompanied al-Mansur on campaign and composed florid odes praising the *hajib*'s piety and military exploits and his "humiliation" of the Christian princes. The poet gloated over the many Christian women, or "fat gazelles," taken back as prisoners to be sold as slaves and concubines.[22] In Ibn Darraj's verses, the *hajib* strikes a dashing figure, charging ahead of his armies on horseback as though he were an Arab warrior-prince of old. In bringing war to the infidel, he bolstered his pious credentials and made it more difficult for the *'ulama'* to criticize him.

No one knew where al-Mansur would strike next or how deep his armies would penetrate Christian territory. He assaulted Astorga in 988, 994, and 997; Zamora in 981, 986, 988, and 994; Coímbra in 987; San Estaban de Gormaz in 994; Simancas in 986; Osma and Toro in 989; Girona in 982. He made incursions deep into the countryside of Galicia, Castile, Navarre, and the Catalan Pyrenees. Neither country nor town was safe, and Ibn Abi 'Amir took particular satisfaction in striking at the capital cities of the Christian princes. León suffered at least five attacks (986, 988, 995, 997, and 999) and Pamplona no fewer than four (978, 994, 999, and 1001). In 985, he launched a major campaign against Barcelona, in which he effectively destroyed the city, carrying a good number of its population off into slavery and killing many others, and destroying churches, monasteries, castles, and fortifications. One chronicle puts the number of captives taken in this campaign at 70,000. Count Borrell II was forced to retreat into the mountains, and the city of Barcelona did not recover for several years. Nor did joining forces help the Christians. In 982, Ramiro III of León, García Fernández of Castile, and al-Mansur's father-in-law, Sancho II of Pamplona, put aside their own differences and marched against him, but they were decisively defeated.

Al-Mansur's signal victory, however, took place in 997, when he marched his Muslim and Christian troops westward to a site near present-day Lisbon and then proceeded north up the Atlantic coast. Their destination was Santiago de Compostela, the most holy Christian shrine in the peninsula and the symbol of emerging Leonese hegemony. Some of the Leonese soldiers in his army apparently had moral reservations and tried to sabotage the campaign, but al-Mansur, as usual, discovered the plot. The *hajib* understood the power of religion in politics and seems to have deliberately targeted major Christian holy sites and monasteries for destruction. Thus, in 997 he sacked Santiago and destroyed its cathedral. But in Santiago, the *hajib* gave strict orders that the tomb of Saint James (Shant Ya'qub), whom Muslims understood to be the brother of the prophet 'Isa' (Jesus), should not be desecrated. Instead, the ponderous chimes of the cathedral (along with much booty and many prisoners) were carried back to Córdoba where they were hung in the great mosque as public symbols of his triumph over the "polytheists" and as testament to his power. Ibn Abi 'Amir had grabbed Spanish Christianity by the bells.

RELENTLESSLY VIOLENT AS al-Mansur's campaigns were, they were driven by pragmatism, as part of a strategy aimed at pushing back against the gradual encroachment by the Christians on Andalusi territory since the ninth century. Ibn Abi 'Amir did not hate Christians or Christianity; he treated well those Christian princes who respected his power, and he did not oppress or attack *dhimmis*. The minority communities were staunchly loyal to the Umayyad state, no matter who was running it. In contrast, it was an era of great fear and uncertainty in the north. Count García Fernández himself would fall victim to the *hajib* in 995, when he was surprised by an Andalusi raiding party while out hunting along the banks of the Duero. Bundled off to Córdoba, he died along the way when his captors stopped at Medinaceli, and in the end only his head made it to al-Mansur.

The windswept plateau of Medinaceli was also, as it happens, the place where Ibn Abi 'Amir would meet his doom. That would come on August 10, 1002, in the waning days of the holy month of Ramadan, when on the way home from sacking the region of La Rioja and the monastery of San Millán de la Cogolla, the patron saint of Castile, the *hajib* fell ill and died. He was in his sixties and afflicted by what may have been a severe case of gout. Unable to even ride a horse, he had been carried on campaign on a palanquin borne by two African slaves. Having striven for a quarter century to establish his own family as the masters of al-Andalus, he had conquered the Maghrib, subdued the Christian princes, and tamed the Arab elite of al-Andalus. But, in doing so, he had undermined the institutions and networks that held al-Andalus together and deepened social and ethnic rifts that had been long apparent within Andalusi society. These would prove impossible to repair, and within less than a decade of his death, the edifice of the Umayyad caliphate would collapse in a bloody civil war, which would transform the political landscape of al-Andalus and herald a new era.

15

The Fall of the House of Umayya

Remarkably, for all the punishment he dealt to the Christian kingdoms, Muhammad ibn Abi 'Amir al-Mansur—"Almanzor"—is rarely mentioned in contemporary sources from Spain or the Frankish lands to the north. Later histories refer to him simply as "king of the Muslims" or "prince," while the Old French epic *The Song of Roland* made his name into a generic synonym for a powerful Muslim warrior, an *almaçur*. Lucas de Tuy's *Chronicle of the World*, a Galician work from 1236, depicts a king, "Almazor," who wages war relentlessly, but portrays him also as a valiant and chivalric figure. This contra-intuitive image of the Andalusi dictator would gradually come into focus in later medieval *cantares de gesta*, the popular songs of chivalric deeds, and eventually be idealized by nineteenth-century Spanish nationalist historians, who saw him as a strong, pragmatic monarch. The *Historia Silense*, a chronicle written about a century after his death, was less charitable. It rehearses al-Mansur's depredations before noting his death with relief: "At last divine piety . . . saw fit to lift this scourge from the necks of the Christians . . . Almanzor was killed in the great city of Medinaceli by the demon who possessed him, and was cast into hell."[23]

The reaction in Córdoba to news of the *hajib*'s death was less celebratory. At Madinat al-Zahira, the courtiers and servants put away their silk to don the dark woolen garb of mourning. Without delay, al-Mansur's son and proclaimed heir, 'Abd al-Malik, hurried from his father's deathbed to Córdoba to be confirmed as *hajib* with no resistance. With characteristic forethought, his father had formally yielded this office to him as early as 997 to ensure a smooth transition. Soon after, the great al-Mansur was laid to rest with the kerchief that he always carried on campaign and that bore the dust of his many raids. After establishing himself as *hajib*, 'Abd al-Malik lost no time in preparing a new mission into the Christian North, and for a moment it may have seemed that life in the caliphate would continue as before. But it was not to be; the kingdom founded in the 750s by 'Abd al-Rahman I and raised to glory under 'Abd al-Rahman III was about to disappear. Islamic unity in Spain would be shattered with the rise of the *taifa* kings; the Christian princes would gain the upper hand; and within a century, al-Andalus would be under the rule of a foreign Berber dynasty. By that point, the Umayyad family, a lineage of caliphs that traced its pedigree back to Mecca at the time of the Prophet, had suffered a drawn-out and ignominious demise.

THE START OF his reign augured well for 'Abd al-Malik, despite his reputation as a somewhat lazy prince with an excessive affection for drink. Following his father's counsel, he kept a steady eye on the treasury and contented himself as *hajib* of the prisoner-caliph, Hisham II. He led a series of successful attacks in the north, and it seemed that the Christian princes were prepared to acknowledge him as their patron and even lend troops to his army. In 1006, a defeat during a campaign against Pamplona together with a series of palace conspiracies prompted him to reform his character, swear off the drink, and take firmer control of the state.

A successful follow-up raid in 1007 calmed the nerves of his subjects and provided the occasion to have Hisham II award him the throne name al-Muzaffar ("the Victorious"). He also had his five-year-old son, Muhammad, appointed as *dhu 'l-wizaratayn*, or double-wazir, the same honor once held by the eminent general Ghalib. 'Abd al-Malik cultivated his own network of clients and associates, making notable use of Saqaliba eunuchs as agents and officials, and depended heavily on his mother, al-Dhalfa', to protect his interests. Conspicuously pious, this widow of al-Mansur would communicate publicly only from behind a curtain and through the medium of a trusted *faqih* she kept at her side. While in rule, al-Mansur had put property in her name to shelter his wealth from view, so she was very rich and became a major political force even beyond the chamberlain's palace. She also happened to have a strong distrust of 'Isa ibn al-Qatta', Abd al-Malik's wazir, confidant, and deputy.

Ibn al-Qatta' had succeeded in marrying one of his sons to a daughter of 'Abd al-Malik, and next he began to turn the *hajib* against his wife Jayal, arranging a new match with Wiyad, the daughter of his own gardener. Al-Dhalfa' was no fool; Jayal had been her ally, and she saw that through Wiyad, Ibn al-Qatta' hoped to control her son. She did not hide her displeasure, causing Ibn al-Qatta' to panic and launch a conspiracy to unseat Hisham II and place another grandson of 'Abd al-Rahman III on the throne, thereby removing 'Abd al-Malik from power. But the plot was foiled, and both the treacherous wazir and the royal pretender were put to death.

But 'Abd al-Malik would not live much longer. Although young, his health was delicate, and while taking shelter in a monastery near Córdoba on his return from campaign in 1008, he died after a short illness. It was whispered that his twenty-five-year-old half brother, 'Abd al-Rahman, was responsible for poisoning him. "Shanjul," as he was known, was then confirmed as the new *hajib* by Hisham II, but he showed little of his brother's caution. He adopted a series of hyperbolic titles—al-Ma'mun ("Protected by God") and Nasir al-Dawla ("the Victor for the Dynasty")—and insisted on referring to the caliph, who became a covert drinking companion, as his "paternal uncle." This was a not-so-subtle suggestion that Hisham's biological father was Ibn Abi 'Amir, and that he and Shanjul were, in fact, half brothers. Acquiring a reputation for vanity, Shanjul made the fatal mistake of going against his father's advice and infringing on the prerogatives of the caliphal family. Shortly after coming to power, he had the childless Hisham formally declare him the heir to the caliphate and appointed his own son 'Abd al-'Aziz, who was only about five years old, as the new *hajib*. The ceremony of investiture took place on January 13, 1009, after which Shanjul gathered the army and headed north to raid Castile.

This turn of events would prove too much for the marginalized yet still-powerful Umayyad elite to bear, and they immediately set the wheels of revolt in motion. They were supported by al-Dhalfa', who, whether or not she believed Shanjul had poisoned her son, had lost her status as queen mother on 'Abd al-Malik's death. She thus diverted much of her considerable wealth to the conspirators in an effort to regain her political influence. But the uprising may have remained merely a palace intrigue had it not been for the discontent among the Andalusi populace. Much of this anger was directed at the Zanata and Sanhaja troops and their families who had continued to arrive in al-Andalus from North Africa in increasing numbers during the rule of the 'Amirids, and who became increasingly comfortable in their adopted land. On February 15, when news reached the capital that Shanjul and his forces had reached Toledo, the people of Córdoba rose in rebellion.

The uprising was led by Muhammad ibn Hisham—a grandson of 'Abd al-Rahman III—whose father had been put to death by 'Abd al-Malik and who had the support of Umayyad loyalists and the Andalusi population of the capital. He enjoined the caliph to abdicate and took the throne himself as al-Mahdi. Shortly afterward, the death of Hisham II was announced. Next, the two palaces were sacked. Madinat al-Zahra' was stripped of its wealth and its furnishings, and the state treasury was seized from Madinat al-Zahira. Shanjul hurried back toward the city, but his Berber troops abandoned him. Captured and killed, his body was taken to Córdoba, where it was put on display in the street for the common people to abuse. His execution marked the beginning of twenty years of *fitna*: the antithesis of the peace and stability of Islam. It would be a mad scramble for power among members of the Umayyad family, palace slaves, Berber warlords, members of the *'ulama'*, and local governors.

Al-Mahdi allowed the people of Córdoba to vent their rage on the Berber neighborhoods, which were the scenes of vicious violence and looting. Withdrawing from the city, some Berber troops rallied to the cause of the 'Amirid family, while others proclaimed their own caliph, another grandson of 'Abd al-Rahman III, with the title al-Rashid. When he was killed, they found another, a great-grandson, whom they acclaimed as al-Musta'in. Intent on taking revenge on the Córdobans, they retook the capital but were soon pushed out again by al-Mahdi, who had appealed to Castile and Barcelona for help. How times had changed! For the first time in four hundred years a Christian prince had entered Córdoba not as a supplicant, but at the head of an army. This proved too much for the populace, who then overthrew al-Mahdi with the connivance of the governor of Toledo, a Saqaliba, who took over the capital and ruled as *hajib* in the name of Hisham II, who was apparently still alive.

In 1013, Berber forces retook Córdoba again, killing Hisham II (again) and wreaking their vengeance on the people of the city for the atrocities that had been carried out against their community. Once they were in control, their puppet, al-Musta'in, began to lose his grip on power, so the Berber army cast about for someone to replace him. They settled on 'Ali ibn Hammud. The Hammudid family were members of the same Idrisid clan the Umayyads had crushed in the 970s, and they based their claim to the caliphate on their descent from Muhammad's cousin 'Ali. With this, Córdoba was now fully in the grip of the Berber mercenary factions, who resumed their anti-Arab, anti-Andalusi policies with increasing intensity. In 1018, the Saqaliba determined to strike back, and Khayran, the slave-king of Málaga, marched on the capital under the banner of his caliph, 'Abd al-Rahman IV al-Murtada—another grandson of 'Abd al-Rahman III. The death of al-Murtada in battle against the Berbers brought an end to the Saqalibas' ambitions.

But Hammudid domination of Córdoba also quickly descended into chaos as various members of that family fought for control before they were ejected from the capital altogether in 1023. The aristocracy of the city, eager to forestall any further unrest, acclaimed another great-grandson of 'Abd al-Rahman III as caliph, but the young 'Abd al-Rahman V was overthrown and killed after just six weeks in power in a coup led by his cousin, who took the throne as Muhammad III. He lasted only sixteenth months before being expelled from the city in 1025, only to be poisoned soon after. At this point, the caliphal title was claimed by Hisham III, an elder brother of 'Abd al-Rahman IV. His incompetent misrule finally cured the people of Córdoba of any further desire to be ruled by a caliph. He was expelled from the city in 1031 and wandered north to Lleida (Larida), in the Upper March, where he died five years later. The era of Umayyad Spain had ended. After twenty-two years of civil war and ethnic strife, of countercoups and pogroms, compounded by flooding and pestilence, Córdoba had been shattered. So thoroughly were its great palaces destroyed that the ruins of Madinat al-Zahra' were not identified until 1843; the site of Madinat al-Zahira has still not been located.

THE CALIPHATE WAS essentially the creation of 'Abd al-Rahman III, who, in the course of subduing his domestic and foreign enemies, seized the opportunity to make a claim of universal sovereignty. His ruthlessness and capacity to delegate made the caliphate possible, as did the good fortune he had to reign for nearly half a century. And although the title gave him, in principle, religious authority, it seems neither the caliphs nor their subjects assigned much weight to that aspect of the office. When the caliphate failed, however, it did so not as the result of the actions of any single individual. It had, after all, lasted less than a century, including the twenty-five years under the rule of al-Mansur. One can blame al-Mansur for its eventual disintegration, but it is not clear that it would not have failed sooner without him. Regionalism, ethnic cleavages, and factionalism within the royal family and their circle of dependents would have undermined the caliphal edifice sooner if not later.

By the same token, no single individual would have been able to save the caliphate. By the 1020s it had largely outlived its usefulness in the eyes of the common folk. By the time the people of Córdoba finished with the Umayyad dynasty in 1031, the rest of al-Andalus had already moved on. There was no formal abolition of the caliphate, only indifference. Various members or purported members of the Umayyad and Hammudid clans continued to claim the title, and many of the rulers of the *taifa* kingdoms also preferred to maintain the fiction of Umayyad authority. But this was not a question of loyalty. By posing as the legitimate agents of a spectral caliph, they neatly side-stepped any questions that might be raised about their own claims as rulers.

At the outset of the *fitna*, over thirty independent *taifa* kingdoms appeared. Most of the smaller ones, many of which consisted of little more than a city and its immediate hinterland, were untenable and were rapidly conquered or absorbed by their larger neighbors. Of those to first break away from Córdoban power, the most viable were the frontier provinces, whose governors had already enjoyed great autonomy. The Upper March, with its capital at Zaragoza, remained under the control of the Banu Tujib until 1039, when the king, al-Mundhir, was killed and the city occupied by his governor of Lleida, Muhammad ibn Hud. A scion of venerable Arab lineage, he established a new dynasty that would annex the various smaller kingdoms of the north. In Toledo, the capital of the Middle March, the wealthiest townsfolk seized power, led by their *qadi*. Lacking an army, they invited a Berber general named 'Abd al-Rahman ibn Dhi 'l-Nun to rule over them. The Lower March, centered on Badajoz, was taken over first by its Saqaliba governor, Sabur; he was succeeded by his wazir, 'Abd Allah ibn al-Aftas, a member of an old Berber family, who established his own dynasty of kings, the Aftasids.

In the densely urbanized south, virtually every city secured its independence, although most would eventually be absorbed by Seville and others by Granada (Gharnata) and Toledo. The second city of al-Andalus, Seville, was initially ruled over by a triumvirate consisting of a *qadi*, a *faqih*, and a wazir. However, the *qadi*, Abu 'l-Qasim Muhammad ibn 'Abbad, soon established himself as a hereditary ruler, taking the formal title of *hajib* and claiming sovereignty in the name of a supposedly absent but still living Hisham II. Southeast of Seville, the largely Jewish population of the area around Lucena (Lujana) petitioned a Sanhaja warlord, Zawi ibn Ziri, for military protection and offered to recognize him as king. Zawi, the brother of the rebel, Bulughghin ibn Ziri, had come with his family and clients to al-Andalus to serve in the caliphal army, but was now fleeing the anti-Berber violence of the *fitna*. He oversaw the founding of the city of

Granada before moving back to Ifriqiya, disillusioned by the hatred of the Andalusis for his people. But his kin stayed on, ruling the kingdom of Granada for most of the century.

After the expulsion of Hisham III, the leading citizens of Córdoba constituted a ruling council to run the city, which became, effectively, an urban republic. Its leading figure was the man who had resolved to expel the Umayyad clan from the city: a *qadi* and wazir named Jahwar ibn Jahwar, whose family would dominate Córdoba for three generations. Although under their rule the city slowly recovered some stability and prosperity, the former capital would never recapture its old glory.

But if Córdoba's light had dimmed, those of the provincial cities flickered to life, and each now boasted a court that provided patronage for artists, poets, and intellectuals, the presence of whom was seen as a sign of authority and prosperity. Scholars and literati who fled the capital found shelter and employment under the *taifa* rulers and among literary and scientific communities that had been incubating in the provinces for generations. Thanks to domination of the Maghrib and the trans-Saharan gold routes, the commercialization of al-Andalus had reached new heights. The smaller cities of al-Andalus, whether port towns or regional centers, had boomed. Agricultural and industrial output remained high, and trade continued even through the chaotic decades of civil war. Thus, the port cities of the Mediterranean coast remained prosperous, and several became durable *taifa* kingdoms. Denia (Daniya), which was ruled by Saqaliba, managed to conquer Mallorca, and even launched an invasion of Christian Sardinia.

The broader populace of al-Andalus was, by the end of the eleventh century, remarkably cohesive in terms of identity and culture. By then, the vast majority of Christians had converted to Islam, while those who had not converted experienced little or no discrimination. Jewish communities, even more deeply assimilated than the Christians, also thrived, both in rural enclaves and in towns. In many day-to-day contexts, people saw themselves as Andalusis first and treated their fellow citizens as such, regardless of their faith. Nor did the conservative *'ulama'* voice concern regarding the non-Muslims living in their midst. For them, the greatest threat remained Islamic heterodoxy, whether in the form of Shi'ism, mystical asceticism, Mu'tazilism, or any of the other dangerous and nonconformist theologies that had percolated westward to al-Andalus and threatened the power of the Maliki elite.

THE EMERGENCE OF urban republics like Córdoba was a phenomenon evident across much of the Islamic world as central authority had broken down and each of the three caliphates failed. This shift represented a soft revolution of the conservative, urban merchant classes from whom so many of the *'ulama'* were drawn. Because Islamic law and institutions for the most part were established by the *'ulama'*, the figure of the ruler in the Sunni Islamic world had become progressively desacralized. His authority, or *sultan*, was essentially secular and quite limited. The role of a *malik* ("king"), a term previously eschewed as un-Muslim and contrary to the notion of Islamic unity, was viewed as a means to maintain order in society through the proper administration of taxes and finances, the maintenance of peace, and the exercise of military force, nothing more.

The greatest threat to order was *fitna*, which by 1031 the Muslims of al-Andalus had suffered for over two decades. Thus, religious credentials were not regarded as the necessary precondition for a ruler's acceptance by a community, as long as he could provide a stable environment in which believers could be faithful under the guidance of the religious elite. For the same reason, many Muslims were willing to accept Jews and Christians serving in the highest levels of royal administration. By the end of the eleventh century, some were even prepared to accept a non-Muslim as their ruler, if they felt he could keep the peace and would vouchsafe the practice of Islamic law.

Thus, as the dust of the *fitna* settled, al-Andalus entered a new age, which might be characterized as one of dynamic instability, or creative destruction. Culturally, Islamic Spain would reach new heights of sophistication; economically, it would continue to thrive, and yet, politically, it would fail. As a contemporary satirical voice implied, for all the *taifa* kings' wealth and all their posturing, they were weak:

They give themselves grandiose names, like "The Powerful,"
　　and "The Invincible," but these are empty titles.
They are like pussycats, who puffing themselves up,
　　imagine they can roar like lions. . . . [24]

This weakness would not be lost on their neighbors—the princes and powerbrokers of Christian Spain and Berber North Africa. In the century following the fall of the caliphate, Islamic Spain would be overrun, and the people of al-Andalus would come under the rule of foreign masters.

PART IV

DISARRAY, 1030–1220

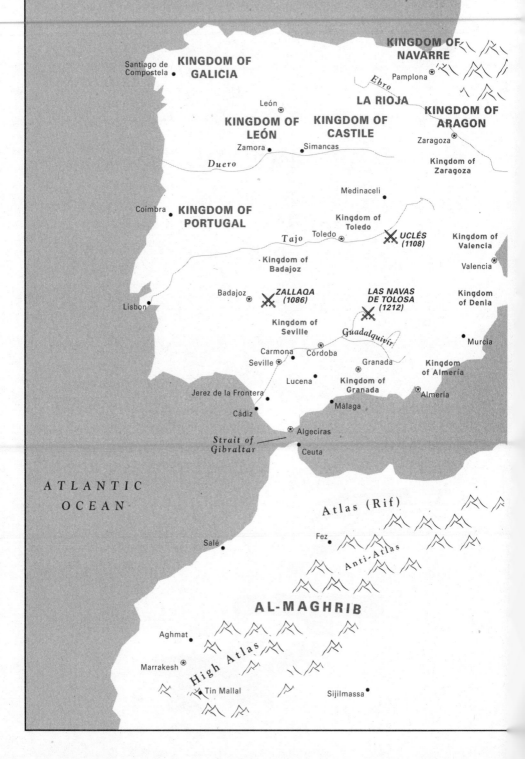

The Taifa Kingdoms & the West, 1030–1230

Pyrenees

COUNTY OF BARCELONA

Barbastro

Lleida

Fraga

Tortosa

Tarragona

Barcelona ⊛

Girona

Minorca

Mallorca

BALEARICS

Denia ⊛

Mediterranean Sea

Tunis ⊛

Tell Atlas

Tell Atlas

IFRIQIYA

Sahara   Desert

| 0 | | 300 mi |
| 0 | | 300 km |

16

The Remembrance of Things Past

I said to my chains,
don't you understand?
I have surrendered to you.
Why, then, have you no pity, no tenderness?[25]

So began the lament of the poet-king al-Mu'tamid—Muhammad ibn 'Abbad, the third and last *taifa* ruler of Seville—which he composed in exile shortly after 1091, the year his kingdom was dissolved by the new rulers of al-Andalus, the Almoravids of North Africa, and he and his family had been carted off as prisoners to Aghmat in central Morocco. Seville had been the capital of the most powerful and prestigious of the *taifa* kingdoms, but, like the caliphate that had preceded it, its glory was fleeting. Less than eighty years after its foundation by al-Mu'tamid's grandfather and namesake, the *qadi* Abu 'l-Qasim, it and all but two of the other kingdoms would be swept away.

With Córdoba and its hinterlands having suffered the most during the *fitna*, Seville had been left as the most populous urban center, a city set in the middle of the fertile Guadalquivir Valley and with a river that was navigable to the Atlantic. Here, ten years after taking power in 1023, Abu 'l-Qasim would brazenly announce that he had found Hisham II alive and that the caliph had appointed him *hajib* with authority over all of al-Andalus. On special occasions the imposter would be paraded out in ceremonial robes to reinforce Abu 'l-Qasim's authority.

As transparent as this gambit may have been, it provided an ideological springboard for the 'Abbadid family's political ambitions and even found support among many of the kingdom's rival dynasties: those close by, like Córdoba, because they feared 'Abbadid conquest, and those further off, like Toledo and Zaragoza, because they were aware that without an explicit connection to caliphal authority, their own legitimacy had no foundation. Hence, Hisham's name continued to be called out in the *khutba*, before the Friday sermon, across much of al-Andalus until 1060, when Abu 'l-Qasim's son and successor, al-Mu'tadid, quietly confessed that Hisham (meaning, evidently, the fake his family had supported) had actually died in 1044. But it was not only the phantom Hisham who had been living on borrowed time. The *taifa* kingdoms, for all their wealth, sophistication, and pretensions to glory, were untenable, and in the century following the disintegration of the caliphate, the balance of political power and military might shifted dramatically from Muslim Spain to the Christian North and Islamic North Africa.

ALTHOUGH THE SON of a respected jurist, Abu 'l-Qasim came to power not on the strength of religious credentials, but on the strength of aristocratic patrimony. He was the richest man in Seville, owning perhaps a third of its territory, and was thus poised to take a leading role in governance. It was the caliph, 'Ali ibn Hammud, who appointed him *qadi*, hoping to curry support; but no sooner had he obtained his position than Abu 'l-Qasim betrayed his patron and shut the gates on the Hammudid ruler. Once in power, and having eliminated the *faqih* and wazir who were his corulers, he set out to absorb the small and weak *taifa* kingdoms of the south. Most went quickly. Algeciras, the last redoubt of the Hammudids, would not fall until the 1050s, and Carmona and Córdoba until the 1060s. Both the Banu Birzal (the Zanata rulers of Carmona, who had immigrated from Ifriqiya as mercenaries in the 960s) and the Andalusi Jahwarids of Córdoba were careful to present themselves as docile subordinates, which allowed them to survive and enabled the war-ravaged former capital to recover a modicum of prosperity.

Under the cautious rule of the wazir, Jahwar ibn Jahwar, and his son, Muhammad al-Rashid, Córdoba's infrastructure was repaired and commerce reestablished, although with the collapse of caliphal patronage, the city was only a shadow of its former self. Thanks in part to the prestige of its name, Córdoba remained home to a constellation of literary and intellectual figures, notably 'Ali ibn Hazm, a jurist, author, poet, historian, and theologian, and perhaps the foremost intellectual and literary figure in the history of Islamic Spain. A number of famous poets served as wazirs of the Jahwarid rulers. One of them, Ibn Zaydun, famous for his love poetry, was disgraced twice by his court intrigues and eventually fled to Seville. He had been spurned by his love, Wallada, the wealthy daughter of the short-lived caliph, Muhammad III. She was a poet herself and maintained a lively literary salon; famous for her affairs, she composed sexually explicit poetry brazenly mocking her unsuccessful suitors. It was the love of another poet-wazir, Ahmad ibn 'Abdus, that displaced Ibn Zaydun in her heart and precipitated his exile. Meanwhile, for ordinary Muslims (as well as the remaining Christians and Jews of the city), life was equally uncertain, but for rather more mundane reasons: persistent economic and financial insecurity. In 1070, twelve years after Muhammad al-Rashid had ceded effective power to his despotic son 'Abd al-Malik, the people of Córdoba, tired of their abusive rule, opened their gates to al-Mu'tamid of Seville and handed the king and his son over as captives.

Seville would experience its greatest glory under Abu 'l-Qasim's son, al-Mu'tadid, whose twenty-seven-year reign, which began in 1042, was characterized by relentless conquest. Al-Mu'tadid justified his campaigns on the basis of his inheritance of the title of *hajib* and on his reputation as a champion of indigenous "Arabs" against foreign North Africans. This posturing has led some historians to characterize the conflicts of *taifa*-era al-Andalus as ethnic or racial in origin, but this is wrong. The *taifa* era witnessed ever-shifting political alliances and rivalries; Zanata and Sanhaja Berbers and Andalusis formed alliances against their fellows as often as they fought against each other, and bloody rivalries appeared even within the ruling families. The political environment of postcaliphal al-Andalus was ruthlessly pragmatic, reflexively opportunistic, and highly atomized. Among the clans, families, and individuals that struggled to hold power, none had a coherent ideological or religious platform, and their internal politics were characterized by regular usurpations, betrayals, revolts, and intrafamilial violence. Indeed, in the world of *taifa* politics, it was in many ways more prudent for Muslim rulers to seek alliances with outsiders who were seen to pose less of a threat and could be, in theory, easily dispensed with, hence the opportunities that opened up for Andalusi Jews in *taifa* courts and the increasing role played by foreign Christians in Andalusi armies during the second half of the eleventh century.

In this volatile atmosphere, the calculating al-Mu'tadid thrived. Bullying the neighboring kingdoms into forming a coalition under his rule, he attacked the minor *taifa* states to his west one by one, extending his territory to the shores of the Atlantic and what is now the south of Portugal. He encountered the stiffest resistance from the kingdom of Badajoz—the former Lower March—an expansive, populous, and well-fortified kingdom that had come under the control of an Arabized Berber family called the Banu 'l-Aftas. Despite some successes, including the brief capture and imprisonment of the kingdom's ruler, Badajoz was simply too strong to conquer. Nor was Seville in a position to wage war against the powerful *taifa* of Toledo to the north.

Thus, as al-Mu'tadid reached his territorial limits to the north and west, he turned on his allies. In 1053 he invited the Berber rulers of Ronda (Runda), Moron (Mawrur), and Arcos (Arkush)—mercenary captains who had carved out tiny principalities in the aftermath of the civil war—together with their households to Seville to attend a banquet. Offering them time in a bathhouse to prepare for the feast, he had his men brick up the entrances and leave them inside to die of hunger in slow agony, their screams echoing in the surrounding streets. In the aftermath, the now-defenseless inhabitants of these towns pledged allegiance to al-Mu'tadid. The king took care to convey to visitors his unflinching brutality: the skulls of his enemies and erstwhile allies were repurposed as flower pots and put on display in his royal garden. In the later 1050s when his son and heir-designate,

Isma'il, tried to break away and found his own kingdom based in Algeciras, al-Mu'tadid had him recalled to the capital, where he put him to death by his own hand and ordered the extermination of his son's family, women and children included.

For all his cold brutality, al-Mu'tadid was no philistine. He composed quite good poetry—although his compositions tended to sing only of warfare and conquest—and like the other *taifa* rulers of the peninsula, he strove to create a culture of extravagant sophistication to reflect his elevated station. Like his contemporaries, he enjoyed wine and women; although he officially married only once, he is said to have had no less than twenty sons and twenty daughters by his various concubines. As Seville's fortunes rose, astronomers, physicians, poets, and scholars flocked in, thanks to al-Mu'tadid's lavish patronage and his championing of Arabic culture. His son Muhammad was tutored by the likes of the exiled Córdoban poet, Ibn Zaydun, who had become a wazir of al-Mu'tadid.

Muhammad became a highly accomplished poet himself and a legendary figure of romance. When he inherited the kingdom in 1069, he took the throne name al-Mu'tamid in honor of his beloved wife, a former slave, I'timad al-Rumaykiyya, herself also a poet. He had encountered I'timad as he strolled incognito with a friend along a riverbank where she was washing clothes. He had extemporized a half-verse of poetry for his companion to finish, but it was I'timad who interrupted, calling out a refrain. Turning to see her, he was smitten. He immediately purchased her from her owner, freed her, and married her. She would be his only wife and would stay at his side even when he was deposed and sent into exile by the Almoravids. Another infatuation, however, had nearly led to disgrace and to the loss of his kingdom.

In 1053, Muhammad ibn 'Ammar, a poet of humble origins from the town of Silves on the Atlantic coast, arrived in Seville and deployed flattering verses to insinuate himself into the good graces of al-Mu'tadid. He became the king's drinking companion and an intimate of the boy-prince, the future al-Mu'tamid, whom he accompanied when the latter was dispatched to Silves as governor at age twelve. Soon, rumors drifted back to Seville that the two had become lovers, and a furious al-Mu'tadid recalled his son, while Ibn

'Ud player at garden party. *Hadith Bayad wa-Riyadh* (early thirteenth century). *Jorge Fernandez-Oronoz (Archivo Oronoz)*

'Ammar fled to Zaragoza. When the adult al-Mu'tamid came to the throne in 1068/69, he welcomed the poet back and made him his closest advisor. But the scheming Ibn 'Ammar led Seville's armies on a series of ill-conceived adventures against the neighboring kingdoms, resulting in a string of defeats that left Seville deeply dependent on expensive military aid from Castile and León. In 1078, Ibn 'Ammar's ambitions were laid bare when, having seized Murcia in the name of Seville, he declared himself an independent king, backed up by Berenguer II of Barcelona. Quickly overthrown, he would spend the next six years stirring up trouble in various *taifa* courts. When al-Mu'tamid finally got ahold of Ibn 'Ammar, he cast

him into prison, where the poet persisted in his attempts at manipulation and intrigue until, in a fit of pique, al-Mu'tamid personally
struck his former lover's head off with an axe.

A capable if somewhat detached ruler, al-Mu'tamid was himself a
highly regarded poet and a legendary bon vivant. The brilliant court
culture he inherited from his father thrived under his rule, particularly
after 1058's annexation of Córdoba, and after 1085, when Alfonso VI's
conquest of Toledo forced the scholars and scientists of that city to seek
new patrons. The renowned astronomer al-Zarqullah, who invented an
improved astrolabe, settled in Seville, as did the physician, botanist,
and pharmacologist Ibn Wafid ("Abenguefit," to Latin Europeans) and
the agronomist Ibn Bassal, who designed al-Mu'tamid's royal garden.
And if Córdoba remained the epicenter of Andalusi theological studies,
Seville was a leader in poetry. The Toledan *qadi* and historian of science Said ibn Said characterized Seville as the "kingdom of poetry,"
Toledo as the "kingdom of science," and Zaragoza as the "kingdom of
philosophy." The poetry of the king was widely admired even after his
death, and he is generally judged to be the finest Andalusi poet of his
generation. While his father had composed self-aggrandizing verses
celebrating his victories and exaggerating his own power, al-Mu'tamid's
poems celebrate sentiment and sensuality. Even his famous victory
poem, composed at his conquest of Córdoba, likened the fallen city to
a bride—a conquest of love, not war.

In *taifa*-era al-Andalus, poetry focused on wine and eroticism (involving both women and boys). Many compositions were inspired by
the all-night wine parties that had become a fixture of aristocratic
culture, where men lounged inebriated in gardens under the moon,
extemporizing verse as their cups were filled by smooth-cheeked
slaves. For a poet in the presence of a king, a flattering couplet might
be rewarded with a rich gift, whereas a lengthy panegyric could lead
to a position in court, a pension, or an estate. Two outstanding figures
who came to Seville late in al-Mu'tamid's reign were Muhammad ibn
al-Labbana, from Denia, and Muhammad ibn Hamdis, who had fled
the Norman conquest of Islamic Sicily. Both were deeply attached to
their lord and followed him into exile at Aghmat.

THE 'ABBADIDS' MAIN adversary, the kingdom of Granada, produced nothing of Arabic culture but was a center of Jewish letters. In the aftermath of the disintegration of the caliphate, the Zirid family, who had come from Ifriqiya to serve in the caliphal army, had consolidated their rule over the plains stretching out to the north and east of the Sierra Nevada and the capital city they founded, Granada. Warriors by vocation, they barely spoke Arabic and were keenly aware of their status as foreigners. They had been invited by the Jews of the region to serve as their kings and ruled over a population of their fellow Sanhaja, as well as Zanata Berbers, with the bulk of their subjects consisting of indigenous Muslim Andalusis, Jews, and a smattering of Christians.

From the outset, the Zirids faced hostile neighbors on virtually every side: 'Abbadid Seville, Hammudid Málaga, and slave-ruled Almería. This was the backdrop for one of the most intriguing episodes of the *taifa* era: the vertiginous rise and fall of the Jewish Banu Naghrilla family. The head of the family, Isma'il ibn Naghrilla, had been raised in the caliphate on the brink of its collapse. A member of the palace elite raised in childhood at Madinat al-Zahra', he had been educated in Arabic, Hebrew, and Latin (as well as, it seems, Amazigh, or Berber) and had been trained in medicine, *adab*, and Islamic and Jewish law and theology by the best teachers in the capital. A refugee from the uprisings in Córdoba, he found safe haven first in Málaga, and then around 1020 in Granada, where his brilliant command of Arabic composition and his knowledge of the Qur'an landed him a position as a secretary in the kingdom's administration.

The first Zirid king, Habbus ibn Maksan, placed great confidence in Isma'il, who served him as an advisor, tax collector, and secretary, and who helped the king defuse a conspiracy within the ruling family to assassinate Habbus's son and heir, Badis. As Isma'il's fortunes rose, he took up the role of leader of the Jewish community—first of Granada and then of al-Andalus. Proclaimed *ha-Nagid*, or "Prince of the Jews," he created an immense network of scholars, and his palace in Granada became a center for Jewish learning and literary production, specifically poetry and legal writings. Jewish thinkers came from far and wide to enjoy his patronage and hospitality. At the time, Hebrew was beginning to reemerge as a living vernacular and literary language, due in large part to the work of scholars including Isma'il and his contemporaries in al-Andalus, who developed a modern Hebrew modeled on Arabic grammatical theory, and who began to compose poetry and prose in this new mode. Like Hasdai ibn Shaprut in the time of 'Abd al-Rahman III, Isma'il saw himself in a messianic light—a "new David"—a protector, patron, and advocate for Jews across the Islamic world. Lamps in Jerusalem burned with oil he had paid for. In this role, he not only lobbied to protect Jewish communities across the Mediterranean and sent alms as far afield as the Holy Land, but waged a bitter struggle against the Rabbinate's enemies, the Karaite Jews.

Under Habbus's successor, Badis, a melancholy drunkard who came to power in 1038, Isma'il's influence continued to rise. He was clearly an extremely charismatic individual and a master strategist. By manipulating divisions within Granada, and playing the middle between the king and his Andalusi Muslim and Zanata rivals, Isma'il gained the trust of virtually every faction in the kingdom. As a consiglieri and tax administrator who effectively squeezed revenue from the kingdom's subjects, particularly his fellow Jews, his personal fortune grew exponentially. After taking a leading role in crushing the army of the slave-ruled *taifa* of Almería when it attacked Granada in 1038, Isma'il soon found himself (at least according to his claims) in charge of the kingdom's (Muslim) army. He spent much of the rest of his career on campaign, as Granada sparred against Seville and conquered Málaga. Such was his fame that when he died in 1058 he was lauded across al-Andalus and much of the Jewish Mediterranean, and was widely praised by Muslim contemporaries as well, who admired his wisdom, gentility, savoir faire, and command of the Arabic language and Qur'an. More than any other of the many Jewish courtiers of the *taifa* period, Isma'il was deeply integrated into the sociocultural milieu of the *khassa*. For all his pious rigor and orthodoxy, he was also famous as a lover of pleasure; he spent many nights at wine parties, and in addition to his sacred and profane Hebrew poetry, wrote verses in Arabic extolling the erotic beauty of the slave girls and boys who served him.

But, not everyone was happy with Isma'il. As in the rest of al-Andalus, the political factions in Granada did not correspond neatly

to religious or ethnic communities, and he had both allies and enemies among the Muslims and Jews of the kingdom. However, his
identity as a Jew gave his Muslim rivals a wedge to use against him,
given that it was considered an offense to Islam for any non-Muslim
to wield authority in a Muslim kingdom or to rise above the subject
status of a *dhimmi*. When Almería attacked Granada in 1038, it was
reported that part of the rationale was to disempower Isma'il. Yet, in
fact, virtually all the larger *taifa* kingdoms employed Jewish subjects
in positions of influence. Almería would also have a Jewish wazir,
and al-Mut'amid of Seville would employ a Jew, Isaac ben Baruch
Albalia, as his court astrologer for two decades. However, at a time
when the fortunes of Islamic al-Andalus seemed to be tilting into decline, and as pious Muslims increasingly attributed this weakening to
the *taifa* kings' lax observation of Islamic law and morality, powerful
Jews could be targeted by reactionary elements among the *'ulama'*.
When Ibn Hazm, who had grown up alongside Isma'il in the caliphal
palace, received a report of an anti-Muslim polemic purportedly (but
almost certainly falsely) penned by the Jewish wazir, he reacted with
fury, composing a scathing tract against Isma'il and Judaism.

After Isma'il's death in 1056, his son, Yusuf, attempted to continue the family's domination of the Zirid kingdom and was eventually able also to serve as wazir. However, he had inherited neither the
prudence nor the charisma of his father and soon made powerful enemies, both among the women of the harem and among the *'ulama'*.
After being driven out of the capital by Yusuf's machinations, the
poet and *'alim* Abu Ishaq of Elvira penned a vitriolic ode to Badis,
shaming him for allowing a Jew to hold such power in his kingdom
and enjoining the king to slaughter him "like a ram" and to humiliate
the "filthy" Jewish *dhimmis* of Granada.[26] However, far from representing an anti-Jewish turn among either the *'ulama'* or the populace,
Abu Ishaq's screed would have been seen by most for what it was—a
personal retaliation against a political rival.

Nevertheless, Yusuf's position became increasingly imperiled,
as factions within the palace vied to succeed the increasingly ineffi-
cacious Badis. When the king's elder son, Buluqqin, collapsed dead
after leaving a wine party at Yusuf's al-Hambra palace, the wazir

was widely blamed for poisoning the prince. Hemmed in by his ever-multiplying enemies and hoping to fulfill his father's messianic ambitions, Yusuf formulated a daring plan. In 1066, he secretly approached al-Mu'tasim, the ruler of the powerful *taifa* of Almería, and offered to open the gates of Granada to him, after which Yusuf would rule the city as his client-king. Al-Mu'tasim agreed, and on the eve of the coup Yusuf held a celebratory banquet and disclosed his plan to his confidants among the elite of Granada.

But, it was not to be. At the last minute, al-Mu'tasim lost his nerve and pulled his army back; once it was revealed that Yusuf had planned to betray Badis and eliminate the Zirid royal family, the loyal people of the city rose up and attacked the al-Hambra, killing Yusuf's confederates, including many Jews, and hunted down the fleeing traitor, whom they crucified. Although the details of the uprising are sketchy at best, modern historians were quick to label it a pogrom and a turning point in Muslim-Jewish relations. This was clearly not the case. Yusuf and those seen as his allies and associates (and who may have indeed included numbers of innocent Jews) were not killed because of their religion but rather because of his treachery. This was a "normal" event in the context of eleventh-century Andalusi politics, little different from the Córdobans' slaughter of the Berber populace in the opening phases of the *fitna*. What was extraordinary is that a Jew could openly wield such tremendous power in a Muslim kingdom, and that a Jew could conceive of becoming a king under the protection of a Muslim sovereign. And while it is true that Yusuf's identity as a *dhimmi* may have lent a certain righteous indignation to the attackers, not all Jews were targeted for retaliation, and Jewish life not only recuperated but thrived in Granada in the immediate years that followed.

THE ELIMINATION OF Yusuf ibn Naghrilla did nothing to stabilize Granada. In 1073, when Badis died and his teenage son, 'Abd Allah, was proclaimed successor, an elder son, Tamim, who held the governorship of Málaga, declared independence. Worse, the ongoing war with Seville had only intensified with the accession of al-Mu'tamid in 1068/69, when the Sevillan king's scheming poet-wazir, Ibn 'Ammar, embarked on a series of military adventures against Córdoba, Granada, and the *taifa* of Toledo. While al-Mu'tamid managed to gain considerable territory, it came at a heavy price: dependency on the king of León and Castile, Alfonso VI. Alfonso provided military support to Seville but demanded a heavy tribute of cash in return. The cost of these payments, or *parias*, would weigh heavily on the subjects of the *taifa* kingdom, who were already struggling under the burden of their ruler's extravagant court. 'Abd Allah of Granada was obliged to respond in kind, and in seeking support from Castile and León was also forced to pay tribute.

And so it was that when the armies of the two *taifa* kingdoms clashed at the Battle of Cabra in 1079, each was led by a detachment of Castilian knights. The commander of those supporting al-Mu'tamid was a seasoned warrior named Rodrigo Díaz de Vivar. When he routed 'Abd Allah's forces and their leader, his bitter enemy García Ordoñez, the Muslim troops of Seville acclaimed Rodrigo as al-sayyid ("lord," in Arabic), which his Castilian countrymen imitated, calling him El Cid. This supposed icon of the "Spanish Reconquest" actually spent much of his career defending Muslim kingdoms against their Muslim and Christian enemies.

17

The Return of the King

Isma'il ibn Dhi 'l-Nun, the king of the *taifa* kingdom of Toledo, was in for a shock. In 1038 he was rallying forces to march on Muslim Zaragoza, where a coup within the ruling family had led to the assassination of his kinsman, King Mundhir II al-Tujibi, and the seizure of the throne by the victim's cousin 'Abd Allah. Isma'il was bent on revenge, and as frontier chiefs had done so many times in the past, he called on the Christians of the north for support. But instead of troops, Fernando I, the young count of Castile, sent a message that reflected the shifting balance of power in the peninsula:

> We . . . demand our land, which a long time ago you conquered and which you have inhabited for as long as had been ordained [by God]. Now He has given us victory over you on account of your wickedness. Depart to your own shores [of North Africa] and give our land up to us. For there is no good in your living with us any longer, nor will we turn away from you until God has judged between you and us.[27]

It was a declaration of war and an early expression of what would eventually become known as *La Reconquista*, or "the Reconquest"— an ideological program supported by the monarchy of Castile and

León and by the papacy, which envisioned the political history of the peninsula as a struggle between Christianity and Islam, endowed it with a moral legitimacy and sense of historical inevitability, and supported the Leonese monarchs' claims to be the heirs of the Visigothic kings and the rulers of all of Hispania, as well as territories beyond. What it was not, and what it would never be, was a call to expel the Muslim population from Spain. When Fernando issued his challenge to the king of Toledo, he was aware that the Dhi 'l-Nun were a clan originating in the Maghrib, and of the decadent reputation of the *taifa* kings. His admonition for them to depart to their own shores was an anti-foreigner, not anti-Muslim, gesture.

In fact, Christian rulers in the following centuries would often go to considerable lengths to tempt the Muslim populations they conquered to remain subjects under Christian rule. Their aim, like that of the Arabs of 711, was to conquer and dominate rather than expel the indigenous peoples. Less than a half century after Fernando's rebuke, Toledo, under the rule of Fernando's son Alfonso VI, would be the first major city of al-Andalus to fall to a Christian ruler since Barcelona in 801. The king would return to the ancient Visigothic capital, but he would not take the city by assault. Rather, he would succeed through the willing connivance of its ruler and the grudging acquiescence of its inhabitants. For his part, Alfonso would style himself not as a king of Christians, but as *al-Imbratur dhu'l-Millatayn*, the "Emperor of the Two Religious Communities": Christianity and Islam.

IN *FITNA*-ERA TOLEDO, as in Seville and Córdoba, the activist local elite—families who owned estates, practiced commerce, and served as *'ulama'*—took control of the city under the stewardship of a *qadi*. They soon found, however, that their factional disputes were weakening the kingdom and they could not defend its territories. Thus, they called on the Banu Dhi 'l-Nun, a Berber family that had come over in the first wave of the conquest in 711 and amassed a distinguished record of serving the Umayyad military. They had often raided Toledo's hinterlands but had now been invited to serve as their *sultans* and protectors. The clan's chief, 'Abd al-Tahman, sent his son Isma'il to the city in 1018/19. Taking the self-aggrandizing title of al-Zafir ("the

Victorious"), the young prince began to rule with the help of a venerable local *shaykh* named Abu Bakr ibn al-Hadidi. Never popular,
al-Zafir managed to consolidate his authority thanks to the rivalries of
local elite families, which he was able to manipulate, and once in
power, he began to wage war against his Muslim neighbors. Taxing
his subjects mercilessly, he funded a court to rival in splendor the
other great *taifas* of al-Andalus.

In the early 1040s, al-Zafir's son, Yahya, or al-Ma'mun, inherited
a kingdom that was ostensibly secure but that in fact suffered from
serious vulnerabilities and was under attack from Badajoz and from
Zaragoza. These conflicts forced al-Ma'mun to appeal to his Christian neighbors for military aid. Zaragoza had begun to pay *parias* to
Fernando I of Castile, so al-Ma'mun turned to Fernando's brother and
rival, García Sánchez III of Pamplona, who himself had designs on
Zaragoza. The alliance, which involved the payment of substantial
tribute, provoked Fernando to unleash his knights on the lands of
Toledo, where they ravaged the countryside, carrying off herds, property, and prisoners. Plunder of this sort had become an important
source of income for the Christian king, and the raids served as an
outlet for his own faction-riven military class. And Fernando's star
was rising. In 1054, his knights killed García Sánchez III in battle,
reducing Pamplona to a dependency. In 1056, he took over León and
assumed the title of "emperor."

In the 1050s and 1060s, Fernando launched raids against almost
every major Muslim kingdom, forcing them to recognize his lordship
and pay *parias*. Through their tribute, *taifa* kings were, in effect, providing Fernando the means to wage war against themselves. Leonese
expansion also met with the approval of Rome. The papacy was beginning to coalesce as an imperial authority, and new reform movements—notably the Burgundian monastic order of Cluny—were
endowing it with an ideological and institutional coherence it had
lacked in the past. Any struggle to broaden the dominion of Christendom was welcome, and before the end of the century, Pope Urban II,
himself a monk of Cluny, would launch what became known as the
First Crusade. Knowing to back a winner, the church supported Fernando's claims of sovereignty over the entire peninsula, and the

clergy, particularly those associated with the papacy and Cluny, actively promoted the notion of a Christian reconquest and the cult of Saint James "the Muslim Killer." In return, and to the growing alarm of the native Spanish clergy, Fernando supported the papacy and the Cluniac order with donations of cash, land, and positions of influence. For all that, Saint James served as the angelic agent only for Castile-León; on those occasions that knights from rival Aragon, Catalonia, and Portugal received divine assistance in battle, it was Saint George who served as their "Muslim Killer."

After consolidating his position as ruler of León, Fernando mounted a sustained series of attacks against the *taifa* of Badajoz, forcing the Banu 'l-Aftas to pay tribute and seizing a strip of land south of the Duero. In 1064 he encircled Muslim Coímbra, in what is now central Portugal. He took the town after a six-month siege. Later chroniclers would claim that Matamoros had given saintly aid to the emperor, but in reality, it was the support of local Mozarabs that made the difference. One native Christian of the region, Sisnando Davídez, had been captured as a young man in a raid by the forces of Seville, where he became a slave of the court and received a thorough education in Arabic. He served as an envoy for al-Mu'tadid until 1064, when he was invited by the victorious Fernando I to return home as "count," or *wazir*, of Coímbra. Sisnando became Fernando's key envoy to the Islamic courts of the peninsula, where his knowledge of Arabic and Andalusi culture, as well as the inner workings of the *taifa* courts, enabled him to skillfully manipulate Fernando's Muslim dependents and extract the maximum tribute.

Fernando preferred raiding and extortion to conquest, as it was less expensive and less risky to set the *taifa* kings against each other, leaving them to face the challenges of rule while he grew rich on the proceeds. The last Zirid king of Granada recalled that Sisnando, when serving as Alfonso VI's bag-man, outlined the king's strategy when he came to collect tribute:

> Al-Andalus originally belonged to the Christians. They were defeated by the Arabs and driven to the most inhospitable region, Galicia. Now that they are strong and capable, the Christians

desire to recover what they have lost by force. This can only be achieved by weakness and encroachment. In the long run, when [al-Andalus] has neither men, nor money, we'll be able to recover it without any difficulty.[28]

Castile would bleed them dry. That said, the tributary relationship between the Christian princes and their Muslim clients was not purely exploitative. Many of the payments came back into the *taifa* kingdoms in the form of purchases of luxury and manufactured goods, thereby helping to sustain the craft industries and commerce in the region, particularly in frontier kingdoms like Toledo. Ironically, many of the *'ulama'* who objected most vociferously to the payment of *parias* were members of the artisanal class who most benefited from this trade.

Back in Toledo, al-Ma'mun was pushed into a double bind. When the war with Zaragoza forced him to seek an alliance with Seville in 1044/45, the urban elite of his city, fearful of 'Abbadid domination, rose up in revolt, and the situation was saved only by the action of his loyal wazir Ibn al-Hadidi. As the neighboring *taifa* rulers increasingly encroached on his kingdom, al-Ma'mun had no choice but to throw himself on Fernando's mercy, bribing him with great treasures, so that the Castilian ruler would put a stop to Zaragoza's incursions. But the exorbitant tribute weighed on his kingdom, as al-Ma'mun passed the burden on to his subjects through ever-heavier taxation. And to the scandal of pious Toledans, the king became a close subordinate of Fernando, going so far as to send troops in support of a punitive mission against the fellow Muslim kingdom of Granada, which had refused to pay *parias*.

Al-Ma'mun's opportunism was laid bare in 1061, when Fernando launched a campaign to conquer the kingdom of Valencia, which was ruled by a grandson of Shanjul. After Fernando fell ill and canceled his invasion, al-Ma'mun did not take the opportunity to shrug off the domination of Castile-León but instead took Valencia for himself, deposing its ruler, 'Abd al-Malik al-Muzaffar—his own son-in-law. He followed up this coup by joining forces with Seville to attack Córdoba in 1069, but once the armies were in place, al-Mu'tamid

double-crossed al-Ma'mun by taking the city and locking out Toledo's forces. It took six years of effort for al-Ma'mun to finally wrest
the former caliphal capital from his treacherous erstwhile ally.

Al-Ma'mun's victories in Valencia and Córdoba provided him
with the resources to people his court with notable poets and scholars,
as was expected of any successful *taifa* king. Thanks to his patronage,
Toledo gained renown as a center for the sciences, including astronomy and astrology, agronomy and botany, pharmaceuticals, medicine, engineering, and the learning of the classical world—what
Muslims had come to call the "science of the ancients." It was said
that after al-Mansur purged the caliphal library in the 990s to satisfy
the conservative *'ulama'*, many scientific texts were smuggled to Toledo where they were incorporated into local libraries, and in the unrest of the *fitna*, learned Jews from the south had taken refuge in the
city, further invigorating the intellectual culture there. Al-Zarqullah,
known as Azarquiel to his Latin readers and the most important European astronomer and astrologer until Copernicus, found an intellectual home here. During his time in the city, he discovered elliptical
planetary orbits; elaborated the "Toledan Tables" (which were used
during the Renaissance to calculate celestial movements); perfected
various astronomical instruments; and constructed a large clepsydra,
or water clock, which could keep time night and day.

Neither poet nor intellectual, al-Ma'mun preferred to spend his
time in a sprawling, rural villa, al-Munya al-Mansurah, which he
constructed outside the walls of Toledo on the banks of the Tagus
River and that featured expansive grounds set with ponds, pavilions,
and fountains. The treatises on pharmacology and agronomy produced by scientists working in the king's gardens here would be regarded as fundamental texts in Europe through the sixteenth century.
It was here that al-Ma'mun welcomed envoys and visitors, held all-
night wine and poetry parties, and marked important royal and personal occasions, earning him the epithet "the lover of gardens." What
the king really loved was flaunting his wealth; the celebration of the
circumcision of his grandson Yahya ibn Isma'il became proverbial
for its excess. Grandees were invited from across al-Andalus, and
guests were sent away with hands full of gold coins. Portentously, in

Brass astrolabe made
by Ibrahim ibn Sa'id
al-Sahli (Toledo, 1068
CE) with Arabic and
Latin inscriptions.
*Museum of the History
of Science, Oxford
(#55331)*

1072, the estate was briefly the home-in-exile to a young prince from
the north, whom his host would have referred to as Alfunsh ibn
Fernando—the future Alfonso VI.

WHY SUCH GENEROSITY to a Christian prince? Al-Ma'mun was riding high. Valencia was his, Zaragoza had been cowed, Badajoz was
reeling from decades of attacks, and he was gaining the upper hand
over Seville. Most importantly, the weight of León was off his back.
As formidable as Fernando's empire had appeared, by 1072 it had
been dismantled. In 1065, Fernando had made it home from Valencia but had died on December 27 of that year. And thus, his accomplishments were nearly undone—not by the strength of his rivals
but by his affinity for the Germanic traditions of his distant Visigothic ancestors. For, rather than passing all his realms on to one
heir, he divided them among his three sons: Sancho, who was given
Castile; García, who inherited Galicia; and Alfonso, the heir to

León. His daughters, Urraca and Elvira, received the towns of Zamora and Toro, respectively.

The brothers immediately set on each other, and Sancho gained an early advantage. Aided by his champion, Rodrigo Díaz de Vivar, and supported by his brother Alfonso, he successfully waged war on Christian Navarre and Aragon, which were ruled over by his cousins Sancho IV and Sancho II, respectively. The pretext was to provide support for *taifa* Zaragoza, which the two kingdoms had been attacking, in an effort to get a piece of the tribute that had been going to Castile. Next, Sancho and Alfonso attacked their brother, García, forcing the defeated king to flee into exile to the court of al-Mu'tamid of Seville, after which his two brothers divided up his lands. But their fraternal concord would be short-lived; Sancho turned on Alfonso and seized the kingdom of León in 1072.

So it was that Sancho ended up with the crowns of his father's three realms, and the young Alfonso wound up in gilded exile in al-Ma'mun's al-Munya al-Mansurah. Although he was there for only a few months, Alfonso, who would have certainly been an Arabic-speaker, had a chance to survey Toledo's weaknesses and get a read on its fractious domestic politics. Unburdened by any sense of gratitude to al-Ma'mun, Alfonso's stay demonstrated to him that the *taifa* kings were unworthy rulers: "clearly all victims of madness, indulging in every manner of vice and iniquity, and passing their lives among a host of singers and lute-players."[29] Not a few of their Muslim subjects were reaching the same conclusion.

Alfonso's sojourn was cut short by events in León. Sancho had attacked their sister Urraca at Zamora in October 1072. During the course of the siege, one of her noblemen feigned betrayal, and when he was being interviewed by Sancho, assassinated the king. Some attribute Urraca's intervention to an incestuous passion she shared with Alfonso. In any event, with Sancho dead, Alfonso hurried back to León to seize the crown. Once he did, he demanded al-Mu'tamid give up his brother García, who would spend the last seventeen years of his life imprisoned in a monastery. The new king controlled a sprawling domain, stretching across the north of the peninsula. He immediately set out to reestablish the tributary relations his father,

Fernando, had forced on the *taifa*. But his noblemen turned against each other; the great families of León, Castile, and Galicia, who dominated the royal court and local churches, regarded nobility from neighboring regions as rivals. The Leonese, in particular, would resist the incorporation of Castilians, like Rodrigo Díaz de Vivar, into the king's inner circles at almost any cost. To maintain peace at home, Alfonso would have to make war abroad.

This was bad news for al-Ma'mun, who was facing increasing resistance from the *'ulama'* of Toledo and the urban patriciate they represented. Unable to strike at their king directly, they weaponized Islamic law to attack his supporters, accusing one of his leading scholars, Ibn al-Hatim, of "heresy" and a litany of offenses, including eating pork, drinking wine, homosexuality, and mocking Islam. What happened next would demonstrate the reach of the religious class in al-Andalus and the effectiveness of the peninsula-wide network they had created.

Condemned to death in Toledo, Ibn al-Hatim escaped to the Lower March, where the king, al-Mutawakkil, gave him shelter. But when the *faqihs* of Toledo forwarded their sentence to their counterparts in Badajoz, al-Mutawakkil withdrew his protection, and Ibn al-Hatim next fled to Córdoba and the protection of al-Mu'tamid of Seville. But al-Mu'tamid saw Ibn al-Hatim as a means of getting revenge on al-Ma'mun, and in 1072 he allowed the death sentence to be carried out. It was a masterstroke: the reprisals a furious al-Ma'mun unleashed against the *'ulama'* of Toledo pushed his capital city into revolt. Al-Mu'tamid finished the job in 1075 by bribing al-Ma'mun's physician to poison him.

The kingdom of Toledo thus passed to al-Ma'mun's grandson Yahya ibn Isma'il, who was placed on the throne with the title al-Qadir ("the Powerful"). Never was a name so ill-chosen. The young boy, coddled in the harem, had no experience and little natural ability. Sensing his weakness, al-Qadir's rivals acted swiftly: Seville seized Córdoba, while Zaragoza attacked Toledo's eastern possessions. Christian forces briefly took Cuenca, and Valencia was recovered by the 'Amirid family. In Toledo itself, riots broke out among the urban aristocracy. Then al-Qadir made the fatal mistake of appealing to Alfonso, who promised help, but only in exchange for a massive payment. When his courtiers and magnates heard this demand, they could not contain their anger. Al-Qadir turned on his own supporters but was then forced to flee, leaving the urban elite to take control of Toledo. But, realizing they were helpless without an army, the patrician families quickly called on al-Mutawakkil of Badajoz, inviting him to rule as their new king.

Like the Banu Dhi 'l-Nun, al-Mutawakkil's family, the Banu 'l-Aftas, were Berbers who had been in al-Andalus since the 700s. Having seized power in Badajoz in 1022 from its Saqaliba governor, they had to contend with attacks from Seville, Toledo, and Fernando I's Empire of León, as well as the intrafamily feuds that characterized the *taifa* dynasties. Nevertheless, they established a prosperous kingdom and supported a court famous for its high culture. Al-Mutawakkil's wazir Ibn 'Abdun was regarded as a leading literary figure of the age, a poet and author whose coterie of followers and students would eventually include 'Iyad ibn Musa, known as "the *Qadi*"—a scholar who would become the premier authority of Malikism in the Muslim West.

For al-Mutawakkil, the death of Fernando I in 1065 had brought little respite, given the continuing aggression of Seville and the renewed attacks of Toledo. To make matters worse, after taking the throne of León in 1072, Alfonso VI mounted his first military campaigns against Badajoz. Thus, rule over Toledo provided an opportunity for al-Mutawakkil to secure his borders and recoup his losses. In the end, however, he proved no more palatable to the urban elite of Toledo than al-Qadir had been, and his ten months in the city were spent emptying the treasury, looting the royal palace, and little more. Meanwhile, al-Qadir sent a petition to Alfonso VI, hoping to renew their alliance and restore himself as king. Alfonso responded with greater demands of tribute, and to drive his point home, he unleashed his warriors on the lands of both Toledo and Badajoz.

Faced with Alfonso's raiding, al-Mutawakkil decided to abandon Toledo, and the urban oligarchy was once again left defenseless and in tenuous control over an increasingly restless populace. As al-Qadir prepared to attack the city, the elite families sent their own envoys to

Alfonso offering to submit, evidently preferring a capable Christian ruler to an incompetent Muslim one. Al-Qadir managed to take back Toledo, but once in power, he could not raise the money he had promised to pay Alfonso as tribute. In response, the Leonese monarch established a gradually shrinking perimeter around the city, until by late 1084 it was cut off from its hinterland. Alfonso was living in the palace of al-Munya al-Mansurah, but now as an occupier rather than a guest. With the populace going hungry as a consequence of the siege and support at an all-time low, al-Qadir offered to hand the city over to Alfonso on the condition that the Leonese ruler install him as client-king in Valencia. For Alfonso, the prospect of taking Toledo without a fight was an appealing one, and a parley was arranged between city leaders and his Mozarab envoy, Sisnando Davídez. The city would surrender.

TOLEDO WAS TAKEN without bloodshed when the leaders of the Muslim populace opened the gates to Alfonso. Their acquiescence was achieved through the combination of the threat of starvation and warfare and the promise of security and prosperity. Some sources claim that to relieve the suffering the inhabitants had endured, Alfonso granted them a massive gift of cash; whether or not that happened, his envoy to the city, Sisnando, went to great lengths to assure them that their lives would continue as much as possible like before. Framing the agreement in terms they would understand, the Muslims of Toledo would become *dhimmis* of the Christians, and in exchange for their subordination and tribute they would be guaranteed security of person and property and the freedom to maintain their religion and live by their own laws. The city's great mosque, it was promised, would remain their place of worship. Crucially for them, and necessarily for Alfonso, the leaders of the community maintained their position and their power over their coreligionists. Likewise, Toledo's Mozarabic and Jewish communities and the newly arrived Latin settlers would be given similar charters and would each be subject to their own legal codes and administered by their community leaders. The message was continuity, not catastrophe; it was a strategy that would be followed almost without exception in the centuries of Christian conquest.

And so it was that on May 25, 1085, the ancient Visigothic capital of Toledo was returned to Christian rule, the first major city of al-Andalus to be lost by the Muslims. It was a curious victory, one that mirrored the Islamic conquest nearly four centuries earlier. And for all its symbolism and historical resonance, it left little mark on the imagination of contemporary Christians. Their histories gloss over it with hardly a detail; they do not even agree on the date. For Muslims, on the other hand, it seemed to be a tragedy of unimaginable proportions and a loss that for many foreshadowed the destruction of al-Andalus.

Despite Alfonso's concessions, it seems that there was considerable migration from the city. Most of the 'ulama' could simply not brook living under Christian rule, a circumstance that was broadly regarded as illicit under Islamic law. Most of the intellectual elite headed for other taifa courts, where they could seek patronage and prosperity. Poets wrote impassioned laments and religious scholars railed at the tragedy of Islam's loss. As for the artisans and the common people, many headed south as refugees, while others seem to have converted to Christianity in resignation of the changing times. Even a few members of the upper classes converted, doubtless inspiring others to follow. One prominent faqih shallowly excused his own apostasy by observing that as a Christian he would still be worshipping the same God. The fact that the substantial Christian community of the city spoke Arabic and identified as Andalusi—many even bore Islamicate names like 'Abd Allah and 'Uthman—would have made conversion easier. Unlikely as the story may be, the conversion of Toledan Muslims is echoed in a later folk tradition that tells of two members of the Dhi 'l-Nun clan, Saint Casilda of Briviesca and Saint Peter of Sopretán, both of whom chose baptism over exile.

With the rapid decline of the Muslim population in Toledo, it should come as no surprise that the original surrender agreement did not hold for long. When Sisnando was called away from the city to other duties, Alfonso sent his Burgundian queen, Constance, to govern with the help of her confessor, the Cluniac monk Bernard of Sahagún, both foreigners with little sympathy for or understanding of their Muslim subjects. He became the new archbishop of Toledo and thus the titular head of the Christians of all of Spain. In short order, the city mosque was appropriated and converted into the new cathedral, and many of the concessions made to the city's Muslims were rolled back.

But if Bernard, Constance, and their fellow Burgundian noblemen and clergy—whom Alfonso was bringing into the kingdom in greater numbers—saw the Christian conquest of al-Andalus in terms of a civilizational conflict, Spanish Christian noblemen and clergy did not. They were more concerned with the Burgundian invasion and the increasing influence of the Roman church, which was infringing on their religious autonomy and political power. Alfonso had married off two of his daughters, Urraca and Teresa, who would inherit Castile-León and Portugal, respectively, to the cousins Raymond and Henri of Burgundy. The papacy and its agents saw their ancient Christian traditions as retrograde, and in 1080, Alfonso would proscribe the Mozarabic liturgy and require services to follow the new rite established by Rome.

For Alfonso, the reconquest, to the extent that he conceived of it as such, was a political mission to restore Christianity to its rightful position at the top of the religious hierarchy. He presented himself as the "Emperor of All of the Spains," the legitimate overlord of both the Christian and the Muslim kingdoms of the peninsula, together with all their Christian, Muslim, and Jewish inhabitants. A thirteenth-century chronicle describes how after Bernard and Constance seized the mosque, Alfonso was furious that they had caused his pledge to be broken and sullied his reputation, and he threatened to execute them both; it was only due to the intervention of the city's Muslims that he was persuaded not to. Apocryphal as the tale may be, it reflects the tenuous nature of political power at the time, and how it was crucial for rulers to maintain the goodwill and trust of their subjects, including infidels. And so, with Toledo under Alfonso's control, Sisnando was dispatched to extort tribute from the now-terrified *taifa* kings of the south, and al-Qadir was installed as king of Valencia after a short siege carried out by a commander

named Álvar Fáñez, a nephew of the emperor's irrepressible if inconstant vassal Rodrigo Díaz de Vivar, El Cid. The emperor himself
marched his army east and assembled it outside the walls of Islamic
Zaragoza, the forces of which Rodrigo Díaz was effectively in
command.

18

A Soldier of Fortune in the Kingdom of Philosophy

Girded by the towering Pyrenees and the rich alluvial plains of the Ebro and its tributaries, the region stretching from Zaragoza to the Mediterranean had a history of independence stretching back into the pre-Roman era. As the caliphate disintegrated after the murder of Shanjul in 1009, the Banu Tujib—the Arab-descended governors of this prosperous, semi-autonomous frontier zone, set far from the upheavals of the south—were easily able to establish themselves as kings, although they followed the same polite fiction as their *taifa* contemporaries and presented themselves as *hajib*s of an absent caliph. This is not to say their succession was untroubled. The clan was beset by the typical internal rivalries, which pitted brother against brother, cousin against cousin, and in which client families intrigued to overthrow their patrons. Compounding the instability, they were nearly surrounded by Christian principalities that had until recently been underpopulated and subdued backwaters. Now, it seemed the balance of power was changing. Locally, the period of Andalusi political disarray coincided with one of Christian dynastic unity, while generally, a warming climate trend was contributing to population growth in the high valleys of the Pyrenees. The resultant demographic pressures would help spur a movement of conquest and colonization, as Christian inhabitants from the increasingly crowded highlands moved down into the Muslim-ruled lowlands.

This fleeting union of the Christian principalities was forged by Sancho III "the Great" of Pamplona, the great-great-grandson of 'Abd al-Rahman III's aunt Toda. Sancho took the throne in 1004, just as al-Andalus was sliding toward chaos. However, rather than waging war against the weakening caliphate, he set out to dominate the Christian principalities of Hispania through a combination of marriage alliances, diplomacy, intrigue, and warfare. By the late 1020s, he was grudgingly recognized as lord by the various counts of the mountain valleys east of Pamplona from Aragon to Barcelona. Conflicts among the ruling families to the west enabled him to seize Castile, where he installed his son Fernando as count, and eventually to take León, where he was crowned emperor in 1034. But, he also regarded the lands to the north as his prerogative and extended his rule over the northern slopes of the Pyrenees and into the plains on the south banks of the Garonne River in Aquitaine. Pamplona thus became a bridge between the isolated Christian Spains and the larger Latin world. It was Sancho who first appreciated the potential of allying with the Roman church and with Cluny, and of drawing on the military potential of the Frankish lands. It was under his reign that ordinary northern Europeans became exposed to the allure of Islamic Spain via the pilgrimage route to Santiago de Compostela, which ran through the breadth of his lands, and the notion that it was God's will they bring it under their power.

FOR THE FIRST decades of the *taifa* era, the Banu Tujib maintained a semblance of the pre-*fitna* balance of power. Mundhir ibn Yahya, the Umayyad governor-cum-king, maintained a loose authority over the towns of his realm through kinsmen and clients, and the title was passed on smoothly to his son Yahya in 1023, and then on to his son Mundhir II in 1029/30. Like the capital, Zaragoza, the robust prosperity of their towns was anchored in local agricultural and craft output, which served regional markets and was not directly dependent on Córdoba. The border between the Muslim-dominated lowlands and the Christian-ruled mountain valleys remained porous; members of the elites continued to intermarry, and common folk raided, traded, and passed their herds through each other's lands. The Tujibids even managed to maintain their role as an intermediary, if not patron, of the neighboring Christian lords. Hence, when, in an effort to stave off the pretensions of their common enemy, Sancho III of Pamplona, Sancho Garcés of Castile married his daughter Sancha to Berengeur Ramon I of Barcelona in 1021, the princely wedding was held in Zaragoza and hosted by Mundhir I. Like the other *taifa* kings, the Tujibids saw their goal as dominating al-Andalus, not the Christian North, and set out to infiltrate their counterparts' kingdoms through marriage alliances and intrigues.

The effects of the unrest in the south, however, would be felt even here, where the counterclaims of the Hammudid caliphs, Seville's pseudo-Hisham II, and the deposed Hisham III constituted an ideological wedge that could be exploited by ambitious members of the ruling clan, with the encouragement of Christian rulers like Sancho III. In 1038/39, Mundhir II was assassinated by his cousin, the *qadi* 'Abd Allah, who then claimed the title of *hajib*. In a foreshadowing of the later uprising in Granada, one of the victims of this revolt was Yequtiel ibn Ishaq, Mundhir's Jewish wazir, who, like Yusuf ibn Naghrella, had been a generous patron of Hebrew letters. 'Abd Allah's reign, however, would last less than a month; the people of Zaragoza rose up against the regicide and attacked his fortress-palace in Zaragoza, forcing him to flee and allowing Sulayman ibn Hud, a Tujibid client who had been governor of Lleida and a respected military commander, to seize the throne. Ruling under the name al-Musta'in, he established a dynasty that would rule here for the next eighty years.

The Banu Hud were an Arab clan that traced their ancestry back to a Companion of the Prophet and had entrenched themselves in the Upper March as clients of the Banu Tujib. With his coup, and after fending off al-Zafir of Toledo, Sulayman took control over a large kingdom that stretched the length of the Ebro and its main tributaries down toward Valencia and included towns like Lleida, Tudela, Huesca, and Calatayud. The capital, famous for the stout,

white Roman walls that still surrounded it, was one of the most cosmopolitan cities of al-Andalus, home to Arab and indigenous Andalusis, as well as large Mozarab and Jewish communities. Merchants,
soldiers, pilgrims, and travelers from the Christian North and Muslim South packed its markets and inns. The region's tremendous
wealth derived from its lushly fertile river valleys, together with
booming craft industries and commerce. Islamic religious and intellectual culture had been firmly established throughout the realm
during the caliphate. Scores of leading Muslim and Jewish scholars,
particularly grammarians, physicians, mathematicians, and philosophers, came to the city in the aftermath of the uprising in Córdoba,
prompting the eleventh-century historian of science Said ibn Said to
call Zaragoza the "Kingdom of Philosophy."

Encircled by competing Christian principalities, including Castile,
Navarre, the Catalan counties, and, from 1035, the newly established
kingdom of Aragon, al-Musta'in did his best to keep these predators at
bay through a combination of diplomacy, intrigue, paying *parias*, and
launching countercampaigns. Although he managed to minimize territorial losses, his increasing dependence on Christian mercenaries and
allies alarmed some of his more pious subjects and ultimately helped
pave the way for the Christian conquest. The heightened awareness of
the frontier here, and the threat of invasion, raids, and capture, contributed to a strong popular investment in the ideal of jihad among his
subjects. However, this did not seem to affect the social and cultural
relations of the court, where intensive collaboration among Muslim,
Jewish, and Christian thinkers continued.

On his death in 1046, al-Musta'in split his realms among his five
sons. It fell to his second son, Ahmad, who was bequeathed the capital, to begin the process of reassembling the kingdom by taking on
his brothers one by one. Reigning for thirty-five years under the so-
briquet al-Muqtadir, Ahmad scored a series of military and political
successes. But the beginning was rocky; soon after he took power,
the people of Zaragoza, "disgusted" by his intrigues against his family, withdrew their loyalty and invited his brother Yusuf to rule over
them. Ahmad was only restored with the help of Sancho Ramírez of
Aragon, to whom he promised to double the *parias* paid by Yusuf.[30]

In the course of defeating his brothers, he also annexed the Slav-ruled *taifa* kingdoms of Tortosa and Denia in 1060 and 1075/76. Tortosa occupied a strategic position at the Mediterranean mouth of the Ebro River; it was an import sea and river port, and its mountainous hinterland was rich in timber. Taking Denia, which was a rich prize in itself, completed al-Muqtadir's encirclement of the *taifa* kingdom of Valencia. In 1063, he defeated and killed King Ramiro I of Aragon at the Battle of Graus, and in 1065, he reconquered Barbastro, a walled town in the foothills of the Pyrenees that had been seized by Norman and Provençal forces the previous year to the great scandal and alarm of the Muslims of al-Andalus.

The Christian conquest of Barbastro was no ordinary raid. The warriors who carried it out were almost all from the European North, and they came armed not only with their weapons and shields but with a pledge from Pope Alexander II that their sins would be forgiven in return for fighting the infidel. This was a sign of a transformation taking place in Latin Europe, with the emergence of the monastic order of Cluny and the reform of the church and the papacy under Pope Gregory VII and his successors. Conscious of the gulf between the church's avowed role as Christendom's religious and moral guide and the corruption, worldliness, and neglect with which its mission was often pursued, a series of popes set out to clean up the clergy and establish a coherent code of canon law, together with a functioning institutional framework of administration, justice, and taxation. The church also endeavored to force the European warrior class to desist from the destructive cycle of internecine warfare that had plagued the continent by imposing a "Peace and Truce of God," which set out to limit how, when, where, and against whom knights could wage war.

But, thanks to an improving climate and better agricultural technology, Europe's population was growing, setting members of the burgeoning noble class on the move in search of lands to rule. A booming economy, meanwhile, helped spark a commercial revolution that saw Italian traders fan out into the Greek and Muslim Mediterranean in search of luxury goods to sell at home. This prompted Western Europeans, who had previously been rather isolated, to come to terms with the existence of a larger world. In the Great Schism of 1054, the Greek and

Latin churches declared each other heretical, just at the time the Western church started to grapple with the challenge Islam posed to Christianity's universalist pretensions. Finally, a "great awakening" was imbuing the lower rural classes of European society, which were only now shaking off their residual pagan ways with a Christian consciousness and an apocalyptic fervor they had not previously possessed.

All these trends would come together in Spain, where monks carved out new settlements on the thinly settled frontiers of al-Andalus, pilgrims trekked toward Compostela to venerate its militant anti-Muslim apostle, and predatory Burgundian knights and noblemen flocked to the court of Castile-León. Although the notion of civilizational struggle between Islam and Christianity hardly informed politics in the Iberian Peninsula on either side, Christianity and Christians in the rest of Europe were defining themselves increasingly in terms of their opposition to and struggle against Islam and Judaism. It is no coincidence that it was at this time that *The Song of Roland*, with its depiction of monstrous, deceitful Saracens, took shape and began to gain popularity across the Frankish lands.

The tumultuous era also saw two other warrior groups make their dramatic appearance in al-Andalus. The first were Normans, the Christianized descendants of the Vikings who had earlier raided the emirate and who were now, with the papacy's blessing, conquering Byzantine and Islamic territory in Italy. The second were Provençals, the people of Aquitaine and Languedoc (the former Septimania), who were united by a common linguistic family, Occitan, but inhabited a mosaic of tiny, overcrowded, and perennially conflicted counties. In 1064, a large force of Norman, Provençal, and Catalan knights, recruited by Sancho Ramírez of Aragon and led by Count William VIII of Aquitaine (the great-grandfather of the troubadour queen Eleanor of Aquitaine), assembled outside the walls of Muslim Barbastro, a town in the foothills of the Pyrenees, which was then ruled by al-Muqtadir's eldest brother, al-Muzaffar of Lleida.

The Latins had been drawn by the prospect of loot and fortified with a benediction from the pope. However, the siege bogged down after meeting a stiff defense from the townsfolk. When the two sides met to parley, it was agreed that the inhabitants could leave in safety with whatever property they could carry in exchange for giving up the town. However, on seeing the long line of refugees burdened with riches, the avaricious protocrusaders could not resist sweeping down on them, truce notwithstanding, massacring the men, and carrying the women and belongings back to the town.

In Barbastro, the victors installed themselves in the homes of the former inhabitants, whose daughters now served them as slaves and concubines, while the conquerors, as reported by a Jewish traveler who passed through the town, enjoyed lives of "Oriental" luxury. The *'ulama'* of al-Andalus were scandalized as news of this outrage swept across Muslim Spain. Seeing an opportunity to capitalize on his brother al-Muzaffar's vulnerability, claim a leadership position among his fellow *taifa* kings, and present himself as a pious *mujahid*, al-Muqtadir seized the moral high ground, proclaiming that the Muslims of al-Andalus should unite under his banner and take vengeance.

The following year, he assembled an army consisting of recruits raised from various *taifa* kingdoms and reinforced by a contingent of knights sent by Fernando I, who was eager to see any Aragonese or Catalan advance forestalled. The attackers quickly overran the town, restoring it to Muslim rule and putting its treacherous conquerors to the sword. By this time, William of Aquitaine had returned home safely, taking with him considerable booty in the shape of silks, furnishings, gold and silver, and slave girls, whom he installed in his court or sent to the pope and other magnates as gifts. These women, some of whom were undoubtedly *qiyan* trained in *adab*, are thought to have been one of the vectors by which Arabo-Andalusi music and lyric entered the Western European tradition, helping to spark the troubadour culture that would emerge soon after in Aquitaine, Languedoc, and the Pyrenees.

Like al-Mu'tamid of Seville, al-Muqtadir of Zaragoza epitomized his age. For all his occasional pious posturing, he was better known for "plying the wine-cups and plucking off heads"—a generous patron of culture, and a ruthless and shrewd monarch.[31] Just to the northwest of Zaragoza's city walls and out of the view of his disapproving subjects, he raised a magnificent and stoutly defended

The "Palace of Pleasures" (Aljafería Palace, Zaragoza); exterior. *Turol Jones, 2004 (Creative Commons)*

fortress-palace as his residence and the center of his court. Its luxury was legendary; the king himself referred to it as his "Palace of Pleasures." It still stands today.

Under his patronage, Zaragoza became an important center of both Arabic and Hebrew letters and home to such literary giants as the poets and grammarians Muhammad ibn Bajja ("Avempace," to the Latin world) and the Jew Solomon ibn Gabirol (who worked mostly in Arabic). Like so many of their fellow Zaragozan men of letters, these two were also physicians and intellectual polymaths: Ibn Bajja, a philosopher, composer, and astronomer, and Ibn Gabirol, a philosopher and grammarian. In fact, the city was most famous as a center of mathematics, astronomy, medicine, and philosophy. It was home to a score of leading twelfth-century Muslim and Jewish scholars who had been swept up by both the rationalistic Aristotelian revolution and the revival of Neoplatonism that were transforming the theological and intellectual landscape of the Islamic world and that would soon provide the foundations for the European Renaissance and the new esoteric movements that developed in all three of the Abrahamic religions.

Al-Muqtadir's son and successor, Yusuf al-Mu'taman, who came to power in 1081/2, was himself one of the most notable mathematicians of his age and emulated his father's support of the sciences. Zaragoza continued to produce top-ranked scholars even as it began to unravel politically in the late eleventh century. Jewish intellectual life was particularly robust in the city. Abu 'l-Hasan Judah ha-Levi, the author of the anti-Aristotelian Jewish apologetic the *Kitab al-Khazari* ("The Book of the Khazar," also known as "The Book of Proof and Defense of the Despised Religion"), lived here. So did his close friend, the poet, exegete, and grammarian Abraham ben Ezra (or Abu Ishaq), regarded second only to his contemporary, the great French rabbi Rashi, for his Biblical commentaries. Abu Fadl ibn Hasday, a poet, musician, astronomer, and mathematician, and a grandson of the great Hasdai ibn Shaprut, was a favorite of al-Muqtadir and al-Mu'taman. He served them as *katib* and wazir and eventually converted to Islam, supposedly out of love, but more likely to advance his career. But if Abu Fadl chose Islam, others would convert to Christianity as the balance of power in the region shifted toward the north. The most notable was Moses Sephardi, baptized in 1106 as Petrus Alfonsi, who wrote both a compilation of Near Eastern fables called the *Disciplina Clericalis* and a seminal anti-Jewish tract, *The Dialogue Against the Jews.* In 1116, he became physician to Henry I, king of England.

But for all the cross-cultural collaborations that characterized the court of the Banu Hud, one of the most curious and portentous exchanges took place between an anonymous Christian cleric and the philosopher Abu'l-Walid Sulayman ibn Baji sometime in the early 1070s. Details are sketchy, but it seems that two Christian monks arrived in Zaragoza from Frankish lands and delivered a courteous, formal letter "to the beloved friend . . . the noble king," al-Muqtadir, politely excoriating Islam as an invention of the Devil and inviting him to convert to Christianity.[32] The author did not disclose his identity, but it may have been (the later Saint) Hugh the Great, Abbot of Cluny. His enormous abbey church in Burgundy, the third largest in

Christendom, had been constructed with funds raised by Fernando I's *parias*, and Hugh's order was then laying the groundwork for its war against Islam.

The monk's letter is remarkable in both its naïve confidence in the supposedly self-evident truth of Christianity and its misunderstanding of the role of religion and the individual in Islamic society. Even if al-Muqtadir had been moved by the letter's feeble arguments and converted, this would have resulted only in the king's deposal, not in his kingdom's conversion. His subjects would remain Muslim. But in any event, al-Muqtadir was not moved, except to turn the letter over to his court philosopher al-Baji, who crafted a lengthy, masterful response that refuted the missionary's arguments and presented a defense of the truth and philosophical consistency of Islam that exhibited a comprehensive grasp of the vulnerabilities of Christian theology and doctrine. But eloquence and ingenuity could not stem the tide of history; Zaragoza would become Christian not long after, when it was conquered by Alfonso I in 1118.

ANOTHER HERALD OF the changing times was the arrival in al-Mu'taman's Zaragoza of the Castilian knight Rodrigo Díaz "El Cid," along with his ragtag band of soldiers of fortune, in 1081. He had been unjustly exiled from the Leonese Empire by a mistrusting Alfonso VI and needed employment. At that time, al-Mu'taman was contending with the hostility of his brother Mundhir, king of Lleida, as well as increasing aggression from Aragon. So, he welcomed the Cid to his court and gave him command over his troops. Al-Mu'taman would not be disappointed. The Cid energetically took the war to Mundhir and his Catalan and Aragonese allies. He scored a series of stunning battlefield successes in which, at Almenar in 1082, Berenguer Ramon II of Barcelona was captured together with his baggage train, and at Morella in 1084, Mundhir and Sancho Ramírez fled the field, leaving a dozen high-ranking Aragonese noblemen and clerics to be captured and ransomed. The Cid became a popular hero in the Muslim kingdom and brought back enough booty to pay his own men and to please his *taifa* liege lord. When the throne of Zaragoza passed from al-Mu'taman to his son al-Musta'in II, the new king renewed Rodrigo's command.

Warriors at the Siege of Jerusalem, *Las Huelgas Apocalypse* (Beatus of Liébana, 1220 CE). Morgan Library and Museum MS M.429 (fols. 149v–150). *The Morgan Library & Museum/Art Resource NY*

But Alfonso VI's conquest of Toledo and al-Qadir's seizure of Valencia had profound implications for the Cid and the kingdom of Zaragoza. Following his success in Toledo, Alfonso VI brought his army to the walls of the capital, putting the Cid in a double bind. He was duty bound to defend the *taifa* kingdom, but he would not fight against Alfonso, who remained, technically, his lord. As it was, the siege came to nothing. Having received word that an invasion force from Muslim North Africa had landed in al-Andalus, Alfonso broke off and hurried south to suffer a near-fatal defeat at the hands of the Almoravids at the Battle of Zallaqa.

For the next few years, Alfonso's concern would be preserving his kingdom as these Sanhaja warriors methodically and relentlessly deposed one *taifa* king after the next, depriving Alfonso of his *parias* and imperiling his imperial ambitions. This respite emboldened al-Musta'in II of Zaragoza, who now considered conquering Muslim Valencia himself. But his mercenary captain, Rodrigo Díaz, tired of his life of exile and despairing of ever returning to Alfonso's good graces and to his homeland of Castile, had settled on the same goal. It was over Valencia that the Cid, Alfonso, al-Musta'in II, the count of Barcelona, and the newly arrived Almoravids would all come to odds.

In Valencia, al-Qadir's rule—a thin veneer over the true authority of Alfonso VI—was quickly proving no more popular than it had been in Toledo. It was only the Cid's power, in the person of his Muslim lieutenant al-Faraj and the presence of a small Christian garrison, all there at Alfonso's request, that kept the local populace in check. As throughout the Islamic Mediterranean, Muslim townsfolk were growing increasingly impatient with abusive princes and turned increasingly toward populist *qadi*-oligarchs as representatives of their interests. In Valencia, the judge Ibn Jahhaf, determined to capitalize on discontent with al-Qadir's misrule and on Alfonso VI's weakness after Zallaqa, led an uprising in 1092 that saw al-Faraj arrested and al-Qadir put to death as a traitor. The luckless, two-time former *taifa* king was apprehended while trying to sneak out of the city disguised as a woman, his *jubba* loaded with jewels. Thus, the once-glorious dynasty of the Banu Dhi 'l-Nun came to a humiliating end.

The coup provided the pretext for the Cid, who cynically presented himself as the defender of al-Qadir's legitimacy and Alfonso VI's authority, to declare war on the kingdom, although by this time it was the Cid rather than the Leonese king who was collecting the *parias* paid by Valencia. The campaign would take two years, during which time the Cid's men mercilessly plundered the Valencian hinterland and tortured wealthy locals to extract the location of hidden treasures. Still officially in the employ of al-Musta'in II, the Cid dared not return to Zaragoza, for fear of arrest. But the *taifa* king was not the only one alarmed by Rodrigo's upstart ambitions; when Berenguer Ramon II of Barcelona, who also had designs on Valencia, took an army south to crush him, once more the Cid schooled the Catalan count with a humiliating and total defeat. It was not for nothing that the Cid was known as Campeador (from the Latin *Campi Doctor*, "Teacher of the Battlefield").

With no one left to stop him, the Cid was finally able to encircle the city of Valencia in the autumn of 1093. Here, even after months of siege, the starving populace (a mouse was said to sell for one *dinar*) was determined to hold out for rescue from the North African Almoravids. As if by some miracle (at least from the Cid's perspective), a massive Almoravid army arrived and set up camp, yet mysteriously withdrew during the night before battle was to be joined. The increasingly unpopular Ibn Jahhaf and the desperate people of Valencia held out briefly, still hoping for relief from the Almoravids or al-Musta'in II of Zaragoza; when this did not materialize, they opened the gates of the city to the Cid in June 1094.

Rodrigo Díaz had become, effectively, a Christian *taifa* king. To secure the city, the Cid adopted a conciliatory approach, allowing Ibn Jahhaf to continue as *qadi*, promising to respect the religious and legal rights of the Muslim inhabitants, installing al-Faraj as his administrator, and garrisoning the town with Arabic-speaking Christian troops who were under orders not to abuse the sensibilities of the citizens. The security these policies gave the Cid enabled him to roundly defeat a large Almoravid force that arrived at the city in September of that year. Once that threat had been dealt with, he adopted more uncompromising and aggressive tactics as a ruler. First, Ibn

Jahhaf was arrested and burned at the stake for the murder of al-Qadir; next, a Christian bishop was installed in the city, a Jewish wazir was appointed to run the finances, and the leading families of the city were levied a heavy fine.

The Cid was now in control, but his rule suffered from the same vulnerabilities as many Muslim *taifa* rulers: he was an outsider with a narrow powerbase and was unpopular among both the city's Islamic elite and the broader populace. Although he managed to hold Valencia until his death in 1099, once he had died, his wife, Jimena, who inherited the kingdom, could not. In 1102, an aging Alfonso VI sent a column of knights south to evacuate her and the small Christian community of Valencia, setting fire to the city as they left to deprive the Almoravids of the prize and to dampen the joy of the local Muslims at their liberation.

In his own time, the Cid was a warrior of legendary stature among both Christians and Muslims of the peninsula, who praised or cursed him not according to their religious affiliation but according to whether he had appeared to them as a liberator or a scourge. This was a culture that glorified brutality in the pursuit of wealth and glory. Ballads extolling his feats, the medieval equivalent of today's *narco-corridas*, which rhapsodize the exploits of modern frontier outlaws, were sung around countless campfires. Over the following centuries these gradually coalesced into a series of chivalric tales that presented Rodrigo as a Christian paladin, a protocrusader, and a hero of the reconquest.

But this was not the Cid of his time; Rodrigo was simply one of a whole class of Christian and Muslim seekers of fortune who hailed from the Christian and Muslim Spains, North Africa, and Europe. Others like him included the Cid's nephew Alvar Fañez, the French count Ebles de Roucy, the Normans Roger Burdet and Robert Crispin, and the Andalusi Sayf al-Dawla ibn Hud. Through the eleventh and twelfth centuries, these men moved among the shifting religious and political sands of postcaliphal al-Andalus, determined to exploit the power vacuum in the peninsula for their own ends. To them, religious community and the notion of holy war may have been ever present in their imaginations, but it only rarely determined their choices and actions.

In the years after the death of the Cid, the kingdom of the Banu Hud collapsed. The kings of Aragon gradually encircled the city of Zaragoza, and in the east, the counts of Barcelona and Urgell began to conquer the lands around Lleida. Al-Musta'in II waged a spirited resistance, dying in battle against Christians near Tudela in 1110—a martyr and *mujahid* in the eyes of his subjects. An increasingly alarmed populace in Zaragoza pressured his son and successor, 'Imad al-Dawla, to cease making alliances with Christian powers, but the vulnerable king had little choice were the kingdom to survive. Thus, as the Aragonese ring continued to tighten, the impatient population overthrew him in 1110 and petitioned the Almoravids who now controlled al-Andalus to send a governor.

Taking with him his treasury and the palace library, 'Imad al-Dawla escaped to his fortress-redoubt at Rueda de Jalón, some thirty miles to the west. From here he would wage war against the Almoravids with the support of Castile. In the meantime, the Aragonese, under the tireless King Alfonso I "the Battler," took town after town. In 1118, the city of Zaragoza would surrender to him, and although Alfonso gave the inhabitants generous terms, which prompted many Muslim commoners to stay, the city's cultural and religious elite departed for exile in the Almoravid-held lands to the south. By his death in 1134, Alfonso had conquered almost the entire *taifa* kingdom.

One notable holdout had been 'Imad al-Dawla, who had weathered the conquests in his fortress perched on a cliff above the Jalón River. When he died in 1130, his son and successor, Sayf al-Dawla ("King Zafadola," to the Christians), submitted to Alfonso VII of Castile and León in exchange for a lordship near Toledo. The last of the proud line of the Banu Hud would spend his remaining sixteen years as an adornment to the court of the Leonese monarch and a commander in the armed struggle against his coreligionists, the Almoravids. He would die in 1146, murdered—to Alfonso VII's annoyance—in a dispute with his Christian allies when he endeavored to carve out for himself a new principality in the lands to the south of Guadalquivir, just as Almoravid power was beginning to unravel.

19

A Terrible, Swift Sword

Aside from Alfonso VI's near-bloodless conquest of Toledo and the Cid's brief occupation of Valencia, the *taifa* kingdoms were not destroyed by Christian aggression but rather at the hands of fellow Muslims. In the 1070s, as Alfonso VI of Castile and León ramped up the pressure on the *taifa* kings—raiding their lands, fomenting internecine strife, and demanding ever-increasing quantities of *parias*—the desperation and despair that ordinary Muslims had long felt finally took root among the ruling classes. The *taifa* kings may have continued to fiddle as each of their Romes burned, but their playing became increasingly unsteady. Their dependence on Christian military support and their payment of tribute had effectively made them *dhimmis* of the Christians in the eyes of the *'ulama'*, with no legitimacy as Islamic rulers. The unifying ideal of the caliphate had dissipated, and in its absence, the *taifa* kings were nothing more than interchangeable strongmen—strongmen who were not even strong. Coímbra, Barbastro, and Toledo had fallen to the infidel; towns defied the authority of their kings; opportunistic wazirs intrigued with enemies; the urban, pious classes resisted; and towns were riven by loyalties to rival rulers.

Meanwhile, the *taifa* kings abandoned themselves to the pursuit of frivolous and immoral pleasures: wine, poetry, sex, and pagan sciences, and patronized and empowered Christians and Jews in their courts. They taxed their subjects in violation of the precepts of the Qur'an and devalued their currencies, hitting the middle classes—the bulwark of the 'ulama'—and the lower classes hard. Still, they could not guarantee order and prosperity in their lands. Raiders ravaged the countryside, and instead of pulling together, the taifa kings paid Christian armies to attack their Muslim rivals. Each, it seemed, would prefer to see the infidels gain ground rather than a fellow Muslim succeed.

And although there was no scapegoating of Mozarabs, there was a growing sense that al-Andalus should be engaged in military jihad against the northerners, particularly as Alfonso articulated his imperial claims over the entire peninsula. Some Andalusis took matters into their own hands, joining taifa military expeditions or serving time in ribats. These fortress-monasteries were springing up along the frontier as "state" and private initiatives, where ordinary Muslims could retire temporarily to engage in pious contemplation and fight in the defense of the dar al-Islam. However, aside from local volunteers and what remained of the caliphal army, the only military the taifa kings could draw on were local troops and northern Christian mercenaries. The era of captive taking had passed, and Berbers were no longer coming over to al-Andalus to serve as soldiers.

So, to whom could al-Andalus turn as Castile-León slowly but steadily gained ground? The northerners were well aware of the animosity of the Andalusis toward Berbers. Back in the 1050s, the people of Toledo had protested to Fernando I that they could not raise the sums he demanded as tribute to defend them against Zaragoza, countering, "if we could raise that much money . . . we would pay the Berbers and bring them over to solve this problem," to which the Leonese monarch scoffed, "you always threaten us with this, but it is impossible, given the enmity there is between you and them."[33]

But, this is precisely what would happen. As early as 1081, when al-Mutawakkil of Badajoz felt he was losing his grip on his kingdom, he sent envoys across the strait to make contact with Yusuf ibn Tashufin, one of the leaders of a confederation of Sanhaja clans from the southern fringes of the Western Sahara that had seized control of the Maghrib. In 1082, al-Mu'tamid, in public in a fit of rage, had ordered

Alfonso's Jewish envoy Ibn Shalib to be crucified. Now fearing reprisals, he also petitioned these al-Murabitun, or Almoravids, for aid.

FEARSOME, BLUE-VEILED desert warriors, who had for generations
lived by either attacking or protecting the desert caravans that brought
African gold, slaves, and exotica up to the Mediterranean, the Almoravids had only just converted from paganism in the 1040s. The
origin of the name is lost in obscurity, but the Arabic root *r-b-t* relates
to tying or binding and may refer to the face veil Almoravid men
wore; the sense of moral duty that bound them to the cause of holy
war; or the ribats of the southwestern Sahara, which were their early
bases. The missionaries who converted them, notably 'Abd Allah ibn
Yasin, were adherents of an extremely strict Maliki persuasion and
envisioned a revolutionary movement that would establish a rigorous
Sunni regime across the region.

Displaying all the uncompromising zeal of the newly converted,
and inspired to establish a "pure" Islam and observe a rigorous and
ascetic orthodoxy, the Lamtuna tribesmen who composed the core
of the movement embodied a determination and moral certainty
that, together with their spartan lifestyle, made them formidable ad-
versaries. As new converts, they had enthusiastically waged holy
war on their pagan neighbors, such that the warrior ethos of these
nomadic tribesmen combined with their newfound religious mission to crystallize as an ideology that emphasized the obligation of
moral struggle, including holy war. Jihad was their raison d'être and
the foundation of their mandate. Emerging from the desert in the
1050s, they had swept across the Maghrib, toppling the Berber
kingdoms that had sprung up after the collapse of the caliphate and
establishing a new capital called Marrakesh beneath the towering
peaks of the Atlas Mountains in central Morocco. In 1086, under the
leadership of an uncultured but brilliant and charismatic *sultan*
named Yusuf ibn Tashufin, they would cross over to al-Andalus,
ostensibly to save the land from Christian conquest.

But Ibn Tashufin did not show great enthusiasm to take his armies
to al-Andalus. Whatever his true intentions, he only appeared convinced to do so after the fall of Toledo, when other *taifa* kings had

joined the chorus calling for help, and when delegations of *'ulama'* shamed him into action lest *al-Rum* ("the Romans," or Christians) conquer al-Andalus as a consequence of Almoravid inaction. It should be noted, the *taifa* kings did not mourn the fall of Toledo out of religious sentimentality or solidarity, but because it demonstrated that the "Emperor of the Two Religions" no longer considered them necessary.

Hence, even old and bitter enemies—the 'Abbadids of Seville and the Zirids of Granada—temporarily laid aside differences in order to counter the power of Castile-León. The *taifa* kings, however, harbored few illusions regarding the Almoravids' ultimate intentions and the danger of invoking their aid. When questioned regarding the advisability of summoning Yusuf ibn Tashufin, al-Mu'tamid of Seville quipped, "Better to be a camel-driver [for Yusuf] than a swineherd [for Alfonso]."[34] Catching wind of the *taifa* kings' appeal, Alfonso VI had a formal letter dispatched to Yusuf in the finest chancery Arabic, challenging him to a battle and promising to trounce him, whether in al-Andalus or the Maghrib. Yusuf did not even deign to have a response written down, but merely instructed his envoys to tell Alfonso "You'll see what'll happen . . ."[35]

And so it was that on Friday, October 23, 1086, the *taifa* kings and their armies gathered uneasily under the command of Yusuf ibn Tashufin, together with his forces of veiled Almoravids, Berber clients, and sub-Saharan African slaves. The great host, borne by horse, dromedary, and elephant, with legions of foot soldiers marching to the boom of war drums, met the Leonese in battle. After withstanding Alfonso's cavalry charge, they rallied and captured his baggage train, annihilated his knights, and forced the king to flee the field. In celebration of the victory, the heads of the thousands of Christian warriors were collected and sent by the cartload on a victory tour through the major towns of al-Andalus and the Maghrib. The people of al-Andalus and the *'ulama'* rejoiced, and poets composed victory odes, but there was an ominous subtext to this grisly advertisement, which served as a warning not so much to the Christians but to fellow Muslims of the consequence of resisting Ibn Tashufin. While the *taifa* kings may have been somewhat more circumspect about the outcome of the battle, it appeared they were safe, for the moment at least.

Rather than press his advantage and march on Toledo or invade León, Yusuf instead took his troops back to Africa.

Thus, in short order, Alfonso began to recover, the Christians started to demand tribute again, and the *taifa* kings renewed their intrigues against each other and the neglect of their subjects. And once again, the *'ulama'* of al-Andalus begged Yusuf, who now styled himself Amir al-Muslimin ("Commander of the Muslims")—like Alfonso, a universal sovereign—to intervene.

In 1088, the Almoravids crossed the strait again and, rallying the *taifa* kings, laid siege to Aledo, a Christian stronghold near Murcia. When the campaign eventually failed due to Andalusi infighting, this only further discredited the local Muslim leaders in Yusuf's eyes. Thus, when he returned for the third time in 1090, he came for good. From his point of view and that of the Andalusi *'ulama'*, the *taifa* kings' return to their previous bad behavior had confirmed their illegitimacy and qualified as treason. To that end, a coalition of Andalusi jurists crafted a *fatwa* annulling any treaties Yusuf had with the *taifa* kings and confirming his duty to depose them. Careful to cover his bases, Yusuf sent this *fatwa* to be ratified by leading authorities in the Islamic East, including Abu Bakr al-Turtushi (himself a refugee from al-Andalus) and the great philosopher and theologian Abu Hamid al-Ghazali. Thus, Yusuf could present himself not as a usurper or a conqueror of fellow Muslims, but as a righteous liberator of the Andalusi faithful. The Almoravids' political platform was simple but appealing: "the spreading of righteousness, the correction of injustice, and the abolition of unlawful taxes"—a populist pledge to make al-Andalus great again that appealed to both the conservative *'ulama'* and the desperate and disenchanted common folk.[36]

Thus armed and once back in al-Andalus, Yusuf confronted the decadent, ungrateful *taifa* kings each in turn, demanding they abdicate or face his righteous wrath. All of them fell: some were pardoned, some were executed, and others were dispatched as prisoners to Aghmat, just south of Marrakesh. Several were betrayed by their own people, who happily handed them over or colluded in the Almoravid conquest. But not all of them went easily. Al-Mu'tamid, for example, had been determined to survive the onslaught, even if it meant submitting to Alfonso. 'Abbadid forces resisted doggedly both at Córdoba, where al-Mu'tamid's son Abu'l-Fatah died defending the city, and at Seville, where al-Mu'tamid himself withstood a heavy siege until the city was finally overrun in September 1091.

Thus, one by one the *taifa* kingdoms fell until only Valencia, under the rule of the Cid, and Zaragoza, under the Banu Hud, were left. By 1110, all of Muslim al-Andalus would be under Almoravid dominion, and by this time, both Alfonso VI and his would-be nemesis, Yusuf ibn Tashufin, were dead. When the amir died in 1106, purportedly at age one hundred, and was succeeded by his son 'Ali ibn Yusuf, al-Andalus had been incorporated into the new imperium based in Marrakesh and with Seville as its regional capital. The integrity and status of Islam had been restored in the peninsula, or so it might have seemed. Two years later, Almoravid forces would deal another crushing defeat to Castile-León, this time at Uclés, just east of Toledo.

Among the many Christian casualties in this battle was Alfonso VI's only son, Sancho, the illegitimate offspring of the king's affair with Sayyida, the widow of Abu'l-Fatah of Córdoba. After her husband had fallen defending the city, the princess had taken refuge first in Alfonso's kingdom and then in his arms. Of Alfonso's eight wives and mistresses, she was the only one to bear him a son. The sixteen-year-old Sancho had escaped the battlefield of Uclés with his life, but he was set upon and killed by Muslim townsfolk in a hamlet he passed through on his way back north. Soon enough, Alfonso's daughters, Urraca and Teresa, who inherited his realms, would begin vying for power, and once again the Christian North fell into bitter infighting.

Fortunately for the Christian kingdoms, the Almoravids once more failed to capitalize on their victory. Historians have puzzled over their apparent lack of interest in taking Toledo, but their reluctance was likely due to their awareness of their own vulnerabilities. They were a foreign army in a foreign land; they did not have the human resources to sustain heavy losses and could not risk imperiling the gains they had made. Moreover, the Almoravids' hold on both al-Andalus and the Maghrib was extremely tenuous. Power was closely held by members of the ruling dynasty and exercised through the appointment of children, cousins, and nephews to key

Almoravid gold *dinar*, minted by Yusuf b. Tashufin at Almería, 1097/98 CE. *Courtesy of the American Numismatic Society (1951.146.6)*

military and administrative positions. But even these individuals exhibited little solidarity, and rivalries and intrigues within the family were a constant threat.

STILL, THE ALMORAVID conquest constituted nothing short of a complete reordering of Muslim Spain. The Almoravid elite, dominated by the family of Ibn Tashufin and composed almost entirely of members of his tribe, the Lamtuna, ruled as a caste apart in al-Andalus. They spoke their own language, were subject to their own laws, and continued to wear the veils that served as a badge of their status. Few came to settle in al-Andalus, but those who did, together with their clients and African slaves, quickly gained a reputation for haughty despotism.

As in the Maghrib, however, the Almoravids realized that they could not govern without the support and collaboration of the religious elite, who found their support for a rigorous interpretation of Maliki law a refreshing change from the laxity of the *taifa* kings. The victory of the Almoravids, then, could be seen as the victory of the pietist, urban patriciate that had vied for power against the *taifa* kings since the collapse of the caliphate. In Andalusi cities, the government would be overseen by councils, each being half Almoravids and the other half Andalusi religious authorities. Civil jurisdiction was left largely in native hands, normally a *qadi,* while military power was held by members of the Tashufin clan.

The Almoravids have gained a reputation among both later Muslim historians and modern scholars as puritanical fundamentalists, particularly with regard to their approach to their Christian and Jewish subjects. Under the new regime, *dhimmis* were expected to pay heavier taxes, to wear the distinctive clothes mandated by the "Pact of 'Umar," and to comport themselves with discretion and humility. In principle, *dhimmis* were to mind their place, although, for all their rigor, the Almoravids continued to employ Jewish wazirs and Christian military commanders. With the changing times, some Andalusi Jews emigrated north to Christian lands, but many stayed. And while the Jewish communities in Granada and Córdoba may have all but disappeared, the rabbinical academy at Lucena continued to thrive under Almoravid rule.

The Almoravids only rarely engaged in what can be described as active persecution, and when they did—such as when the Mozarab population of the Guadalquivir region was transported en masse to North Africa in 1126—they were careful to justify their policies under Islamic law. On the other hand, when Christian communities were abused contrary to the spirit of Islamic law, both the Almoravids and the Andalusi judiciary intervened to protect them: the amir 'Ali ibn Yusuf once deposed and arrested an Almoravid governor of Granada after local Christians complained of his abuses.

The same strictness was applied to their Muslim subjects, and the new rulers were hostile both to the non-Maliki schools of Islam and to the esoteric and mystical currents of Islam that had been gaining ground in al-Andalus over the previous two centuries. Committed to the ideal of Islamic unity, and conscious of the need to establish their own religious and political legitimacy, in 1098 they submitted nominally to the 'Abbasid ruler al-Mustazhir, in Baghdad—himself a puppet of the Central Asian Seljuq warlords who had taken control of the caliphate—and received in exchange a formal investiture as his governors in the west.

IN SUM, ALMORAVID policies regarding non-Muslims derived not so much from an anti-*dhimmi* animus as from a determination to observe the precise letter of Islamic law, enforced by the now-unfettered power of the Maliki *fuqaha'*, who became the ideological bulwark of the regime. Given a free hand in the judicial administration of al-Andalus, patronized and supported by the Almoravid elite, and no longer inhibited by the laissez-faire heterodoxy of the *taifa* royal courts, many leading jurists developed an uncompromising approach. Nor was the influence of these religious scholars limited to al-Andalus; even before Ibn Tashufin's conquest of al-Andalus, they had been installed in high positions in the court at Marrakesh.

Appointed as *qadis* across al-Andalus and in the cities of the Maghrib, and with official support, conservative Andalusi jurists endeavored to impose their inflexible interpretation of the law on the populace. They clamped down on public behavior and moral laxity, conducted purges of the judiciary, and attacked the work of scholars of rival theological schools, such as Ibn Hazm, and the writings of esoterics, such as al-Ghazali, both of whose books were burned in public. Born in 1058 in Khurasan, Abu Hamid Muhammad al-Ghazali was one of the most innovative, original, and influential scholars of Islam, famous both for his attacks on philosophy and for his affection for the mysticism of the Sufis, and therefore an enemy of the more conservative Malikis. Such was the reputation the Andalusi *'ulama'* had gained that when 'Iyad ibn Musa of Ceuta (known as al-Qadi 'Iyad, "'Iyad the Magistrate"), who would become the greatest Maliki scholar of his time, embarked on his mission of scholarly education, he would not travel to the east in search of masters, but to al-Andalus.

Until recently, histories of medieval Spain have near-unanimously described the Almoravids as "intolerant," "fundamentalist," or "puritanical"—dour anti-intellectual philistines who destroyed the effervescent culture of the *taifa* period. Historians have uncritically accepted the anti-Berber and anti-Almoravid prejudices of later Andalusi writers, who vilified them, and have chosen to ignore or misunderstand the dynasty's relationship with culture. The Almoravids did patronize culture; however, their support was largely limited to the religious sciences and Maliki law, and it is for this reason that Western scholars have not recognized their intellectual achievements.

But a number of important figures emerged in al-Andalus during or right after their reign, including Abu Bakr ibn al-'Arabi and

Muhammad ibn Bajja. Ibn al-'Arabi was famous for working to reconcile Malikism with the mysticism of al-Ghazali, while Ibn Bajja ("Avempace") produced influential works on medicine, botany, and astronomy. However, caution was required amid the atmosphere of strict orthodoxy of the Almoravid period, and many scholars straddled a fine line between acclamation and condemnation. Even widely admired thinkers like Ibn Bajja could be charged with heresy, and sometimes could just as suddenly be rehabilitated. Their students, thinkers such as Ibn Tufayl and Ibn Rushd, would produce startlingly innovative philosophical works, and although these were composed during the rule of the Almohads, who came to power in the 1140s, they were very much a legacy of the rationalism and Malikism of the Almoravid era.

DESPITE THE UPHEAVALS of the period, urban and commercial life continued to thrive, thanks to al-Andalus's tremendous agricultural output and its large population base, which created a robust domestic market for craft and industrial production. The Almoravid imperium extended deep into Central Africa, and the flow of gold from the Niger Delta that had driven the Umayyad economy increased under their rule. The fine gold *dinars* they minted became the new "dollars" of the Western Mediterranean, accepted and recognized everywhere. Christian rulers would quickly produce their own imitations—referred to as "Morabetís" or "Maravedís"—complete with genuine or ersatz Arabo-Islamic inscriptions. Under the Almoravids, tribute to the Christian kings declined, trade with the north abated, and the economy was reoriented toward the Maghrib, which was the true center of their empire. Indeed, after 1100, money from al-Andalus was being diverted to support Almoravid struggles against North African insurgencies that began to rise against them in North Africa—a dynamic that would further complicate collaboration between natives and their new rulers and lay bare the colonial dynamic that underlay their relationship.

The subsidiary nature of al-Andalus became clear under the anemic rule of Yusuf's son and successor, 'Ali ibn Yusuf. The child of a

Christian slave, who had been raised not as a desert warrior but as a coddled, urban prince, 'Ali had neither the charisma nor the competence of his father. Ensconced in Marrakesh as Commander of the Faithful, he rarely ventured out, and visited al-Andalus only four times, leaving it first in the hands of his brother Tamim and later of his own son Tashufin.

Despite the Christian disarray, the campaigns undertaken against León proved largely inconsequential even when they were successful. After 1118, when Alfonso I, king of Aragon and Navarre (Pamplona), captured the city of Zaragoza, the losses piled up. By the time of his death in 1134, after being shot through the eye by a Muslim archer while he was directing the siege of Fraga, Alfonso had conquered the entire former *taifa* kingdom of Zaragoza. To make matters worse, the Aragonese king, as a show of force and to forestall Leonese claims, had led a raid deep into the Muslim South in 1125. And by the late 1130s, León was back on the offensive, launching a raid that reached Córdoba in 1144.

While Alfonso I's campaign of 1125 did not take any territory, it did expose Almoravid vulnerabilities. It also helped to foment tensions between Andalusi Muslims and Christians. The latter seemed to have colluded with Alfonso, and a large number followed his forces back to Aragon, where they settled in the former kingdom of Zaragoza. It was this act of betrayal that nullified the Christians' status as *dhimmis* in the eyes of the Almoravids and led to the forced transportation of the remaining Mozarabs of the south to Morocco the following year. Although the dictate came from an enraged 'Ali ibn Yusuf, the *fatwa* on which the policy was based had been promulgated by Muhammad ibn Rushd, an Andalusi jurist from Córdoba, who lobbied 'Ali to enforce it.

In other words, the expulsion is evidence of Andalusi, rather than Almoravid, "intolerance." Ironically, these exiled Mozarabs became an integral part of the regime, serving as soldiers in the Almoravids' struggle against the local tribes that had risen up in rebellion against them. So important was their role that their leader, a Catalan nobleman known as Reverter, who had been captured in a separate campaign in the

1130s, was appointed commander of 'Ali's military forces in the Maghrib. It was largely thanks to his regiments of Christian captives and mercenaries that the Almoravids would endure for as long as they did. But this was not very long at all. As early as 1149, the emirate founded by Yusuf ibn Tashufin would be no more.

20

Faith and Power

As tired as many Andalusis had become of the *taifa* kings' decadent misrule, most had only opted for the Almoravids as a last resort, and only thanks to the lobbying of certain elements of the religious elite— the *faqihs* and, increasingly, the mystical holy men who were coming to represent the face of Islam to the common people. Thus, when the Almoravids sought *fatwas* to justify their invasion of al-Andalus, it was not so much a means of putting a pious gloss on their conquest as of gauging Andalusi opinion as to whether their authority and strict ideology would be welcomed.

Much of the appeal of the Almoravids was that they could protect the Andalusis from the Christians. Thus, when public opinion shifted against the Almoravids after their military defeats in the 1120s, the Maliki judiciary, whose power was founded on popular recognition, was obliged to respond, and many moderates withdrew their support. But the popularity of the Maliki religious elite had already been declining, as members of both the *'ulama'* and the common folk were drawn increasingly to Sufism and other mystical approaches to Islam.

These modes of piety had been gaining ground since the early tenth century, an esotericism fueled by the millenarian sentiments that were sweeping up Christian, Muslim, and Jewish society across Europe and the Mediterranean at this time. The work of al-Ghazali, which had been burned under the Almoravids, was championed by the Andalusi ascetics who came to form the core of the religio-political resistance that would help bring down the Almoravids and usher in Almohad rule. Some of the same privately founded ribats that earlier were points of dissemination of religio-political resistance against Christian kings and those Muslims who collaborated with them, now became nodes of religious and military resistance to the Almoravids. Lacking any alternative, the Muslims who rebelled against Almoravid authority now actively sought out Christian rulers as patrons, allies, and protectors. They did not necessarily see their political or religious world as defined by a clash of Islam and Christianity but as a clash of rival visions of Islam.

The first open revolts against the Almoravids broke out in the 1130s; urban populations rose up against and cast out their governors and assassinated unpopular *qadis*. In 1133, the people of Seville approached Alfonso VII of Castile-León, offering to become his tributaries under the rule of Sayf al-Dawla—the last in the line of the Banu Hud of Zaragoza, who as "King Zafadola" now formed part of Alfonso VII of Castile's court—in exchange for liberation from the predatory Almoravids. In 1144, Ahmad ibn Qasi, a Sufi convert from Christianity who had served as a tax collector for the Almoravids, seized a fortress near Silves and declared himself "imam." Cobbling together an unstable "kingdom" of fellow rebels, known as the Muridun ("Disciples"), he marched on Seville. The Andalusi capital itself was fought over by three parties: Yahya ibn Ghaniya, the Almoravid governor of al-Andalus; the reactionary Maliki *qadi* Abu Ja'far ibn Hamdin; and the supporters of the Hudid king Sayf al-Dawla. Briefly occupying the city, the Christians in Sayf al-Dawla's army sacked its great mosque, stripping it of most of its precious ornamentation.

FOR THEIR PART, the Christian princes were well aware of this anti-Almoravid sentiment and did their best to exploit it. In the 1130s, Alfonso I of Aragon overran what had been the *taifa* kingdom of Zaragoza and successfully appealed to ordinary Muslims to remain in their lands as subjects of his kingdom. He offered them protection of their persons and goods, religious freedom, and the right to continue to live under Islamic law—to become, in effect, *dhimmis* of the Christians. The upper classes and cultural elite, who could afford to uproot and who practiced vocations in demand elsewhere in the Islamic world, and the pious, who could not brook infidel rule, departed. But, most of the common folk—tradesmen, artisans, and farmers—stayed in their ancestral lands and became *mudajjan* ("those who remained," known in Spanish as *mudéjares*). Distasteful as living under infidel rule may have been, it would have brought respite from the raiding and captive taking that rural Andalusis had been suffering with increasing frequency at the hands of Christian militias and adventurers.

But the death of the childless Alfonso I in 1134 plunged Aragon into a succession crisis that was only fully resolved in 1146, after his brother Ramiro II's infant daughter, Petronila, was betrothed to the twenty-four-year-old count of Barcelona, Ramon Berenguer IV. With this, the foundation was laid for the "Crown of Aragon"—the dynastic union of the county of Catalonia and the kingdom of Aragon that was created when Ramon Berenguer and Petronila's son, Alfons, inherited both titles in 1164. Already a seasoned ruler, Ramon would take up where Alfonso I had left off and complete the conquest of the Andalusi territory north of the Ebro River.

Meanwhile, the other Christian kings had resumed their advances. In 1146, Alfonso VII of León attacked Córdoba, forcing Yahya ibn Ghaniya, who resisted fiercely, to submit. The king himself was said to have attended a mass held in the great mosque. Ibn Ghaniya agreed to hold the city in Alfonso's name, but no sooner had the emperor departed than the Almoravid general reasserted his loyalty to his own dynasty. By this point, however, the Almoravid regime was on its last legs. The insurgent Almohad movement was overrunning North Africa, exterminating the dynasty as it went. Marrakesh, the Almoravid capital, fell in the summer of 1146, and later that year Almohad forces would cross over to al-Andalus for the first time.

AT THE VERY moment the religio-political consensus in the Islamic West was disintegrating, leading to dissension and revolt, it was coalescing in the Christian West, endowing princes there with a unity of purpose. The church was coming into its own as an institution thanks, in part, to the reforms of the later eleventh century introduced under the influence of the Cluniac Order: disengaging itself from the influence of secular rulers and developing a coherent theology, a code of canon law, and an institutional framework that would allow the papacy to function as a metamonarchy.

In 1095, Urban II, a former monk of Cluny, unwittingly launched what would become the Crusade movement when he enjoined the warriors of Europe to cease fighting each other and instead go to the aid of their fellow Christians of Byzantium, whose eastern possessions had been overrun by the Seljuq Turks. If they would do that, he said, God would forgive their sins. His call to crusade provided a pious outlet for the apocalyptic anxieties of the common folk and the military energies of the noble classes, combining three established pillars of contemporary Christianity: pilgrimage, penance, and holy war. In July 1099, Christian forces conquered Jerusalem, the Holy City, cleansing it of its Muslim presence in a genocidal orgy of killing. Christendom rejoiced.

This was part of a broader process that was taking place within Latin Christendom. The combination of a better climate, increased agricultural output, and population growth had put the European backwater on the path to progress and prosperity. The European interior and its fringes (including the frontier lands of Spain) had been colonized by Cistercian monks and lordless peasants in search of new land, and town and city culture began to reemerge in a way not seen since the fading days of the Roman Empire. Money was reintroduced into circulation, and industry, trade, and commerce came to rival landholding as sources of prosperity for the upper classes. The maritime trading republics that dotted the Italian coast—Venice, Pisa, Genoa, and Amalfi—began to send their ships into Islamic and Byzantine waters to trade for or seize luxury goods, spices, and exotica that they could sell to the increasingly cash-rich nobility and upper clergy of the Latin lands.

People—both common and noble—became more mobile and worldly, trekking across Christendom to visit the shrine of Saint James "the Muslim Killer" at Compostela or braving the sea to journey on pilgrimage to the Muslim-ruled Holy Land. Population growth and pressure for resources stirred up popular unrest, particularly among the marginalized underclass, as did competition among an increasingly land-starved nobility. The looming crisis of the dispossessed, together with the zeal with which they embraced the Christianity that had finally penetrated the lower strata of European society, fed a desperate millenarianism that manifested itself in protorevolutionary social unrest, apocalypticism, and anti-Jewish violence.

Most European Christians knew nothing about Islam, but they were increasingly convinced it was their mission to vanquish it, and the miracle of the conquest of Jerusalem was seen as manifest proof of God's favor. In the aftermath of this success, crusading fervor gripped Europe, and Bernard of Clairvaux, a Cistercian abbot who enjoyed the ear of popes and kings, promoted a muscular view of the faith, which saw it as virtuous to wage war against all unbelievers in order to extend the dominion of Roman Christendom. He also wrote in praise of "the new knighthood"—the military orders, including the Templars and Hospitallers. Founded in the Holy Land for the protection of pilgrims, these orders combined knightly ethos with Christian virtue and monastic discipline in the service of the church and its ruler, the pope.

The princes of the Christian Spains quickly appreciated the potential of the Crusade movement. Six years before issuing the call to crusade, Urban II had encouraged warriors to join a Catalan campaign against Muslim Tarragona with the promise of the redemption of their sins, and after 1095's Council of Clermont, when the pope launched what would be later known as the First Crusade, he issued another letter permitting Spanish knights to fulfill their crusade vows against Islam in the peninsula rather than the Holy Land. Thus, from the twelfth century onward, Spanish rulers sought to qualify their campaigns as crusades in order to attract foreign knights and utilize the financial resources of the church.

Afonso Henriquez, Alfonso VII, Ramon Berenguer IV, and Alfonso I of Aragon all supported the Templars and the Hospitallers, donating lands and fortresses in their newly conquered territories. By doing so, they gained a dedicated, standing military force untainted in principle by the divided loyalties and perennial rebelliousness of their aristocratic nobility. Alfonso I even founded his own short-lived orders: the Order of Monreal and the Confraternity of Belchite. These soon disappeared, but in the later twelfth century, three more successful orders would be established in Castile and León: Alcántara, Catatrava, and Santiago.

As well as serving as a counterweight to the local nobility, the military orders also helped compensate for the dwindling supply of Christian settlers the Spanish kings had at their disposal. In the early phases of their advance southward, these rulers could draw on the growing population of their mountain valleys to populate the lands they conquered, but as they pushed further south, they found it increasingly difficult to find colonists. Thus, across the peninsula the military orders were allotted substantial territories to govern and hold, lands that were populated in some cases almost exclusively by Muslim subjects. Ironically, the commanders of orders founded to fight the infidel soon found themselves in a position where it was in their best interest to protect and defend their Muslim tenants and vassals against other Christian powers, notably the communities of Christian settlers that also appeared in the newly conquered territories.

To entice immigration to the dangerous and unstable frontier zone, Christian rulers granted the inhabitants of new towns they founded generous privileges. Unlike in the rigidly structured society of the feudal European heartland, where peasants were forbidden from the military vocation, here, ordinary townsfolk were required to serve in local militias as either foot soldiers or horsemen in exchange for their right to keep all but a fifth of whatever plunder they took when raiding enemy territory. A brave and lucky peasant could rise from being a foot soldier to a horseman and eventually attain lower nobility. Settlers were recruited from as far away as France and Germany, and amnesties were established so that fugitives and outlaws would gain their freedom once they had lived for a year and a day in a frontier settlement. In the later twelfth century, the municipal militias of these towns would prove to be a key element in both the defense of Christian territory and the expansion into al-Andalus. Although these militias spent as much time fighting each other as they did Muslims, this helped to inculcate ordinary Spanish Christians with a sense that they were engaged in a grand struggle against Islam. Christian Spain became, in effect, a society organized for war.

AND SO IT was that in the mid-1140s, circumstances would align in Spain, Europe, and the east to bring down the Almoravid regime. 'Ali ibn Yusuf, the son and successor of Yusuf ibn Tashufin who had struggled to control the intrigues and competition within his own family, died in 1143, having failed to establish an institutionally stable regime or to confront the rebellions that had been brewing in his kingdom. In turn, 'Ali's son Tashufin ibn Yusuf, who had proven his worth as a military commander in al-Andalus, came to the throne, but he was killed only two years later while organizing a defensive campaign against the Almohads, leaving his son Ibrahim ibn Yusuf holding the title of "Commander of the Faithful." Soon after, the infant amir was deposed and his uncle Ishaq ibn 'Ali acclaimed in his place.

Taking advantage of this unforeseen turn of events, the Almohads marched on and captured Fez before encircling Marrakesh in 1145. The city would withstand the siege for two years, falling to the forces of the self-proclaimed Almohad caliph, 'Abd al-Ma'mun, in March 1147. In the aftermath, Ishaq and other members of the ruling family were hunted down and killed.

Back in al-Andalus, the major towns and cities once again became independent in what became known as the second *taifa* period; the Christian kings were on the march, and Yusuf ibn Ghaniya was desperately trying to maintain a nucleus of Almoravid authority around Córdoba, Carmona, and Jaén. Further north in Murcia, a neo-muwallad named Muhammad ibn Mardanish, who had served the Almoravids as a military commander, would do the same as he sought to carve out his own principality in eastern and southern al-Andalus.

But events in the Islamic East would prove just as crucial. In 1144, the Seljuq warlord 'Imad al-Din Zengi, who had cultivated an ideology of anti-Frankish jihad, captured the city of Edessa in Anatolia, the capital of the earliest crusader principality. In response, Pope Eugenius III called for a Second Crusade, which, thanks in part to the energetic preaching of Bernard of Clairvaux, drew the interest of many knights from England, Flanders, and other northern regions. In

1147, Afonso of Portugal convinced a crusader fleet that was sailing down the Atlantic coast en route to the Holy Land to join him in an attack on Muslim Lisbon. In July of that year, a siege was established, and the Christian forces ringed the city determined to force the inhabitants into submission. Appeals for help to neighboring Muslim leaders were ignored or refused, and finally, in late October, the inhabitants agreed to the generous terms of surrender the Portuguese king had offered them. Despite this, the Crusader army breached the walls and swept into the city, looting and indiscriminately massacring the inhabitants, both Muslim and Christian, including the city's bishop.

Only a week earlier, similar events had played out in the city of Almería, the most important port of southern al-Andalus. In late July 1147, Alfonso VII, with the aid of forces sent by García Ramírez of Navarre and Ramon Berenguer IV, had assembled an army outside the city walls, while Pisan and Genoan fleets blockaded the harbor, having been promised control of the city in compensation. As the siege dragged on, Alfonso VII opened secret surrender negotiations, but once the Italian forces got wind of this betrayal, they stormed the city and put its inhabitants to the sword. Only those who reached the safety of the fortress were saved. The once great port was left devastated and near empty, and now under the control of Castile and Genoa.

Ramon Berenguer then decided to use the same approach to conquer Tortosa, the Andalusi port situated at the mouth of the Ebro River. In July 1148, aided by the Templars and the Genoese, each of whom were promised one-third of the city as their reward, he encircled Tortosa by land and sea. Having endured some five months of privation and artillery fire, the inhabitants agreed in November that if no relief force had arrived after one month, they would surrender. And so, on December 30, Ramon Berenguer took control of the city, granting the Muslim inhabitants the same generous terms of submission that Alfonso I had offered at Zaragoza thirty years earlier.

With the lower Ebro Valley now cut off from the sea, the city of Lleida surrendered in October 1149 after a fiercely resisted siege. In 1151, the victorious count and his counterpart, Alfonso VII of Castile, signed the Treaty of Tudilén, an agreement that divided the Iberian Peninsula, including yet-to-be-conquered al-Andalus, into two zones of control: all that was below Murcia would go to Castile-León and all that was above to the Catalan-ruled Crown of Aragon. Al-Andalus, however, was far from finished. Over the course of the next decades, the Almohads would convert it into a key province of their new caliphate, once again halting the Christian advance and profoundly transforming the society and culture of Islamic Spain.

21

An African Caliphate

In the end, what brought down the Almoravids was neither the increasingly aggressive Christian North nor the rebellious and discontented Andalusis, but a lone holy man from the rural highlands above their capital of Marrakesh. Born around 1080 in the Anti-Atlas Mountains of central Morocco, Muhammad ibn Tumart was schooled in Córdoba before embarking to the east, where he studied under al-Turtushi in Alexandria and allegedly met and received the blessing of the great al-Ghazali himself. The theology Ibn Tumart developed combined elements of the various strands of Islam, including Sunnism, Shi'ism, Kharijism, and Sufism, with a stark moral and theological simplicity. After returning to the Maghrib in 1116 or 1117, he retreated to the alpine valley of Tinmallal, south of Marrakesh. Here he preached among the recently Islamized tribesmen of the High Atlas, promoting a view of the religion in which Berber culture was praised and that downplayed the centrality of the Arab East to Islam. His followers became known as *al-Muwahiddun*, or Almohads, whose name signifies a true, unified, and uncompromising monotheism.

The Almohads may have remained merely another narrow, Berber nativist movement had it not been for the death of Ibn Tumart in 1130. The Almohad founder was succeeded by his right-hand man, 'Abd al-Mu'min, a Zanata from Algeria. 'Abd al-Mu'min would play Saint

Paul to Ibn Tumart's Jesus, crystallizing and formalizing the vague, Berber-oriented Almohad mission into a coherent and universal ideology and claiming the ultimate authority as the caliph of Islam—the Amir al-Mu'minin, the "Commander of the Faithful." Like the Almoravids, the Almohads have been characterized traditionally as "fundamentalist" and "puritan," but neither label fits. Focusing on a strict *tawhid* (monotheism), Almohadism was a synthetic creed developed in response to conditions in the twelfth-century Islamic West and was presented as superseding and rendering obsolete traditional Islam.

To broaden its appeal beyond its Berber base, 'Abd al-Mu'min Arabized it (and manufactured an Arabic lineage for himself), and cultivated Tinmallal and the tomb of Ibn Tumart as an alternate site of pious pilgrimage to Mecca. Almohadism was held to be the only legitimate interpretation of Islam—indeed, the only legitimate form of Abrahamic monotheism—a position that would complicate the movement's relations not only with Christians and Jews but with the majority of its Muslim subjects, who were expected to convert to the particular brand of *tawhid* the movement preached.

As leader, 'Abd al-Mu'min's first mission was to dismantle the vulnerable Almoravid imperium, which was completed when Marrakesh fell to an assault in the spring of 1147. The Almoravid capital was purged of the defenders and their supporters with thorough brutality; thousands were put to death, including the last amir, Ishaq ibn 'Ali. 'Abd al-Mu'min established his new capital here, marking the occasion by razing the religious installations of his vanquished enemies and founding a new congregational mosque, al-Kutubiyya ("Of the Booksellers"), adjacent to the royal palace he had commandeered. In 1151, his forces would strike out eastward, wresting the coastal cities of the Maghrib from local Muslim rulers and recovering Islamic Ifriqiya from the Norman kings of Sicily.

The Almohads had arrived in al-Andalus as early as 1145 at the invitation of the Sufi rebel Ibn Qasi. But, although they found supporters among some of the esoterically inclined *'ulama'*, they lacked the means to carry out a large-scale invasion. This situation would change after their capture of the Almoravid's African fleet and with establishment of a major naval base and shipyards at Salé on the

Atlantic coast. In 1146, Cádiz and Jerez (Sharish) recognized Almohad rule, and Seville was forced to yield in 1147. The surrender of the former Almoravid capital was followed by bloody reprisals against the inhabitants, violence that focused disproportionately, but far from exclusively, on the city's Christians and Jews. At this point, Andalusi resistance intensified. Although Granada held out until 1154, Almohad forces swept across the region to the west and south of Seville in 1157, culminating in their conquest of Castilian-held Almería later that year. With their presence in the peninsula thus secured, the caliph 'Abd al-Mu'min crossed the strait and set up headquarters at Gibraltar.

THE IMMEDIATE CHALLENGE the Almohads faced as they endeavored to establish domination over al-Andalus was not from the ever-more confident Christian kingdoms but from fellow Muslims, including those Andalusi warlords who had worked to overthrow the Almoravids, and from the Banu Ghaniya, who constituted the remnants of the dynasty. Chief among the former was Muhammad ibn Mardanish, a neo-muwallad of Navarrese origin and former Almoravid military commander, known to the Christian chroniclers as the "Wolf King." In the chaos that followed the collapse of the regime, he carved out a short-lived kingdom centered on the cities of Murcia and Valencia, minting his own coins, developing infrastructure, and cultivating commercial contacts across the Western Mediterranean, particularly with Pisan and Genoan merchants. He was a larger-than-life figure, famed as a gallant and imposing warrior, a copious drinker, and legendarily tireless lover. Brutal and pragmatic, the Wolf King was very much in the mold of the *taifas* of old—an unflinching authoritarian who brooked no dissent and crushed his subjects with taxes to support his own regime and further his own lineage.

And like the *taifas* of old, he was utterly dependent on Christian support, for which he was obliged to pay enormous sums in tribute. In return, both Ramon Berenguer IV and Alfonso VII of Castile lent him troops and protection. His army became closely integrated with theirs, such that in 1158, for example, Ibn Mardanish led the forces of the urban militia of Christian Ávila against Seville, which had been established as the Almohads' Andalusi capital. And so, as the Christian kingdoms faltered, so did Ibn Mardanish.

After the death of Alfonso VIII, Castile and León went to separate heirs, provoking a war between the two kingdoms that was also joined by Afonso Henriques of Portugal. 'Abd al-Mu'min skillfully played the warring Christian rulers against each other, securing León as an ally. He had moved his base of operations to al-Andalus, and drawing reinforcements from recently conquered Ifriqiya, extended his power in the peninsula. A massive invasion was planned for 1163, but 'Abd al-Mu'min fell ill and died the year before it was to be launched.

His son, Abu Ya'qub Yusuf, quickly imposed his authority over his rebellious brothers and quashed a rebellion by his father's early Berber supporters. They had realized too late that the Almohad movement had been hijacked by the Mu'minid family, and that it was now dynastic rather than ideological factors that drove policy. With this resistance behind him, Abu Ya'qub Yusuf set out for al-Andalus to attack Ibn Mardanish. In the face of the Almohad onslaught, the Wolf King was abandoned by his allies; he died of natural causes in 1171, just as his kingdom was about to be overwhelmed. A pragmatic Abu Ya'qub Yusuf accepted the surrender of Ibn Mardanish's son Hilal, and to seal their alliance, he married one of Hilal's sisters and wed the other to his son and heir, Abu Yusuf Ya'qub. Now as uncontested ruler of al-Andalus, Abu Ya'qub Yusuf officially took the title Amir al-Mu'minin.

THE ALMOHADS PRESENTED their wars of conquest as jihad. But, behind this pious posturing they were no less pragmatic than their Andalusi enemies when it came to dealing with Christian powers. As allies of Fernando II of León, their troops supported the king's campaigns, including his raids into northern Castile. Fernando reciprocated in kind, lending his forces to Almohad operations against their Christian enemies in the south. In addition, many Christian noblemen and soldiers of fortune enlisted in the Almohad army in both Spain and North Africa. When Geraldo Sem Pavor ("the Fearless"), a hero of the Portuguese "Reconquest," fell out of favor with Afonso Henriques, 'Abu Ya'qub welcomed his company into his

forces, first in Spain and then in North Africa, although he ultimately had him beheaded in 1174 when it was suspected he was
going to switch sides again. In the same era, a Leonese lord, Fernando Rodriguez de Castro, joined the Almohads to fight against his
own people, and fifteen years later, his son Pedro Fernandez de Castro provided support for their raids against Portugal and Castile.
Around 1198, Sancho VII of Navarre fought on behalf of the Almohads in the Maghrib in an effort to court their support in his struggle
against Castile. And in 1219, the Portuguese king Afonso II's own
brother Pedro enlisted in the Almohad forces. By the mid-thirteenth
century and the twilight of the dynasty, it was said there were some
12,000 Christian soldiers living in Marrakesh alone. Like the Almoravids before them, the Almohads had become all but dependent
on Christian mercenaries for their survival.

In the final quarter of the twelfth century, the war between the
Christian rulers and the Almohads intensified across the broad band
of territory between the Tagus and Guadalquivir rivers, and in 1184,
Abu Ya'qub launched a major campaign to retake Santarém, in Portugal. Unfortunately for the caliph, Afonso Henriques and Fernando II
had signed a truce, and together they secured a decisive victory over
the caliph. Abu Ya'qub was mortally wounded in the engagement,
and on his return to Seville his son Abu Yusuf Ya'qub hurried back to
Marrakesh to claim the caliphal title.

But, despite the Christian kings' posturing as crusaders, diplomatic contacts with the Almohads intensified. León remained an inconstant ally; Navarre, another rival of Castile, sent envoys to Seville;
and in the thirteenth century, even England's King John proposed an
alliance. As the rulers of al-Andalus, the Maghrib, and Ifriqiya, and
with their domination of the trans-Saharan gold routes, the Almohads
controlled an immense economy and were thus courted by the competing Italian merchant powers, Genoa and Pisa. Envoys were sent,
treaties signed, and trading colonies established in their ports. Even
as the popes preached crusade against the Almohads, they exchanged
letters with the caliphs and sent diplomatic missions to Marrakesh.

The Almohads are usually viewed as reactionary and intolerant
rulers who actively oppressed their Christian and Jewish subjects. At

the conquest of Marrakesh, for example, they were said to have rebuffed Jewish and Christian offers of *jizya*, declaring that they had no need for money. 'Abd al-Mu'min is said to have decreed that the institution of *dhimma* was now considered void and that Christians and Jews would need to convert or leave—a radical departure from established Islamic law. Córdoba was the scene of the repression around 1149, leading many Jews—most famously, the great philosopher Musa ibn 'Ubayd Allah ibn Maymun (Moses Maimonides) and his family—to feign conversion to Islam and emigrate to Fez before eventually escaping to Egypt and reasserting their Judaism. Abraham ben Meir ibn Ezra, an Andalusi poet, penned a lamentation for the destruction of the Jewish communities of the peninsula, but he had fled al-Andalus during the Almoravid period and his perspective cannot be viewed as reliable.

While there were undoubtedly periodic acts of violence and repression, destruction of synagogues, and conversion of Jews to Islam, and while many fled to Christian lands or the Islamic East, neither forced conversion nor the abrogation of *dhimma* were pursued consistently after the reign of 'Abd al-Mu'min. Nevertheless, the Almohads' commitment to a very strict observation of *dhimma*, emphasizing the humiliation of non-Muslims, would have emboldened some Muslims to engage in sectarian violence, but this was likely motivated by economic rather than religious factors. During Abu Ya'qub Yusuf's reign, not only Jews but also converts from Judaism were obliged to wear special attire and were prohibited from serving in certain professions—a reflection of suspicions that many had converted falsely and continued to secretly practice their original faith. On the other hand, some Jewish converts rose to positions of high influence and trust in the caliphal house, and there is considerable evidence that Jewish life continued to thrive openly under Almohad rule. Eventually, Jews were fully rehabilitated as subjects when the Mu'minid dynasty formally abolished the Almohad creed in the 1220s.

In any event, Almohad policy toward non-Muslims was not so much anti-Jewish or anti-Christian as a consequence of the revolutionary nature of their faith. For them, the arrival of Ibn Tumart had established a new age, one in which everyone would be called on to accept their brand of monotheism. It was not enough even to be Muslim; one had to be Almohad. Existing mosques were required to be either rebuilt or repurified and to have their direction of prayer "corrected" to the Almohad standard. Those Muslims who did not conform, at least outwardly, ran the danger of being seen effectively as apostates and became the focus of the Almohad jihad. Consequently, many pious, orthodox Muslims also fled from the Almohad caliphate and returned to Sunni Islam.

The Almohads' confidence that their rise marked the dawn of a new era is reflected in their coinage. Although they continued to mint Almoravid-style round gold *dinars* and half-*dinars*, their silver *dirhams* were square, a radical departure from established norms. Moreover, none of their coins were dated, and most did not bear the name of the ruler who minted them. In the new era, time and temporal rulership were seen as incidental, and their inscriptions evoked the singularity and uniqueness of God and the role of the Mahdi as imam. Due to their quality, these coins became the standard throughout the Maghrib, al-Andalus, and the Western Mediterranean and served to reinforce and advertise the revolutionary creed, as did the enormous silk and filigree banners they carried before them into battle and the carefully choreographed pageantry of the public appearances of the caliphs. In fact, in a war of propaganda carried out through competing currencies, the Almohads were obliged to raise the gold content of their own coins to curtail the growing popularity of Spanish Christian imitations, which bore inscriptions in Arabic lauding the Christian kings and their faith.

For all its egalitarian pretensions, Almohad rule was intended as a vehicle to power first for the regime's core supporters and then for the Mu'minid dynasty. The Almohad state, which they called a *makhzan* ("treasure chest") as opposed to a *dawla* ("dynasty"), was enriched by the confiscation of the properties of *dhimmis* and Muslims who resisted acknowledging the new orthodoxy and sustained by the trans-Saharan gold trade and the tremendous commercial and industrial output of their territories. Power was exercised by the caliphs through a hierarchy of councils of Almohad *shaykhs* and outsiders who had shown their commitment to the cause and who served as ideological cadres, whereas the nuts-and-bolts administration was in the hands of scribes or bureaucrats, many of whom were Maliki *'ulama'* whose families had been in the service of the Almoravids.

In order to rule, the Almohads depended on the collaboration of native elites, but to a lesser extent than their predecessors. Local religious men served as scribes—mere functionaries—and did not dictate or shape law and policy as they had under the Almoravids. In al-Andalus, which quickly became the front line of the Almohad jihad, governors were typically appointed from among the royal *sayyid*s (princes) or other trusted denizens of the inner circle, but these privileged members of the elite frequently neglected or abused the Andalusi populace, which served to soon turn the popular tide against the regime.

The dynasty reached its zenith under Abu Ya'qub Yusuf and his son Abu Yusuf Ya'qub, each of whom was serving as governor of Seville, the Almohads' second capital, when they came to power. Both invested heavily in the city, constructing lavish palaces and gardens intended to reinforce to both subjects and rivals the regime's majesty and legitimacy, and to provide a setting for the ostentatious ceremonies that the Almohads developed as a means of advertising their power. It was under Abu Yusuf that the minaret known as La Giralda, the magnificent seventy-five-meter structure modeled on the tower of the al-Kutubiyya mosque in Marrakesh, was added to the city's congregational mosque.

During his youth as governor in Seville, Abu Ya'qub Yusuf cultivated a taste for higher learning, specifically medicine and philosophy. He began to compile a library that would be said to rival that of the Umayyad caliph al-Hakam II and supported a salon that included such revolutionary thinkers as the physician-philosophers Ibn Tufayl and Ibn Rushd. Abu Bakr Muhammad ibn Tufayl ("Abubacer") is best known for his remarkable allegorical novel, *Hayy ibn Yaqzan*, a parable of a boy who grows up alone on a desert island and who, tabula rasa, must construct his own ideas of the world and himself. The brilliantly original story—the inspiration for Defoe's *Robinson Crusoe* and an anticipation of Descartes's *Discourse on Method*—set out to reconcile faith and philosophy through the application of reason and would exercise a profound influence on European thought after its translation into Latin in 1671.

It also piqued the caliph's interest in Aristotle and spurred his patronage of the controversial Córdoban scholar and *qadi* Muhammad ibn Rushd ("Averroës," to the Latin world), who, in a series of treatises, set out to codify Islamic philosophy and law through the systematic application of logic. One of the great intellects of the Middle Ages, Ibn Rushd transformed Muslim, Christian, and Jewish thought. His work served as the inspiration for Maimonides' own codification of Jewish law and reintroduced Aristotle to Latin Christian philosophy, energizing the Scholastic movement, which revolutionized European thought and laid the foundations for the Scientific Revolution.

But Ibn Rushd was not popular among many of the Andalusi religious elite, who were enraged by his advocacy for philosophy and his opposition to al-Ghazali. Al-Ghazali had written a tract called *The Incoherence of Philosophy*, which Ibn Rushd directly rebutted in his *The Incoherence of the Incoherence*. It was only due to the patronage and protection of Abu Ya'qub Yusuf and Abu Yusuf Ya'qub that Ibn Rushd was able to continue his work, at least until 1195, when bowing to political pressure from Andalusi *'ulama'*, the pious-minded Abu Yusuf decreed his works to be burned and ordered the philosopher into internal exile at Lucena, which had remained a Jewish enclave and center of learning. In 1198, the caliph reconsidered and rehabilitated him, but Ibn Rushd died that same year, shortly after his return to Marrakesh.

DURING THE REIGN of Abu Yusuf, the situation in al-Andalus became increasingly fraught. The continuing depredations of the Christian powers and a series of inconclusive Almohad campaigns undermined the dynasty's claim as protectors of Islam and as rulers vouchsafed by God. Popular anti-Berber sentiment and resistance to the imposition of a foreign ruling elite contributed to a growing grassroots resistance and popular hatred of the regime. Although Mu'minid rule became increasingly moderate and pragmatic over the course of his and his father's reigns, the memory of the brutality of the conquest lived on among Andalusis and was revived by occasional excesses against the populace committed at the hands of Almohad commanders and troops.

In the meantime, another node of anti-Almohad resistance in al-Andalus had coalesced around the Banu Ghaniya family—the last remnants of the Almoravid imperial clan. Muhammad ibn Ghaniya had been installed as governor of the Balearic Islands in 1126, and when the Almoravid regime collapsed, he became an independent king. Mallorca, with a considerable fleet at its disposal, was established as a thriving entrepôt, exporting salt and slaves to Africa and produce to Italy, and alternatively clashing and forming alliances with the Christian maritime powers of the Western Mediterranean.

Muhammad's son, Ishaq, who inherited the throne in 1155, raided Provence and secured favorable, bilateral treaties with Genoa and Pisa. By the time the Almohads finally conquered Mallorca in 1203, the Banu Ghaniya had taken over much of Ifriqiya and shifted operations there. In response, the Almohads sent the Banu Hafs, descendants of one of Ibn Tumart's closest disciples, to defeat them; but after they had accomplished this, their leader, Abu Zakariyya Yahya, declared his own independence. The Hafsid emirate (later, caliphate) of Tunis that he established in 1237 would dominate Ifriqiya through the next century.

Meanwhile, the rulers of León, Castile, and Portugal were effecting a piecemeal conquest of the territory north and west of the Guadalquivir River through the 1170s and 1180s and raiding with near impunity. In 1189, Abu Yusuf brought a huge army across the strait and set out to tame the Christian powers and recapture the towns that had been lost before returning to Marrakesh. He was determined to teach them a lesson, which he did in July 1195 outside a small fortress halfway between Córdoba and Toledo, called al-Arak in Arabic and Alarcos by the Christians. Here, with the help of the Castilian nobleman Pedro Fernandez de Castro, the Almohad army dealt Castile a devastating defeat in which several bishops, a number of important lords, and the commanders of two military orders lost their lives.

The caliph, who adopted the honorific al-Mansur bi-Llah ("Victorious by God") to commemorate the victory, followed up this battle by raiding far and wide. Castile was crippled, and it was further isolated by treaties Abu Yusuf concluded with León and Navarre. But no significant or lasting territorial gains were made, and having returned to Marrakesh, the aging and exhausted caliph died in 1199. His young heir, Muhammad, who rashly assumed the throne name al-Nasir ("the Victor"), was singularly unequipped to take the reins of a complex empire that was slowly being torn apart by centrifugal forces: North Africa was fragmenting, the caliph's subjects both here and in al-Andalus were increasingly resisting the heavy and capricious Almohad rule, and the intrigues of palace officials and provincial governors undermined the efficacy and coherence of the *makhzan.*

It would take eighteen years, but Alfonso VIII of Castile would take his vengeance for his defeat at Alarcos. Gathering together a coalition of all the Christian kingdoms (except León), fortified by a Crusade bull from Pope Innocent III and promoted eloquently by the indefatigable warrior-archbishop Rodrigo Jiménez de Rada of Toledo, the Castilian king raised a massive army. In anticipation of the clash, preparations took place over the course of nearly two years. Alfonso VIII amassed Spanish knights and foreign crusaders at Toledo, and the caliph mustered his own forces at Seville, including Berber and Arab troops from North Africa, Turkic warriors from the east, and legions of volunteers—*mujahidun* eager to fight the infidel. The gathering clouds of war hung ominously over al-Andalus.

The storm would break on July 16, 1212, at a place not far from Alarcos, which the Spanish call Las Navas de Tolosa. Having confidently established his base in a broad valley backed by mountains, al-Nasir was completely surprised when the Castilian-led forces threaded a little-known pass and descended in full assault on his camp. The rout was complete. Al-Nasir, who was barely able to escape with his life, humiliatingly abandoned his tent, his treasure, and his battle standards, which were seized as prizes by the victorious Alfonso. The Almohad army was destroyed and the Christian forces suffered only light casualties. Returning to Marrakesh in defeat, the caliph retreated into his palace until his death in 1213, likely murdered by his own courtiers. The victory, transformed through the propaganda of Archbishop Rodrigo into a divine triumph and a vindication of Castilian manifest destiny, has traditionally been seen by historians as precipitating the decline of the Almohads. But al-Nasir's defeat at Las Navas was a symptom, more than a cause, of the failure of his dynasty and the collapse of Almohad power in al-Andalus, and the battle was not regarded as a watershed by most contemporaries.

As for Alfonso VIII of Castile, his exhausted army quickly disbanded, much to Archbishop Rodrigo's frustration, and he was unable to capitalize on his success at Las Navas. Nor were his counterparts in the peninsula. Alfonso died in 1214, followed by his son Enrique only three years later. In Portugal, the teenage Afonso II, who had come to the throne in 1211, was too preoccupied with consolidating his own position to wage war on al-Andalus. Pere (Peter) "the Catholic," count of Barcelona and king of Aragón, who had distinguished himself at Las Navas, was killed in battle in 1213 by crusaders sent by Innocent III to crush the Cathar heretics of Languedoc. As for Sancho VII of Navarre, geographical position had effectively locked his kingdom out of the opportunity to conquer Islamic Spain, and therefore he remained focused on his rivalry with Castile.

After al-Nasir's death, the Almohad dynasty's decline accelerated, characterized by the accession of young, inexperienced caliphs, a number of whom were murdered and all of whom were prey to the increasingly predatory internal politics of the palace. Eventually, al-Ma'mun, the ninth caliph, who was only able to come to power in 1228 with the aid of Castile, would return to Sunni Islam and declare that Jesus, rather than Ibn Tumart, was the Mahdi of scripture. His reign marked the effective end of Almohad power in al-Andalus. The dynasty would persevere in the Maghrib, ruling over an ever-diminishing zone around Marrakesh, until their capital was conquered in 1269 by a nomadic Zanata clan called the Banu Marin. Tinmallal would fall in 1276.

In al-Andalus, there had been a pregnant, decade-long pause after Las Navas de Tolosa, in which the status quo endured only because of inertia. In the interim, native Andalusi strongmen and disaffected Almohad commanders each endeavored to establish local powerbases, until in the 1220s the rise of Castile-León under Fernando III and the Crown of Aragon under Jaume I, and the entrenchment of a new indigenous dynasty, the Banu 'l-Ahmar, or Nasrids, would once more transform al-Andalus and the lives of the Muslims of the Iberian Peninsula.

22

Golden Ages

After the nobles of the west, how can I find pleasure
   in sleep, and how will my heart find rest
May my right hand be forgotten if I forget it, and if
I will desire to rejoice not in their presence
If ever God returns me to the Glory
   of the Pomegranate [Granada] my way will be successful
I will quench my thirst in the waters of Snir
   which were clear on the day
   that the rivers of Eden were muddy
A land in which my life was pleasurable and the waters
   of the cheeks of time were flat for me. . . . [37]

The lament of the self-exiled Jewish poet Moses ben Ezra, who left al-Andalus in 1090 in the wake of the Almoravid conquest, found echo with Muslim contemporaries, whose elegies bemoaned the conquest of al-Andalus, whether by Christian "polytheists" or uncultured Berbers, and the disappearance of the vibrant and open culture of the *taifa* age. Their nostalgia has struck a deep chord with modern scholars, who have lauded the eleventh century in al-Andalus as a "Golden Age" of tolerance, diversity, creativity, sophistication, and sensuality—one that was destroyed as a consequence of the invasion of the foreign Almoravids and the Almohads. Appealing as this portrayal may be, it is an oversimplification. The intellectual culture of al-Andalus did not come to an end with the destruction of the *taifa* kingdoms, and although it was transformed, many strands of continuity can be traced through to the end of Almohad rule and beyond. Similarly, the profound influence that this culture exerted on the Christian Spains and on Latin Europe was not limited to a single moment but played out over the course of centuries.

The *taifa* era is famous for being an age of verse. Poetry was profoundly political and, for its practitioners, a pathway to material and social success. A clever poem addressed to the right patron could catapult a humble man to riches or power. The ability to compose in classical Arabic was prized by rulers, among whom elegance in correspondence was a hallmark of authority. Poetry was used both as political propaganda and to voice popular discontent. While Isma'il ibn Naghrilla sang of his own power in Hebrew and that of his king, Badis of Granada, in Arabic, enemies, like Abu Ishaq of Elvira, fought back in kind by aiming vicious lampoons at the Jewish wazir and his king. Verse served as the medium for broadcasting news, disseminating political ideology, and expressing dissent. Court poets lauded the triumphs of their kings in classical Arabic, while anonymous popular poets composed earthy verses in the spoken Andalusi dialect.

Love, sex, longing, and death were favorite subjects among both Muslim poets and their Jewish counterparts, the latter favoring Arabic for more profane themes and the sacred tongue, Hebrew, for liturgical compositions and other works—including anti-Muslim polemics—that were intended for a narrowly Jewish audience. Although Hebrew reemerged as a living literary language and vernacular at this time, Arabic remained throughout these centuries the main spoken and written language for Jews across the *dar al-Islam*. Many Jewish scholars were so thoroughly acculturated that they regarded Arabic as inherently superior to Hebrew for poetry and science.

But, poetry did not disappear with the destruction of the *taifa* courts. Writers merely adapted to the changing times, and despite the more modest patronage they received from the Andalusi *khassa* under Almoravid rule, poets continued to thrive. For example, Ibn Khafaja, an aristocrat from Valencia, wrote classical-styled poetry and rhymed prose in praise of nature and human emotion that was admired even in the Islamic East, establishing an idiom that was imitated through the fifteenth century. Eventually, Mu'minid patronage, particularly of panegyrics in their own honor, became a platform for the revival of Andalusi poetry in the later twelfth century. This was part of a general florescence under the Almohad caliphs and their governors in Seville, which saw Andalusi scholars once more heading to the Islamic East and returning with new books that were then copied and distributed among the learned classes.

In addition to their literary patronage, *taifa* rulers also continued to support the scholarship that had been popular under Umayyad rule, notably the "sciences of the ancients," astrology and astronomy, medicine, philosophy, mathematics, geometry, botany, and agronomy, all of which reached new levels of sophistication. Competition among the various *taifa* kings stimulated the market for education and knowledge, and in the same manner as poets, scholars crisscrossed the peninsula, moving from court to court depending on the various kings' intellectual predilections, the vicissitudes of politics, and the opportunities for patronage.

While support for the "sciences of the ancients" dried up after the *taifa* era, in the Almoravid and Almohad periods, genres such as historical writing, geographical treatises, and biographical dictionaries became more popular. Muhammad ibn Ghalib, for example, wrote a history of the time of Creation to the reign of 'Abd al-Mu'min, while the Jewish Aristotelian Abraham ibn Daud composed his *Book of Tradition*, recounting the history of the Jews in the peninsula for the same period. This was also the period in which important biographical dictionaries of Andalusi *'ulama'* were compiled, notably the sequel to al-Faradi's tenth-century *History of the 'Ulama' of al-Andalus* called *The Book of the Continuation of the History of the Sages of al-Andalus*. Written by Ibn Bashkuwal ("the son of Pascual"), it contains over 1,500 entries. Remarkable personal travel accounts were written in the Almohad period by Muhammad ibn Jubayr of Xàtiva, who passed through the Crusader kingdom of Jerusalem and Norman-ruled Sicily on his way back from the *hajj*, and Abu Hamid al-Gharnati, who traveled to Central Asia and settled briefly in Hungary.

In science and philosophy, as in literature, Jewish scholars were highly active within both specifically Jewish circles and the broader Arabo-Andalusi environment. Many works were translated from Arabic to Hebrew and from Hebrew to Arabic, and Jewish scholars were treated, in circumstances where the socioreligious hierarchy could be set aside or ignored, as effective equals. Learned Muslims trained under Jewish masters and vice versa, and intellectual battle lines were drawn not between Judaism and Islam, but rather between, for example, Platonists and Aristotelians of both faiths. So intellectually integrated were Jews and Muslims that their work was sometimes indistinguishable. For example, until the mid-nineteenth century it was assumed that *The Fountain of Life*, a seminal Neoplatonist work in Arabic written by Solomon ibn Gabirol ("Avicebron," to Latin Europeans), had been authored by a Muslim or a Christian. In fact, Mozarab Christians rarely distinguished themselves as intellectuals in this era and, with the exception of translation or production of religious texts in Arabic, are notable for their absence. But, for Jewish and Muslim courtly scholars, this was a heady, effervescent time; they wrote poems praising the power of reason, imagining themselves as soaring falcons and the conservative *faqihs* who opposed them as venomous serpents.

That said, not all intellectuals were enamored of the rational sciences as practiced by these courtly scholars or of the palace milieu in which they thrived. As the power of the *taifa* kings declined, some scholars condemned their decadence and acquiescence to the Christian kings. Muslim and Jewish pietists composed their own poems criticizing this effete culture. However, it would be wrong to think that there were two, clearly defined cultural-intellectual camps in al-Andalus—a secular one and a religious one. Many of the court scholars were also deeply religious and active in theological pursuits, despite the apparent self-contradictions that this could involve. For example, Isma'il ibn Naghrilla was at once an eminently respected theologian and stalwart defender of orthodox Rabbinical Judaism and an author of erotic and homoerotic verse. Homoerotic verse, as well as poetry celebrating illicit interfaith relationships, was also penned by Muslim intellectuals and religious scholars. Nor should one imagine that Maliki scholars composed a unified party or that they were, as a group, reactionary conservatives. They were rationalists: many explored alternative religious paths, including mysticism, and many who advocated for the application of a rigorous Maliki law were also engaged in nonreligious sciences.

If there was one individual who embodied the creativity and tensions of the *taifa* period, it was Abu Muhammad 'Ali ibn Hazm (d. 1064). The scion of a family of well-connected courtiers fiercely loyal to the Umayyad dynasty, Ibn Hazm grew up in the palace harem and was educated with an eye to a career in the caliphal administration. The collapse of the regime and the *fitna* that followed destroyed his family's fortune and threw Ibn Hazm into a tumultuous political career as he worked in vain to support the reestablishment of the dynasty. He distinguished himself as a scholar and theologian, championing the rigorously literalist Zahiri school of Islam and producing hundreds of works ranging from theology to jurisprudence, physics, astronomy, medicine, law, logic, ethics, history, and philosophy. In fact, he is credited as being a pioneer of comparative religion, thanks to his encyclopedic work *Fisal* ("Detailed Critical Examination"), which compared moral and religious beliefs from Antiquity to his own time. He was also a poet and is best known for his treatise on love, *The Dove's Neckring*. He was a convinced rationalist and a vehement critic not only of Shi'ism, mysticism, and philosophy, but of rival schools of Islam. This set him against the reactionary Maliki *'ulama'*, who persecuted him, burning his books, banning his teaching, and occasionally imprisoning him. Although with the Almoravids the Maliki *'ulama'* would gain the political support they needed to persecute their rivals, the Zahirism championed by Ibn Hazm continued to acquire adherents and would eventually find patronage and official support under Abu Ya'qub Yusuf, the third Almohad caliph.

In any event, *taifa*-style court culture was not driven to extinction by the Almoravids but merely driven underground, and it helped fuel nativist resistance against them. Through patronage, the courts of the "second *taifas*"—the Banu Hud of Castile, Ibn Mardanish of Sharq al-Andalus, and the Banu Ghaniya in Mallorca—gave new life to the sciences and arts that the Almoravids had deliberately neglected, although their means were much reduced. Nor did Jewish intellectual life disappear; under Almoravid rule, Jewish religious and scientific culture remained robust, with Granada, Córdoba, and Lucena continuing as the principal centers of activity.

Even in pious Muslim circles, nonreligious literary pursuits were not abandoned. *Adab* remained important because it was the foundation of the high literary style that was indispensable to the chancery, diplomacy, and the projection of authority. Grammar continued to be a key to understanding Qur'anic scripture (and, thereby, the world). History and geography were also viewed as tools for maintaining and extending the power of the dynasty. In any case, the power of the Maliki *'ulama'* was largely restricted to al-Andalus; thus, persecuted intellectuals and literati could take refuge in the Maghrib in the households of the ruling elite in places such as Tunis, Salé, Marrakesh, and Fez, whose ninth-century Qarawayyin University is the oldest in the world.

Despite the official Malikism of the dynasty, Almoravid rulers and aristocrats personally, if discreetly, supported thinkers, including many former denizens of the courts of the defeated *taifa* kings, whose work did not toe the official line. The Almoravids were also energetic mosque builders. The earliest were constructed in a sober, unadorned style that reflected their stark ideology and recalled the whitewashed adobe of Moroccan *qasba*s and ribats. But this was soon encroached on by the elaborate vegetal and geometric designs typical of Andalusi tastes, as the regime and its Maliki enforcers could not suppress the distinct and by now entrenched artistic cultures of al-Andalus. In other words, the cultural turn under the Almoravids was not regressive, but one wholly consistent with their ideology and their priorities, including the entrenchment of orthodox Islam in the still very heterodox Maghrib.

MOST IMPORTANTLY, THE Maliki *'ulama'* and the Almoravids were unable to stem the growing tide of mysticism in al-Andalus. The public burning of al-Ghazali's books in Seville by the *qadi* Ibn Hamdin did not extinguish the flames of Sufism in al-Andalus but fanned them. Asceticism and mysticism were gaining ground among the populace, as attested to by the proliferation of esoteric holy men, the establishment of local shrines, and the growing popularity of magic. By the early thirteenth century, the tombs of local saints were becoming centers for pilgrimage and popular devotional rituals, as well as favored sites for religious colonies. Sufi-inspired rebels like Ibn Qasi presented themselves as *mahdis* and raised the local revolts against the Almoravids that paved the way for Almohad domination.

Indigenous movements such as these were reflections of a broader mystical and millenarian turn that can be seen also among the peninsula's Jews. By the mid-twelfth century, the Rabbinate party, which can be seen in some ways as analogous to the Maliki *'ulama'*, had all but extinguished Karaism in Spain, but a new challenge was emerging in the form of Kabbala, or Jewish mysticism, which was itself influenced by Sufi movements. In the early 1100s, a certain Moshe al-Darri arrived in al-Andalus claiming that the Messiah had revealed himself in a dream and would appear in Fez in 1130. His unfortunate followers sold off all their worldly goods in anticipation of the coming apocalypse.

Like the Almoravid elite, members of the Almohad upper classes began to discreetly patronize dissident scholars. And so it was that under the rule of Abu Ya'qub Yusuf, Andalusi rational philosophy, particularly Aristotelianism, reached its zenith with the work of luminaries such as Ibn Rushd and Maimonides (both from Córdoba), Ibn Tufayl (from Guadix), the astronomer al-Bitruji ("Alpetragius," to Latin Europe), and the physician and poet Abu Marwan ibn Zuhr. Indeed, the caliph's own daughter Zaynab gained renown as a rationalist theologian. For rationalists like Ibn Rushd, Ibn Zuhr, and Ibn Tufayl, there could be no conflict between Reason and Revelation—between *falsafa* ("Philosophy") and *kalam* ("the Word"), and between natural law and divine law—a position that resonated with the Almohads' holistic approach to theology (and knowledge in general), while appealing to their notion of a higher, inner truth accessible to only a spiritual or intellectual elite.

In fact, the experience of the Banu Zuhr provides an illustration of how intellectual culture persevered through the regime changes of the

eleventh and twelfth centuries, and how families cultivated intellectual "trade secrets" that could sustain their prosperity. The family first
came to prominence in the era of the *fitna*, when Zuhr al-'Iyadi
(d. 1030/1) gained fame as a legal scholar. His son Abu Marwan ibn
Zuhr (d. 1078) began as a jurist but ended his career as a renowned
physician at the *taifa* court of Denia. His son Abu'l-'Ala' Zuhr ("Abo-
eli," to the Latin world; d. 1130) trained in *hadith* and *adab* and served
as a wazir in 'Abbadid Seville, but he was most famous as a medical
doctor and pharmacologist. Abu Marwan ibn Zuhr ("Avenzoar"), a
son of Abu'l-'Ala', was a prolific author who served as an Almoravid
and Almohad court physician and befriended Ibn Rushd. His daughter Umm 'Amr was appointed court physician for treating the royal
women, children, and female slaves.

Abu Marwan's son Abu Bakr ibn Zuhr, "the Grandson," carried on
the family medical practice (specializing in ophthalmology) while
studying Maliki law and *adab*. In the manner of an old-style Andalusi
aristocrat, he was a man of learning, faith, and culture who composed
muwashshah poetry and took up noble pursuits, including chess and
archery. While physician to Abu Ya'qub Yusuf, he was ordered by the
caliph to purge the realm of all works on logic and philosophy, but the
Almohad ruler allowed him to keep his own collection, which Ibn
Zuhr discreetly made available to trusted students. After he was poisoned by a rival courtier in 1198/9, his son Abu Muhammad would
briefly serve as physician to the caliph al-Nasir, but he also was poisoned in 1205/6. The careers of the Banu Zuhr reflect the reorienta-
tion of intellectual patronage in al-Andalus toward the Maghrib. For
all of their wanderings, every member of the family after Zuhr al-
'Iyadi was born in Seville, and every member was buried there.

Almohad artistic and craft production was also at odds with what
one might expect of simple "fundamentalists." Their mosque and
palace building and their construction of grand gardens were, like
their public ceremonial, intended to reinforce the power and legitimacy of the regime and collaterally drove innovation in Andalusi
craft and construction industries. In contrast to mostly sober Almoravid styles, under Almohad rule flamboyant vegetal and geometric
designs returned to architectural decoration (notably, brickwork

patterns, tile inlay, and stamped stucco), textiles (especially silk), glass, and ceramics. Often featuring flowers, and sometimes animals and even human forms, these were more elaborate, complex, and delicate than those of the caliphal and *taifa* periods and laid the foundations for the arts and crafts of the Nasrid kingdom of Granada. As in the caliphal period, Qur'anic inscriptions were used to reinforce the new religious orthodoxy. The epigraph on the elaborately carved portal of the mosque of Seville read, "Praise be to God of his graces. Thanks be to God. Sovereignty belongs to God (alone). Glory is for God."[38] Not surprisingly, arts associated with the Word were heavily patronized. Córdoba became a major center for bookbinding, and new techniques of decorative calligraphy were developed, while Xàtiva, near Valencia, became a center for paper production as early as 1100; it was from here that this technology would spread across Western Europe.

OVER THE COURSE of the eleventh and twelfth centuries, Latin Europeans became intensely interested in Islamic knowledge and culture. Beginning in this period, "lost" classical treatises by authors such as Ptolemy, Galen, Plato, and Aristotle (and Arabic commentaries on and corrections of these), as well as original works in virtually every discipline of science—philosophy, theology, mathematics, optics, alchemy, geometry, music, medicine, magic, astronomy, and botany— and works of literature and popular culture were suddenly made available to European intellectuals in the newly established universities that were sprouting up across the continent. Among the many seminal works translated here was the *Qanun*, a medical manual written by the eleventh-century Persian scholar Ibn Sina ("Avicenna," to the Latins), which remained the standard medical textbook in Europe into the eighteenth century. The translation movement, a massive project of intellectual appropriation, was possible thanks to the collaboration of Mozarab Christians and Arabic-speaking Jews who came north in increasing numbers in the wake of the Almohad conquest, as well as free and enslaved Muslims, and Jewish and Muslim converts to Christianity, who worked together with Latin clergymen under the patronage of the city's archbishops.

The earlier appropriations of scholars like Gerbert of Aurillac had already fired the imaginations of the European clergy, who had begun to enthusiastically apply the tools of reason to previously unsystematized Catholic theology, and this would now reach a fevered pitch. The effect on European culture cannot be overstated; it was here the foundations for the Renaissance, the Enlightenment, and modernity itself were laid.

The translation of philosophical and theological works had the greatest immediate impact. For centuries, Muslim, and eventually Jewish, thinkers had been wrestling to reconcile pagan Aristotelianism and Neoplatonic thought with Abrahamic monotheism, and Christian religious scholars appropriated the resulting ideas, making adjustments mainly to account for their own doctrinal particularities, such as the incarnation of God as Jesus and the notion of the Trinity. Even if for most Christian thinkers Islam was perceived as diabolical and threatening, this also fueled interest in Islamic theology, if only to better refute it. Hence, in the 1140s, Peter the Venerable, the Abbot of Cluny, commissioned the English canon Robert of Ketton, who was based in Tudela, to produce the first Latin translation of the Qur'an, which Robert candidly titled *The Law of the False Prophet Muhammad*.

By the early 1200s, within only a generation of his own death, the works of Averroës (Ibn Rushd)—notably, his commentaries on Aristotle—would be rendered into Latin by the likes of Michael Scot, a canon of Toledo who was known not only as a prolific translator but as an accomplished sorcerer. Leading European Scholastic theologians applied Ibn Rushd's method with such enthusiasm that they became known as "Latin Averroists." Like their Islamic and Jewish counterparts, however, their unbridled rationalism soon led them into conflict with doctrinaire theologians, who understood that by questioning the eternality of scripture and the world, and the nature of divine creation, these philosophers threatened the very foundations of the faith.

As early as 1210, the church began an attempt to limit the teaching of Aristotelian philosophy; by 1277, no fewer than 219 propositions of the Latin Averroists had been denounced as heretical. Nevertheless, the greatest of the theologians influenced by Ibn Rushd, the Dominican friar Thomas Aquinas (d. 1274), escaped direct condemnation and

Ibn Rushd (Averroës) and Porphyry in an imagined debate in Monfredo
de Monte Imperiali's *Liber de herbis et plantis* (fourteenth century).
*Reproduction in "Inventions et decouvertes au Moyen-Age," Samuel
Sadaune (Wikipedia/Creative Commons)*

direct censure, and even in his own day he was recognized as having
revolutionized Catholic thought. The "Angelic Doctor" was canonized
in 1323. Christians did not hesitate to give credit to the infidel philosopher Ibn Rushd, whom they hailed as "the Commentator." When Dante
composed his *Divine Comedy* in the early fourteenth century, he portrayed Ibn Rushd in Limbo, having escaped by grace of his wisdom the
eternal damnation that was his just fate as a Muslim.

As well as ideas, sophisticated material goods made their way
north into Latin lands through trade, tribute, plunder, and eventually
imitation. Delicately sculpted ivory boxes and fine silk brocade created for Muslim aristocrats were repurposed as reliquaries and clerical vestments in the Christian North. High-quality ceramic plates
made by Muslim craftsmen for European markets often featured Arabic script or nonsensical pseudo-Arabic inscriptions. Elaborately
carved African tusks, or "olifants," were so prized in the north in the
twelfth century that by the thirteenth century, cheap knock-offs were

being manufactured for sale. One of the most intriguing examples of material exchange is the so-called Eleanor Vase, which once belonged to Eleanor of Aquitaine and is now held in the Louvre in Paris. What began as a carved, rock crystal ewer in eleventh-century Fatimid Egypt (or perhaps Persia) was acquired by the Banu Hud of Zaragoza. Evacuated with the rest of the royal treasury in 1110, it was apparently presented by 'Imad al-Dawla ("Mitadolus," in the vase's Latin inscription) as a gift to William IX of Aquitaine, when both were allies-in-arms supporting Alfonso I of Aragon in his campaign against the Almoravids. Such was the enthusiasm for all things Islamic that the twelfth-century rational theologian Peter Abelard (d. 1142) gave the name "Astrolabe" to the illegitimate son he had with his pupil and lover, Héloïse—the approximate equivalent of naming one's child "iPhone" today.

In sum, as the Islamic and Christian worlds became more engaged, cultural influence intensified. Through the medium of alliances, immigration, conquest, slavery, and collaboration, Christians and Muslims borrowed, adopted, and absorbed from each other. Owing to its relative sophistication, its urbanity, and its global reach, Islamic culture had more to give in this era. And the Christian West took eagerly, adopting styles of clothing, food, dance, music, poetry, song, and literature. A striking example is modern Spanish, the language of Castile and León, which, excluding place-names, features some four thousand words of Arabic origin, from scientific and technical terms, to foods, to popular idioms—nearly 10 percent of its lexicon. Much in the same way that the new linguistic variant known as Spanglish is developing in the modern United States by adapting English vocabulary to Spanish grammar, the names for new concepts and objects were appropriated from Arabic and Latinized, thus coming to form part of the Spanish, or Castilian, language that was emerging at this time. Even English, a language that did not achieve its modern form until the fourteenth century, contains over nine hundred words of Arabic origin, mostly technical and scientific terms, ranging from "alcohol" (from *al-kohl*, or "antimony") to "zenith" (from *samt al-ra'is*, or "upper direction").

But over the course of the following centuries, the balance of political and cultural power would slowly shift. From the mid-thirteenth century onward, it would be the Muslim princes of a greatly diminished al-Andalus who ruled as clients and tributaries of the ever-stronger Christian kings and not the reverse. While Islamic culture would continue to exercise fascination and appeal to the Christian upper classes, the Muslim aristocracy also began to borrow from the Latin world. Those Muslims who lived as legitimate but second-class subjects—*mudajjan*—of infidel regimes slowly took on the manners and appearance of their Christian neighbors, even as they were determined to maintain their identity as members of the *umma*.

PART V

ROMANCE, 1220–1482

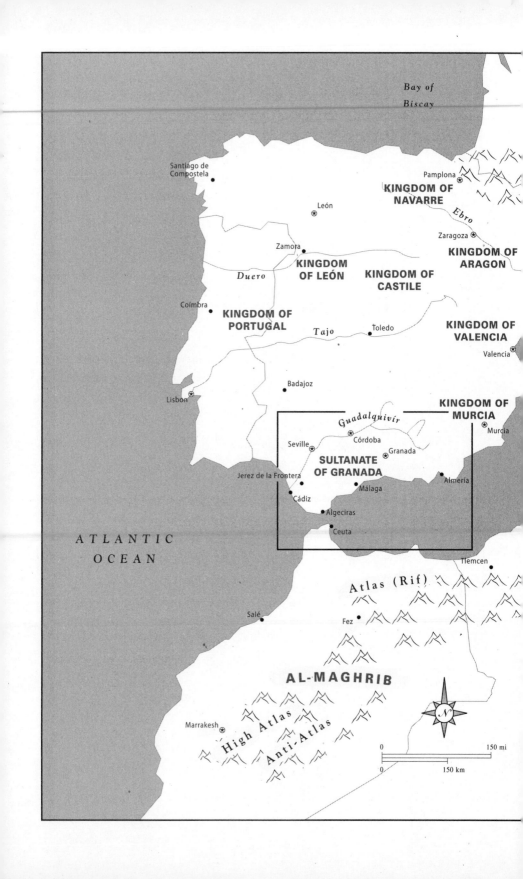

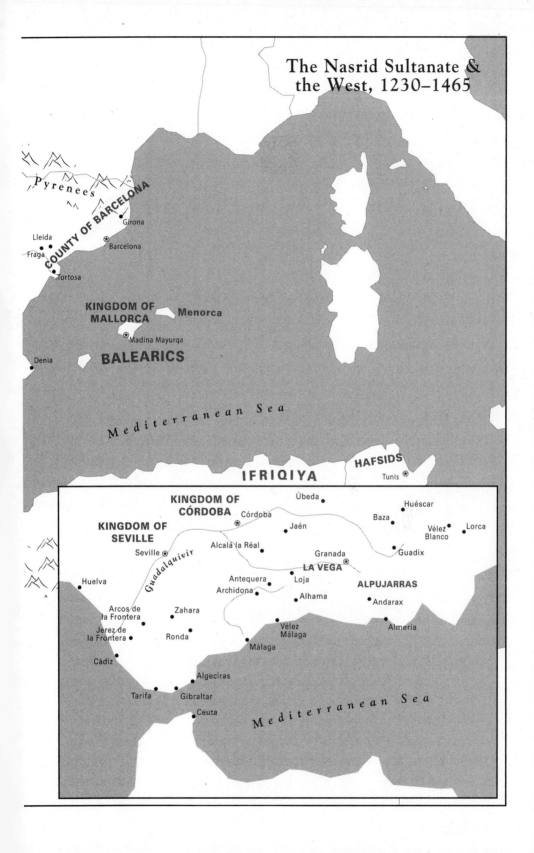

The Nasrid Sultanate &
the West, 1230–1465

Pyrenees

COUNTY OF BARCELONA

Girona

Lleida

Fraga

Barcelona

Tortosa

KINGDOM OF
MALLORCA

Menorca

Madina Mayurqa

Denia

BALEARICS

Mediterranean Sea

IFRIQIYA

HAFSIDS

Tunis

KINGDOM OF
CÓRDOBA

Úbeda

Huéscar

Córdoba

Baza

KINGDOM OF
SEVILLE

Jaén

Vélez
Blanco

Lorca

Guadalquivir

Alcalá la Réal

Granada

Guadix

Seville

LA VEGA

Huelva

Antequera

Loja

ALPUJARRAS

Archidona

Alhama

Andarax

Arcos de
la Frontera

Zahara

Vélez
Málaga

Almería

Jerez de
la Frontera

Ronda

Cádiz

Málaga

Algeciras

Tarifa

Gibraltar

Ceuta

Mediterranean Sea

23

The Great Game

And rejecting the lordship of the Almohads, the Andalusis followed Ibn Hud as if king and lord, who . . . pounced viciously on
the Almohads, capturing men, cutting their throats, striking off the
penises of some, cutting off the breasts of women, and wretchedly
putting children to death.[39]

The words of an anonymous thirteenth-century Castilian cleric
capture the disorder that accompanied the disintegration of Almohad
rule in the 1220s. Cities and towns were cast adrift as orphaned Almohad officials and commanders, local strongmen, and members of the
religious classes and landed aristocracy each endeavored to impose
order on their own locales. As the fourteenth-century historian Ibn
Khaldun put it, "every commander and man of influence, who could
command a few score of followers or possessed a castle to retreat to
in time of need, styled himself sultan and assumed the insignia of
royalty."[40] Remarkably, amid the chaos, the fabric of Islamic law, the
vigor of Arabo-Islamic culture, and the resilience of the Andalusi
economy continued to provide a foundation for prosperity and a platform for the ambitions of the ruling elite. The *'ulama'* remained a
potent force. And to the extent that there was a consensus as to what
Andalusis expected from their overlords, it was a respite from the

plundering of Christian and Muslim raiders, the expulsion of the Al-mohads, a return to Sunni orthodoxy, and an end to the cycle of alli-ance, dependence, and domination by Christian princes.

Several warlords would position themselves as champions of these causes, but none could deliver. Each, for all their posturing as *muja-hidun*, fell into the same cycle of internecine conflict and dependence on outside powers, whether from North Africa or the Christian North. Ultimately, Jaume I of Aragon and Fernando IV of Castile and León seized the advantage, and as al-Andalus appeared to crumble before them, the two rulers raced against each other to seize as much Muslim territory as they could. From this point, the survival of Muslim princes would depend on their ability to exploit Christian competition. The Great Game had begun.

IN 1228, MUHAMMAD ibn Hud al-Mutawakkil, who claimed descent from the Banu Hud of Zaragoza, formally raised the flag of rebellion against the Almohads. Seizing Murcia, he sent envoys to the 'Ab-basid caliph al-Mustansir in distant Baghdad and received a formal acclamation as amir of al-Andalus in 1232 with the express charge of waging war against the Christians. Symbolic as the caliphal patent may have been, it gave Ibn Hud support among the *'ulama'* and a claim to authority over all that remained of al-Andalus. He minted coins advertising his legitimacy and set about to establish a formal apparatus of rule. The people of al-Andalus, however, expected him to deliver on his pledge to stave off the Christians, and there were troubling signs he might not be up to the task.

And he had more to contend with than Christian foes. To his north was Valencia, ruled by Abu Zayd, a great-grandson of 'Abd al-Mu'min, who served as governor and remained nominally loyal to the Almohad dynasty. Abu Zayd's distant kinsman Abu Yahya Muham-mad al-Tinmalli, who ruled in Mallorca, was too far removed to par-ticipate in peninsular politics. To fulfill his calling as a *mujahid*, Ibn Hud waged holy war not only against the Christians, but also against those Muslims who rejected his authority. As a result, he was drawn into conflict with the Aragonese and into a relationship of tributary dependence with now-united Castile-León. This provided an opening for two of his subordinates, Muhammad ibn al-Ahmar and Zayyan ibn Mardanish. Ibn al-Ahmar was a frontier *mujahid* who ruled a small territory stretching from Arjona, some forty miles east of Córdoba, to Guadix (Wadi 'Ash), twenty miles east of Granada. Zayyan ibn Mardanish, a kinsman of the Wolf King, was a commander based near Valencia who served Ibn Hud as a thorn in the side of Abu Zayd and the Crown of Aragon.

No sooner had Ibn Hud received his title from the 'Abbasids than Ibn al-Ahmar revolted, quickly gaining the support of Jaén and Córdoba and forcing the new amir to appeal to Fernando III of Castile for aid. This cost Ibn Hud land and cash, but also his reputation as a holy warrior, undermining his popularity among his subjects. Worse, Fernando soon betrayed him by switching his support to Ibn al-Ahmar. This enabled the Castilian king to move on Córdoba, where he arrived in February 1236 with a large army, sealing off the city. The siege would spell the end of both Islamic Córdoba and Ibn Hud.

After five harsh months of deprivation, the city opened its gates to the Christian king. The Muslim population was required to leave with whatever property they could carry, while Fernando took up residence in the fortress and proclaimed his new kingdom of Córdoba. Although the former capital's age of glory had long passed, the loss was a powerful blow to the Muslims of the peninsula. The great mosque, founded by 'Abd al-Rahman I over four hundred years earlier, was promptly reconsecrated as the new cathedral, and the bells of Santiago that the *hajib* al-Mansur had hung there as a trophy in 997 were borne back to Compostela in triumph on the shoulders of Muslim captives. To their credit, neither Fernando nor his successors destroyed the mosque; instead, its minaret was repurposed as a bell tower, and gradually across two centuries, a hulking cathedral was raised up incongruously within it, like a stake stabbing upward through what had been for a half millennium the heart of Islam in Spain.

After the fall of Córdoba, Muhammad ibn al-Ahmar moved quickly to consolidate his position, taking Granada as his new base and sending out subordinates to secure the obedience of the towns of the south. This marked the beginnings of the new sultanate, or kingdom, of Granada, which would be ruled over by his descendants, the

Banu Nasr, or Nasrids, for the next two and a half centuries. As for Ibn Hud—his reputation in tatters and his men deserting him—he eventually made for Almería, hoping to take refuge within its stoutly fortified walls, only to be murdered outside its gates in 1237 by the governor of the city that he himself had appointed.

ALTHOUGH IT PUT Córdoba at risk, Ibn Hud had every reason to be focused on the frontier in the northeast, which had been an arena for raiding and piecemeal conquest by the Aragonese nobility and municipal militias since the 1220s. The situation had become acute by the end of that decade, as there was every sign that Jaume (James) I, the count-king of Barcelona-Aragon, was gathering forces for a major campaign. In the face of Aragonese aggression, Abu Zayd of Valencia had signed a truce with Fernando III of Castile. This prompted outrage among the populace, who cast him out and invited Zayyan ibn Mardanish to rule over them. The exiled Almohad *sayyid* Abu Zayd made his way with his family and entourage to Jaume's court. There, he was welcomed by the king, who recognized him as the true "King of Valencia" and pledged to restore him to power as his client. In return, Abu Zayd handed over a string of fortresses that would serve as a launching pad for Jaume's invasion, and he became a member of the king's entourage. Abu Zayd and those soldiers who remained loyal to him would fight alongside the Aragonese forces, provide intelligence, and facilitate Jaume's negotiations with the indigenous population.

In the early 1230s Jaume was in a strong position, fresh from his conquest of Muslim Mallorca. Two decades earlier that had not been the case. After the death of his father, Pere the Catholic, at the hands of anti-Cathar crusaders in 1213, the seven-year-old heir to Aragon had been whisked away under the protection of the papacy and the Knights Templar. Then, at only thirteen, Jaume defied his wards by asserting his title as count and king and set out to wage war on the Catalan nobility who had taken advantage of his minority to shake off royal authority. Having forced them into submission by the late 1220s, he was eager to undertake a project that would provide an outlet for their military energy and generate wealth for his kingdom and glory for his name.

Thus, all eyes turned to Mallorca, including those of the merchant families of Barcelona who had come to form one of the pillars of the Crown of Aragon's prosperity. Positioned midway between the Iberian Peninsula, the Italian mainland, Sicily, and North Africa, and with a large and well-protected port at the capital, Madina Mayurqa, the island kingdom was a prize sought after by both Muslim princes and the Italian trading republics. Jaume determined to take the island, and having recruited Genoans and Pisans, and armed with a papal bull that cast the expedition as a crusade, on September 5, 1229, his fleet set sail from Barcelona.

His timing was auspicious. The island's Almohad king, Abu Yahya al-Tinmalli, had been contending with an influx of hostile Andalusi refugees, who rose up in revolt in August of 1229. Some of these greeted the invasion force when they landed and guided them to the capital; others in the countryside provided supplies to the invaders.

Undeterred by the thick walls of Madina Mayurqa, Jaume refused al-Tinmalli's offers first of tribute and then of surrender and ordered his men to begin undermining the fortifications. When the walls were breached on December 31, Christian knights poured in and dogged house-to-house fighting began. After Abu Yahya himself was captured, Jaume pledged to respect his life if he would order the city to surrender but then murdered the king's teenage son in front of Abu Yahya's eyes to encourage him to divulge the location of his treasure. The city's surviving population was claimed by the king as slaves, and their persons and all their moveable property were auctioned off or distributed among the victorious forces.

Next, Jaume moved on Menorca, but because his booty-laden troops had little interest in further risk, the count-king resorted to a gambit. Landing at night not far from Menorca's main city, he ordered his small party to light campfires all along the beach so that the defenders would believe a large army invasion force had landed. The ruse worked. The governor of the island and a delegation of *shaykhs* invited the king to parley, and they ended up concluding an arrangement in which Menorca would become an autonomous tributary and Jaume's knights would occupy the island's fortresses. The tiny island protectorate would survive for another half century, becoming a magnet for Andalusi refugees, particularly members of the religious and cultural elite.

Meanwhile on the mainland, the noblemen and municipal militias of Aragon, which had been largely left out of the Mallorcan campaign, were mounting incursions into the northern reaches of Sharq al-Andalus, and Ibn Mardanish was launching counterattacks. Jaume needed to take control of the situation. But Sharq al-Andalus was far larger and more populous than compact Mallorca, and it would require nine years of fighting for Jaume to reach the walls of Valencia. During this time, the count-king perfected a carrot-and-stick strategy for dealing with his Muslim foes: to those communities that surrendered and supported him, Jaume offered protection, peace, and respect for their religion and customs in exchange for loyalty and tribute. Those who resisted, on the other hand—and Jaume's forces often met very fierce resistance—were rewarded with expulsion.

It is clear the king went to great lengths to establish a rapport with his Muslim foes and subjects by treating them as near equals (or at least pretending to), respecting their traditions, scrupulously honoring the agreements he made with them (as long as it suited him), and not hesitating to punish his own subjects should they break his treaties. This, together with his great personal valor in battle and his unyielding determination, made him a figure respected and feared by the inhabitants of Sharq al-Andalus but one they felt they could do business with.

Jaume was also a deeply convinced Christian, a proud crusader, and a champion of the church, and there were very practical reasons behind this strategy. Sharq al-Andalus was an extremely wealthy region, thanks to the highly productive market gardening and craft industries its inhabitants had perfected. Jaume needed the Muslim population to stay in place in order to maintain the economy and to provide a base for tax and tribute, and so he had to accommodate them on terms they would accept. He could not engage in ethnic cleansing here as he had in Mallorca; once a market is saturated, slaves become a burden and their value decreases. Likewise, unproductive territory would be a liability. Nor could he afford to tolerate a restive Muslim population intent on rebellion and revolt.

As the campaign slowly progressed down the coast toward Valencia, it became clear that reinstating Abu Zayd was not in the cards, and the Almohad prince astutely converted to Christianity together with his children, taking the name Vincent, after the patron saint of Valencia. In reward, he and his daughters were married into leading families of the Aragonese nobility, and he was assigned an estate in the interior. Abu Zayd, who it is said continued to wear the clothes and follow the customs of his infidel days, apparently lived to a respectable age, moving back and forth between the royal court, his landed estates in Aragon, and the city of Murcia, which was held by the Castilian vassals, the Banu Hud. How he conceived of his apostasy, one can only speculate. It may have been an act of genuine inspiration or one of hollow cynicism. Perhaps he saw it in the light of the late-Almohad affirmation of Jesus as *mahdi*, or the esoteric conviction that God is above any doctrine. Whatever the case, in 1264, he was prompted to write a letter to Urban IV and received in return a message of blessing from the pope in recognition of the great material sacrifices he had made as a consequence of his conversion.

IN 1237, JAUME'S forces arrived at Valencia, encircling it by land and blockading it by sea. It was soon clear the siege would not be broken without outside help. After the Hafsid amir Abu Zakariyya of Tunis sent a fleet but was unable to breach the blockade, negotiations were opened and on September 29, 1238, it was agreed that the entire Muslim population of the city would depart within five days, taking only what property they could carry. They would be given safe conduct either south to the ports of Cullera and Denia, where they could sail off into exile, or to anywhere else in the king's lands to settle there as free subjects.

Ten days later, Jaume entered the abandoned city in great ceremony to see the congregational mosque purified and consecrated as the new cathedral of Saint Vincent. In what was becoming established procedure for the Christian rulers of the peninsula, the homes, shops, and properties of the former inhabitants were shared out among the victors—the knights, soldiers, and military orders—as spoils, or apportioned to settlers on the condition they reside in the city for at least one year. A Jewish colony was established. Mosques and religious properties were given to the church. All of this was recorded in a *Llibre del repartiment*, a "Book of Distribution," in which every property was recorded and its new owner registered. Quickly, parishes were created and monasteries and convents founded. Muslim homes were razed and rebuilt according to Christian tastes, and slowly the now-Christian city rumbled back to life as the capital of Jaume's new kingdom of Valencia.

Ibn Mardanish and his troops moved south to Murcia, which had drifted into chaos after the death of Ibn Hud. The palace had been sacked by the populace, who had elected a popular but ineffective *faqih*, Ibn Hattab, as ruler. Ibn Mardanish seized the city, arrested and executed Ibn Hattab, and declared loyalty to the Hafsids, who were now carrying the ideological torch of Almohadism. When that proved ineffectual, he turned to Fernando III and his powerful mother, Berengaria of Castile, proposing an alliance against the Crown of Aragon. It was the same trap Ibn Hud had been pushed into, and in 1241 when the people of Murcia got wind of the proposal, they overthrew Ibn Mardanish, who escaped to Tunis, and invited an uncle of Ibn Hud al-Mutawakkil named Baha' al-Dawla to rule over them.

WITH THE CONQUEST of Valencia, Jaume's campaign ran out of momentum. Although he could still count on the military orders for manpower and to administrate the territory he managed to conquer, he lacked knights and was running out of Christian colonizers. Nevertheless, he continued to cajole, bribe, and bluff the local Muslim commanders, *qadis*, and *shaykhs* who governed the towns south of his new capital to recognize him as their lord. Thus, in 1240, Jaume besieged Xátiva and convinced the local strongmen, the Banu 'Isa, to gradually cede control of the strongly fortified town in exchange for a nearby castle. In 1252, with the handover complete, the population was ejected from the walled precinct but allowed to build a new settlement adjacent to it. The Banu 'Isa had left their townsfolk to their fate, but in exchange they were able to live as effectively independent, if modest, lords until 1275.

Not all local magnates were so compliant, however. 'Abd Allah ibn Hudayl, an enigmatic figure known as al-Azraq ("the Blue," presumably after the color of his eyes), would lead a series of stubborn insurrections against Jaume through the 1240s and 1250s, at times with Castilian backing. In the scrubby and inaccessible valleys in the highlands above Denia, this self-styled *mujahid* attracted considerable popular support and proved enormously difficult to defeat. A series of truces and treaties only prolonged the rebellion until 1258, when Jaume defeated al-Azraq, and then only after one of the rebel's Muslim allies secretly betrayed him. Al-Azraq and the king made their peace, and in exchange for handing over his last fortresses he was given safe passage to Ifriqiya.

Meanwhile, Baha' al-Dawla ibn Hud had held out in Murcia until 1243 when, isolated and under threat, he had little choice but to declare formal vassalship to Castile, swearing to honor the crown prince Alfonso, the son and heir Fernando III, as his lord. So it was that Murcia was formally incorporated into the Crown of Castile as a Muslim-ruled client-kingdom. Through all this, Fernando III continued to make gains in the Muslim South where his main concern remained the Portuguese, who were also racing to conquer as much Andalusi territory as possible. As early as 1217, they had taken the strategic Alcácer do Sal, south of Lisbon, in contravention of their treaty with the Almohads, and in 1225 a Portuguese force dealt a bruising defeat to the army of Seville. And, although in 1230 León deprived Sancho II of Portugal the opportunity of taking Mérida and Badajoz, the Portuguese king would regain the initiative and overrun the Algarve, the south of modern Portugal, by 1250. This was only possible because of the generous offers he made to the Muslim inhabitants. Ordinary folk were granted protection for their property and persons and guarantees that their law and religion would be respected, while members of the elite were invited to serve in the king's forces.

By then, the Great Game for the south of al-Andalus appeared to be all but over, and it was clear that Castile-León was the winner. In the 1240s, Fernando III had stepped up the pace of conquest, launching a series of ferocious campaigns, aided by his Muslim dependents, against the lands of the Guadalquivir. The countryside was ravaged, Muslim peasants were taken prisoner or put to the sword, and one by one the towns of the south fell. Little quarter was shown. The slave markets swelled as masses of Muslim captives were sent northward, while in the south, the larger towns were purged of their native inhabitants, who were banished to the countryside if not condemned outright to exile. In the race against his rivals, Fernando could not afford a gradual conquest by negotiation, and although the violence of the campaign might cripple the economy of the Muslim South, that Muslim South would at least belong to him and his heirs. The strategy paid off. By the time Alicante fell in 1248, the king, together with his son Alfonso, had set up camp outside the former Almohad capital, Seville.

ALTHOUGH IT WAS no longer the official capital of al-Andalus, Seville, endowed with a formidable fortress and ringed by thick walls studded with over 150 towers, was its largest city by far. It had remained the center of economic, religious, and cultural life here and the home to scores of poets, intellectuals, and men of religion. But, since the departure of the last Almohad caliph in 1228, it had suffered from repeated raids by Muslim and Christian forces and from the internal unrest characteristic of al-Andalus. As various factions battled each other, the city passed under the control of a succession of warlords and *qadis* who recognized either Ibn Hud, the Almohads, the Hafsids, or no one but themselves as their rulers, prompting a series of coups, countercoups, purges, and executions that played out as Fernando prepared to attack. In 1242, the Hafsids sent a military commander to the city, an occasion marked by the great poets of Seville with elegies praising the arrival of the "Arabs" and the hope they would rescue al-Andalus, but this only intensified the violent partisanship that held the city in its grip.

By summer 1247, Fernando's siege was in place, and among the Castilian forces was Ibn al-Ahmar, who had come at the head of a body of troops to assist the attack. For their part, the Sevillans were determined to resist, and their counterattacks temporarily forced Fernando back. Meanwhile, the countryside was devastated by the

Castilians and their allies, and little food was getting into the city. A Hafsid fleet sailed up the Guadalquivir but was turned back by the Castilian admiral. As the months wore on, famine stalked the city, and the weakened populace—"walking around as if in a drunken stupor"—began to succumb to starvation.[41] Proper funeral rituals were neglected, even for prestigious citizens, because there were simply not enough people to participate. Over the course of the winter of 1248, more and more Christian troops arrived, establishing a ring of siege camps around the city. In May, Castilian ships moved on the city, breaching the two pontoon bridges that linked it to the fortified suburb of Triana (Atrayna, in Arabic) on the left bank of the Guadalquivir. The city was now completely cut off, and it would only be a matter of time until the hardship of the siege proved too heavy to bear.

And so it was that on November 23, 1248, the royal standard of Castile was raised over the *alcázar* of Seville, and on December 22, King Fernando rode victorious into the vanquished city. Under the terms of their capitulation, the surviving Muslim population would abandon the city, taking with them what they could carry, having been given the period of one month to sell off whatever they could not. It took a further three weeks for the last Muslims to depart—tens of thousands of refugees heading southwest toward Cádiz under escort of Fernando's knights. Ibn al-Ahmar's kingdom of Granada was the final destination for most, but many eventually ended up in the Maghrib and some in Menorca, in a process that for most refugees took part in stages—a series of dislocations they suffered as the Castilian conquest slowly continued to advance.

Given the terrible duration and conditions of the siege, and the fact neither rich nor poor escaped its consequences, the fall of Seville—the last capital of al-Andalus—left a traumatic wound on the Andalusi psyche. Nowhere is this more evident than in the poetry of lament it generated, both among exiles and across the Muslim West. From Tunis, the Valencian poet Ibn al-Abbar decried the "profaning" of the city, while years later in Ceuta, the Sevillan Salih ibn Sharif al-Rundi wrote a lengthy elegy on the conquest of al-Andalus in which his home town figured prominently:

Almohad troops and Christian allies march against the Marinids under the banner of the Virgin Mary. From Alfonso X's *Cantigas de Santa María* (Cantiga 181, Codex Rico, Ms TI1. Biblioteca de El Escorial, ca. 1280 CE). *Jorge Fernandez-Oronoz (Archivo Oronoz)*

Who, who can help avert the mortal shaming of a once mighty folk,
Whom tyranny and outrage now in humility cloak?
For yesterday as monarchs they reviewed their rich domains;
Today they are but slaves, and bound in Unbelievers' chains.[42]

The poem was read across the Islamic world and is regarded as a classic even today. These works formed part of the distinctive genre known as *ritha' al-mudun* ("lamentations for cities"), the nostalgically overwrought remembrances of the lost glory of al-Andalus.

For the Christians, the conquest of Seville was a triumph, and in the aftermath, the urban landscape was quickly transformed to suit the conquerors. The great Almohad mosque was consecrated as the city's cathedral, a ceremony that Ibn al-Ahmar's dignitaries participated in. For the following century and a half, Christians worshipped in chapels erected within its vast prayer hall, until in 1401 a decision was made to raze the Almohad building and construct a new church in its place. The nearby royal fortress-palace complex became the residence of the Castilian king. And although it would be centuries before the population of the city recovered to its preconquest level, Seville would remain one of the leading cities and favored capitals of the Spanish kings. So proud was Fernando of the accomplishment that he arranged to be interred in the former mosque, and after his death in 1252, a funerary monument was constructed there that bore epitaphs praising the king in Spanish Romance, Latin, Arabic, and Hebrew.

FERNANDO WAS SUCCEEDED as king of León, Castile, Galicia, Murcia, Jaén, Córdoba, and Seville by his son Alfonso X, who had ridden in battle beside his father since the age of sixteen. His first campaign as king would be an invasion of Portugal, and the next was an aborted attack on Navarre, but by 1259, Alfonso was planning a new campaign of conquest in Muslim lands. With the encouragement of his vassal Ibn al-Ahmar, the Castilian king had envisioned a crusade that would bring the Maghrib under his power. Here, the last remnants of the Almohad state were being conquered by the Banu Marin, a clan of Zanata Berbers from the western Sahara, who had seized Fez in 1248. Desperate to save himself, the Almohad governor of Salé on the Atlantic coast—a son of Abu Zayd of Valencia—offered to convert to Christianity if Alfonso would send help. A Castilian fleet arrived at the Moroccan port in 1260, but rather than defending the city, the troops who disembarked brutally sacked it, killing many men and old women, plundering homes and shops, and defiling the main mosque by raping the women and girls they had corralled within its precinct. Some 3,000 captives were carried back to the slave market of Seville.

Although Alfonso would abandon his plans for Africa, they served as a catalyst for further conquests in al-Andalus, namely, the last independent zone in the southwest. This area, which included the Atlantic port of Cádiz and the tiny Muslim kingdoms of Jerez de la

Frontera and Niebla (or Labla, with its capital at Huelva), had been made to pay tribute by Fernando III. But now looking southward, Alfonso was determined to finish the job. Violating the treaty with Jerez, Alfonso's troops seized the city's fortress, prompting its ruler, Ibn Abi Khalid, and his court to decamp to Morocco. Lacking settlers to repopulate the region, Alfonso accepted a proposal by the inhabitants to allow them to stay on their lands, if they surrendered. Strongly fortified Niebla, on the other hand, put up a fight. In early 1262, the lord, Ibn Mahfuz, surrendered after nine and a half months under siege, accepting Alfonso's offer of an honorable retirement in Seville in exchange for the evacuation of the city. And with that, Castilian domination of the lower Guadalquivir was complete—or so it seemed. Only two years later the subject Muslims of Andalucía, the Christian South, would rise in revolt against their Christian overlords.

The fact that Alfonso X embarked on his African campaigns while so much of al-Andalus remained under Muslim rule gives lie to the suggestion he was driven by an impulse to "reconquer" pre-Islamic Hispania. In fact, his great ambition was to secure the title of Holy Roman Emperor. By the same token, the Catalan-Aragonese Crusades were not limited to recovering the conquered lands of Christian Iberia. As part of their imperial strategy, the count-kings would take advantage of any opportunity to extend their power. Thus, in 1284, Jaume I's son and successor, Pere the Great, would conquer Jerba, a large island just off the coast of Ifriqiya. Two years earlier, Pere had seized Sicily from its Angevin rulers, provoking a crusade from which the Crown of Aragon would be saved in no small measure thanks to the Muslim soldiers who fought to defend it against the papal forces. As the 1200s drew to a close, the Great Game was on again, as both the Christian powers and Ibn al-Ahmar's new Nasrid sultanate of Granada struggled against each other for domination and survival.

24

Crescent Under Cross

The dramatic Christian conquests of the thirteenth century were made possible by the divisions within Andalusi society in the wake of the Almohad collapse. The populace had lost faith in the local strongmen who governed them. Many commoners were determined to resist the Christian invaders, while others simply fled. Most of the *'ulama'*, together with those more pious layfolk, would have felt a strong compulsion to leave rather than live under infidel rule, particularly if they had money or the prospect of patronage elsewhere. Thus, many of the great aristocratic clans who had anchored the urban culture and economy in southern al-Andalus, families like Seville's Banu Khaldun, abandoned the peninsula in the face of the infidel advance. Most went to North Africa and many to Tunis, where they were welcomed for their erudition and cultural sophistication. But, the local inhabitants did not necessarily welcome the Andalusi refugees, whom they saw as burdensome foreigners who had failed to defend the faith and who brought with them instability and economic competition.

Most Andalusis took a more practical approach to the conquest. Abandoned or betrayed by their own elites, the *'amma* was left to its fate. Political Islam and the orthodox clergy had failed them, and they turned increasingly to local mystics and holy men and women. For these humble folk, their lands were their home, and many were prepared to make whatever compromise was necessary to stay, even if that meant living under the rule of an infidel king.

AND SO IT was that by the 1260s, the majority of the Muslim population of the peninsula had become *mudéjares*. For the most part, these "stay-behinds" lived as free subjects in autonomous communities, or as *aljamas*, governed by their own officials under the direct jurisdiction of the Christian kings, under the terms of surrender agreements negotiated by the local Muslim leadership that guaranteed their religious rights and communal autonomy in exchange for tribute. This was effectively the same arrangement Jewish communities lived under. This legal and administrative segregation was necessary because religion in this era was conceived of not so much as a matter of individual conscience as the legal community to which one belonged. A Muslim was someone who followed "the law of the Muslims." This was an arrangement that recalled the Islamic institution of *dhimma*, and it reflected precisely how *mudéjares* understood their place in Christian society: a legitimate, but subordinate, community.

Initially, the shift to Christian rule may have been all but imperceptible, especially in the rural world. Christian settlers arrived slowly and the rhythm of life would have continued much as before, as *mudéjar* society gradually evolved to reflect its subordinate status and its place in the new Christian order. Most Muslims worked as farmers, craftsmen, and merchants, with some practicing specialized professions, including medicine, horse care, military vocations, music and dance, architecture, and engineering. Their work in agriculture was crucial, as was their proficiency in certain crafts and industries, such as luxury tailoring, silversmithing, decorative arts, and weapons manufacture. For example, Muslims were so prominent in the building trades that they built the great majority of churches and palaces constructed in Castilian and Aragonese lands in the twelfth and thirteenth centuries, many in their signature *mudéjar* style, characterized by elaborate geometric brick patterns and the use of glazed tile.

Education in Arabic and on Islam continued on a local scale, and *mudéjares* traveled, although in fewer numbers than before, to the

Islamic world for religious, educational, and economic reasons. Wealthier individuals even managed to perform the *hajj*, sometimes with their families. As free subjects, *mudéjar* men and women bought and sold property, borrowed money, invested in commercial ventures, and moved from one town or kingdom to another in response to economic opportunities. Although Muslims circulated throughout the Christian lands, generally their communities tended to become self-contained, dominated by local families who used the wealth they generated through craft and commerce to acquire appointments from the royal court as judicial or administrative officials within their *aljamas*. The intense competition for these positions often generated factional disputes that led *mudéjar* leaders to seek out allies among local Christians.

Their formal autonomy and subordinate status notwithstanding, *mudéjares* became enmeshed within Christian society, integrating economically as tenants, suppliers, customers, service providers, and business partners, while Jewish lenders provided access to credit. *Mudéjares* served under arms with Christians in municipal militias and royal armies, formed local political alliances, and even committed crimes together. This interdependence helped to stabilize relations between members of the two communities, who frequently saw their interests as coinciding. Although there were often tensions, local Muslim and Christian communities would band together to defend each other when threatened from the outside, whether by rival towns, raiders, or predatory royal or church officials or noblemen.

Muslims also formed mutually beneficial relationships with noblemen and the church. The nobility, monasteries, cathedral chapters, and military orders often preferred *mudéjares* as tenants on their lands; consequently, they protected and defended their Muslim subjects and vassals against local Christians, predacious lords, the king, and even their own *aljamas*. Whether supported by Christian patrons or on their own, *mudéjares* vigorously defended their rights and property, both in arms and in the courts. In fact, *mudéjares* became extremely adept at using both their own and the Christian legal system, whether in disputes against fellow Muslims, Christians, Jews, their communities, or their lords, including the king himself. Interminable

legal conflicts between Jewish lenders and Muslim debtors were frequent but never descended into communal violence.

Cultural and social integration was also widespread. In some areas
Romance vernaculars began to edge out Arabic as the spoken language of *mudéjares* as early as the late twelfth century, and many
became proficient in Latin. In many regions, they adopted the styles
of dress of their Christian neighbors, which facilitated interaction but
carried its own dangers. Although at the time of the conquest Christians and Muslims lived in separate neighborhoods, over the years
these tended to become mixed, and members of different faiths could
find themselves living side by side or even in the same buildings. The
resulting fraternization posed a dilemma for both *mudéjar* and Christian authorities, particularly due to the prospect that members of the
two faiths might engage in sexual relations, which was considered a
capital crime in both communities. Both Christian and Muslim religious leaders, concerned by the prospect of losing the faithful through
conversion, viewed interfaith socializing with unease.

Legal and moral prohibitions notwithstanding, although Christians, Jews, and Muslims attended each other's celebrations, drank,
gambled, went to the baths, and frequented prostitutes together, it was
rare that such interactions led to censure. At least for men. *Mudéjar*
women, for whom the slightest misconduct could bring condemnation, were particularly vulnerable. When they were charged with violating sexual norms they were liable to enslavement by royal
authorities and often condemned to slavery and service in royal broth-
els. Corrupt Muslim and Christian officials at times colluded to profit
by falsely accusing them of sex crimes.

Mudéjares' formal classification as legal subordinates served to
mitigate Christians' fears of the Muslim minority, while the broad
rights and opportunities they enjoyed helped make these Muslims
willing subjects of the Christian kings. As for jihad, subject Muslims
pursued this as an inner moral struggle, not armed resistance. Thus, in
the lands conquered prior to the thirteenth century, there are almost
no recorded instances of uprisings or popular violence between Christians and *mudéjares*—nor, for that matter, between *mudéjares* and
Jews—until the end of the Middle Ages.

IN THE MID-THIRTEENTH century, both church and royal authorities began to elaborate coherent, comprehensive law codes, modeled on imperial Roman law, and were thus forced to formally articulate the place of Muslims and Jews in Christian society in detail. Hence, at the Council of Lateran IV held by Innocent III in 1215, it was ordered that Jews and "pagans" (meaning also Muslims) should wear distinctive badges or articles of clothing to mark them off as non-Christians, the aim being to prevent sexual contact with unwitting Christians who might thus be tempted to leave the flock. It was also ordered that they should not serve in positions of authority over Christians. Synagogues and mosques were not to be constructed or repaired—restrictions that resembled, but were not inspired by, those of the "Pact of 'Umar." However, each of these decrees went largely ignored in the Spanish kingdoms, as did the prohibition, promulgated at the Council of Vienne in 1311–1312, on muezzins calling the Muslim faithful to prayer. Indeed, except for the clergy's use of Muslim tenants and slaves, the church all but ignored the *mudéjar* population. Efforts at missionizing and conversion were almost nonexistent; preaching to Muslims was strictly limited by royal authorities, given its potential to provoke unrest.

Through all of this Islam remained a force of cohesion, and there is very little evidence of *mudéjares* converting to Christianity, apart from slaves hoping for manumission, convicts seeking a pardon, or individuals wanting to join the privileged Christian community. But the cost of apostasy was high: loss of one's social network, family, and religious community. Moreover, converts tended to be seen as turncoats by Christians as well as Muslims.

Slavery was common in Christian Spain, and the majority of slaves were Muslim. Most were foreign captives—prisoners of war, victims of shipwrecks, or captives taken in raids on al-Andalus or Africa. Many were used as domestic servants, including women, who were subject to rape at the will of their owners. In a few regions, slaves were used as a rural labor force and lived under quite harsh conditions, but most were put to work in domestic or urban situations according to their skills and abilities. Craftsmen and artisans were most prized, as they could bring considerable income to their owners. In some cases, the master-slave relationship could resemble a collaboration, one that might continue after the slave had been freed. Terms for manumission were often established so that slaves could work, save, or beg to obtain their freedom. Sometimes *mudéjares* sold themselves as slaves to a third party for a fixed period of time in order to work off a debt, an arrangement sadly little different in essence from employment arrangements today. As royal subjects, slaves could even sue their masters in the king's court for failing to free them as agreed or for other abuses. *Mudéjares* sometimes raised money for slaves' ransoms and aided slaves on the run.

As it was, conversion to Christianity did not bring freedom to slaves; legal obstacles were put in place to discourage it, and even slaves of Jews who converted to Christianity remained enslaved until they could buy their freedom. Even some wealthy *mudéjares* kept Muslim slaves. Debt and judicial slavery was also common; as subjects of the kings, free *mudéjares* who committed capital crimes tended to be enslaved instead. However, notwithstanding the terrible suffering and abuse it often entailed, slavery performed important functions for *mudéjar* society. It helped sustain communal solidarity and provided a conduit for the rejuvenation of Arabo-Islamic culture among *mudéjares* through the integration of foreign Muslims, who served as a bridge between Christendom and the *dar al-Islam*.

ENSLAVED AND FREE Muslims also transformed the culture of Spanish Christians, habituating them to Andalusi styles through the use of Muslim-made craft goods and Arabo-Islamic cuisine. Christians took recourse to Muslim physicians and barbers and to their folk cures and magic. *Mudéjar* musicians and dancers were popular fixtures at Christian celebrations, including the royal and municipal events and the religious processions held to mark the most important holidays. Andalusi folktales, oral traditions, and styles of song were also picked up by Christian listeners, together with the hundreds of common Arabic words that made their way into colloquial Spanish—common expressions like *Ojalá!* ("God willing," from *law sha' Allah*), *Alá* or *Olé* ("Wow!," from *Allah!*), and *fulano* ("so-and-so," from *fulan*).

The robust Andalusi literary traditions of both poetry and prose exercised a fascination on Christian audiences. Whereas previously

Christian scholars had focused for the most part on scientific, technical, and philosophical texts, now Arabo-Islamic epics, romances, and folktales—many of South Asian and Persian origin—were translated, adapted, or otherwise made their way into popular literature. These included the *Kalila wa-dimna*, a collection of fables; *Sindibad*, or *Sendebar*, the tales of Sinbad the Sailor; the epic of Alexander the Great; and tales from *The One Thousand and One Nights*. Popular and didactic literature of the era, such as Ramon Llull's *Book of the Beasts* (1280s) and *The Tales of Count Lucanor*, written in 1335 by Don Juan Manuel, a nephew of Alfonso X, were strongly influenced by these texts. In fact, Arabic literature transformed European fiction, both through the borrowing of narratives and through the appropriation of the literary device of the *maqamat*, or frame tale, the story-within-a-story—the same device used by Boccaccio in his *Decameron* and by Chaucer in *The Canterbury Tales*.

The translation initiative that had begun in Toledo and Tudela in the twelfth century picked up pace in the thirteenth under the patronage of Alfonso X. Known as El Sabio ("the Learned"), the king sponsored a vigorous cultural agenda, which included the composition of religious poetry (his own *Cántigas de Santa María*) and the translation or adaptation of works on music, astronomy, chess, hunting, law, politics and rulership, history, and a range of other subjects. Toledo was the center of this initiative, but schools of Arabic sprung up around his kingdom, and translators, typically working in teams (with a Jew or Muslim checking the Arabic and a Christian composing the Latin or Romance), carried out their labor under royal patronage or on their own initiative. Alfonso X established an academy open to Muslims, Christians, and Jews, in either Murcia or Seville, under the direction of the physician Abu Bakr al-Riquti.

The thirteenth century was the great era of universities in Christian Europe, institutions that kings supported to cultivate the knowledge they saw as emblematic of their power and to train both the clergy and the members of their growing bureaucracies. Universities in Castile-León, Portugal, and the Crown of Aragon became centers for the dissemination of Arabo-Islamic intellectual traditions. It was in this period that the royalty and aristocracy began to admire,

Women playing chess. From Alfonso X's Book of Games (1283). *Jorge Fernandez-Oronoz (Archivo Oronoz)*

imitate, and fetishize Arabo-Islamic high culture, as they came to dominate al-Andalus and domesticate Arabo-Islamic society politically. In fact, it has been suggested that Alfonso X's commitment to high culture and to reordering society, and his conception of a universal monarchy, was influenced by Almohad notions of kingship, sovereignty, and knowledge.

The thirteenth-century royal legal codes formalized the place of both free and enslaved Muslims in these societies, explicitly reinforcing their inferior status and legal disadvantage but also enshrining their rights and protections. However, the more discriminatory aspects of these laws—such as the obligation to wear certain distinguishing clothing, the laws against building mosques and publicly practicing Islam, and the prohibition to practice certain trades—were often never or only fitfully enforced. As a rule, medieval law codes reflected the ideals of legal scholars, not social or legal realities. Moreover, because of the direct jurisdiction Christian kings had over their Muslims (as opposed to Christian subjects, who also came under seigneurial, church, and municipal authority), *mudéjaras* constituted an important source of revenue for the monarchy through taxation, fees, and licenses. Therefore, the monarchy protected them. In the fourteenth century, Pere the Ceremonious of Aragon would refer to the *mudéjares* of his realms as his "royal treasure."

The prosperity and confidence of the *mudéjar* population of northern Spain throughout the mid-fourteenth century was a consequence, to no small extent, of the general prosperity of this period, which saw an improving climate, demographic growth, commercial expansion, the proliferation of towns and cities, and increased agricultural production across Christian Europe. And in this period, Muslims circulated among the Christian kingdoms, including Castile and León, the Crown of Aragon, Navarre, and Portugal, moving in response to opportunities and even settling in areas that had never been under Muslim rule. Even foreign Muslims occasionally immigrated to Christian lands.

But the official position of the Nasrid sultans, as expounded by the Granadan *'ulama'* and widely echoed across the Islamic West, was that it was unacceptable for Muslims to live under infidel rule, where Islamic law and institutions could not function with integrity; where Muslims were in danger of acculturation and subject to oppression; and where, most importantly, their women were vulnerable to coercion and abuse. However, even as conditions for them harshened in the fourteenth century, few *mudéjares* took up the call to escape "the land of humiliation," and by the fifteenth century, some Islamic legal authorities in the Islamic West were softening their stance in this regard. In the meantime, as a demonstration of the sovereignty they claimed over all Muslims in the peninsula, the Nasrid kings lobbied the Christian kings for *mudéjar* rights, particularly the right to emigrate freely.

True social integration of the Muslim minority was not possible, nor was it a goal for either community. With religious prohibitions against intermarriage in effect on both the Christian and the Muslim side, the two communities remained genealogically self-contained. Because property and power in this era were passed down through families, and families joined through marriage, this meant that inevitably Muslims and Christians would come to see each other as competitors. In a society based on a hierarchy of closed religious communities, it would be the dominant group, the Christians, that would hold the advantage and be able to impose its will on and dispose of non-Christian competitors. This occurred through peaceful means or through violence—violence that may have been economically motivated but that could be expressed in the self-righteous and morally reaffirming language of religious superiority.

And so, as the European and Islamic West collapsed into crisis in the mid-fourteenth century, and as a succession of famines, plague, and warfare pushed their economies to the brink of collapse and their societies into pessimistic despair, *mudéjares* would begin to see their rights eroded and come to be viewed by their Christian neighbors with increasing suspicion and hostility, whether as dangerous enemies or as objects of exploitation.

THIS PANORAMA CONTRASTS with the situation in the south of the peninsula in the aftermath of the thirteenth-century conquests. Here, the violence of the Christian campaigns and the killing, enslavement, and dislocations that accompanied them, together with the destruction of the infrastructure of the rural economy, had left the local Muslim population in disarray but determined to resist. They did not wait long to act. In 1264, Alfonso X was overextended. Distracted by his campaign to claim the title of Holy Roman Emperor, he was driving his kingdom into bankruptcy and the nobility to rebellion. Tensions with his Muslim vassals were also mounting. In Granada, Ibn al-Ahmar was determined to resist Alfonso's demands that he hand over the strategic port towns that commanded control of the Strait of Gibraltar. Meanwhile in Murcia, which was still under the rule of Alfonso's vassals, the Banu Hud, Christian colonists had been abusing the terms of the Castilian-Murcian treaty, and communal tensions were nearing the breaking point. The two Muslim-ruled kingdoms, therefore, put aside their own enmity, and finding common cause with the Marinids of Morocco and the *mudéjares* of the recently conquered Guadalquivir, launched a region-wide uprising.

Apparently, the plan had been to seize the king and assassinate him when he convened the *cortes*, or parliament, in Seville in 1264, which Ibn al-Ahmar was obliged to attend. The plot failed, but meanwhile the Marinid sultan, Abu Yusuf Ya'qub, had dispatched a large force of cavalry and infantry to al-Andalus to take up the jihad against Castile. These were joined by the Nasrid army under the leadership of Ibn al-Ahmar's kinsman 'Ali ibn Ashqilula and numbers of *ghuzat* ("holy raiders," or "Volunteers of the Faith") who had come over from North Africa under the command of exiled Marinid princes. The Christian garrisons of the region were taken by surprise and overwhelmed; a number of major towns were seized and the local Christian settlers put to flight or massacred. Reeling from the loss, Alfonso petitioned Pope Clement V to authorize a crusade and marched on Granada itself. Although his forces caused great damage to the hinterland around the Nasrid capital, they suffered a bloody defeat at the hands of the Marinid cavalry.

Next Murcia rose up, at which point Jaume I of Aragon, fearing that the uprising might spread to his kingdom of Valencia, personally led his forces to pacify the rebellion. Rolling southward, he took the major towns of the kingdom of Murcia with the same carrot-and-stick approach he had taken when conquering Valencia. Local warlords and leaders were intimidated, bribed, or crushed, and assurances were given to those Muslims prepared to accept Christian overlordship. According to Jaume's autobiography, which describes the campaign in vivid, personal detail, no reprisals were taken by the chivalrous king; Muslim accounts, however, record looting, killing, and the abduction and abuse of inhabitants by the Aragonese forces. Arriving at Murcia, Jaume obtained the surrender of the city in January 1266 after granting generous privileges to the Muslim authorities there but demanding that the main mosque be handed over and that Ibn al-Ahmar's military commander be expelled.

Subsequently, the city and most of the territory Jaume had taken were duly handed over to Alfonso X, who promptly rescinded Jaume's concessions and dissolved the kingdom of Murcia, establishing instead the tiny "Kingdom of Arrixaca"—in reality, a suburb of the capital—under the rule of the Banu Hud. This would survive until 1295, when its last ruler, Abu Ishaq Ibrahim, sold his properties to the Castilian king, Fernando IV, and left for exile in North Africa. In the intervening years, the harsh policies initiated by Alfonso X had provoked the flight of Muslims southward to Granada, leaving a much-reduced population of *mudéjares*. Fernando IV offered concessions in an effort to put a brake on the exodus, but the damage was done and the economy of Murcia was irreversibly crippled.

As Jaume I was pacifying Murcia, Alfonso X was regaining control over the southwest. The success of the Marinid forces and the growing influence of the *ghuzat* in the kingdom of Granada had provoked unease among the Banu Ashqilula and other members of the Nasrid elite. Up until then, the Banu Ashqilula had been a bulwark of the sultanate, but they were losing territory and influence to the newcomers. 'Ali ibn Ashqilula's two sons had married the two daughters of Muhammad I and perhaps held hopes of inheriting the kingdom. Now, they felt betrayed. Sensing an opportunity, Alfonso sent envoys pledging support to the clan and prompting the Banu Ashqilula to turn against Ibn al-Ahmar, which forced the sultan to sue Alfonso for peace. A treaty was signed in 1267 obliging the Ibn al-Ahmar to hand over some of his territory and resume paying *parias*.

Through all of this, trouble had been brewing to the north in Jaume I's kingdom of Valencia. Here, fueled by crusade propaganda and intimidated by the overwhelming numbers of subject Muslims among whom they lived, Christian settlers had been contravening the guarantees of protection Jaume had given to the *mudéjares* of the kingdom, abusing them and driving them to the point of insurrection. The spark came in 1276 when, following up on a Marinid raid of the previous year, Granadan and Moroccan forces, led by the exiled and aged rebel al-Azraq, attacked the kingdom and soon found support among the subject Muslims. Although al-Azraq was killed in battle that same year, it was not until 1277 that the insurgency was suppressed. Sporadic acts of local resistance would continue until as late as 1304. Jaume viewed the uprising, the War of the Muslims, as a personal betrayal, and when he abdicated in 1276, he advised his heir, Pere, to expel the kingdom's *mudéjares*. Economically and politically, however, this was impossible: Pere needed the Muslims of Valencia, who constituted perhaps 90 percent of the total population at that time and nearly the entire agricultural workforce. Thus, instead of taking reprisals, he offered them broad amnesties and did his best to encourage refugees and emigrants who had fled south to Granada to return.

The uprising and its aftermath, however, contributed to the development of a distinct *mudéjar* society in Valencia and a particularly fraught relationship with its Christian neighbors. *Mudéjares* were expelled from some of the larger towns, and their communities were pushed inland, in part so that they might not collaborate with North African invaders, but also because the best land for grain production, which is what Christian farmers and lords preferred, was located along the coast. These forced relocations tore apart long-established communities and relegated Muslim farmers to the poorest lands. Christian colonists feared the *mudéjares* and consequently avoided social contact with them, while often infringing on their legal privileges or committing acts of violence against them. Occasionally, as in 1309 in the capital city, Christian mobs attacked Muslim neighborhoods. Ironically, the *mudéjares* who did best were the many who lived as tenants of the military orders, which, despite their genesis as instruments of crusade, cultivated and protected their Muslim subjects both from popular violence and from abuse at the hands of officials.

The Muslims of the kingdom, for their part, resisted assimilation. Although they learned the local vernacular, Arabic remained very much a living language, and outside of the cities, where Muslims and

Christians were forced to rub shoulders, acculturation came slowly. There were disproportionately more foreign Muslim slaves in Valencia than in other parts of the Crown of Aragon, and this entrenched the Christians' view of Muslims as outsiders and enemies, as well as the *mudéjares'* determination to resist. Tensions would simmer through the fourteenth century, aggravated by the stresses brought on by crop failures and famine and the lethal advent of the Black Death, which first struck in 1348. In 1360, another significant revolt flared up in rural Valencia, this time under the leadership of a would-be messiah named Salim. He was soon captured and burned at the stake, but smaller uprisings and Christian reprisals continued in the following years.

A further blow to the *mudéjares* of the kingdom came in the second half of the fourteenth century with the War of the Two Peters. This struggle between Castile and Aragon, which lasted from 1356 to 1375, took a particular toll on the rural Muslim communities in the southern reaches of the kingdom of Valencia, who were subjected to abduction by Castilian and Granadan raiders and whose Christian neighbors at times took advantage of the disorder to drive them further into distress. As the chaotic fourteenth century closed, *mudéjares* once more became the focus of popular violence, inspired by the rabble-rousing sermons of charismatic millenarian preachers like (Saint) Vicent Ferrer of Valencia, who characterized Muslims as a "contagion" within Christian society that needed to be eliminated.

DESPITE THESE TROUBLES, Valencian *mudéjares*, like their better-integrated counterparts in the north of the peninsula, continued to see themselves as subjects of their Christian kings and legitimate members of the larger society in which they lived. This is perhaps most obvious in the military service they rendered the count-kings of Barcelona. The best example of the importance of Muslim troops can be seen in the events of 1285, only a few years after the conclusion of the War of the Muslims. In 1282, the inhabitants of Sicily overthrew their Angevin king, Charles I, and invited Pere the Great to rule the island kingdom. In response, Pope Martin IV, an ally of the Angevins, called a crusade against the Crown of Aragon, and in 1285 an invasion force of French and Mallorcan forces invaded Catalonia. While many of Pere's own perennially rebellious noblemen offered only lukewarm support, a detachment of six hundred Muslim crossbowmen arrived from Valencia and played a key role in breaking the crusaders' siege of Girona, bringing victory to their king. In fact, through the late 1200s and early 1300s, the Aragonese kings depended repeatedly on Muslim troops, whether Aragonese or Valencian *mudéjares* or foreign Muslim mercenaries. Throughout this period, Granadan and North African exiles and soldiers of fortune could be found fighting under the Aragonese banner against the Crown's Christian rivals, Navarre and Castile, and they were received as honored vassals in the court of Barcelona.

The fate of Muslim Menorca was less happy. In 1286, Pere the Great's son Alfons the Liberal found a pretext to annex the island protectorate. He could not simply break the treaty he had with the island's Muslims, so he accused them of violating its terms by passing intelligence to their North African coreligionists. Having obtained papal approval to qualify the invasion as a crusade, Alfons's forces landed on January 5, 1287. Despite initial resistance, the Aragonese swept over the island, which surrendered on January 21. The king, Abu 'Umar, his family, and two hundred followers, together with their belongings, were given safe passage to North Africa. The remaining population—or at least those who could not pay their own ransom—were considered captives and sent to the slave markets of the mainland, where families were torn apart as men, women, and children were sold to the highest bidder.

IN THE FINAL analysis, as far as subject minorities were concerned, the main difference between the Christian and Islamic world was that in Islam, *dhimmi* status was enshrined in scripture, thereby providing minority communities with certain minimal "constitutional" rights that could not (in theory) be violated. Christianity made no such guarantees and was instead, by its nature, unaccommodating to minority communities. But in fact there was little difference in practice between the two approaches.

Although it is true that some Muslim communities in Christian Spain suffered catastrophic violence and repression, in many regions they enjoyed broad rights and lived in peace, security, and contentment, integrated to a remarkable degree with their Christian neighbors and overlords. Thus, it was not ideology or doctrine that most shaped policies toward *mudéjares*, but practical concerns. Where Muslims were seen as reinforcing the power of rulers and the prosperity of their kingdoms, their communities were protected and cultivated; when they were perceived of as threatening, or as a liability, or when it was simply more convenient to dispose of them, their rights were eroded or simply abrogated. This volatility was built in to the *mudéjar* experience and all but guaranteed that, sooner or later, the Muslim communities of Christian Spain would disappear. This was a process, however, that would take some four centuries to play out.

25

The Pearl in the Necklace

On January 22, 1273, Abu 'Abd Allah Muhammad ibn Yusuf ibn Nasr ibn al-Ahmar, who preferred to be known as al-Ghalib bi-Llah ("the Conqueror by God") but was referred to by his followers as al-Shaykh (meaning "the Old Man" or "Boss," as well as "holy man"), fell from his horse and died. Out of all the local strongmen who had struggled to carve a kingdom out of the ruins of post-Almohad al-Andalus, he alone had succeeded on the strength of his natural cunning and political instincts; his determination to establish a kingdom at any cost, allying with and fighting against Christians and Muslims alike; and his longevity.

By the time he passed away at age seventy-eight, quite literally still in the saddle, he was not only the last Muslim ruler in al-Andalus, but he had managed to lay the groundwork for the succession of his thirty-eight-year-old son Muhammad II. True, his sultanate of Granada was a pale shadow of the old caliphate of Córdoba, but his dynasty would rule for the next 250 years through what would be the final cycle of glory and dissipation of Islamic Spain. The first century would be particularly fraught, and the family would fight tooth and nail to survive. Among those who lent strength to the struggle was a royal princess—Muhammad's brilliant granddaughter Fatima bint al-Ahmar, whose maneuvers behind the scenes helped ensure the survival of the royal line.

Muhammad I's power had been founded on his defiance of Ibn Hud al-Mutawakkil in 1232 and his alliance with Fernando III in 1236. During his uprising, he tapped into powerful currents of Andalusi religiosity, presenting himself in different contexts as a charismatic, ascetic figure, a holy warrior, or a guardian of Maliki orthodoxy, thus attracting the support of a wide group of common folk across the south. But, whether his piety was genuine or mere posture, if the people believed they were gaining an uncompromising champion of Islam, they were mistaken. In 1246, he was forced to let Jaén be taken by Fernando after a harrowing siege. He then became a tributary of the Castilian king, promising territory and a heavy cash tribute, as well as to attend the king's council and *cortes*, and to march in war alongside the armies of Castile. Castilian sources present the agreement in terms of feudal submission, emphasizing the requirement that Muhammad kiss Fernando's hand as a token of his vassalage and his obligation to render *consilium et auxilium* ("counsel and aid"). Ibn al-Ahmar and his supporters, meanwhile, likely preferred to see it as a set of mutual obligations between independent equals. Nevertheless, when Fernando died, Muhammad, whether out of esteem or respect for protocol, ordered a period of public mourning in his realms and dispatched an honor guard to attend the funeral in Seville. Subsequently, he journeyed personally to Toledo to conclude a treaty with the new king, Alfonso X.

The two decades of peace with Castile bought by the truce gave the Nasrid king the opportunity to consolidate his rule. But after Alfonso X obliged him to support his invasion of Africa and demanded more territory, Muhammad decided to resist, and in 1264 he rose up together with the *mudéjares* of Murcia and Jerez, and the Banu Hud of Murcia, and with the aid of the Marinids. The sultan had been emboldened by this alliance and the arrival of the *ghuzat* from the Maghrib, who soon took a leading role in his army. When the Banu Ashqilula rebelled as a consequence, Alfonso brought them over to his side by promising to support them against the sultan. Muhammad then countered by supporting the Castilian noblemen who were seeking to overthrow Alfonso. Nuño González de Lara, who commanded the same knights Alfonso had sent to aid the Banu Ashqilula, betrayed his king and joined with Granada. But when Alfonso made overtures to the Marinids regarding an alliance against Granada, Muhammad was forced to sue for peace and reluctantly agreed to reestablish his vassalship. With his sudden death in 1273, the conclusion of the agreement fell to his son Muhammad II. For Alfonso X, it appeared to be "check" and "mate."

BY THE TIME Muhammad II came to the throne, the chessboard of the Western Mediterranean had been transformed. If it had ever been clearly divided into Islamic and Christian zones, it was now fractured by rivalries and crisscrossed by alliances that bore little relation to religious identity. The next three-quarters of a century would see Castile-León, Granada, the Crown of Aragon, Hafsid Ifriqiya, the Marinid sultanate (with its capital at Fez), and the trading emporia of Genoa and Pisa each maneuvering against the other in the fight for individual survival and expansion. Each of the kingdoms was plagued by internal tensions: rebellious aristocracies whose members at times challenged their own rulers, and when they did so, sought help from neighboring powers, whether Christian or Muslim. Aragon was also interested in weakening Castile and at times allied with Granada against it. The Marinids looked to al-Andalus with an eye to dominate Nasrid Granada and take whatever other territory they could from Castile while contending with their own enemies in North Africa. Meanwhile, Genoa and Pisa were working to obtain trading privileges in the Islamic world and consequently often supported the Muslim powers against their Christian would-be overlords.

The newcomers on the political scene were the Marinids, the descendants of the Zanata *shaykh* 'Abd al-Haqq al-Marini, who had begun to gradually overthrow the Almohad caliphate soon after the defeat at Las Navas, concluding with the conquest of Marrakesh in 1269. These recently converted herdsmen from the desert regions on the northeastern slopes of the Atlas Mountains—the famous Merino sheep bear their name—had been sending warriors to al-Andalus since the late twelfth century. In the Maghrib, the Marinid sultans empowered the Maliki *'ulama'*, including many Andalusi exiles, disseminating the latter's ideology. They also supported Sufism and the cults of local saints and holy men, which were gaining popularity among the common folk of the Maghrib, especially in the country-side. In the absence of a revolutionary Islamic doctrine to underpin their legitimacy, the call to jihad against the Christians, which reso-nated increasingly with the populace, became one of the Marinids' raisons d'être. The popular reverence for local warrior "saints" mir-rored, in a sense, the Spanish Christian veneration of Saint James "the Muslim Killer."

But at bottom, the Marinid rulers were pragmatic. Their army de-pended heavily on Christian mercenaries, and they carried out a ro-bust program of diplomacy with Christian powers, aimed at encouraging commercial development of both the trans-Saharan gold routes and the Mediterranean markets. They invested heavily in inno-vative military technologies, including artillery and firearms, but failed to establish a fleet that could counter those of the European powers, a weakness that contributed to their failures in al-Andalus.

The result of the tangled agendas of these various players in West-ern Mediterranean politics was an ever-shifting array of alliances and rivalries characterized by military clashes, commercial agreements and partnerships, the exchange of embassies, and lending of troops. Marinid and Granadan knights could be found fighting under the ban-ners of Castile and Aragon, and the Aragonese and Castilian fleets, renegades, and mercenaries serving the North African powers. Mus-lim, Christian, and Jewish traders competed and collaborated on both shores of the Mediterranean, and rebels and insurgents—including the Banu Ashqilula, elements of the Castilian nobility, and the in-creasingly independent and divided "Volunteers of the Faith"—courted foreign powers for support.

But however little the doctrine of jihad actually informed real pol-icy, the war against the infidel was crucial to acknowledge on an ideal level. Hence, Muhammad I, vassal of Castile and consummate realist, and who was an accomplice to the Christian conquest of Muslim Jaén, Seville, and Jerez, would be presented without irony in the epi-taph carved on his tomb as

> the greatness of Islam . . . the aider of the *umma*, the source of
> mercy and pole of the Community, the light of the Shari'a, the

protector of the Sunna, the Sword of Truth . . . the guardian of the
frontier, the shatterer of armies, the subjugator of non-Muslim
rulers, the victor over unbelief and rebels . . . the holy warrior in
the service of God.[43]

WHILE MUHAMMAD MAY not have been, in fact, much of a "subjugator of non-Muslim rulers," he did leave a formidable and defensible
kingdom to his heir. Its craggy coastline, stretching some 300 miles
from Tarifa in the southwest to Pulpí in the northeast, provided a series
of natural harbors, each of which gave access to the narrow valleys
that rose up steeply into the highlands that stretched along the kingdom's length. At its midpoint, the Sierra Nevada, the summit of which,
Mulhacén, rises nearly 12,000 feet above sea level, shelters the city of
Granada on its northern slopes. Slumbering after its ephemeral days of
glory as the capital of the eleventh-century Zirid *taifa* kingdom, the
city burgeoned under the Nasrids as refugees from the north of al-
Andalus flocked to this new capital. Almería and Málaga were also
thriving commercial ports and industrial centers, and the former was
home to massive shipyards. Further south, Tarifa, Gibraltar, and Algeciras guarded the strait.

The interior, featuring broad plains and verdant valleys punctuated by rocky and difficult-to-cross ridges and hills, was at once fertile and foreboding. Larger, fortified inland towns, such as Ronda,
Guadix, Loja, and Baza, served both as military strongpoints and agricultural and artisanal hubs, while the northern frontier was studded
by castles, strongholds, and walled settlements, which served as a
deterrent and first line of defense to Castilian raiders and invaders.
All of this contrasted with the sparsely populated Christian lands to
the immediate north, an economically depressed region given over
largely to herding and punctuated by large seigneurial estates, and
where urban life had largely atrophied.

The kingdom of Granada, by contrast, boomed, owing to the farmers and craftsmen who flocked to it beginning in the thirteenth century, providing both a labor force and a domestic consumer base, and
to its connection to the markets of Christian Europe and North Africa.
Agricultural production was robust as a consequence of centuries of
Andalusi experimentation and innovation in irrigation, fertilization,

and farming techniques. A broad range of high-value fruits, including oranges and figs, were grown in intensively irrigated river valleys, while wetlands were used for rice and sugarcane. Saffron, extremely sought-after in both the Islamic and the Christian worlds, was an important cash crop. Alongside the staple crops grew olives, grapes (only for raisins and never wine, had the jurists had their way, which they did not), nuts (notably almonds), flax for linen production, and mulberry trees—the habitat of the *Bombyx mori* larvae that provided the raw material for the silk industry that drove the Granadan export economy.

Silk production and weaving was undoubtedly the single most important sector of the industrial economy. Expensive Nasrid textiles, famous for their high quality, bright colors, and rich brocade and filigree were exported across Europe. Other craft industries were also highly developed, including metal- and leatherworking, papermaking, crystal, and ceramics, notably lusterware, with production geared for both domestic consumption and export. It was these manufactured goods that attracted the greatest interest of foreign merchants, particularly Catalans and Italians, who by bringing them home and distributing them across Christendom transformed European tastes and techniques. This too contributed to the kingdom's political security, given that Catalan and Italian merchants were eager to maintain an independent Granada to avoid having to pay taxes or duties to Castile and were prepared to defend its interests to the extent that it reinforced their own.

There was also much trade across the land border with Castile, and in the fourteenth and fifteenth centuries a series of truces and agreements were concluded with the Nasrids with the aim of regulating it. Muslim merchants who traveled north were protected by these agreements even in time of war. The border was also the scene of smuggling, notably of livestock, whose seasonal grazing routes often crossed the boundary between the kingdoms. Similar commercial and political treaties were enacted with the Crown of Aragon and the Italian trading cities, providing European traders with access to Nasrid ports and the Granadans with protection against piracy and abduction at the hands of Christian corsairs. In the late thirteenth and early fourteenth centuries, a handful of powerful Jewish families in the Crown of Aragon dominated the diplomatic service and shuttled back and forth to Granada, negotiating agreements, hiring mercenaries, and redeeming captives taken in violation of treaties.

The Nasrids also used slaves, some brought up by Muslim traders from Africa but many captured on raids against Christian territory and ships, or as prisoners of war in battles on land and at sea. Some were forced into hard labor, particularly the construction of defensive works, and agricultural work. The conditions they lived under were often brutal, characterized by confinement in dungeons, back-breaking toil, and the ever-present threat of execution. Women were typically destined for domestic service or concubinage. Their fate should not be romanticized: abducted and uprooted, sold as chattel and subject to rape at the will of their owners, these women, like their Muslim counterparts in Christian lands, suffered through their own tragic "Handmaid's Tales." Captives taken on raids into Christian territory, occasionally including Muslims from Murcia or the kingdom of Valencia, were processed in border towns before being sold onward, often for resale in Granada. Many converted to Islam, particularly those who had little prospect of emancipation and repatriation to their homelands, those in domestic service, and concubines.

Apart from captives, foreign merchants (who lived primarily in Málaga and Almería), mercenaries, and soldiers of fortune, many people of the Nasrid kingdom would have had little contact with non-Muslims, except in the context of war. The small number of native Christians who remained in the kingdom seem to have been mostly poor farmers living in a handful of hamlets in the Alpujarras, on the southern slopes of the Sierra Nevada. The few Jewish communities, whose total population was probably less than two thousand, were confined to larger towns, including Granada, Guadix, Ronda, Baza, and Almería. Although a small Jewish intellectual and literary elite persisted in Granada (and continued to write in Arabic), it seems they did not occupy official positions in the Nasrid administration. Castilian Jews were active in commerce along the frontier but do not seem to have established colonies in the Nasrid kingdom. After pogroms ravaged the Jewish communities of the Christian kingdoms in

1391, some Jews came to the kingdom of Granada as refugees; those who had been baptized out of fear or under threat were thereby able to return to Judaism.

The population of the kingdom was fairly homogenous, united by Islam, Arabic, and Arabo-Andalusi culture, the three poles of identity the Nasrids deliberately cultivated. Although the bulk of the population was made up of native Muslims, even in this late period there were still families who proudly traced their pedigree back to the Arabian Peninsula. And while there was a considerable Berber element (including recent arrivals), it was Arabic language and Andalusi culture that defined Granadan society. Moreover, because the kingdom was home to refugees from across the peninsula, its culture comprised a supraregional melting pot that included elements from all over al-Andalus. The greatest influx came during the thirteenth-century era of conquest, but *mudéjares* continued to arrive in the early fourteenth century, thanks in part to a 1325 treaty with Aragon that guaranteed Valencian Muslims the right to emigrate. The presence of so many exiles in the Nasrid kingdom, together with intermittent cross-border raiding, engendered a heightened sense of Muslim-Christian conflict among the populace, many of whom were, of course, refugees or the descendants of refugees, had suffered in Christian attacks, or had spent time as captives in infidel lands. To bolster their claims of legitimacy, the Nasrid kings would present the kingdom of Granada as the last refuge of Islam in al-Andalus.

WITH ALL OF this, Muhammad II, who would be known as al-Faqih ("the legal scholar"), was not dealt an easy hand. But he played it masterfully. He inherited a kingdom beset by revolt, burdened by *parias*, and faced with the cost of building and maintaining its fortifications and patronizing a demanding and fickle elite. When he came to power, his most powerful forces were the less-than-trustworthy rebellious Castilian knights commanded by Nuño González de Lara. His potential allies, the Banu Marin, were casting hungry eyes at al-Andalus, and the North African *mujahidun* who had come over during the reign of his father were operating independently along the northern frontier, irritating the local populace and local aristocratic dynasties and causing their support to waver.

Yet, by skillfully playing these various parties off each other, and capitalizing on the disarray in Castile caused by the rebellion of Alfonso's son and heir, who would come to the throne in 1284 as Sancho IV, Muhammad II managed not only to persevere, but to consolidate his kingdom. In a decade-long flurry of invasions, uprisings, betrayals, and alliances involving the major Christian and Muslim powers and the various rebel parties, the Banu Ashqilula were neutralized, the Marinids were driven out of al-Andalus, Castile was contained, and the military might of the *ghuzat* was harnessed. This came at some cost. The Marinids killed Muhammad's ally Nuño González (whose head they sent preserved in camphor as a gift to Muhammad, who in turn sent it on to Alfonso), and the Moroccan *ghuzat* brought their own problems. Chief among these was the struggle between two rival branches of the Marinid clan to control this militia—the Banu Abi 'l-'Ula and the Banu Rahhu. As the Banu Abi 'l-'Ula gained the upper hand, the Banu Rahhu headed north to Barcelona, where they were welcomed into the royal court and placed in charge of the Crown of Aragon's mercenaries.

For its part, Castile was again thrust into crisis with the succession of the ten-year-old Fernando IV in 1295. And so it was that Muhammad was left, in effect, the last man standing in the south. In 1296, he cast in his lot with Aragon in exchange for a free hand to invade the south of Castile. But the Nasrid ruler did not long enjoy his advantage: in 1302 Muhammad II died, poisoned, it seems, by his own son and successor.

Ruthless as he may have been, Muhammad III proved far less capable a king than his father or grandfather, and in the seven years of his rule, he squandered many of their gains. If later, unsympathetic chroniclers are to be believed, he embarked on a series of violent purges, shaking the confidence of the *khassa*. Next, despite the fact that the *ghuzat* had scored victories in the region of Jaén, he signed a treaty reaffirming his own vassalship to Castile, which included the payment of *parias* and the cessation of fortresses. The treaty was approved by Aragon (which would soon conclude a secret pact with

Castile to divide up a conquered Granada), leaving Muhammad's enemies, the Marinids, vulnerable, but troubling both the common folk
and the *ghuzat*, who were opposed on principle to treaties with the
infidel. Then, emboldened by the weakness of the Marinids, the sultan encouraged the people of Ceuta to revolt and in 1306 seized the
city, thus gaining control of the Strait of Gibraltar.

This alarmed all the powers of the Western Mediterranean, provoking a triple alliance of Castile, Aragon, and the Marinids, which
left Muhammad III isolated. To be fair, all of this may not have been
entirely the sultan's doing. His eyesight had begun to fail early in his
reign, and he had begun to depend heavily on an advisor named Abu
'Abd Allah, a poet who had charmed his way into the service of Muhammad II as *katib* by way of some flattering verses. Abu 'Abd Allah
subsequently gained the trust of Muhammad III, and as the sultan's
double-wazir (prime minister for civil and military affairs) he ran the
state and amassed a great fortune. But the resentment Abu 'Abd Allah's policies provoked among the common folk and the envy his
wealth sparked among his fellow officials led to the outbreak of a
revolt in March 1309. The uprising, led by a rival official and supported by the sultan's younger brother Nasr, saw the wazir killed, his
body profaned, and his palace sacked. Muhammad III was sent off
into a gilded internal exile at Almuñecar on the southern coast.

Nasr came to power in a time of crisis, with Aragon launching an
attack on Almería and Castile on Algeciras and Gibraltar. By September 1309, Gibraltar had fallen, after which its inhabitants were expelled. Algeciras and Ronda opened their gates to the Marinids, who
had landed troops in al-Andalus in support of Castile. Nasr responded
by formally ceding these territories to the Banu Marin, thus reconcil-
ing with them and driving a wedge into the triple alliance against him.
Soon after, Don Juan Manuel (the same prince who would later compose *The Tales of Count Lucanor*) and his sizable body of troops abandoned Fernando IV and returned to Castile, thus saving Algeciras from
conquest. At Almería, the Aragonese crusaders fared even worse. They
surrounded the city with a massive army and a naval blockade in August 1309, but the Muslim commanders had spent months strengthen-
ing its fortifications and stockpiling food. The defenders held off

several assaults with the aid of boiling oil and at one point (and to great effect) pelted the dashingly decked out Christian knights with raw sewage. The attackers rained tens of thousands of stones fired by catapults on the city and even breached the walls in one instance, but to no avail. In early 1310, the Aragonese withdrew.

Significant as this victory may have been, it did little to satisfy the populace of Granada, who were increasingly disappointed with both Nasr and his wazir 'Atiq ibn al-Mawl. Nasr also had powerful enemies within the royal family. His half sister, Fatima bint al-Ahmar, had been a strong supporter of her brother Muhammad III. Both had been born to their father's first wife and maternal cousin. Fatima was married to her own paternal uncle Abu Sa'id Faraj ibn Isma'il, a nephew of Muhammad I, who had rendered crucial service to the dynasty as the long-serving governor of Málaga. Thus, from the point of view of bloodline, Nasr, born to Muhammad's second wife, Shams al-Duha, a Christian and former slave, was an interloper. His inclination toward Christian styles of dress and his appointment of a former *mozarab*, Muhammad ibn al-Hajj, as a wazir did not help his image. And so the stage was set for conflict.

Fatima's husband, Abu Sa'id, had no claim to the throne himself, but their son, Isma'il, was now the most full-blooded heir of the Nasrid dynasty—a descendant of Muhammad I through both his father and his mother. Nasr would see him as a threat, and rightly so; as such, Fatima needed to act. Thus, with the support of Abu Sa'id's old comrade, the *ghuzat* commander 'Uthman ibn Abi 'l-'Ula, and sympathetic elements within the urban elite of Granada, Fatima helped to engineer the overthrow of Nasr. Dislodged from the capital by rebel forces in February 1314, he was permitted to retreat into a luxurious exile in Guadix, accompanied by his personal bodyguard. No sooner had he arrived than he sent out feelers to Castile, hoping to make an alliance that would place him back on the throne.

Fernando IV of Castile had died in 1312 and been succeeded by his one-year-old son, Alfonso XI, who had come under the tutelage of his grandmother Maria de Molina and two powerful princes, Juan (a son of Alfonso X) and Pedro (a son of Sancho IV). When they heard Nasr's offer, the two princes led a large column of knights down to

Guadix, scoring a hard-fought victory in 1316 over forces led by the ·
ghuzat commander 'Uthman ibn Abi 'l-'Ula. Three years later, they
followed it up with a massive expedition into the fertile Vega, or hinterland, of Granada. It was a disaster. Both Pedro and Juan were
killed, and the Christian troops were routed by Granadan forces; the
shaykh al-ghuzat, 'Uthman, had taken his revenge.

With Castile now in disarray, Alfonso XI's wards sued for an eight-
year truce, and when this expired in 1323, Isma'il went on the attack,
personally leading his forces in the capture of a string of sizable towns
along the northern frontier and apparently making use of cannon for the
first time in the Iberian Peninsula. In the meantime, he had fallen out
with his father, who was suspected of plotting to hand over Málaga to
the Marinids. Abu Sa'id was thus deprived of his position and cast into
the royal prison, where he died in 1320. Perhaps sensing Isma'il's increasing isolation, or fearing his own fate, 'Uthman ibn Abi 'l-'Ula
decided to act and incited Isma'il's cousin Muhammad ibn Isma'il, the
governor of Algeciras, to assassinate him. Muhammad and his brother
stabbed the sultan in his own palace but nearly botched the job, and the
wounded Isma'il survived long enough for the assassins and their supporters to be arrested and put to death. But 'Uthman, the man behind
the plot, escaped detection, and when the dead king's eldest son, the
ten-year-old Muhammad IV, was proclaimed as successor the very
same day his father died, 'Uthman assented, undoubtedly sure that he
would wield the real power behind the boy-king.

Fatima was now in her mid-sixties but still a force to be reckoned
with. She had stood by Isma'il and had been instrumental in securing
the succession of her grandson Muhammad IV, whom she served as
regent, alongside an official guardian. Now she worked to assure the
continuity of the dynasty while 'Uthman ibn Abi 'l-'Ula and the wazir Muhammad ibn al-Mahruq intrigued against each other with the
aim of taking control of the kingdom. Things came to a head quickly.
'Uthman set about to isolate Ibn al-Mahruq from the rest of the court,
in reaction to which the wazir invited Yahya ibn 'Umar, of the rival
Ibn Rahhu clan, to come to Granada and take command of the *ghuzat*
in 1326. 'Uthman found himself abandoned by the bulk of his own
troops, who went over to the new commander, sparking a war among

the Moroccan *ghuzat*. Casting about for a figurehead for his ambitions to take control of al-Andalus, 'Uthman turned to Muhammad ibn Abi Sa'id, an uncle of Muhammad IV, who had escaped to Tlemcen when his brother, the murdered sultan Isma'il, had come to power. Crossing over to al-Andalus and settling in Andarax (Andrash) in the Alpujarras, Muhammad ibn Abi Sa'id was declared the rightful sultan by 'Uthman. In response, and with the connivance of Fatima, who was alarmed by Ibn al-Mahruq's success and by this latest uprising, Muhammad IV ordered Ibn al-Mahruq assassinated. 'Uthman promptly abandoned his pretender to the throne and was restored as commander of the *ghuzat*.

With stability reestablished, by 1330 Muhammad was able to launch a series of attacks against Alfonso XI, aided by the *ghuzat*, who were now led by 'Uthman's son Abu Tabit. But when the Castilians struck back in force, the sultan buckled, pledging to renew his tribute to Alfonso and hurrying off to Fez to personally petition the sultan, Abu 'Ali 'Umar, for aid. In response, the Marinids landed a significant force in the south with the aid of the Genoese and recaptured Gibraltar from Castile in June 1333. Alfonso XI arrived soon after and mounted a counterattack, but after three months he had failed to dislodge the defenders.

When news of new rebellions among the Castilian nobility (captained by the irrepressible Don Juan Manuel) reached him, the king resolved to negotiate, and he and Muhammad settled their differences in person over a lavish banquet and the exchange of gifts. Alfonso would withdraw from al-Andalus, Muhammad would pay tribute to Castile, and trade would be reopened along their land border. A satisfied Muhammad IV then prepared to return to Granada. But Abu Tabit, the commander of the *ghuzat*, who had fought through the two sieges of Gibraltar, was less content. With peace restored with Castile and an alliance forged between Nasrid Granada and Marinid Fez, he had become less useful and undoubtedly feared his family might be extradited to Morocco. And so, he arranged for the eighteen-year-old Muhammad IV to be ambushed as he journeyed back in triumph to Granada.

Muhammad's loyal wazir Abu Nu'aym Ridwan was there when the sultan was killed. He rode straight back to the capital, arriving that day, and with the assent and collaboration of the queen mother, Fatima, immediately declared Muhammad's fifteen-year-old brother, Yusuf, the new sultan. Their pledges of loyalty to the new king notwithstanding, Abu Tabit and his family were arrested and sent off into exile to Hafsid Tunis, while Yusuf ibn 'Umar ibn Rahhu was restored as commander of the *ghuzat*. Despite this rocky start, it would be under Yusuf I and his eldest son Muhammad V that Nasrid Granada would enjoy its era of greatest glory—thanks in part to the vision and constancy of Fatima bint al-Ahmar, who had for three generations worked to support the Nasrid line and provided vision and experience for its young and ill-fated sultans. Her stature was evident to her contemporaries, not the least the courtier, poet, and historian Ibn al-Khatib, who at her death in 1349 at age ninety, praised her as

> the cream of the cream of the kingdom, the great pearl at the center of the dynasty's necklace, the pride of the harem, aspiring to honor and respect, the chain binding its subjects, the protector of the kings, and the living memory of the royal family's birthright.[44]

26

Prosperous by God

When Yusuf I took the throne in 1332, the Nasrid kingdom of Granada faced formidable challenges, not the least being the deep factional divisions that characterized the royal family and aristocracy, the palace bureaucracy, and the army. The sultanate was vulnerable in other ways too. It was surrounded by larger and more populous rivals in the peninsula: Castile and Aragon, each of which could legitimize any aggression against the Nasrids with the veneer of crusade. Its only effective Muslim ally, Marinid Morocco, also eyed it as a prize and needed to be kept off-balance. The costs of defense, including constructing fortifications, maintaining an army and navy, and paying *parias* to its Christian neighbors, were high.

And because their subjects had suffered so much from Christian aggression, and so much of the Nasrids' popular support and legitimacy were grounded in their self-promotion as champions of Islam and holy war against the infidel, they risked popular reaction when they were inevitably forced to make compromises with their Christian neighbors. But the religious ground in the sultanate was shifting as mysticism gained traction not only among the common folk but also among the elite, threatening the consensus of the kingdom's *'ulama'*. In the end, the success of Yusuf I and his son Muhammad V was due

as much to the circumstances that kept their rivals divided and distracted as to their own significant skill as diplomats and monarchs.

YUSUF'S REIGN BEGAN unevenly. A three-way peace with Castile
and Morocco ended in 1340 when a combined Marinid-Nasrid naval
force crushed the Castilian fleet off the coast of Gibraltar. Determined
to maintain the initiative, the Marinid amir Abu 'l-Hasan 'Ali gathered his forces and crossed over to al-Andalus with the aim of retaking Tarifa. Such was his confidence that he not only led the invasion
himself but brought over his entire household with him. This would
prove to be a mistake. The Castilian defenders managed to fend off
the initial attacks, and, owing in part to a well-coordinated heavy
cavalry charge, Alfonso's relief forces put the Marinid and Granadan
troops to flight, killing them as they fled and overrunning the amir's
camp. Abu 'l-Hasan escaped back to Ceuta, but his household, including his wives, children, and personal treasure, was seized, together with precious metal of such quantity that the European gold
markets dipped significantly. Although the Marinids continued to en-
tertain ambitions in al-Andalus, their defeat at the Battle of Rio Sal-
ado marked the end of any threat they posed to the Nasrids. After the
death of Abu 'l-Hasan in 1351, the dynasty spiraled into a cycle of
rebellions, coups, and regicides that would see no fewer than sixteen
amirs take the throne in the second half of the fourteenth century.

Following his victory, Alfonso proceeded to the strong point of
Alcalá la Real (al-Qal'a), just thirty miles northwest of Granada,
which surrendered after a prolonged siege, before turning back west
toward Algeciras in 1342. Here he gathered an immense force, including crusaders from across Europe; notables, including Carlos III
of Navarre; and ships from Genoa. The siege would last two and a
half years as the Christian forces worked relentlessly to undermine
the city's fortifications and to storm its walls, and the defenders doggedly repulsed the enemy, striking terror into the attackers with their
use of cannon. Both sides became worn down by fatigue, hunger, and
disease, and Alfonso's foreign allies gradually abandoned him. Yusuf
had sued Alfonso for peace, but the Castilian king's demand that he
break his alliance with the Marinids was a compromise the sultan

could not make. Without an influx of African troops, his kingdom would be doomed. Finally, Alfonso yielded, agreeing to a ten-year truce and the receipt of an immense annual payment of cash, in exchange for allowing the garrison and inhabitants to leave the town peacefully. The respite would allow Yusuf to focus on state building and the entrenchment of his dynasty.

Just prior to the treaty, Alfonso had laid siege to Gibraltar. It would be his undoing. At the siege camp in March 1350, "the tyrant" met his end, struck down not by the sword of some valiant Muslim warrior, but felled instead by a tiny, invisible enemy: the bacillus *Yersinia pestis*. The Black Death had arrived. It would strike the Iberian Peninsula and the rest of the Mediterranean mercilessly—in some areas mortality rates reached nearly 90 percent.

In a gesture of chivalry to his former lord and implacable enemy, Yusuf gave safe passage to the deceased king's funeral cortege as it wound its way back to Córdoba, where he was interred in the former great mosque alongside his father, Fernando IV. Four years later, Yusuf himself fell, stabbed while at prayer by a stablehand slave who had apparently lost his wits, although the assassination may well have been orchestrated by the sultan's enemies in Fez. Despite his losses on the battlefield, Yusuf had been a popular king, adored by his subjects and respected by the Christian rulers, diplomats, and merchants he received and with whom he corresponded.

In the short term, the Plague, which would bring about the transformation of both the Christian and the Islamic worlds, would benefit Granada, contributing to upheavals among the neighboring powers that the Nasrids were able to use to their advantage. Crucial was their relationship with Castile and its new king, Pedro I. A polarizing figure, known to his supporters as "the Just" and to his opponents as "the Cruel," Pedro plunged the Christian powers of the peninsula into a series of wars that would last until almost the end of the century, placing the kingdom of Granada in a position of new strength.

With Yusuf's unexpected demise, the long-serving wazir Ridwan quickly had the deceased sultan's sixteen-year-old son, Muhammad, put on the throne. Yusuf had long favored another son, Isma'il, who had been born to his second wife, a slave named Rim, or Maryam, but had designated Muhammad his heir just before his death. Together with Ridwan as *hajib*, the young sultan could count on the loyalty and talents of Yahya ibn 'Umar ibn Rahhu, who headed the *ghuzat*, and Muhammad ibn al-Khatib—the preeminent writer and intellectual of fourteenth-century al-Andalus, known as Lisan al-Din ("the Voice of the Faith")—who served as chancellor and held the double wazirate. But powerful forces within the palace were arrayed against them, namely, Rim and her children, particularly Isma'il. In 1359, the conspirators struck, sending a large force of assassins to invade Ridwan's house and murder the *hajib*. Thanks to the quick action of the Banu Rahhu, the sultan Muhammad was spirited out of the city, first to Guadix and then on to exile in the Marinid court at Fez, together with his loyal officials, including Ibn al-Khatib; the poet-courtier Muhammad ibn Zamrak; and his personal bodyguard, made up of two hundred Christian slave soldiers. The Banu Rahhu rallied their troops and battled their way north to Castile, where they took refuge with Pedro I and fought alongside his knights against Aragon.

Isma'il settled onto the throne quickly, putting the Banu Abi 'l-'Ula in charge of the *ghuzat* once more and demanding Muhammad V's wife, who had remained in Granada, divorce her husband and marry him. The city had already suffered considerably because of the Plague and the economic crisis that rippled across the western world, creating a situation of general malaise that had undoubtedly helped fuel discontent with Muhammad V. But under Isma'il things were hardly more stable, and many inhabitants, including both the elite and the commoners, fled the capital in alarm. Moreover, his vanity and effeminate appearance (he scandalously wore his long hair in braids tied with ribbons of silk) led many to feel he was not regal material. Meanwhile, his brother-in-law, a great-grandson of Fatima bint al-Ahmar named Muhammad, who had aided Isma'il in the coup of 1359, took power behind the scenes.

Known to the Castilians as El Bermejo ("the Red Head"), by 1360 Muhammad had consolidated his position such that he could overthrow and murder Isma'il, along with the sultan's closest family members and advisors. El Bermejo then claimed the throne as Muhammad VI al-Ghalib bi-Llah ("the Victor by the Help of God"). But El Bermejo, said to be slovenly and addicted to hashish, did not inspire much confidence either, and the unrest that followed his coup provided an opportunity for Muhammad V to return from exile. Gathering his faithful followers and troops at Ronda, and calling on the support of his old ally and friend Pedro of Castile, the deposed sultan began the fight to regain his crown in 1361.

Court intrigues aside, powerful geopolitical forces were at work in the peninsula. Tension had been simmering between Pere the Ceremonious of Aragon and Pedro I of Castile since the death of Alfonso XI in 1350. Both monarchs had to contend with rebellious noblemen and city governments, and each was supporting the other's half brothers' attempts to seize the throne. In 1356 when Pedro attacked the Crown of Aragon, initiating what would be called the War of the Two Peters, his ally Muhammad V had lent ships and troops, and in response, Pere established an alliance with the Marinids against Granada and Castile. Now, with the two Muhammads battling for the throne of Granada, Pedro I supported Muhammad V, while Muhammad VI joined the Aragonese alliance. Concerned that his kingdom might lose control of Granada, Pedro sought a temporary truce with Aragon using the expedient of a Crusade bull obtained from Innocent IV to fight Islam (which in this case meant to support his own Muslim ally) and sent his forces to Granada to aid Muhammad V.

With Castilian attacks dividing the forces of El Bermejo, Muhammad V gained the initiative and in March 1362 seized Málaga, taking control of access between Granada and Morocco, while Pedro's Christian forces claimed a series of towns and fortresses along the frontier. At this, the increasingly unpopular El Bermejo panicked and fled Granada, with his household, his treasure, and five hundred troops, to throw himself at the mercy of Pedro I.

What followed was one of the many occasions that Pedro would live up to his infamous nickname, "the Cruel." The day after Muhammad and thirty-six of his dignitaries were treated by the Castilian king to a welcome feast, Pedro had them taken out to a field where he personally drove his lance into El Bermejo before ordering the rest to be slaughtered in cold blood. As an act of amicable courtesy, Pedro had their heads send back to Muhammad V as gifts, and the surviving Granadan courtiers and commanders were thrown in the dungeons of

Seville. As for the abundant treasure El Bermejo had brought with him, Pedro kept that for himself.

Once restored, Muhammad V would remain on the throne until 1390, as once more the two Peters of Castile and Aragon resumed their mortal struggle. As for the sultan, he would use all his considerable diplomatic skills to avoid becoming fatally embroiled in the conflict, and turn it to his own and his kingdom's advantage. Initially things went well for the allies. In 1363, with the help of Navarre and Portugal, Pedro made considerable territorial gains in Aragon, while Granada cavalry were unleashed on Murcia and southern Valencia, ravaging the countryside and taking Christian captives. But the length and cost of the war pushed his kingdom further into debt, sapping Pedro's already flagging popularity. The increasingly unstable king inflicted his subjects with ever more burdensome taxes and tortured and executed anyone suspected of disloyalty, including members of his own family. Soon, he faced open revolt by his nobility and the main towns of his realm.

Meanwhile, Pere of Aragon's fortune turned when, thanks to a lull in the fighting in England and France's Hundred Years' War, Pedro's illegitimate half brother Enrique de Trastámara, whose claim to the throne of Castile Pere supported, was able to recruit to his side the notorious mercenary White Companies, which had caused so much havoc in their native France. As the White Companies invaded Castile and Pedro's position crumbled, Muhammad stayed loyal, rebuffing offers of an Aragonese alliance and continuing to send his knights into battle under the banner of Castile. However, stung by the Crusade bull of 1361, which he saw as proof of a papal plot to overthrow him, and anxious to reinforce his own reputation as a warrior of the faith and mobilize his divided subjects, Muhammad declared a jihad and personally led his troops as they recaptured a string of Castilian fortresses and towns that were in revolt against Pedro, nearly retaking Córdoba. Sending envoys to the various rulers of the Islamic world from Fez to Mecca, Muhammad rationalized his alliance with Pedro as part of a grander strategy for battling Christendom.

By 1369, Pedro's domestic support had all but evaporated. In March of that year, when he suffered a defeat at the hands of Enrique and the White Companies at Montiel, among the few troops who had stood steadfastly by him were the fifteen hundred Granadan cavalry whom Muhammad V had sent. In the aftermath of the battle, the Castilian king was lured into a trap by the mercenary captain Bertrand de Guesclin, who took him to a tent where Enrique de Trastámara lay in wait. After a brief exchange of words, the rebellious royal bastard fatally drove his dagger into his half brother, Pedro. Thus began the era of the Trastámara dynasty, the line from which both Isabel and Fernando "the Catholic" would descend. But rather than bringing peace to the peninsula, Enrique's victory and his coronation as king of Castile embroiled the Christian kingdoms of the peninsula in a new series of wars that would last decades.

These conflicts provided a much-needed respite for the Nasrid sultanate, and Muhammad V was determined to take full advantage. In July 1369, he arrived with a large army at the gates of Castilian-held Algeciras. After only two days, the fortifications of the "new town" were breached, and the Nasrid troops flooded in and massacred the inhabitants. The next day, the petrified garrison in the more strongly fortified "old town" offered to surrender in exchange for safe passage. Thus, Muhammad, who adopted the title al-Ghani bi-Llah ("Prosperous by God") in honor of the victory, entered the city in triumph. He restored its congregational mosque, which had been converted into a church, and then embarked on a series of lucrative raids against the lands south of Seville and Córdoba. With this, the sultan's reputation as *mujahid* was sealed, and poets, such as Ibn al-Khatib, advertised this feat far and wide. But even a victory of this scale could not change the reality of Granada's vulnerability. Muhammad recognized this and in 1379 made the decision to dismantle the three miles of walls that surrounded Algeciras and abandon the city to prevent its being used by his enemies in the future.

In the interim, the embattled Christian kingdoms were in little position to respond to Granada's newfound confidence. Both Aragon and Castile were eager to have Muhammad V as an ally, and as neither was in a position to demand exclusive loyalty, relations with both remained cordial and productive. Nasrid knights won glory and loot, whether raiding the war-weakened Christian-held lands or riding alongside Christian knights against Christian enemies, while Christian and Muslim merchants plied the land and sea routes between the kingdoms. Through the skillful manipulation of rivalries within the royal family and the exercise of soft power, Muhammad ensured that the Marinids and the various other dynasties of North Africa would cause him no difficulty as they slipped into decadence and slowly lost their grip on the Maghrib. By 1372, he had brought the *ghuzat* under the control of Nasrid commanders, and in 1374 after he took Gibraltar, it was he who was sending military aid to his Marinid clients. In 1384, he occupied Ceuta, taking control of the strait.

The latter part of Muhammad's reign was an era of great prosperity and stability, and the king strove to present himself as a ruler of the first rank. He engaged in diplomacy with the Mamelukes of Egypt (who since the Mongol sack of Baghdad in 1258 had served as protectors for the 'Abbasid caliphate-in-exile) and claimed to be the true sovereign of the subject Muslims of the Christian kings. Nasrid courtier-propagandists had been working since at least the reign of Yusuf to legitimize the claims of the dynasty, fabricating a genealogy that had them descend from a venerable Arabic lineage of the Ansar and encouraging the sultans to adopt the title "caliph," if only in discreet and limited contexts.

THE MOST VISIBLE manifestation of the Nasrid's confidence was and remains the great Alhambra Palace at Granada. It was constructed on the Sabika, a hill on the southeastern edge of the city overlooking the Darro River, where the palace of eleventh-century Jewish wazirs, the Banu Naghrella, had once stood. After taking Granada in 1238, Muhammad I had begun by repairing and rebuilding the existing fortress on this site, and construction continued under Muhammad II and Muhammad III. During the latter's reign, the Jannat al-'Arif ("the Master's Paradise," today's *Generalife*)—a formal garden and farm graced by a palatial pavilion—was laid out slightly further up the slope, and a congregational mosque and public baths were built in the suburb below.

It was under Yusuf I and Muhammad V that much of the Alhambra one visits today was laid out. The monumental "Gate of Justice"

The Patio of the Lions (Alhambra Palace, Granada). *Courtesy Alamy*

constructed by Yusuf still stands, but the throne room, the royal residences, and many of the regal audience chambers he built were largely replaced by Muhammad in the 1360s. Two conjoined complexes, known today as the Comares Palace and the Palace of the Lions, were constructed. The latter, it has been suggested, was a combination *madrasa* (a religious academy), *zawiya* (a convent for Sufis), and future mausoleum for the sultan.

Using an innovative plaster-casting technique, Nasrid, Maghribi, and Castilian *mudéjar* artisans crafted an interior of gravity-defying and graceful high-relief screens and stalactites, featuring dizzyingly complex geometric and vegetal patterns interspersed with inscriptions taken from panegyric verses penned by the sultanate's poets-laureate and wazirs, Ibn al-Khatib and his student Ibn Zamrak. The dazzling parget was complemented by brilliantly colored ceramic tiles, elaborately carved woodwork, and expanses of translucent marble. Christian artists from Castile added paintings depicting scenes of chivalry and the hunt. Grand reception halls were interspersed with gurgling fountains, and breezy balconies looked out over Granada and the slopes of the Sierra Nevada. The effect was (and remains) transcendental. In the words of Ibn Zamrak, the Sabika was "the crown on the forehead of Granada, and the Alhambra (May God safeguard it!), the ruby at the peak of this crown."[45]

The Alhambra, however, was far from singular, except perhaps in its scale. In fact, it epitomized a vibrant post-Almohad Islamicate aristocratic culture and aesthetic that bridged not only Granada and the Maghrib but also Castile. Muslim and Christian princes, diplomats, noblemen, and knights who traveled or settled across their respective frontiers formed close personal relationships based on their common values and shared vocations, and these served as a conduit for cultural dissemination and integration. The sultans understood that this could serve as a form of soft power and took care that palatial accommodation, the Diyar al-Diyafa ("the House of Hospitality"), was provided to visiting dignitaries.

Hence, like many members of the Castilian frontier aristocracy, Muhammad V's ally Pedro the Cruel developed a fascination with Arabo-Islamic culture. He maintained a close, personal bond with the sultan; adopted "Oriental" affectations and fashions; and built a series of palaces in a lavish fusion of Islamic and Latinate styles, constructed by *mudéjar*, Nasrid, and Castilian craftsmen. Emblematic of this was the royal palace in Seville. Whereas Pedro's predecessors had each renovated parts of the *alcázar*, or palace-fortress, in an Islamic fashion to commemorate their victories and celebrate their domination of the infidel, his extensive remodeling was an exuberant celebration of Islamicate taste on its own terms—an only slightly paler reflection of the Alhambra that Muhammad was constructing at the same time 150 miles to the east.

Indeed, Pedro cemented a fashion among the Castilian upper classes for *maurophilia* (the affection for and affectation of Arabo-Islamic styles) that would last into the reign of Isabel the Catholic. Across Castile, royal and noble palaces, as well as convents, were built according to the same general plan as Granadan palaces or decorated in *mudéjar* and Nasrid styles. Aristocratic Jews, who moved in the same circles, also emulated these styles, as can be seen both in the modest fourteenth-century synagogue at Córdoba and in the

Synagogue of El Transito—the opulent house of prayer commissioned in Toledo by Pedro's Jewish treasurer, Samuel ha-Levi, and dedicated to the Castilian king.

Why would a Castilian king model his palaces after the styles of his infidel enemies? For the simple reason that he did not see them as such. His political survival depended on his good relations with Granada and the Marinids, whereas the threats to his throne came from Christians—whether members of his own family and nobility or neighboring kings. Moreover, despite advances in Latin Europe, the Arabo-Islamic world remained more technologically advanced, intellectually dynamic, and cosmopolitan. Thus, the cultural entente established between Castile and the Muslim West was not confined to ephemera or "mere" decoration but ran far deeper, and the three kingdoms were bridged by a "community of letters" and an intellectual culture that spanned the Western Mediterranean.

This can be seen in the encounter that took place at the *alcázar* of Seville in 1364 between Pedro I and a Granadan emissary named 'Abd al-Rahman ibn Khaldun. Ibn Khaldun was a scholar and historian who authored a sophisticated universal history and is often credited today as the founder of sociology and a pioneer of political science. His family, members of the old Arabic aristocracy of Seville, had fled al-Andalus during the time of Fernando III and settled in Ifriqiya. From there, he had moved to Fez in the service of the Marinid sultan in 1352. Here, he had on several occasions met Muhammad V's Jewish physician and astronomer, Ibrahim ibn Zarzar, who served the sultan as an envoy to the Marinids. Seven years later, when Muhammad was overthrown and took refuge at the Marinid court, Ibn Khaldun befriended the Granadan wazir Ibn al-Khatib, who had accompanied the king into exile.

Lisan al-Din ibn al-Khatib was Muhammad V's most influential courtier, a scholar from Loja who first served Yusuf I as a secretary and then rose to be Muhammad's double-wazir. When the king returned from exile in 1362, Ibn al-Khatib took over the day-to-day running of the sultanate, working to raise the standing of the Nasrid sultans through the poetry he composed and the policies he promoted. In addition, he corresponded with leading literary, religious, and scholarly figures across the Islamic West and wrote prodigiously in a range of genres, including philosophy and theology, *adab*, history, medicine, and science, as well as fiction in prose and verse, emerging as the greatest intellectual of his age.

Back in Granada, Ibn al-Khatib helped Ibn Khaldun, who was tiring of the intrigues of the Marinid court, receive an appointment from the Nasrid ruler. And, soon after his arrival at the Alhambra, Ibn Khaldun was dispatched as an envoy to Pedro I to ratify a treaty between Castile and Granada. When he arrived in Seville, he was met by none other than Ibn Zarzar, who had fled the intrigues of Granada and now welcomed Ibn Khaldun generously, singing his praises to the Castilian king. Pedro was so taken, and so determined to add this jewel to his royal court, that he not only offered Ibn Khaldun a position in his palace but promised to restore to him the properties his ancestors had owned in and around Seville before its conquest, which were now in the hands of Christian noblemen.

Ibn Khaldun, who demurred and returned to Granada, and subsequently to Fez, would repay Ibn al-Khatib's earlier kindness by giving him shelter in 1371. That year, the wazir fled Granada as his enemies, the chief *qadi* of Granada, al-Bunnahi, and his erstwhile protégé, Ibn Zamrak, colluded to accuse him of apostasy and to turn Muhammad V against him. Ibn al-Khatib had many enemies, and these were now emboldened to act. In 1372, al-Bunnahi had the wazir's books burned in public, and Ibn al-Khatib was tried and sentenced to death in absentia for apostasy. He was arrested in Fez, subjected to torture, and in 1374 was found guilty at a second trial. However, before the official sentence could be carried out, Lisan al-Din ibn al-Khatib was strangled in his jail cell—a stunning end for the leading literary and intellectual figure of fourteenth-century Granada.

Although the literary culture of the Nasrid kingdom may not have been as innovative as that of the caliphate or the *taifa* period, it was incredibly robust. This was due in part to the sultans themselves, who actively patronized the culture of knowledge both as a dimension of their monarchy and out of personal interest. Muhammad II al-Faqih, for example, had a passion for Islamic law; Nasr was an accomplished astronomer and mathematician; and several, notably Muhammad V's grandson Yusuf III, composed poetry. The court at Granada became a hothouse of literary and scholarly production, driven by the patronage of the royal family, the aristocracy, and the bureaucracy, many members of which—particularly those who were secretaries, *qadis*, or *faqihs*—were scholars and writers themselves.

The vigor of the intellectual culture here grew in part because Granada was the destination for so many members of the Andalusi cultural elite who were fleeing the Christian conquests of the thirteenth century. Scholars from the Maghrib who found themselves on the wrong side of political intrigues, or who simply traveled back and forth across the strait in search of knowledge and patronage, were also drawn to the sultanate. Consequently, cultural production was not limited to the capital: cities like Málaga, Almería, Ronda, and even smaller provincial towns boasted robust intellectual scenes. Smaller towns would be given a further boost by Yusuf I, who took an active interest in ensuring there was access to education across his realm; in 1343 he ordered schools to be established in every town. Likewise, the *maristan*, a hospital primarily for treating mental illness, was established in Granada by Muhammad V beginning in 1365; it not only served patients but also bolstered the city's medical culture.

THE NASRID RULERS also took an active interest in religion. Muhammad I's claim to authority had been based on his self-professed identity as an orthodox *mujahid*, and many of the families that supported his uprising were the same local urban and rural elites who had acquired power and property as members of the Maliki *'ulama'* over the previous centuries and weathered the Almohad occupation. In exchange for their blessing and support, the second sultan, Muhammad al-Faqih, effectively ensconced the Maliki *fuqaha'* in the administration of the kingdom, enabling them to battle against their Zahiri rivals. But as Muslim jurists had long understood, patronage can lead to dependence, and rather than empowering the *'ulama'*, this served as a means of controlling them. Leading legal scholars and magistrates were expected to assent at the acclamation ceremonies of new sultans in order to reinforce their legitimacy. Meanwhile, Nasrid rulers deprived the chief *qadi* of his power to appoint lower judges and worked to convert the judiciary into a branch of the bureaucracy that served at the sultan's pleasure.

The challenge to the rigid legalism favored by some of the more conservative Maliki scholars came not from a rival legal-theological school but from the rising tide of mysticism engulfing the Islamic West. Common folk were turning increasingly to alternative forms of spirituality and to unorthodox and charismatic religious leaders, some of whom were venerated and credited with miracle working, even after death. Exuberant spiritual exercises that included ecstatic chanting, dancing, singing, and the mortification of the flesh gained popularity, to the increasing alarm of orthodox religious authorities.

On the one hand, this new popular piety contributed to the establishment of ribats along the frontier and encouraged a certain grassroots dedication to jihad against the Christians. Indeed, Muhammad I had counted on the support of such ascetics when he launched the kingdom. But on the other hand, mysticism, by claiming access to a divine truth that transcended doctrine, could be seen as threatening to the very notion of orthodoxy. Contacts with Morocco, where Sufism exercised a profound appeal, both through direct rule over Andalusi territory and through the influence of the *ghuzat* and other high-status Moroccan exiles in al-Andalus, acted as a further catalyst for the spread of Sufism, and *zawiyas* and *qubbas* (saintly tombs) proliferated across the countryside and in the capital. By 1340, a privately founded *madrasa* had been established by Sufis in Málaga, the first in al-Andalus—a signal not only of the increasing popularity of Sufism, but of the creeping religious and political influence of the Marinids. Moreover, some of the leading families of the kingdom, such as the Banu Mahruq, had very publicly embraced the new piety. It was clear that the sultans needed to confront this increasingly popular form of devotion; if controlled, it could be used as a counterweight against the Maliki *'ulama'* and as an alternative source of religious legitimacy.

Yusuf—or, rather, his wazir Ibn al-Khatib—began by inviting the Banu Sidi Bona to the Alhambra. A venerable Sufi clan that traced its influence back to twelfth-century Sharq al-Andalus, the family had come to Granada in the mid-1250s; they settled in Valencia and its environs, where they established a ribat, or convent, as the home for their spiritual brotherhood. Yusuf had shown an early inclination toward Sufi-tinged piety when in 1333, the first year of his reign, he instituted the official and public celebration of the *mawlid*, the birthday of the Prophet. Now, with the encouragement of his wazir, the Sidi Bono began teaching their spiritual exercises to the king.

In 1348, Yusuf, through his *hajib* Abu Nu'aym Ridwan, would go a step further by founding a royal *madrasa* in Granada, which featured classes in orthodox and established theological disciplines as well as instruction by Sufi masters. The *madrasa*—an academy of religious instruction that provided free tuition and board to qualified students— was an institution that had developed in the eleventh-century Seljuq sultanate as a means of ensuring that religious education stayed on-message politically. By the early 1300s, the Marinids had embraced it enthusiastically, founding a series of *madrasas* across their realm. This posed a danger for the Nasrids, who in the absence of their own theological colleges would see their own *'ulama'* head to Morocco to be inculcated with the Marinid-oriented religious doctrine.

After Yusuf, Muhammad V continued the trend of normalizing Sufism in Granada, most dramatically with his hosting of the *mawlid* celebration of 1362 in the Alhambra itself. This shift of royal favor was taken as an affront by the Maliki *fuqaha'*, who had seen their political weight decrease and their own numbers thin through defection. And so, they went on the attack. The legal scholar Abu Ishaq al-Shatibi produced a two-volume *Book of Adherence*, an encyclopedic condemnation of *bida'* ("innovation"), which declared that the new mysticism was effectively *kufr*, or "unbelief." Meanwhile, the chief *qadi*, al-Bunnahi, took aim at the individual whom he regarded as responsible for the shift in royal favor: Lisan al-Din ibn al-Khatib. The double-wazir had been wrestling with his own attraction to Sufism for some time and as early as 1367 had written an essay called *The Garden of Knowledge of Noble Love* as a defense of mysticism. At the time it garnered little attention, but as Ibn al-Khatib's political power wavered in the years that followed, al-Bunnahi and his fellow *faqihs* combed through it meticulously, looking for any statements that could be used to condemn the author. Based on a series of what they regarded as incriminating passages, they asserted the book was proof of Ibn al-Khatib's apostasy—a capital crime. The case was far from open and shut, but this was at bottom a political trial, and thus, his condemnation and execution were all but inevitable.

27

Tales of the Alhambra

The execution of Ibn al-Khatib in 1374 laid bare the tensions fracturing the Nasrid kingdom among both the political elite and the ruling family itself. The long-reigning Muhammad V would die in 1391 in circumstances that are far from clear. The apparent stability of his later reign would quickly dissipate into rebellions and intrigues, and the last century of Nasrid rule would see no fewer than fourteen sultans claim the throne. Potential rivals within the family were frequently forced to escape into exile or faced imprisonment or death. The Marinids intervened when they could, and never for the better. When Muhammad V's son Yusuf II died in 1392, the cause was most likely a poisoned shirt the Marinid amir Abu 'l-'Abbas Ahmad had sent as a gift and that caused the king's "flesh to drop off in pieces" over the course of an agonizing month.[46] In 1410, the Marinids seized Gibraltar after its garrison rebelled against Yusuf III, who regained it the following year only after a prolonged and costly campaign. Otherwise, they intrigued behind the scenes, fomenting discontent within the royal family and backing rebellious princes who they felt would serve their purposes, just as Granada had done to them in the previous century. As for Tunis, it was locked into the Christian sphere of political and economic influence and effectively incapable and unwilling to either help or harm.

Throughout the 1470s, Castile and Aragon each remained absorbed in their own struggles, including a series of succession crises and uprisings, as well as wars against their Christian neighbors. Granada's trade and diplomatic relations with both kingdoms remained robust, and contacts were also maintained with Navarre. For the most part, Castilian rulers were not in a position to take advantage of Nasrid disarray, nor did they show much interest in doing so, aside from stirring the pot and encouraging rebellions. Castile did score a handful of signal military victories; however, Granada not only managed a spirited defense but also went on the attack. Nevertheless, in his fourteenth-century treatise on holy war, the Granadan scholar Ibn Hudayl had characterized al-Andalus as the "land of *jihad*," but also as "a country stuck between a stormy ocean and an enemy with terrible weapons"—an observation that foreshadowed the doom that would soon befall it.[47]

The death of Muhammad V's former prime minister also marks a turning point in our understanding of the history of the Nasrid kingdom. Thanks to Ibn al-Khatib, as well as to other Granadan scholars of his era, we have a detailed picture of life in the sultanate in the fourteenth century. Our view of the fifteenth is much narrower. There are few surviving sources in Arabic, and historians have had to depend on often confused Christian records. The picture is so unclear, for example, that only recently it has been determined that the so-called Muhammad X "the Lame," a sultan thought to have ruled from 1445 to 1457, never reigned at all. The dynasty's complex genealogical tree becomes so muddled, it is sometimes impossible to say with certainty how individuals were related.

Untangling the histories of the leading courtly families is even more challenging, not the least because the history of the final century of Muslim rule was so quickly and thoroughly romanticized. For example, the epic struggle between the chivalrous "Spanish" Banu 'l-Sarraj (here, the "Abencerrajes") and the villainous North African "Zegries" (perhaps from *Thaghri*, or "frontier warrior"), which is recounted as fact and in grisly detail by tour guides at the Alhambra Palace even today, is pure Orientalist fantasy. The tale originated in Ginés Pérez de Hita's novel known as *The Civil Wars of Granada*, written between 1595 and 1619, and eventually spread to the English-speaking world in the form of Washington Irving's 1832 *Tales of the Alhambra*. The cohesiveness and unity of purpose of the Banu 'l-Sarraj has almost certainly been exaggerated, and the origin story of their rival, Ridwan Bannigash—said to have been the son of a Christian nobleman, Egas Venegas—may also be a figment of romance. But, although the intrigues of the kingdom's leading families may have undermined the power of the Nasrid dynasty, it was an unforeseen royal marriage in Castile and Aragon that would seal Granada's fate.

THE NASRID CLAIM to power had never been particularly strong. The family had no caliphal pedigree, and the other noble families of the south had seen Ibn al-Ahmar as a "first among equals" rather than some sort of divinely ordained king. Hence the Banu Ashqilula's sense of betrayal when the sultan passed his title on to his son Muhammad II, or the propensity of local nobles, such as the Banu 'l-Hakim of Ronda, to support either the Marinids or the rebellious Nasrid princes against whoever wore the royal turban in Granada. Some of these aristocratic clans claimed to descend from the early Arab settlers; others emerged in the fourteenth and fifteenth centuries, and still others originated with converted former captives who had risen to power in the palace. In any case, their authority rested on a combination of their wealth based in landed estates they controlled, their influence through the occupation of powerful administrative and judicial posts, their lineage and religious prestige, and their capacity to raise and lead troops in battle.

Together, the great families of the realm made up a "one percent"—a *khassa* within the *khassa*—who used the mechanism of *musahara*, or intermarriage, typically through the betrothal of their daughters and sons, to control who gained membership to this loose, elite group. They saw al-Andalus as their own, and as cynical as their pursuit of power might seem, the risks they took to run it were high. A political miscalculation or failed intrigue could easily lead to death. And whatever their propensity for forming alliances of convenience with Christian frontier lords and kings, many members of the elite, including scholars and jurists, fought on the front lines, and not a few met their death in battle against Castile, a circumstance that, whatever their motivations, qualified them as martyrs in the jihad.

The Nasrids themselves practiced *musahara* only rarely. Unlike their Maghribi counterparts, they did not marry into other royal families but jealously guarded their influence and worked to maintain a stable line of succession through intrafamily matrimonies and the practice of concubinage. Only occasionally did they offer a princess or accept a daughter in marriage to cement the loyalty of an aristocratic clan. But, such a concession of royal pedigree could put the dynasty at risk.

For example, Yusuf III's betrothal of Zahr al-Riyadh to his cousin Muhammad set in motion a chain of events that would lead to civil war. The marriage was a reward to Zahr's father, a trusted former Christian slave who had served Yusuf as a military commander. However, Zahr, it turned out, was a force to be reckoned with, and once she was married, she began to cultivate the Banu 'l-Sarraj as allies. Then, when Yusuf died in 1417 and his eight-year-old son, Muhammad VIII al-Saghir ("the Little One"), came to the throne, Zahr ordered the young sultan's guardian, the wazir 'Ali al-'Amin, assassinated, and with the help of the Banu 'l-Sarraj she had her own husband Muhammad IX al-'Aysar ("Lefty") made sultan.

Al-'Aysar would reign until 1453, enduring a series of coups that would see him pushed from power and returned three times. During his troubled early reign, Zahr was widely regarded as the effective sovereign and even carried out correspondence under her own name with foreign rulers, including Alfons the Magnanimous of Aragon and his queen, María of Castile. Al-Saghir would briefly retake the throne in 1427 with the support of his wazir Ridwan Bannigash, but by 1429, the Banu 'l-Sarraj, aided by Castile, had forced him out of power and into the royal prison at Salobreña, on the Málagan coast, where he was discreetly put to death.

Around the time of Zahr's marriage, a daughter of Muhammad VI El Bermejo had been given as wife to the wazir Ibrahim ibn al-Mawl, a match that proved no less destabilizing. In 1432, with the backing of his allies and in-laws, the Banu Bannigash, Ibn al-Mawl's son, Yusuf (IV), would be proclaimed king, claiming royal descent through his mother. A puppet of Juan II of Castile, who was hated by the populace who saw him as a traitor, Yusuf's authority never extended beyond the capital. When he was cornered in the palace by Yusuf's enemies only four months later and captured, Muhammad IX al-'Aysar, the sultan he had deposed, was able to retake the throne supported by the Banu 'l-Sarraj, leaving their rivals, the Banu Bannigash, to flee to exile in Castile. But stability was elusive, and a new challenge soon appeared in the person of Muhammad IX's kinsman Yusuf V, known to Castilian chroniclers as El Cojo, or "the Lame." Yusuf had been biding his time as governor of Almería, feigning loyalty while quietly laying the foundations of a separate state: minting his own coins, taking control of state revenue, and carrying out an independent diplomatic relationship with Aragon.

When Muhammad came to Almería at the head of a delegation of *qadis* and a body of troops to discipline the rebellious Yusuf in 1445, the latter countered by declaring himself sultan, once again pushing al-'Aysar out of power and into exile in Salobreña. Meanwhile, the Banu Bannigash returned from exile with a new Castilian-backed usurper, a son of Yusuf II named Isma'il. This Isma'il III briefly took Granada in 1446, but once again the people would not support a king who was so clearly a creature of Juan II. Moreover, Yusuf fought back, drawing the support of members of the Castilian royal family and nobility who were opposed to their own king, Juan II. The three-way struggle was resolved when Yusuf was murdered by his own wazir and Isma'il's support collapsed, allowing Muhammad IX al-'Aysar to once more assume the throne.

Muhammad, who had no sons of his own, was anxious to prevent further fighting and to reconcile with the branch of the dynasty represented by his cousins, the descendants of Yusuf II. Thus, the sultan betrothed Umm al-Fath (his daughter by Zahr) to the son of Muhammad VIII al-Saghir, the sultan whom he had first deposed in 1419 and had executed in 1430. This prince, also named Muhammad (X) and known as "the Little Boy" (El Chiquito, to the Castilians) would co-rule with al-'Aysar until the latter's death in 1453, when he would take the throne himself. For all of this, the most enduring effect of Muhammad IX's reinstatement was that it cemented the ascendancy of the Banu 'l-Sarraj, who now attracted other leading clans, including the Banu Kumasha and the al-Amins, to their faction. Although their role was almost certainly exaggerated by later historians, it seems that it was members of the Banu 'l-Sarraj clan who drove the politics in the final half century of Nasrid rule, and that their efforts and intrigues in the name of saving the kingdom actually helped push al-Andalus to extinction.

UP TO THIS point, relations between the Granadans and their Castilian neighbors had settled into what was essentially a hot peace, in which there were relatively few episodes of formal warfare after the taking of Antequera (Antaqara) by the prince-regent, Fernando, in 1410. One exception was when in 1431 the all-powerful Castilian constable, Álvaro de Luna, launched an invasion of the sultanate. His goal was to distract the perennially restive Castilian nobility and force the unwilling populace of Granada to accept Yusuf IV ibn al-Mawl, a grandson of the former wazir 'Atiq ibn al-Mawl, as their ruler. A massive battle was joined at Higueruela, just outside the capital. Great feats of chivalry and derring-do were performed on both sides, and although the inhabitants of the capital were forced to open their gates to the Castilian-backed "Abenalmao," no territory was taken. Over the following several years, Castile conquered a series of frontier towns, including Huéscar, Huelma, Vélez Blanco, and Vélez Rubio, but the Granadans also mounted a number of successful operations. By 1438, the border had stabilized, and the two kingdoms resumed their pattern of negotiating a series of short truces, often only of one year.

Given the succession of peace treaties, the fifteenth century was for the most part an era of intermittent, small-scale raiding rather than campaigns of conquest. Aside from those mounted under royal authority, raids were usually undertaken as independent initiatives by Christian and Muslim border lords or municipal authorities, sometimes in breach of the established treaties. At other times, common folk struck out of mere opportunity, waylaying merchants, capturing herdsmen, and rustling livestock. However, the various kingdoms went to great lengths to prevent this sort of illegal activity, especially the kind that might damage the flow of trade, disrupt the transit of herds who pastured on both sides of the frontier, spark violent reprisals, or justify the annulment of a truce.

The Castilian crown developed the office of the "Judges for Complaints" and the "Superior Commander between Christians and Muslims" to reinforce the rule of law and arbitrate disputes involving cross-border exchanges in conjunction with their Nasrid counterparts, the "Magistrates between Kingdoms." Frontier deputies, known as *fieles de rastro* ("trackers"), went after bandits, raiders, and other criminals. Professional ransomers and go-betweens, known in Castilian as *alfaqueques* or *exeas* (from the Arabic *al-fakkak*, or "redemptor," and *al-shi'a*, or "guide"), crisscrossed the frontier—many were ex-Muslim or ex-Christian converts and some were Jews—as did representatives of the Trinitarians and the Mercedarians, two clerical orders dedicated to redeeming captives.

There is no doubt that the broad frontier lands were a place of violence and fear for ordinary Christians and Muslims, a fact that contributed to a heightened awareness of religious difference on both sides and the sense of a larger religious struggle. Thus, when the common folk of the Nasrid kingdom demanded their rulers refrain from submitting to Christian overlordship or wage jihad against the unbelievers, this was not merely some ideological posture. It was a very pragmatic reaction to the realities of the frontier, where the rule of a weak or compliant sultan might encourage Christian raiding, resulting in death, economic ruin, or the loss of family and property for ordinary Muslims, or burden the sultanate with heavy *parias*, which would inevitably be passed on to the common folk. Similar fears gripped the Christian lands. Here, the idea of Christian-Muslim conflict came to be enshrined in the celebration of religious holidays and municipal celebrations, featuring processions and reenactments of battles between Christian and Muslim forces—simulations in which local *mudéjares* often participated as voluntary or paid enactors, as well as musicians, dancers, and acrobats, and which survive today as popular *fiestas de moros y cristianos*.

Paradoxically, the conflict on the frontier also bred a deep intimacy among the Muslims and Christians who lived along it. Traders, travelers, and herders were constantly moving back and forth. Prisoners were taken, and sometimes returned. Both captives and free subjects converted to the other faith—sometimes freely, out of conviction or even for love; sometimes under duress; and sometimes for political convenience. These converts, in turn, served as intermediaries with their former people, or perhaps betrayed them, but they inevitably transformed their new faith community through the cultural influence they brought. Multilingualism was widespread. Many Christians who spent time in or around the Nasrid kingdom picked up at least some Arabic (sometimes quite a bit), and Castilian-inflected Romance could be heard throughout the sultanate. Common social mores, customs, songs and stories, and appetites bound even common Castilians and Andalusis.

There were parallels also within their religions: just as Sufism and esotericism had taken root among the peninsula's Muslims, spiritualism was sweeping over Christian Europe. The established church order there had been challenged in the thirteenth century not only by heretics but by new religious orders like the Franciscans, whose spiritual inclinations could be remarkably similar to those of Sufis. However, this did not necessarily lead to mutual sympathy. In the Christian lands, the tilt toward mysticism and apocalypticism intensified in the era of anxiety and upheaval following the Black Death. It contributed to the peninsula-wide attacks on Jewish communities in 1391 and the emergence of influential preachers, like Vicent Ferrer, who championed aggressive missionizing.

The increasingly strident and confrontational tone of Muslim and Christian ideologues was not necessarily reflected in actual Christian-Muslim relations, particularly in Castile and Granada. In practice, warfare was rarely a Christian versus Muslim affair, and there were few battles in which there were not knights and soldiers of each faith fighting on both sides. In 1449 when the Granadan and Navarrese allies were raiding the territory around Cuenca, they were met by Castilian forces that included the Guardia Morisca—a cavalry regiment made up largely of Granadan Muslims, some who had converted, and a few wealthier *mudéjares*. A year later, Alonso Fajardo "the Brave," who as Commander of the Frontier had spent much of his career inflicting grievous aggression on the eastern territories of the Nasrid kingdom, found himself calling on the aid of his Muslim counterparts in Almería and on the wazir Yusuf ibn al-Sarraj for help against his enemy Pedro Fajardo, the Commander of Murcia, who also happened to be his cousin.

By the following year, the situation had shifted again, and when faced with a massive raiding party sent by Muhammad IX, Alonso made peace with his Christian rivals and dealt the Granadans a massive defeat at the Battle of Alporchones in 1452. Thousands of Muslim prisoners were taken to Lorca (Lurqa), Alonso's home base, which was overwhelmed by the influx, leading the captives and local Muslims to rise up and seize the town by force. Fajardo responded without quarter, retaking Lorca and slaughtering the prisoners and the town's *mudéjares*. If Alonso and his ilk are any measure, it sometimes seems there were *only* atheists in the foxholes in medieval Spain.

WHETHER IN FRIENDSHIP or at odds, the Christian and Muslim warriors of the peninsula recognized that they shared a common set of values. When Christian knights chose to hold tournaments or settle disputes via duels, they often asked Muslim warriors to arbitrate or even host these events. Muslim and Christian soldiers competed against each other in the *juego de cañas*, a Nasrid game that consisted of teams of riders throwing special lances at each other. When knights and lords of either faith came on business or to parlay, they were treated with great honor and respect, given gifts—particularly articles of luxury clothing, tack, and weaponry—and feted with banquets and receptions. Even when defeated they were often treated with honor. For example, when Fernando de Antequera accepted the surrender of the garrison of Zahara in 1407, he lent the defeated Muslims horses on which to ride out of the city. Whether as hostages, refugees, or soldiers of fortune, they spent extended periods of time in each other's courts and palaces, establishing friendships that could transcend politics and religion. Hence, in the 1360s when the choleric and impulsive Pedro the Cruel had planned to execute Martín López, the commander of the crusading Order of Calatrava, Muhammad V intervened to save his Christian friend.

A number of sultans were granted knighthoods by Castile, including Muhammad II and Yusuf IV, whom Juan II inducted into his chivalric fraternity, the Order of the Sash. Respect on the battlefield was acknowledged through imitation. Some Andalusi warriors began to use the heavier armor and weapons that were favored by Christian knights, whereas among Castilian aristocrats the fashion of riding *al la jinete* ("like a Zanata") became a favored affectation in the fifteenth century. Enrique IV delighted in appearing in brocaded silken robes and mounted on a Maghribi saddle with short stirrups, brandishing the light lance of the Andalusi cavalry.

This shared ethos of the frontier warrior is most dramatically expressed in the *romances fronterizos*, anonymous popular frontier ballads that came to be sung across the region. Many refer to actual people and real events. One of the most popular was the tale of Abenámar, a fictionalized dialogue between Juan II and Yusuf IV ibn al-Mawl at the time of the Battle of Higueruela. Granada is personified as a beautiful woman, whom Abenámar has shown to Juan, and whom the Castilian king longs to possess, but who rejects him because she is already taken:

> I am married, King *Don* Juan
> I am married, and no widow;
> the Muslim who holds me
> so tightly, loves me very dearly.[48]

Although it was sung in Romance, it seems that the author was likely a Muslim from Granada who was adept in both poetic traditions. Conversely, Castilian literary modes were also appropriated by poets writing in Arabic: in late fourteenth-century Almería, the religious scholar Ibn Khatima wrote verses using Castilian poetic structures (as well as a *muwashshah* to a "Christian buck"—"His love has caught me").[49] A half century earlier, his fellow townsman Ibn Luyun, who was best known as an agronomist, also wrote rhyming proverbs and *muwashshah* poetry that incorporated Romance language.

Naturally, the greatest degree of acculturation and contact took place among Muslims living in Christian lands. In the fifteenth century, *mudéjar* communities were found across the peninsula. In the south of Portugal and northern Castile and Navarre, Muslims continued to live as substantial minorities in both urban and rural settings, with little indication of tensions with Christians. Navarrese *mudéjares* were particularly well-integrated, with a number serving in the royal administration and as specialists in the kingdom's military, some as far afield as France. In addition, the kingdom of Aragon and southern Catalonia retained a substantial rural population, and there were few signs of tension or aggression aimed at Muslim communities or individuals—even as Jews figured increasingly as victims of Christian violence. Not so in Valencia and Murcia, lands vulnerable to attack both from Nasrid raiders and increasingly from corsairs based in Ifriqiya and the Maghrib. Here, there was a growing sense among some (although certainly not all) Christians that *mudéjares* were disloyal outsiders who constituted a "fifth column" for foreign Islamic powers, a suspicion stoked by the growing power of the Ottomans in the Eastern Mediterranean.

Such accusations were not entirely unfounded, given that *mudéjares* sometimes did collaborate with Muslim raiders. In both Valencia and Castilian Andalucía, the bond between monarch and *mudéjar* that had traditionally served as a pillar for Muslim communities was eroding. Now it was seigneurs, whether landed aristocrats or military orders, whose interests aligned with rural Muslims and who became their protectors. In Castile, the growing estrangement was aggravated by the imposition of the *servicio* and *medio servicio*—royal taxes levied on Muslims only for the purpose, of all things, of paying for the war on Muslim Granada. And so, in these areas, Christian-Muslim relations began to spiral downward as occasional acts of disloyalty led to repression, which encouraged further acts of disloyalty, which prompted further resistance, and so on. In 1455, the first major act of popular anti-Muslim violence in the Christian kingdoms took place: the *moreria* of Valencia was sacked and many *mudéjares* were forced under threat of death to convert.

THE ATTACK IN Valencia coincided with further convulsions in the Nasrid court. Alonso Fajardo's stunning victory at Alporchones in 1452 struck a blow against the aging al-'Aysar and undermined the reputation of his heir-in-waiting, Muhammad X El Chiquito. Moreover, the king-making Banu 'l-Sarraj clan looked on El Chiquito with suspicion on account of the time he had spent as an exile in Juan II's court, where he may have been contaminated by Castilian influence.

Thus, not long after al-'Aysar died and his son-in-law took the throne (which happened by early 1454), the Banu 'l-Sarraj put forward their own candidate, Sa'd, a fifty-five-year-old grandson of Yusuf II. Sa'd had just sent his son Abu 'l-Hasan 'Ali to attend the coronation of the new Castilian king, Enrique IV, who promised to help his cause but required Abu 'l-Hasan 'Ali to remain behind in his kingdom as a "guest." As Sa'd and El Chiquito's forces began to clash, an opportunistic Enrique IV unleashed his forces to devastate the countryside along the central frontier under the banner of a Crusading bull, until a new rebellion by Alonso Fajardo in Murcia forced him to make peace with Granada in exchange for a substantial payment in cash from Sa'd. El Chiquito was turned out of Granada and fled south to the Alpujarras in 1456 but was captured there with his sons by Abu 'l-Hasan 'Ali, who had been released from his gilded captivity in Castile. Taken back to the Alhambra, El Chiquito and his sons were put to death.

But Sa'd's victory would not bring peace, caught as he was between Enrique IV and the Banu 'l-Sarraj, and vacillating between yielding to the Castilian king's demands and defying him. The price of not being seen as a tributary of the Christian was the resumption of devastating Castilian raids in 1462. Abu 'l-Hasan 'Ali and other military commanders fought back with determination and valor, but tremendous damage was done, culminating in the fall of Gibraltar that July. It was at this moment that Sa'd chose to rid himself of the domination of the Banu 'l-Sarraj and murdered several members of the clan after luring them to what they thought was to be a banquet. The dead included Abu Surrur al-Mufarrij, who had been the true power behind the sultan, and the wazir Yusuf ibn al-Sarraj. In the aftermath, the surviving grandees of the family gathered in their base at Málaga, where after an aborted attempt to displace Sa'd with another Nasrid prince, they headed north, seeking shelter among the Christian warlords of the Guadalquivir, from where they continued to intrigue. They would not have to wait long. After Enrique attacked the Vega of Granada in 1464 and forced Sa'd to submit to another truce, the sultan was overthrown by his own son Abu 'l-Hasan 'Ali, who had forged an alliance with the Banu 'l-Sarraj against his father. The stage was now set for the final collapse of the dynasty.

IF THE ALHAMBRA Palace was the canvas on which the lurid intrigues of fifteenth-century Nasrid Granada were painted, the kingdom of Castile was the frame upon which that canvas was stretched. When not engaged in direct warfare against the sultanate, the Castilian kings did what they could to destabilize and force it into vassalage. Fortunately for the Nasrids, Castile had problems of its own to deal with. The fifteenth century had started off well enough for the Christian kingdom, with a capable Enrique III taming his nobility, cowing his peninsular rivals, attacking Morocco, and preparing an offensive against Granada. But his health was poor, and when he died in 1406 at age twenty-seven, he left a one-year-old son as his heir. The infant Juan II came under the guardianship of his mother, the English dowager Catherine of Lancaster, and his uncle, the *infante* Fernando. The two hated each other and effectively divided the kingdom, with Fernando taking control of the south and Catherine the north. Muhammad VII responded to the divisions in Castile by going on the attack, helping his popularity at home but provoking the ire of the *infante*.

By 1407, Fernando responded in force, capturing the frontier town of Zahara with his devastating use of cannon, only to see it retaken and its garrison massacred in 1409. In 1410, the *infante* would take his revenge and seal his reputation by conquering the ancient, fortified town of Antequera, only sixty miles west of Granada and just thirty north of Málaga. In doing so, he took control not only of the town itself but of its fertile hinterland, sapping the economy of the sultanate and interrupting communications between the capital and its main port—effectively driving a wedge in the Nasrid heartland. Having a forward Christian base here threatened not only the capital, but also the prosperity of the entire kingdom, and Castilian forces began to engage in deliberate scorched-earth attacks intended to damage crops and infrastructure, thereby undermining Granada's wealth and the will of the populace.

The siege had been long and hard-fought, and negotiations had been intense. Fernando had been determined to reestablish Granada's obligation to pay tribute, which had not been enforced since 1370, but this was a concession the new king, Yusuf III, could not make without losing his domestic support and putting his rule in peril. In the end, Fernando kept Zahara and departed from Nasrid territory, taking with him one hundred Christian captives freed by the sultan (very specifically qualified as a gift rather than tribute). Then fate intervened on what appeared to be the side of the Nasrids. In 1410, the Catalan dynasty that had ruled the Crown of Aragon since its creation in the twelfth century became extinct when King Martí I died leaving no legitimate heir. A clutch of claimants to the throne came forward, but none was strong enough to seize it. After two years of upheaval, a conclave of bishops, grandees, and city councilors convened at the town of Caspe in Aragon and declared the *infante* Fernando, "He of Antequera," the new king of the Crown of Aragon.

With the departure of Fernando to Barcelona, the political situation in Castile came to mirror that of Granada—a battleground for factions within the royal family and ambitious and grasping courtiers. Fernando of Antequera, now king of Aragon, fueled the unrest by encouraging his children, who held land in Castile, to rebel against the weak-willed Juan, who himself fell under the spell of his scheming constable, Álvaro de Luna. Álvaro was a political mastermind who, by ruthlessly eliminating his rivals, became the king's sole confidant and the true power behind the throne. Holding the king in his thrall, Álvaro accumulated unprecedented wealth and influence, until in 1453 he met his match in Juan's second wife, Isabel of Portugal, who had the constable arrested on trumped-up charges of treason, tried, and executed.

When Juan died the following year, he passed the Crown of Castile on to his son Enrique IV. At age twenty-nine, Enrique was no boy when he took the throne, but neither was he regarded as much of a man. Ridiculed widely by his own nobility, he was humiliated by public accusations of impotence. When his queen, Joana of Portugal, gave him a daughter, the *infanta* Juana, the king's many enemies referred to the princess as La Beltraneja, putting it about that she was, in fact, the result of an adulterous affair between the queen and

Enrique's royal favorite, the courtier Beltrán de la Cueva, whom they viewed as a parvenu and a threat to their own ambitions.

This turn of events would have profound ramifications for Castile, Aragon, and Granada. Juana was Enrique's only child, and so the rebellious nobility took up the banner of the king's half brother, Alfonso, presenting him as the legitimate heir to the throne of Castile. They were supported by Fernando of Antequera's son Joan, who not only ruled over Navarre but would inherit the Crown of Aragon after the death of his brother Alfons the Magnanimous in 1458. For the next sixteen years, Castile was swept up in a fitful civil war, which Joan II of Aragon did his best to fuel. The death of the young insurgent prince, Alfonso, in 1468, brought no resolution: his testament named his sister, Isabel, as his successor, which the Castilian nobility accepted. However, contrary to the will of both Enrique and her own supporters, Isabel eloped with Joan II's son Fernando (or Ferran) in 1469. Five years later, Enrique would be dead, and when Isabel was acclaimed as queen of Castile in January 1475, the seventeen-year-old Fernando was at her side.

Crowned king of Sicily the previous year, the young king-consort of Castile would reveal himself to be a prodigy, endowed with a native political and military instinct that would eventually earn him the praise of Niccoló Machiavelli, whose notorious 1513 treatise on realpolitik, *The Prince*, presented Fernando as the ideal "Renaissance king." The year 1479 would prove pivotal. Isabel was recognized as queen, and with the death of Joan II of Aragon, Fernando inherited the Crown of Aragon, including Aragon itself, Catalonia, Valencia, Sardinia, and Mallorca. At that point, the fate of Granada was sealed. The marriage of Fernando and Isabel, two young and capable rulers united in purpose if not temperament, put an end to the rivalry between Aragon and Castile—a rivalry that both the Castilian nobility and the Nasrid sultans had been exploiting to their own advantage for the previous two centuries. Granada was now very truly on its own.

PART VI

SHARDS, 1482–1614

HOLY ROMAN EMPIRE

Augsburg

North Atlantic Ocean

KINGDOM OF FRANCE

DUCHY OF SAVOY

ITALIAN STATES

PAPAL STATES

A Coruña

Pamplona

Burgos

CROWN OF CASTILE

Zaragoza

CROWN OF ARAGON

Agde

Marseille

Barcelona

Rome

Naples

KINGDOM OF PORTUGAL

El Escorial

Madrid

VICEROYALTY OF SARDINIA

KINGDOM OF TWO SICILIES

Toledo

Valencia

KINGDOM OF SPAIN

Denia

Lisbon

Granada

Cartagena

Cádiz

Málaga

Ceuta

Oran

Algiers

Tunis

KINGDOM OF FEZ

OTTOMAN EMPIRE

Salé

Fez

KINGDOM OF MOROCCO

0   300 mi

0   300 km

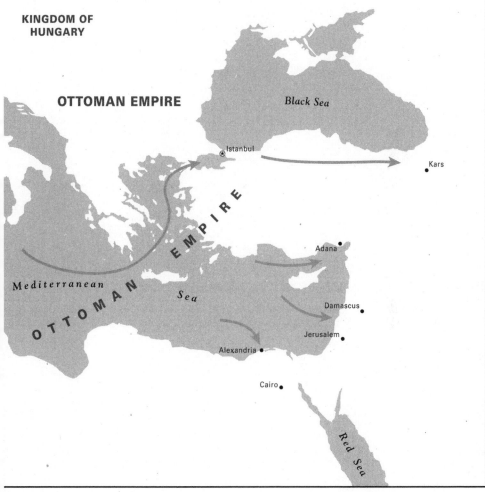

Spain & the Morisco Diaspora,
1609–1614

KINGDOM OF
HUNGARY

OTTOMAN EMPIRE

Black Sea

Istanbul

Kars

OTTOMAN EMPIRE

Mediterranean

Sea

Adana

Damascus

Jerusalem

Alexandria

Cairo

Red Sea

28

A Last Sigh

If the supporters of Abu 'l-Hasan 'Ali, or Muley Hacén as he was known to Castilian chroniclers, were hoping for a muscular sultan who would take the war back to the Christians, they would not be disappointed. But Abu 'l-Hasan's reign was complicated by the same factors that plagued his predecessors—endless intrigue in the palace and among the magnates of the sultanate, and the relentless pressure of paying for either war or tribute as Castilian forces set about to destroy the economic infrastructure of the kingdom. Within his own family, he would face challenges from his brother, Muhammad ibn Sa'd, and his son Abu 'Abd Allah Muhammad ("Boabdil" to the Christians). Rivalries within the *khassa* continued also, as the two main factions, led by the Banu 'l-Sarraj and the Banu Mawl, pursued their agendas with fickle opportunism. Although the marriage of Fernando and Isabel would bring an end to the rivalry between Aragon and Castile, the two rulers were embroiled in a number of foreign conflicts, and their own nobility remained divided, focused on their struggles against each other rather than the conquest of Muslim lands.

No sooner did Abu 'l-Hasan take the throne in 1464 than his brother, Muhammad ibn Sa'd, rebelled in Málaga supported by the Banu 'l-Sarraj, who were now based in the city and had already abandoned Abu 'l-Hasan in retribution for his having taken Abu 'l-Qasim ibn Bannigash, the son of their rival Ridwan, as his wazir. Having repressed this uprising, and taking advantage of open warfare that had broken out in Seville between two leading noblemen, the count of Cabra and Rodrigo Ponce de León, Abu 'l-Hasan began to launch raids against Castilian territory. Robust fighting continued into 1471, with each side scoring victories; a number of treaties were signed, including one in 1475 that called for five years of peace. Meanwhile, raiding continued on both sides of the frontier—crops were destroyed, cattle were rustled, and many prisoners were taken. By this point, Fernando had embarked on his strategy of turning members of the Granadan royal family against each other. In 1474, he opened secret negotiations with Abu Salim ibn Najjar, a son of Yusuf IV ibn al-Mawl, the governor of Almería, offering him a protectorate in the east of the kingdom should he rebel.

No sooner had the 1475 treaty expired than Abu 'l-Hasan went on the attack, retaking Zahara in 1481 to the elation of his subjects. But, Fernando maintained the initiative and had Ponce de León launch a sneak attack on the fortified city of Alhama, on the road between Málaga and the capital. Breaching the walls, the Christians surprised the townsfolk, who then put up a desperate fight, even as their families fell dead around them. When the last defenders took refuge in the mosque, it was set alight, and they rushed out to be slaughtered or captured. When the sultan's massive relief force arrived four days later, they saw dogs feasting on the dead, which lay in heaps around the town walls. Amid great losses, the Granadans repeatedly stormed the city until they were forced to break off because of the arrival of Christian reinforcements and news of an attack by Fernando on Loja to the east. Here, Abu 'l-Hasan fared better, firmly repulsing the Aragonese king and launching diversion raids in the southwest, which brought him considerable plunder.

While Abu 'l-Hasan was thus occupied, his sons fled Granada and installed themselves in Guadix, where the eldest, Boabdil, proclaimed himself sultan against his father with the support of the Banu 'l-Sarraj. This was said to have been done at the instigation of his mother, 'Aisha (or Fatima—historians do not agree), a daughter of Muhammad IX. Sometime previously, a young, captive girl of noble birth named Isabel de Solís had arrived in the royal harem.

Converted to Islam under the name Turaya, she caught the eye of Abu 'l-Hasan and soon became his favorite and his new wife, displacing his affection for 'Aisha and her children, whom he then spurned. Whatever emotional distress this may have caused 'Aisha is moot. That Turaya gave Abu 'l-Hasan two sons, Sa'd and Nasr, who could serve as potential heirs, put 'Aisha and her children in mortal danger. For them, the palace had become a prison, and once they had escaped, they had little choice but to rebel. Later historians romanticized this episode, encouraged in part by contemporary allegations that Abu 'l-Hasan had suffered a breakdown in 1478 and had thereafter given himself over to a dissolute life of sensual pleasures. But the sultan's military record hardly bears this out. It remained robust, despite his evident suffering from some sort of degenerative condition that affected his sight and other faculties.

In 1483, Abu 'l-Hasan, now supported by his brother, Muhammad ibn Sa'd, ambushed and annihilated a major Castilian raiding party that had ravaged the area north of Málaga, taking many prisoners. Anxious to claim his own share of glory, Boabdil launched a raid on Christian Lucena. But, because a traitorous Granadan had forewarned the defenders, Boabdil lost the element of surprise and suffered a crushing defeat, in which several commanders were killed and he was taken prisoner. Abu 'l-Hasan was once again the sole ruler of the sultanate, but as Fernando relentlessly continued to devastate the countryside, many of his subjects were becoming exhausted.

After keeping Boabdil prisoner and refusing him an audience for some time, Fernando finally agreed to free the young prince in exchange for a massive cash payment, a pledge to redeem seven hundred captive Christians per year, and a formal vow of vassalship. Obliged to leave his son and heir, Ahmad; his brother, Yusuf; and other children of leading families as hostages, Boabdil returned to Guadix, still claiming the throne. On hearing of the pledge of vassalship, however, and his humiliation at having to kneel and kiss Fernando's hand, the leading *qadis* of Granada provided Abu 'l-Hasan with a *fatwa* decreeing Boabdil ineligible to rule.

Meanwhile, Fernando kept up the pressure. In 1483, Zahara was retaken, and by 1484, Ronda was encircled. The once-impregnable city would fall to Castilian cannon in only two weeks. In accepting the surrender, Fernando gave the city's grandees a choice—they could either emigrate to Muslim North Africa or retire with honor in his lands. The local commander, the last of the venerable Banu 'l-Hakim, accepted the latter and settled in Seville. In effect, Fernando was following the same stratagem as had his predecessors Jaume I and, before him, Alfonso I of Aragon. He co-opted or displaced the Muslim elite and then negotiated the surrender of the now-leaderless and defenseless towns and hamlets of the countryside, promising to respect their rights and traditions and to give them his protection as *mudéjares* in exchange for their submission. Thus, the west of the kingdom fell into Fernando's hands. Keeping up the devastating raiding and destruction of the countryside, the king quickly took Loja and the other main towns of the Vega in 1486, depriving Granada of its breadbasket and bringing his forces all but to the gates of the capital. Then, hunkering down, he began to lay in supplies for the final battle.

Fernando's stunning successes were due to two factors: the unity he and Isabel imposed on the Christian noble families of the frontier and his effective use of a game-changing technology—the cannon. From the time it was first used here by Granadans in the previous century, the manufacture and use of heavy artillery had been refined to the point that it would spell the end of al-Andalus. Previously, Granada had enjoyed certain tactical advantages that made conquest very difficult. The sultanate's compact geography meant that rulers could muster forces from across the kingdom on short notice and move them from point to point rapidly without overextending supply or communication lines. Towns and cities could be stocked with years' worth of provisions to outlast besiegers, and their thick, towering walls could withstand almost any assault by cavalry and foot soldiers, while crossbows, including massive versions worked by crews, rained death on the attackers from the safety of the parapets. Not so, now. The immense bombards Fernando brought to the front, some of which were crewed by hundreds of soldiers and overseen by expert gunners from France and Italy, could open a breach in any wall no matter how thick—and the taller the wall, the better the target. What had been impregnable was suddenly vulnerable.

Carrying out this costly type of warfare was possible because of the unprecedented resources Fernando and Isabel could draw on as rulers of most of the peninsula and parts of Italy. This gave them tremendous financial leverage, which was exploited by their financiers and tax collectors, notably the Jewish courtiers Abraham Senior and Isaac Abravanel. In addition, popes Sixtus IV and Innocent VIII promulgated a series of Crusade bulls from 1479 to 1491, thus allowing "the Catholic Kings" (as Pope Alexander IV would honor Isabel and Fernando in 1494) to divert ecclesiastical taxes and assets to the war. Finally, this was supplemented by the *parias* they collected, the *servicio y medio servicio*, and the proceeds of their raids. Fernando and Isabel's manifest wealth and power, and their unity of purpose, also dissuaded the nobility from causing problems and encouraged them to collaborate in this larger cause. By contrast, Granada's resources and population were shrinking, its potential allies in North Africa were afraid of the Catholic Kings, and the Christian blockade of the strait prevented any but a trickle of volunteers and material from reaching al-Andalus.

Through all this, Muhammad ibn Sa'd fought on in the name of his ailing brother, Abu 'l-Hasan, taking Almería from Boabdil in 1485 and counter attacking Fernando as he could, earning popular admiration among those intent on resisting the Christian advance. Emboldened by this acclaim and supported by Ibn Bannigash, Muhammad deposed his ailing brother and took the throne as al-Zaghal ("the Brave"). As his territory in the east shrank, Boabdil turned to Christian Murcia for support and appealed to those inhabitants of Granada who now wanted peace at any price. Tensions were running high, and fighting broke out in the capital itself in 1486 between his supporters and those of al-Zaghal. Ultimately, al-Zaghal's men gained the upper hand and Boabdil reluctantly recognized his uncle as king. Shortly thereafter, Fernando and Isabel pledged to recognize Boabdil's rule of the eastern part of the sultanate if he would hold it in their name. Thus emboldened, he returned to Granada and after several weeks of fighting, seized the city in April 1487 and executed his uncle's leading supporters.

Meanwhile, Fernando's forces headed south to the coast and took Velez-Málaga (Balish). The defenders, led by Ibn Bannigash, fought valiantly but ultimately surrendered, after which Fernando allowed the inhabitants to evacuate the city with their possessions and head to either North Africa or elsewhere within the sultanate. With this, Málaga was isolated, and the Aragonese king drew up his forces around the kingdom's second city and major port in the spring of 1487. As Boabdil stood by impassively in Granada, the defenders endured three and a half months of artillery fire and starvation, counterattacking valiantly and determined to fight to the last man. At one point, an infiltrator posing as a turncoat nearly succeeded in assassinating Fernando in his tent. But, ultimately, the city was betrayed by a leading citizen, Ali Dordux, whom the Catholic Kings rewarded by making him ruler of the *mudéjar* communities of Málaga and Ronda and the surrounding countryside. Whatever his motives, Dordux remained steadfast in his faith, refusing to abjure Islam and even disinheriting one of his sons who did. The rest of the starving and desperate citizens were either put to death or enslaved. Most of these ten thousand survivors were women, many of whom were sent off by the score as gifts to the courts of the pope and various rulers of Europe. The atrocities committed at Málaga were meant to send a message: to strike fear into the hearts of the remaining populace of the sultanate and tempt the leadership to defect or despair.

And this was precisely the effect it had. Corralled in Almería after the loss of Málaga, al-Zaghal went on the attack in 1488, seizing numerous towns in Boabdil's domains and along the eastern frontier. But Fernando responded by laying siege to Baza, a key inland city in the east, constructing a massive series of earthworks and strongpoints that totally encircled the town. It would be impossible for al-Zaghal to lift the siege. Thus, perhaps fearing another Málaga, or perhaps merely fearing for himself, the commander Yahya al-Najjar (a son of Abu Salim), secretly negotiated the city's surrender, thereby saving the lives of the inhabitants, who were allowed to evacuate in safety with their belongings, leaving "nothing but the rooftops behind."[50] As for Yahya, he converted to Christianity as Pedro de Granada Venegas, taking up the preconversion surname of Ridwan Bannigash, the father of his wife, Cetti Maryam, and appropriating the noble status conferred by this alleged Christian pedigree. Whatever regrets he may have felt would have been softened by the cash reward he received from his new king and the lands that he now held as lord.

At this point, al-Zaghal gave up hope, ceding Almería and Guadix to Castile in return for a large sum of money and the lordship over a small principality based at Andarax in the Alpujarras. It was to be a Muslim-only kingdom, in which al-Zaghal could continue to maintain his own army (as long as he didn't cause any trouble). At first, either out of resignation or to spite his nephew Boabdil, al-Zaghal and his commanders dutifully took up the cause of their new lords and assisted in the pacification of the sultanate. But he soon lost heart and resolved to abandon al-Andalus, selling his remaining lands and boarding ship for the Maghrib.

Now was the moment for Boabdil's conscience to be stirred, and, swept up by the desperate determination of his subjects, he struck out at the Catholic Kings in 1490. It was far too little and far too late; the only consequence of this irruption was that the noose on the capital city tightened, and Fernando and Isabel could now label him a rebel. This is the position they would take. In 1502, when the Mameluke sultan al-Ashraf threatened retaliation against Eastern Christians in reprisal for the conquest of Granada, the Castilian ambassador assured him that Fernando and Isabel had not conquered Granada for religious reasons but to punish their rebellious vassal Boabdil, as was their legal right. A few years earlier, an envoy had been sent by the Nasrids to Cairo to petition al-Ashraf's predecessor, Qa'it Bey, in a vain attempt to rally outside support. Although the sultan could not offer direct help, he did threaten to destroy the Church of the Holy Sepulcher in retaliation. This alarmed the pope, who wrote to Fernando, begging him to leave Granada in peace, but the Aragonese king replied that he had every right to eject the foreigners from his land, and that those who wished to stay would be fortunate enough to enjoy his protection and generosity as their lord.

In 1490, Fernando and Isabel now began to assemble a massive siege camp—Santa Fe, virtually a city in itself—below the walls of Granada. There could be little doubt as to how the war would end, and scores of Christian glory seekers poured in, emboldened by the guarantee of victory and the patina of moral vindication provided by the Crusade bull. In the city itself, the inhabitants, now resigned to their fate, appointed a committee consisting of Abu 'l-Qasim ibn Bannigash and two respected *faqihs* to negotiate the best possible terms of surrender. But, unbeknownst to all, Boabdil had opened up his own secret negotiations aimed at achieving the best possible outcome for himself.

In November 1491, the official, public surrender agreement was signed and arrangements made to hand over control of the city. However, to ensure there would be no disruptions, Boabdil moved up the date and on January 1, 1492, in a carefully choreographed ceremony of submission, handed the keys of the Alhambra to Fernando and Isabel. On the following day, the Catholic Kings entered the city in pompous triumph. A new Christian kingdom of Granada had been founded—al-Andalus was no more.

Whatever the symbolic or ideological value of the conquest was, Fernando was a hard-nosed pragmatist. Now that Granada was his, he wanted it to remain an economic powerhouse. And it was: the income generated by the new kingdom for the royal treasury of Castile far exceeded that of all the rest of the crown's territories. For that reason, the *Capitulaciones de Granada* granted extremely generous terms to the vanquished, aimed at encouraging the productive classes to stay by refraining from taking reprisals and giving broad assurances that Islamic law would remain in force and that there would be no pressure to convert. At the same time, he encouraged the potentially troublesome upper classes to convert or to leave. By respecting their preconquest property rights, he thereby provided them with a means to integrate into the Castilian elite or to raise money to depart. The *elches*, Christians who had converted to Islam after being taken captive, were permitted to remain Muslim or return to their old faith without punishment.

As for Boabdil, he departed—doubtless with a heavy heart, but likely not as Washington Irving imagined, blubbering while his bitter mother scolded him for his lack of virility. The last king of Granada accepted what was essentially the same offer his uncle, al-Zaghal, had taken and ultimately rejected—his own little puppet principality in the Alpujarras. But he too soon tired of playing at king and, taking his possessions and family, crossed the sea to Morocco, living out the rest of his years in modest luxury in Fez, where he died in 1533/34.

Many among the landed elite were prepared to follow the example of Yahya al-Najjar and convert to Christianity to take their place among the Christian aristocracy of Andalucía. The close bonds formed over two centuries of conflict and collaboration had served as a bridge across the religious gulf that separated the military aristocracies of the two realms. Nobility is nobility; it is a question of class. Foremost among these converts was Abu 'l-Hasan 'Ali's favorite concubine, Turaya. Although she changed her name back to Isabel de Solís, she continued to proudly style herself as "Queen of Granada" and moved to Seville, where she litigated to recover ownership of the many estates she had received from her husband, but which had been confiscated during the conquest. She gained the sympathy of Isabel herself, and married her

Hilt of a sword attributed to Boabdil, with the inscription "There is no conqueror but God . . ." (late fifteenth/early sixteenth century). *Bibliothèque Nationale, Paris, Cabinet des Medailles*

sons, Sa'd and Nasr, who were baptized as Pedro and Juan de Granada, into respectable Old Christian families.

Surprisingly, many of the religious elite stayed behind also, having been given the opportunity to become the rulers and administrators of the new kingdom's robust *mudéjar* society. Through their official positions, and control of pious endowments and the communal property of the Muslims, these *alfaquíes* came to compose a prosperous and influential upper class of royal functionaries, helping smooth the transition to Christian rule.

Meanwhile, the ordinary Muslim inhabitants of the capital found themselves under the dual authority of a military governor, Iñigo López de Mendoza, and the royal confessor, Archbishop Hernando de Talavera. Known affectionately, if ironically, as El Santo Faquí ("the Holy *Faqih*"), Talavera, the descendant of Jewish *conversos*, endeared himself to his charges by taking a soft approach to proselytizing, by showing sympathy and interest in the nonreligious aspects of Arabo-Islamic culture, and by scrupulously abiding by the terms of the surrender. However, tensions across the kingdom of Granada were soon on the rise. The Catholic Kings imposed a crippling tax burden on the *mudéjares*, adding to the already heavy Nasrid-era taxes. Unscrupulous colonial administrators mistreated Muslims, arbitrarily confiscating their property and bringing false charges against them. Finally, there was growing friction with the haughty and overbearing Christian settlers who were pouring into prosperous cities like Granada, social powder kegs already overcrowded with discontented Muslim refugees.

A brief tax revolt flared in 1497, but in December 1499, a full-blown uprising took place in the capital. This was prompted by Talavera's fellow cleric Francisco Jiménez Cisneros, who had succeeded him as confessor to the Catholic Kings and served as archbishop of Toledo, Castile's senior-ranking churchman. Cisneros was in every way the opposite of Talavera: ruthless, uncompromising, and unhesitant to deploy violence, cruelty, and terror in the name of the higher good. He arrived in Granada with the Inquisition in 1499 and immediately began to harass and abuse the city's Muslims in open violation of the *Capitulaciones*—persecuting *elches*, imprisoning and torturing *mudéjar* leaders to induce them to convert, ordering the social segregation of Muslims and Christians, passing ordinances that discriminated economically against *mudéjares*, and waging a culture war on the Arabo-Islamic customs of the natives. Commanding all the books in Arabic in the city to be confiscated, Cisneros had them burned in a public bonfire. This was the flame that sparked the rebellion.

Talavera quickly defused the situation by promising amnesty to any rebels who embraced Christianity, leading some 50,000 to convert. But this shredded the social fabric of the city as neighbors and family members became apostates, mosques were turned into churches, and former Muslims immediately clamored to be accorded full rights as Christian subjects. In any event, the revolt had spread to the countryside—first to the Alpujarras, and then in 1500 to major towns across the kingdom, including Ronda, Málaga, and Almería. The rebels were led by a *mudéjar* official named Ibrahim ibn Umayya ("Abrahem aben Humeya"). Rallying under the banner of the caliphal name, they attacked Christian officials, settlers, and clergy. Fernando's forces responded with commensurate brutality, deliberately massacring men, women, and children to break the insurgents' will. But, more serious damage than this was done: the revolt provided a legal pretext for the monarchy to abrogate the *Capitulaciones* and proscribe Islam altogether.

In desperation, *mudéjar* leaders sent plaintive letters to the Ottoman sultan Bayezid II. But to no avail: not only was no help forthcoming, but the existence of the embassy only confirmed Christian fears that the *mudéjares* were traitors. By 1501, the rebellion had been put down and the kingdom placed under quarantine—no Muslims could come or go. The *mudéjars* of the kingdom were then given the same choice the Jews of Castile and Aragon had been presented with nine years earlier: accept baptism or face exile. Most, who would have been in no position to leave even had they wanted to, went reluctantly and unbelievingly to the font.

Castilian church authorities were only too aware of the problems that forced conversion could provoke, particularly if the converts continued to have access to or contact with their former coreligionists. This had been the heart of Spain's "Jewish Problem" in the previous century. The continuing presence of Jewish communities provided clandestine access for *conversos* to the Jewish faith and

Ecce servus meus, suscipiam eum, electus meus, complacuit sibi in illo anima mea, dedi spiritum meum super eum, iudicium gentibus proferet. Isa. 42.

eduxit eos in spe, & inimicos eorum operuit mare Et induxit eos in Mon.

Mudéjares baptized in Granada (F. Heylan). *Biblioteca de la Universidad de Granada (Colección de láminas alusivas a los libros de plomo y reliquias del Sacro Monte de Granada)* rituals, while some nonconverts secretly proselytized with the aim of tempting *conversos* back to the faith. It was because of this that the Catholic Kings had requested permission in 1478 to establish what would become known as the Spanish Inquisition, a body that had no jurisdiction over non-Christians but was meant to root out "crypto," or secret, Jews. But the Inquisition did not prove up to the task, and it was as a result of its perceived failure that Isabel's counsellors prevailed upon her to order the conversion or expulsion of the remaining Jews of her lands in January 1492. Fernando may have had little interest in pursuing such a policy in the Crown of Aragon, but he was obliged by the terms of his marriage contract to follow suit.

To prevent such a situation from developing, hard-liner clerics like Cisneros urged Isabel to break her promises to her Muslim subjects in Castile. Although she had assured them as late as 1493 that they would not be subject to an order of conversion, just such an order was issued in February 1502. With that, all the Muslims of the Crown of Castile were obliged to convert to Christianity or depart. The order applied to Isabel's lands and therefore did not affect the *mudéjar* communities of the Crown of Aragon or the kingdom of Navarre. The Muslims of Portugal, or nearly all of them, had been quietly expelled in the years prior to 1500.

Fernando, who was both king of Aragon and the real power in Navarre, had no interest in harassing the *mudéjares*, who made up such a large and valuable community in these lands. However, in Navarre, his hands would be tied as a consequence of the terms of his marriage to Isabel. Thus, when he conquered Pamplona in 1513, nine years after the queen's death, and was acclaimed king of Navarre, that kingdom was automatically absorbed by and became subject to all the laws of Castile, including the edict of conversion. Overnight, and without any particular church, royal, or popular impetus, the *mudéjares* of the kingdom were obliged to abjure their faith or depart.

Naturally, the Crown of Aragon, where it remained completely legal to practice Islam, became the destination for many Muslims of Castile and Navarre who opted not to convert. Here, particularly in the kingdoms of Aragon and Valencia, Muslims continued to constitute numerous dynamic and vibrant communities. In Aragon, they had become extremely well integrated into Christian society, and although they suffered from vulnerabilities and occasional abuses as a consequence of their secondary status, they were, on the whole, confident, secure, and safe. In Valencia, the situation was somewhat less stable. Here, the history of *mudéjar*-Christian relations was much more confrontational, and the two communities tended to see each other as rivals and retreated into social isolation. This was aggravated here by the perception of *mudéjares* as foreign sympathizers or agents and by the volatility of the urban craft classes, who saw Muslims as competitors and as symbols of the royal and noble authority they resented.

When Fernando died in 1516, the stage was set for the demise of Islam in the Crown. Fernando's second marriage had not produced children, so Juana, a daughter he had with Isabel, inherited Aragon as well as Castile. She had been married to the Hapsburg prince Philip the Fair. When he died in 1506, Juana—who would be known as "the Mad"—retreated into melancholy despair and was removed from the throne to be succeeded by one of her sons, the Holy Roman Emperor (from 1519) Charles V, or Carlos I in Spain. For Charles, the Crown of Aragon was merely another of his many dominions. The "New World" was the economic engine of his empire. He had no dynastic memory of or sympathy for his *mudéjar* subjects, and he was engaged in an existential struggle with the Ottoman sultans, who presumed to be both caliphs of Islam and emperors of Rome.

Thus, when the Valencian craftsmen took up arms in 1520 in the revolt known as the Brotherhoods (*Germanies*) and attacked the kingdom's *mudéjares*, killing some and forcing many at gun- and sword-point to baptism, Charles reacted with indiscriminate brutality, and the foreign imperial troops sent in to quell the disturbance committed their own atrocities against his Muslim subjects. By 1522, the uprising had been suppressed, but mop-up operations would continue for another six years.

In the meantime, Charles, who had little sympathy for the troublesome Aragonese and Valencian nobility whose prosperity was built on *mudéjar* labor, passed an edict on January 5, 1526, ordering all his Muslim subjects to convert to Christianity and all mosques to be closed. Those who opted not to convert were given only seventeen days to reach A Coruña, in the far northwest, where they could in theory embark into exile. But this was clearly impossible, and the provision was included in the order only so that it might be claimed that those *mudéjares* who stayed and were baptized did so out of choice. Faced with the edict, a few stalwarts holed up in the town of Benaguasil, in the hills northwest of Valencia, and prepared to fight to the death. But when the full weight of the imperial army had been thrust upon them in the form of shells and bombardments, the rebels yielded and marched in resigned despair to the baptismal font. With that, the *mudéjares* of Spain became "Moriscos"—"Muslim-ish Christians." Islam had come to an end in the Iberian Peninsula . . . at least officially.

29

The Virgin and the Veil

Construction on a new cathedral of Granada had begun in 1518. Slowly, the old Nasrid congregational mosque was dismantled, and over the course of the next century and a half, a hulking church was raised over its foundations, first in chunky Gothic and eventually in extravagant Spanish Baroque style. In March 1588, as one of the old towers was being demolished, an incredible discovery was made. Buried beneath the rubble was a lead box containing a handwritten parchment, a piece of cloth, and human remains. The authorities excitedly began to examine the text, which was written in Latin, a strange form of Arabic, and a smattering of Greek. Two Morisco physician-courtiers, Alonso del Castillo and Miguel de Luna, were called in to assist. Difficult as it was to decipher, the general thrust was clear. The cloth was nothing less than a kerchief or veil that the Virgin Mary had held as Jesus was crucified, and the remains—a bone—a relic of Saint Stephen, the first martyr in the Christian tradition.

These objects had been conveyed here by early Christians soon after the crucifixion and hidden away from the Roman authorities. It was a sensational find. This meant that Granada was, in fact, the original Christian city in the peninsula. Not only this, but the parchment established that these early Christians spoke Arabic, and that this had been a language of Christianity a thousand years before Castilian had evolved. Arabic, therefore, was a language that was more Christian and more "Spanish" than Spanish itself!

More mysterious discoveries followed when, beginning in 1596, the first of twenty-two enigmatic objects that would be unearthed over the next eleven years around the Sacromonte neighborhood overlooking Granada were encountered. Referred to as the "Lead Books," they are, in fact, gatherings of discs or plates of lead inscribed with a strange Arabic-style script, as well as mysterious, perhaps magical symbols. Fortunately, the Moriscos Alonso del Castillo and Miguel de Luna were always close at hand and set to work deciphering them. Among what they could make out was a series of prophecies by the Apostles and instructions from the Virgin for the evangelization of Roman Hispania. Needless to say, this generated considerable interest and immediately provoked debates over the books' authenticity. Papal authorities quickly stepped in and carried the tablets off to the Vatican. They would be condemned as false in 1682 and have remained under lock and key to this day—quietly forgotten and all but totally inaccessible, even to scholars, until very recently.

BY 1588, SPAIN had been, according to the law, uniformly Christian for over half a century, and Granada for over three generations. Some elements of the *mudéjar* population had made a successful transition to the new order. Many members of the Nasrid nobility, including local commanders and the great families who had dominated the Granadan court, had converted and been welcomed into the Castilian aristocracy. Notable among these were the Banu Mawl—the family of Yusuf IV—and their in-laws, the Banu Bannigash, some of whom had reasserted (or reinvented) their Castilian Christian origin as the Venegas, the noble family that Ridwan Bannigash was said to have belonged to as a boy when he was captured in a Nasrid raid in the early 1400s. Those men of religion who had become the *alfaquies* of the postconquest era had now become Christian, but they retained their positions as administrators of the Morisco population.

Some of those members of the educated upper class of Muslim Granada who stayed in 1492, and their descendants, known as "Arabic Christians," made the transition not only into the elite of the kingdom of Granada but even into the royal court. Alonso del Castillo and Miguel de Luna are two of the best examples. They each received excellent training at the University of Granada as physicians, but it was also their Arabo-Islamic linguistic and scholarly abilities that were the foundation of their success.

Both were well versed in classical Arabic, of which they were intensely proud, and both became royal translators for the Hapsburg kings. In 1573 Alonso had been charged with collecting Arabic manuscripts from around the realm and cataloging them in Felipe II's library at his palace-monastery, El Escorial. Miguel wrote a best seller called *The True History of King Rodrigo*, a history of Spain that laid the blame for the conquest on the Visigoths and presented the Islamic period in an extremely sympathetic light, and which he presented in 1605 as the alleged translation of an Arabic text by a certain "Abulcacim Tarif Abentarique." The two Morisco courtiers were also close; until recently it was thought that Miguel had married Alonso's daughter. There is little doubt, then, that Alonso and Miguel not only "discovered" and translated the Lead Books, but also played a role in creating them. But why?

Neither the *True History* nor the Lead Books are defenses of Islam per se; rather, they sought to support the notion that there is nothing un-Christian or un-Spanish about Arabic language and culture, and that the people who identified with them could be truly pious and loyal Christian subjects. It was a necessary argument to make because although the *mudéjares* had been baptized so many decades earlier, they continued to be treated as second-class citizens. They were regarded with suspicion and disdain, and officially, their folk culture was seen as dangerous and aberrant. Except for those of the upper classes, conversion had brought little benefit to most Moriscos, and generally, there was very little religious, social, or administrative integration with the Old Christian majority.

Moriscos continued to live in insular communities, subject to distinct laws. In the absence of educational initiatives, Spanish was slow to gain traction in areas where Arabic was the spoken language. Arabo-Islamic folk customs remained deeply entrenched, whether mores and values, ways of dress, music and dance, and so on. Much to the Morisco peasants' disappointment, especially in the kingdom of Granada, conversion did not bring them relief from the oppressive *mudéjar* tax system. Thanks to the legacy of Jewish-Christian relations in the peninsula, a notion of "blood purity" had developed. One's religious identity now was not merely a function of one's beliefs or the legal community one belonged to, it was transmitted by blood and was therefore all but impossible to change.

Like formerly Jewish *conversos*, Moriscos were left in a biological double bind. As "New Christians," they were discriminated against legally and socially by privileged "Old Christians." This, in turn, discouraged marriage across the two groups and contributed to an ever-deeper estrangement. In other words, the forced conversion did not make the Muslims more Spanish, it seemed to make them less Spanish. In coastal areas subject to corsair raids, Moriscos were suspected (sometimes deservedly) of collusion with foreign Muslim powers. They came to be seen by many Old Christians as foreigners of suspect loyalty—a people apart. In areas where large Morisco populations worked the fields, this was compounded by the view of them as underprivileged laborers and objects of exploitation. They were seen as dirty, scheming, noisy, lustful, and "black"—a bundle of stereotypes that people often apply to groups they actively oppress.[51] The objectification of rural Muslims had been noted by the German scholar Jeronimo Münzer, who traveled around the peninsula in the years following the conquest of Granada and who noted the popular saying *Quien no tiene moro, no tiene oro*—"If you don't have Muslims, you can't be rich."[52]

Like their *mudéjar* ancestors, Moriscos remained a potent economic force, particularly in the Granadan countryside and the Crown of Aragon, and substantial Morisco enclaves survived in these regions. In towns, where Moriscos and Old Christians engaged in all sorts of mutually beneficial relationships, economic and social integration was much greater, even more so than had been the case in these settings during the *mudéjar* period. In these environments, the social distance between Moriscos and Old Christians was less. At times, their shared municipal citizenship provided them with a sense of common identity, and class diversity among both groups opened avenues for solidarity that crossed ethnic lines. But in times of competition or scarcity, prosperous urban Moriscos were caricaturized as grasping, greedy, and overprivileged.

Moriscos, like their ancestors, dominated certain key professions and crafts, which gave them value within the Spanish socioeconomic environment and contributed to their prosperity. Many muleteers were Morisco—not a glamorous profession, but necessary. Artisanal skills continued to be passed through families, and thus many crafts remained Morisco-dominated. And finally, Moriscos continued to practice high-status professions, such as medicine, even as laws were passed designed to exclude them. Muslim female obstetricians were particularly sought after by wealthy Christian women. That said, much like has happened with African Americans in the aftermath of the Civil Rights movement, the theoretical removal of Muslims' subordinate status provoked a hostile reaction among those nonnoble Christians who saw Moriscos as economic competitors and who no longer enjoyed an advantage over them as a consequence of Christian religious and legal superiority. In sixteenth-century Spain, this provided an opening for the Tribunal of the Holy Office—the Inquisition—which was ready to investigate any suggestion of Morisco impropriety no matter how thin the evidence and could be easily deployed by Old Christians against uppity or challenging Moriscos. Everyone may have been Christian now, but some Christians were seen as more Christian than others.

There are similarities also to our own society regarding the relationship between Morisco and Old Christian culture in sixteenth-century Spain. The flamboyant, high-culture *maurophilia* of the fifteenth century had been left behind and was now regarded with some embarrassment. After all, Islam had "lost," and its people were seen now as a poor underclass. Castilian culture had emerged in full-blown imperial glory and was enjoying its "Golden Age" of artistic and literary production, which was consciously rooted in European Christian traditions. Nevertheless, Arabo-Islamic popular culture continued to exercise great appeal. The songs, dances, and culinary traditions of the Moriscos were embraced across the Old Christian social spectrum, even as they were formally prohibited. Morisco musicians and acrobats provided the entertainment at both private and

Morisco dancers and musicians. From Christopher Weiditz's *Trachten-buk* (1530/40). *Germanisches Nationalmuseum, Digitale Bibliothek, Germanisches Nationalmuseum Nürnberg, Hs. 22474. Bl. 107–108 Der Moriskentanz*

public functions, while the *zambra*, a traditional Andalusi dance, was decried as scandalous by moralists and prudes, even as bishops glee-fully hiked up their cassocks at parties and kicked up their heels. As the experience of African Americans in the "white" twentieth-century United States shows, a people do not have to be loved, or even ad-mired, for their culture to be appropriated by those in a position of privilege—quite the contrary. The act of appropriation can feel addi-tionally empowering, while its illicit flavor adds to the attraction.

However, for every churchman who was sympathetic to Morisco culture, there was one who saw it as a threat and an impediment to the successful missionization of the convert population. In the after-math of the conquest of Granada, Cisneros believed it was necessary to destroy the indigenous culture of Granada for the benefit of both Christian Spain and the Muslims themselves, who would therefore be driven to embrace Christianity, and to do so fully. This found an echo in the Hapsburg court, whose functionaries and rulers increasingly came to see the persistence of Arabo-Islamic culture among the Moriscos as a political threat linking them to the foreign Muslim powers, whether the Sa'di dynasty of Morocco or the Hapsburgs' existential enemy, the Ottomans.

The edicts of conversion had been a huge blow to Islamicate culture in the peninsula. In the Crown of Aragon, for example, in January 1526, with the swipe of a pen, ancient places of worship were shut down or destroyed, the social elite was disempowered and the religious elite driven underground, religious books were hurriedly ferreted away, and first and family names were changed. Entire communities were pressed into a society that would not accept them and forced under obedience to a clergy that, with rare exceptions, did not sympathize with them. Were this not enough, six months later a conclave of clergy—the *Congregación*—proposed measures that would effectively outlaw Morisco culture, mandating the suppression of folk customs, the prohibition of "Moorish" costume (notably the veil, for women) and the use of Arabic, restrictions on the practice of medicine and midwifery, and the requirement that Moriscos take "Christian" names. Hurriedly, the Morisco communities across the realm raised a massive bribe of 8,000 ducats, which convinced the emperor, Charles, to suspend enforcement of these laws for forty years.[53]

But, whatever Morisco culture's role might have been in interfering with conversion or inspiring crypto-Muslim resistance to the edicts, a far greater obstacle was posed by the church's and the crown's own policies and attitudes. The continuation of the *mudéjar* tax regime and other discriminatory laws prevented the social and economic integration necessary for religious conversion and cultural assimilation. But, worse, the church failed to provide religious leadership, convert communities, or educate Muslims in the Christian faith. In other words, Islam was prohibited, but nothing substantial was provided to take its place, even to those Muslims who willingly and genuinely opted for baptism.

In the absence of such instruction (and surveillance), many Morisco communities, particularly those that were geographically isolated or large enough to maintain a stable social structure, either secretly persisted in Islam or discreetly developed their own religious traditions. And without parish priests, crucial sacraments could not be administered—a failure that, according to doctrine, would condemn even truly convinced New Christians to Hell. It placed the Moriscos in another double bind, a theological one that left them "damned if they did, and damned if they didn't." From the perspective of the church, this should have been extremely alarming, if not for the sake of the souls of the faithful, then for the body of the church. The previous century's Jewish "*converso* problem" was being duplicated with the Moriscos.

This was not lost on all clergymen. Hernando de Talavera, for example, clearly felt that it was instruction and compassion, not coercion and neglect, that would bring about the successful evangelization of the Muslims. But as the sixteenth century progressed, there were few who shared his sense of mission. The Castilian aristocracy and upper clergy, flush with their triumphs on the global stage—the "discovery" and colonization of the "Indies," and the riches this had brought the empire—were swollen with moral self-assurance and ethnoreligious hubris. The underclass of former Muslims held little interest for them.

Not so, however, for those clergy committed to their mission among the Moriscos, although those were few and far between. Upwardly mobile Moriscos tended to go into royal service rather than the church, and it is easy to see why, given that Catholic culture, faced with the continuing challenge of heresy, and now the Reformation, was becoming increasingly reactionary. A rare voice in the wilderness was that of Ignacio de las Casas, a Jesuit of Morisco origin who between 1606 and 1607 wrote a series of essays that he sent to Pope Clement VII, decrying the church's failures to its New Christian congregation. De las Casas specifically pointed to factors including the chauvinistic attitude of the Old Christian clergy, the repression and marginalization of Moriscos, the policies of the Inquisition, the failure to use Arabic effectively as a missionizing tool and to educate young Moriscos, and the continuing appeal of the crypto-Muslim religious authorities to Morisco communities. But, not only did the church fail to act, it stepped up its discrimination against Moriscos. In 1593, Ignacio's own order adopted "blood purity" laws that prevented the recruitment and ordination of clergy, like himself, who had *mudé-jar* ancestors.

Such tensions and frustrations were not limited to the church. They were also felt by the Morisco courtiers who served in the heart of the imperial administration, and who were indignant at the attacks on the Morisco culture that even genuine New Christians still identified or sympathized with. In 1554, a synod in Granada passed laws surpassing those of the *Congregación* of 1526, additionally prohibiting Morisco dance and music, the use of Arab-style baths, and the ownership of slaves, and ordering Moriscos to keep their doors open on Fridays and Sundays to ensure they were observing the correct sabbath day. In 1567, a year after the forty-year moratorium on the anti-Morisco laws laid out by the *Congregación* had expired, a Morisco courtier named Francisco Núñez Muley, whose surname signaled his descent from Marinid royalty, drafted a lengthy letter of protest to the Real Audiencia (the high court), railing at the injustice of these restrictions.

Nothing less than a manifesto of Morisco dignity and loyalty, Núñez Muley's *Memorandum* emphasized that Moriscos were not foreigners but natives of the peninsula and that they had served the Hapsburgs loyally as soldiers, quelling the uprisings of Christian rebels. Their dances, music, and dress, he said, were not African or Turkish, but Spanish. Moreover, what else could poor Moriscos wear but the clothes they had, many of which were made of the now-prohibited silk? And if they spoke Arabic, it was the same Arabic Eastern Christians had spoken since almost the time of Christ. The greatest indignation, however, was that African slaves—"Can we say there is a lower race than the black slaves of Guinea?"—were allowed to perform their songs and dances, but free, native-born Moriscos were not.[54] Even prior to the conversions of the early 1500s, *mudéjares* across the peninsula had emphasized their condition as "naturals," which is to say, native born, to stake their claim to their legitimate status as subjects—a foreshadowing of the European concept of nation and nationality that was only beginning to take shape in this era.

Not all members of the Christian aristocracy were hostile to Moriscos. Quite the contrary. Many of the aristocracy of rural Valencia and Aragon continued to depend on a Morisco workforce, and just as had been the case prior to the edicts of conversion, rural lords went to great lengths to ensure that their Morisco tenants and vassals were content and productive, even if it meant turning a blind eye to those who very deliberately persisted in their Islamic faith.

The most sensational example is that of Sancho of Cardona, the royal admiral, who had extensive landholdings in the kingdom of Valencia. The Inquisition caught up with Sancho in the 1540s, discovering that he had been allowing his Morisco peasants to live openly as Muslims and colluding with them to avoid detection by church authorities. They kept Arabic books, including the Qur'an; the women continued to cover their faces; and they circumcised their children, who went unbaptized. It was in his lands that the founder of the Banu Sidi Bono line of Sufis was buried. His tomb at Azteneta had been a popular site of pilgrimage for centuries, and now with Sancho's blessing, Moriscos had built a new mosque, where they would gather "to conduct their ceremonies and other rituals just like Muslims."[55] Once convicted, the admiral was spared the stake due to his high birth but was sentenced to life imprisonment, during which he was to wear the *sanbenito*—a humiliating outfit consisting of a long, yellow robe emblazoned with a red crucifix and topped by a tall, conical hat.

One of the consequences of the forced conversions was that Spain's Muslims came for the first time under the legal jurisdiction of the church and its prosecutory arm, the Inquisition. From the time of its inception, the mission of the Inquisition had broadened to include enforcement of orthodoxy in general, including public and private morality. The inquisitors had their work cut out for them. The sixteenth century was a time of great religious creativity and instability, with the irruption of the Protestant Reformation, the emergence of new Catholic spiritual and theological movements, and the growing popularity of mysticism, all of which presented challenges to the church's authority. This was also the age that saw the first stirrings of European Absolutism and notions of divine kingship, initiating an era in which the church and the monarchy saw their interests as identical. Thus, the Inquisition became a key instrument for maintaining political and religious conformity, and the Moriscos were an obvious target.

Although the violence of the Inquisition has been exaggerated, there is no doubt that it was an institution that struck fear into the hearts of even those innocent of dissent. A mobile court that circulated regularly through the realms, part of its power was that *everybody* expected the Spanish Inquisition. Its arrival in a town was preceded by an exhortation for individuals to step forward themselves or to inform on their guilty neighbors. Those who confessed freely were generally shown mercy, but those who did not could be crushed by the weight of what very quickly became a totalitarian-type apparatus of repression.

Accusations could be made in secret, and no concrete evidence was required. The accused would be arrested without warning, tortured, and pressured to turn in real or imaginary accomplices. If found guilty, one could be condemned to prison or public execution, typically at the stake. Fortunate and repentant convicts might be mercifully strangled to death on the pyre, while those who denied their guilt were burned alive. Condemnation would normally be accompanied by confiscation of one's property (part of which would go to the accuser). Those who were released were forbidden from disclosing any of the proceedings they underwent, or even the arrest itself. Like any institution, its goal became its own self-perpetuation, which only entrenched the potential for abuse that was already inherent in the system.

Naturally, Moriscos came under close scrutiny. Rural communities were somewhat better protected from the Inquisition because of their homogeneity and the solidarity this bred among their inhabitants. Without an accuser, it was difficult for the Inquisition to make progress, and these communities often resisted. The urban setting was much more promising. Here, where Old Christians and New Christians mixed, there was a greater chance forbidden behavior would be observed or reported. Even the innocent lived in the fear that a bitter neighbor or unscrupulous business competitor might lodge a false accusation, which, given the Inquisition's presumption of guilt, could be devastating. And even genuine Christians could be found guilty. The Inquisition sometimes focused their interrogations on fine points of doctrine that ordinary Christians were simply unaware of, trapping them into admitting heretical beliefs they did not even realize were heretical. Even today, many people are ignorant or misinformed about the doctrine of their own religion—theology is simply not an important aspect of most people's lived religious experience.

The establishment of the Inquisition was a symptom of the great political, religious, and social transformations that Spain, Europe, and the Islamic world were undergoing at this time. Under the Hapsburgs, Spain had become a global empire. Felipe II, whose imperium was funded by massive infusions of New World silver, reigned for almost the entire second half of the sixteenth century, ruling over an empire "on which the sun never set." In fact, the Hapsburgs, particularly the German branch, who inherited the title Holy Roman Emperor, came to conceive of themselves in Messianic terms: universal rulers who were to usher in a new era of divinely sanctioned order. In Europe, the dynasty was opposed by the French, English, and Dutch, but their greatest rival was the Ottomans, whose own universalist, messianic pretensions directly challenged the Hapsburgs. Under Felipe's contemporary, Sulayman the Magnificent, who claimed the titles "Caliph of Islam" and "Emperor of Rome," the Ottomans annexed almost the entire Islamic Mediterranean and sent their armies to the gates of Vienna.

Spanish society was changing too. With the mission of the Reconquest accomplished, the religio-political imperative evolved into a justification for the conquest of Muslim North Africa and the pagan lands of the New World. The social, economic, and cultural foundations of the peninsula were transforming, as what had long been regarded as an aggregate of distinct kingdoms and peoples was now conceived of increasingly as "Spain." Although the principled medieval age of chivalry may never have been more than a figment of the imagination, its passing was mourned by the old Spanish aristocracy, who did not adapt to the opportunities of the ruthless mercenary era that had begun. The landed nobility, whose agricultural estates had once been the foundation of the Spanish economy and the pillar of their own political power, were becoming increasingly incidental in the face of the tremendous wealth that was flowing in from the Americas. And as this proudly independent aristocracy was seen increasingly as an obstacle to the power of the monarchy, these lords and their Morisco subjects both became more vulnerable.

The malaise provoked by these changes is portrayed in what is universally regarded as the greatest work of Spanish literature, Miguel de Cervantes's novel *The Ingenious Nobleman Don Quixote of La Mancha*, the story of an aging and scatterbrained knight who vainly sets out with his bumbling page, Sancho Panza, to recapture the vanished age of chivalric romance. The book was written at a key moment in the history of the Muslims of Spain. The first part was published in 1605, when the weak-willed Felipe III was being pressured by his ministers to end the Morisco problem, and the second in 1615, the year after the last Moriscos had been expelled. Tellingly, the book is structured like an Andalusi *maqamat*, in which Cervantes fictitiously recounts the story as provided to him by "Cide Hamete Benengeli," a Castilian Morisco who translated the Arabic manuscripts in which the tale was said to be recorded—a fictionalized representation of Cervantes's fellow courtier, the royal translator Miguel de Luna, the forger of the Lead Books and the author of *The True History of King Rodrigo in Which the Main Reason for the Conquest of Spain Is Explained*.

30

On the Road with Ricote

The implementation of the anti-Morisco laws of 1567's *Congregación* may have provoked the "Arabized Christian" and royal courtier Núñez Muley to compose his *Memorandum* in defense of the Arabic language and Andalusi customs, but others were prepared to go much further. The crushing of Aben Humeya's revolt in the Alpujarras in 1501 had not ended Muslim resistance, only crystallized it. It was continued in the kingdom of Granada by bands of renegade Muslims, whom the authorities dismissed as *monfíes*, after the Arabic word for "bandit." Others conspired with foreign powers. In 1526, the year of the edict of conversion, the Muslims of the Espadà mountains in Valencia, still simmering after the Brotherhoods, rose up and attacked Christian towns, killing inhabitants and defiling churches. Soon after, the Ottoman governor of Algiers sent a series of clandestine flotillas to the Granadan coast to evacuate tens of thousands of New Christians. Throughout the century, Moriscos remained a numerous and strongly armed community in the peninsula, and when they were pushed to the point of desperation, they would turn to violence. The authorities were well aware of this danger, as reflected in an edict published by the Aragonese Inquisition in 1559, prohibiting "converted Muslims and their descendants" from owning crossbows and any firearms, on the basis of their sympathy for Ottoman raiders.[56]

So it was that in 1568, just one year after the edicts of the *Congregación* were imposed, an armed insurrection broke out in Granada's Alpujarras. The innocent protestations of the Arabized Christian courtiers were not for these rebels, who proudly declared they were "Muslims" and claimed that their leader, Francisco de Valor, had been crowned according to the "rite of the Granadan kings."[57] The scion of a prominent Morisco family, Francisco had fallen afoul of the law and now took up his rebel great-grandfather's legacy and name: Aben Humeya. The uprising began with an incursion into the capital city, Granada, and then attacks on the Old Christian settlers of the hinterland. Soon after, the rebels' numbers were augmented by Ottoman troops and volunteer *mujahidun* from North Africa. Felipe II's response was to crush the rebels with the full weight of his army, led by his bastard half brother, Don Juan of Austria, who responded to the guerilla tactics of the Muslims with brute force and terrible reprisals. In the end, divisions within the rebel camp proved its own undoing. Aben Humeya was murdered in 1569 and succeeded by his cousin Aben Abóo. The new rebel leader was determined to fight on, but he was killed in 1571 by a faction who advocated negotiating a peace.

In the aftermath of the War of the Alpujarras, Felipe determined to solve the problem by ridding Granada of its Moriscos. Some 84,000 were sent into internal exile, settling among the communities of Castile, Aragon, and Valencia. But this diaspora had the opposite effect that the king hoped for. Instead of being absorbed into the complacent communities of the north, these "Granadan Moriscos" scattered among the Morisco communities of Spain, reenergizing the Islamic consciousness of the "Old Moriscos" and inspiring them to resist.

PRIOR TO THE sixteenth century, the *mudéjares* of the Spanish Christian kingdoms had been living in something of a religious predicament. With few exceptions, the overwhelming majority of jurists of the Islamic world concurred that it was illicit for Muslims to willingly live under infidel rule. But, the edicts of conversion had moved Spanish Muslims into even more problematic territory, given that the alternative to apostasy was, effectively, death. Islamic law, however, had developed a legitimate response to such situations: *taqiyya*, which means "prudence" or "dissimulation." The idea was that as long as they remained faithful in their hearts, Muslims who were under threat of death could pretend to have converted to another religion and participate in its rituals and customs, even if these involved eating pork and drinking wine. This provided a morally sanctioned "out," particularly for Muslims living in towns or mixed communities, where they were subject to greater surveillance, and it enabled Islam to survive illicitly among Moriscos. At the same time, crypto-Muslim religious authorities in Spain enjoined the faithful to commit themselves to the inner, moral jihad, rather than resisting Christianity with arms. When in the early 1500s a *mudéjar* delegation from Aragon posed the question to four *muftis* of Cairo, representing the four schools of Sunni law, as to whether Muslims could legitimately live in Spain, the Sha'fi'i judge replied that Islam was so robust there even as practiced in secret that he saw no issue for Muslims who wished to remain there.

And so, Islam did not disappear with the edicts of conversion but survived, sustained by a clandestine class of *alfakis* (from the Arabic *al-faqih*)—the pre-1526 *'ulama'* and their successors. Many of these were prosperous artisans or landholders, who continued to teach, write, and discreetly guide their communities, hold prayer services, observe their holidays, and even run underground *madrasas*, while secret Morisco *scriptoria* turned out prohibited works to order. Networks of *faqihs* were discovered by the Inquisition in several regions, and communities also kept in contact through the mediation of Morisco mule drovers who crisscrossed the peninsula and wandering holy men and women.

The best known of these was Mancebo ("Lad") de Arévalo, a prolific crypto-Muslim theologian who traveled around the Spanish communities in the early sixteenth century. In 1534, the community in Zaragoza, conscious that they were forgetting their doctrine, commissioned him to produce a guide, the *Tafçira* (from the Arabic *tafsir*, or "exegesis"). He also wrote or co-wrote a number of other works, including *The Short Compendium of Our Holy Law and Sunna*, a summary of Islamic law. Moriscos also managed to keep in touch with the larger Islamic world, where they traveled as merchants, soldiers, and agents of the crown. In 1603, an Aragonese Morisco, Puey de

A manuscript in Aljamiado of Mancebo de Arévalo's
Tafçira, f. 1v (sixteenth century). *Biblioteca Tomás
Navarro Tomás (CSIC: Madrid)*

Monzón, not only made the pilgrimage to Mecca but composed a
rhymed account of his journey.

Women also played an important role in maintaining Islamic consciousness and traditions, thanks in part to the increasing popularity
of mysticism, which gave women in the peninsula—both Christian
and Muslim—who had been excluded from the masculine-dominated
exercise of formal theology, a greater role in the religion. Among
Moriscos, the suppression of formal Islam further undermined the
established male religious elite, without which legalism could no

longer put a brake on mysticism. Thus, if Spanish Catholicism produced figures such as Saint Teresa de Ávila, contemporary Spanish crypto-Islam engendered holy women such as the Mora ("Muslim Woman") de Úbeda and Nozaita Kalderán. Both served as mentors to the Mancebo. The enigmatic Mora, despite her advanced age and illiteracy, had great knowledge of the Qur'an and mysticism and was regarded as the leading religious scholar in Granada and its environs. Nozaita gave religious counsel to communities across Castile and was also a famous midwife.

But ordinary women were also crucial in the survival of Islam. With their lower public profile, it was women who found it easier to resist linguistic acculturation and the pressure to appear "Spanish." Women carried out key rituals that marked the life cycle, such as washing the dead. They cooked traditional foods, said prayers, sang songs, educated young children, and established Islamic domestic environments. When the agents of the Inquisition came, women resisted. There are many reports of their fighting off the soldiers searching their houses, even hiding copies of the Qur'an up their skirts. In Valencia, over a quarter of those brought to trial by the Inquisition were Morisco women, and almost all claimed to speak only Arabic, a ploy that effectively disarmed the inquisitors' strategy of verbal entrapment. Lived experience and daily ritual are key to the survival of religion, as much as theology or law, and it was women who most actively sustained these.

BUT CULTURE, RELIGIOUS or otherwise, does not exist in a vacuum. Even though religious ties were maintained with the larger Muslim world, it was inevitable that Morisco Islam would continue to evolve and be influenced by the Christian world in which it was now immersed. This can be seen most clearly in the evolution of its literature. Classical written Arabic had been declining in some regions of Spain even in the fifteenth century, when religious works began to be translated into Castilian for the benefit of *mudéjares*. Now in the sixteenth, it all but disappeared, with the exception of the Qur'an. Moriscos produced some works in their idiosyncratic colloquial Arabic, but most of their literature was written in Aljamiado, a hybrid of spoken Castilian (or other Romance vernaculars) written in Andalusi Arabic script. Despite their prohibition, numerous works in Aljami-ado have survived, including treatises on Islamic law, mysticism and theology, prayers, Qur'an commentaries and translations, magic, folktales, medicine, and poetry and prose. Many of these books have only been discovered in the last century or so, plastered into the walls of former Morisco homes. In fact, Moriscos became so intuitively Hispanified that they even produced versions of crusade romances (complete with heroic Christians and villainous Muslims) in Alja-miado. As well, they read (or listened to) the popular literature of the day in Spanish and produced editions of Islamic religious texts, in-cluding the Qur'an, in Latin script.

Morisco religiosity was also heavily influenced by Christian and crypto-Jewish thought. The Mancebo, for example, claimed to have been educated in Hebrew, as well as Greek, Latin, Castilian, and Al-jamiado. He may have been of Judeo-*converso* origin; secret conver-sions between the two prohibited religions were not unknown. But, he and other educated crypto-Muslims were also reading the Chris-tian devotionals and Humanist literature of the day. The Mancebo and other Morisco thinkers were, for example, clearly influenced by the German theologian Thomas à Kempis, whose 1427 blockbuster, *The Imitation of Christ*, marked the pulse of popular "Modern Devotion" across Christian Europe on the eve of the Reformation. Secular, mor-alizing literature, particularly 1499's *La Celestina*, a sensational par-able of sexual transgression, was also influential.

Moriscos were also swept up in the growing tide of Marianism that was affecting Spain and the wider Catholic world. Mary is not the mother of God to Muslims, but she is the mother of Jesus, who is considered a prophet. In fact, she is the only woman referred to by name in the Qur'an, which recounts the Annunciation and affirms the virgin birth. Thus, venerating her presented a middle ground to Moriscos, who could thereby participate openly in public Christian devotional exercises, processions, and pilgrimages dedicated to her without engaging in the worship of Jesus as God, which they consid-ered anthropomorphism and polytheism. Moriscos raised her almost to prophethood, and the adoration of "the Most Holy Virgin of the

Rosary" provided common religious ground with Christian neighbors and a framework for social and economic engagement through membership in confraternities and other popular religious institutions. In some parts of rural Valencia, a hotbed of Islamic resistance, new Morisco brides were customarily taken to the capital to participate in the feasts of Corpus Christi and the Assumption of the Virgin.

In fact, acculturation was so profound that in some circumstances it becomes difficult to analyze contemporary Spanish popular piety in terms of Christianity and Islam. What evolved was to some appearances a hybrid religion that heterodox Christians, crypto-Jews, and crypto-Muslims engaged in together. Christian esoteric movements, such as the Illuminados and Alumbrados, which were considered heretical, advocated for an enlightenment rooted in a truth higher than any doctrine, ceremony, or religious institution. This resonated strongly with Sufism and Jewish mystical trends but was a threat to the apparatus of orthodoxy. Dreams and miraculous journeys, whether literal or symbolic, and angelic interventions figured prominently in the popular imagination in all three faiths. The political messianism of the sixteenth-century empires was echoed by millenary expectations that were blossoming across the Mediterranean, manifested by would-be messiahs whose missions often crossed religious lines. In Spain, rabble-rousing popular prophets, who appealed to both Christians and Muslims, were pursued by the Inquisition, whose mission was to reinforce rigidly defined doctrine.

The task of the Holy Office was complicated further by social forces that combined to blur the lines between religious communities. Even within Morisco rural enclaves, mixed households of Christians and crypto-Muslims could be found, and fraternization between Old and New Christians, together with people's natural impulse to draw on whatever magical and religious approaches they find, contributed to a general atmosphere of organic heterodoxy. Moreover, in this increasingly mobile world, people often crossed back and forth between Christendom and the *dar al-Islam* as merchants, travelers, soldiers, prisoners, and slaves. It was not unusual for a single individual in such circumstances to change religions several times, although the price for getting caught might be condemnation and the stake. Such religious commuting may have seemed outrageous to the church, but it seemed natural to many. At the trial of a serial apostate from Portugal, exasperated Inquisitors rejected his defense that he was at once an adherent of two faiths by categorically stating what was to them obvious: "It is not possible to be both a Jew and a Christian."[58]

INDEED, FROM THE perspective of the law, whether secular or ecclesiastic, there were no gray areas. All Moriscos were considered Christians, but they were New Christians of secondary status and with fewer rights. And because their legal status shaped the sort of marriage and economic partnerships Moriscos developed, it helped maintain them—in both their own view and that of the Old Christians—as a people apart on the communal level, regardless of whatever syncretic tendencies might blur the lines between the faiths. Thus, in times of social stress or economic competition, Moriscos became convenient scapegoats.

In the decades following the War of the Alpujarras, Spain was gripped with anxiety as it endured renewed conflict with Portugal, the debacle of the Spanish Armada, and famine and plague at home. Moriscos came to be seen at once as poor but avaricious, cowardly but threatening, and enjoying advantages denied to loyal Old Christians. Not unlike the disenfranchised white working class in the post–Civil Rights era of the early twenty-first-century United States, Old Christians' sense of entitlement was threatened because as Christians, Moriscos were no longer clearly a class below them. In the tangled logic of desperate bigotry, the underclass was perceived as unduly privileged. Suspicions of Morisco disloyalty increased. It was said they were stockpiling arms. In Seville and Valencia, false rumors of impending revolts led to vigilante assaults on Moriscos, while in Aragon, rural revolutionaries came down from the mountains and attacked their villages.

Morisco leaders responded in kind. As early as 1575, it emerged that some had been in contact with Spain's enemies—not only the Ottomans but the French Protestants, who were engaged in the bloody civil war with their Catholic monarchy, which came to be known as the Wars of Religion. When the Huguenots, under Henri of Navarre, triumphed in 1589, the king, who converted to Catholicism in order to take the French crown as Henri IV, instituted a multireligious legal regime in France. Thus, the Moriscos looked with vain hope to France as a new model of a multireligious kingdom. Likewise, the 1555 Peace of Augsberg, which recognized the legitimacy of Protestantism and Catholicism and was signed by none other than Spain's emperor, Charles V, had seemed to hold the possibility of a return to religious plurality. But it was not to be. And as a consequence, Moriscos were driven to seek Spain's enemies as their allies. Navarrese Moriscos let it be known to Henri IV that they would welcome him as king, should he invade Spanish Navarre, while other agents contacted the Protestant English and Dutch, who were encouraging a Moroccan invasion of the peninsula.

By 1581 Felipe II was entertaining the possibility of eliminating the Moriscos, but the task would fall to his only surviving son, Felipe III, an anemic monarch who was dominated by a clutch of reactionary magnates and churchmen. Various stratagems were considered, including genocide by drowning and forced sterilization, coupled with deportation to far-off and inhospitable Labrador. But, in the end, it was decided to simply send them into exile. And because it could not be determined which, if any, Moriscos were genuine Christians, it was better to deport them all. Moderate voices in the church and court were drowned out. At this point, it was difficult to make an economic argument for sparing them. Their contributions to the royal treasury were not crucial, and in any case, the confiscation of their property would generate a windfall for the cash-strapped royal treasury. Politically, their removal would also favor the monarchy by dealing a blow to the troublesome landed aristocracy of Valencia and Aragon, who depended on Morisco labor.

Some moderate clergymen made a moral argument, noting that this constituted collective punishment and that good Christians would be sent into an exile in which they would certainly be forced to abjure their faith and invite damnation. To no avail; the best they could achieve was a reprieve for the youngest children, who would be separated from their own parents and given to Old Christian families. Such was the tenor of the time. The voice of the church was Felipe's viceroy of Valencia, the archbishop (and later, Saint) Juan de Ribera.

The most merciful approach he could envision was the mass enslavement of the entire Morisco population.

ONCE IT WAS resolved to take action, preparations were made in secret so as to prevent resistance. Then, on January 22, 1609, the Moriscos of Valencia were informed that they had three days to assemble in their hometowns with whatever goods they could carry and prepare for deportation. The penalty for noncompliance was death.

By November of that year, the expulsion was all but complete, with 116,000 individuals having been conveyed to Oran, a Spanish enclave in Algeria, where they were simply marched to the city limits and told to keep walking. The expulsion from Aragon and Catalonia began in April 1610 and saw over 60,000 New Christians trudge either to Tortosa or to Agde in France to board ships for North Africa or the Ottoman East. Henri IV offered any who would pledge to be good Catholics the option of becoming French subjects, but few showed any interest.

The Castilian Moriscos were expelled in stages between September 1609 and July 1610. In some areas, they were given up to thirty days to dispose of the property they could not carry, in others, only ten. In any event, all the exiles were subject to a 50 percent exit tax, levied on whatever cash they carried out of the kingdom. By late 1610, it was just a matter of mopping up, and royal agents fanned out to scour the countryside for fugitives and for deportees who had sneaked back in to Spain after being expelled. On February 20, 1614, the count of Salazar, who had been entrusted by Felipe III with the responsibility for carrying out the policy, reported that his mission was complete. Nine hundred and three years after Tariq ibn Ziyad had landed at Gibraltar, the age of Islam in Spain had come to an end.

The scale of this undertaking and the human suffering it entailed are difficult to appreciate. In total, some 320,000 individuals were deported, embodying emotions ranging from regret to resignation, to hatred, to sadness. After suffering the immediate loss of most of their property, they were subjected to the repeated abuses of bandits, officials, and opportunists as they made their way, disoriented and traumatized, across inhospitable land and treacherous sea into exile. Whole villages were uprooted and neighborhoods emptied. People

The Expulsion from the Port of Denia (Vicent Mostre, 1613). *Auraco.org (Fundació Bancaja, València)*

whose ancestors had never known any other homeland were thrust into exile in foreign lands where they did not speak the language or understand the culture, and where they were rarely welcome.

From the point of view of the North Africans among whom most of them landed, any such influx of refugees would have been threatening and unwelcome. Moreover, in the eyes of many Muslims, the Moriscos were foreigners, infidels, and apostates: "Christians of Castile" who did not deserve mercy, charity, or consideration. These feelings would have been reciprocated by those Moriscos who were convinced Christians. There was considerable resistance, sometimes violent, to the arrival of the refugees in some areas, and Moriscos were at times forced to fight for their survival or face death.

But there were also displays of compassion and solidarity, both in Spain and in the lands of exile. Many Old Christians behaved with honor and compassion, helping their Morisco neighbors dispose of their properties, some even continuing their friendships by corre-spondence after the deportations were complete. Bishops and lords sought to intervene to save their tenants and subjects, fiercely defend-ing them as loyal subjects and good Christians, but to little avail. Officially, almost no exceptions were made. Some of the aristocratic Morisco families were given leave to stay, as were the slaves of Chris-tian masters and recently converted North African renegades, but few others. Nevertheless, many individuals, and some entire communi-ties, were able to either evade the official dragnet or return secretly in the years that followed.

The transition to exile was also facilitated by the Morisco elite, who in the years previous to the edict had built up networks of con-tacts in the Maghrib, Ifriqiya, and the Ottoman East. Here, they used their influence to protect their countrymen and preserve the "nation" of al-Andalus. Exiled Andalusis were particularly welcome in Otto-man territories, both in Tunis and the east. Here, the divide-and-rule strategy of the sultans depended on having an array of distinct eth-noreligious communities, so the Moriscos were a valuable addition to the mix for the sultans. And in Morocco, the Sa'di regime welcomed the exiles as soldiers to support it in its wars against the rebellious Berber tribes of the interior. Eventually, these Moriscos revolted against their Sa'di overlords and seized the port city of Salé, which they then established as an independent republic. From here they waged jihad in the form of piracy on Spanish shipping for much of the seventeenth century.

Some Moriscos could not bear their exile and sneaked back into Spain, where they lived as permanent fugitives or were arrested and either executed or sent into exile again. A group from the Valley of Ricote, near Murcia, which was the final locale in Spain to be evacu-ated, returned to their villages and set fire to the local archives, hop-ing to avoid expulsion by destroying any evidence of who precisely they were. But to no avail. It is no accident that the Morisco encoun-tered in Don Quixote is named Ricote. Having gone off to exile in Augsberg—that model of Early Modern diversity—Cervantes's Ric-ote, once a prosperous shopkeeper, slips back into Spain disguised as a pilgrim as he searches for his daughter, Ana Félix, and his wife, who have been deported to Algeria. It is here he bumps into his old friend, Sancho Panza. As the two sit down to a meal of ham and wine, Ricote regretfully contemplates his own fate and that of his fellow country- men. Most of these were Christians descended from Muslims de- scended from Christians, who had lived in their lands since before the time of the Romans, before the birth of Christ, and, therefore, long before the arrival of the foreign Hapsburg kings who would eventu- ally condemn them to exile.

I think it was a divine inspiration that prompted his Majesty to put in effect such an elegant solution; not that we were all guilty, since some were steadfast Christians; but they were so few that they couldn't stand up against those who were not. . . . In the end, it was with just cause that we were punished with the penalty of exile, gentle and lenient in the eyes of some, but to us the most terrible that we could be given. Wherever we are we weep for Spain; for after all we were born there and it is our native land.[59]

EPILOGUE

Al-Andalus Unmoored

And so it was that over the course of nearly one thousand years, Tariq ibn Ziyad, the valiant Berber conqueror, was transformed into Ricote, the skulking Spanish exile, and the Muslim presence that had transformed the peninsula came to an end with the forced exile of the Moriscos of 1609 to 1614. But the expulsions did not, of course, mark the end of the peninsula's engagement with Islam, which continues to this day. Almost two million Muslims live in Spain today: some native converts but most of North African origin, many who are completely integrated in Spanish urban society and many others who labor in the fields picking fruit or in other menial tasks. Intrepid North Africans still cross the strait, but now as economic refugees, not warriors, and in flimsy *pateras*, not war galleys. And the memory of al-Andalus continues to loom large—a lost paradise, symbolized by the profaned magnificient mosque of Córdoba and the magnificent palace of the Alhambra.

The history of al-Andalus is not one of a foreign occupation. It is not an anomaly, nor is it an exception. It represents, rather, an integral part of the historical process that created not only modern Spain and Portugal but modern Europe as well. The history of al-Andalus is European history, but also Islamic history and Jewish history. Islam, Christianity, and Judaism do not represent three independent civilizations. They are

all inextricably linked elements, or dimensions, of the larger venture
we call "the West"—the product of the ancient Near East and Hebrew,
Greek, Persian, and Roman influences that combined in the Mediterranean over the course of the last few thousand years, drawing in peoples
and cultures from Africa, Europe, western Asia, and beyond.

Al-Andalus and the Christian Spains that subsumed it occupy a
central place in this historical process. Chronologically, the era of
Islamic Spain bridges Late Antiquity, which saw the decline of the
classical world and the emergence of Abrahamic monotheism, and
the era of Modernity, with its new notions of race, nation, religion,
progress, and knowledge. Geographically, it comprised a hinge between Christendom and the *dar al-Islam*. Creatively, it was the point
where Africa, Europe, and western Asia met, and where the most profound processes of cultural innovation took place; it was the most
important and enduring point of their diffusion. If one takes Islamic
Spain out of the equation, European history simply does not add up.

Looking back on the history of al-Andalus and its interaction with
its Christian neighbors, this appears obvious. From the time the Arab-
led conquerors arrived in Hispania in the early 700s to the time their
descendants were expelled in the 1600s, the political, cultural, and
social history of the region was not characterized by separation or
isolation but by integration and collaboration among Christians, Muslims, and Jews. This is not to say that religious identity was not important or that it did not inform action or shape experience—the often
viscerally hostile rhetoric of religious difference makes this clear. In
fact, it may well have been the single most important element of people's identity. But even so, it was only one factor out of many that
contributed to people's sense of who they were and how they should
interact with others and move in the world.

Much ink has been spilled as to whether al-Andalus was an idyll
of enlightened tolerance and *convivencia* or the arena of a brutal clash
of civilizations. It was neither. Tolerance is hardly regarded as a virtue today, let alone in the Middle Ages, and most of the clashing took
place within, not between, "civilizations." The great cultural historian Amerigo Castro popularized the notion that Medieval Spain was
a land of *convivencia*—of Christians, Muslims, and Jews "living

together." But it is better to think of it as a land of *conveniencia* where members of different ethnic and faith communities "came together" and worked together not in the name of some ideal of tolerance but out of convenience—that is, for their own perceived benefit. Even before Tariq's forces had landed in Hispania, he had come to a political understanding with factions within the Visigothic elite.

Although Christians and Muslims regarded each other's religions as ill-founded, they did not necessarily see them as ill-intentioned, and they understood that they all worshipped the same God. The Christians, Muslims, and Jews who lived around the Mediterranean all shared in a common culture grounded in Abrahamic monotheism, Persian and Greek learning, Roman institutions, Egyptian esotericism, a common sense of history, and folk traditions and cultural mores that had developed as a consequence of thousands of years of trade, migration, conquest, and colonization involving peoples living around the sea and beyond. They moved in an environment of "mutual intelligibility," which enabled them to find common ground despite whatever differences they had, and which made it possible for them not only to communicate but to adapt and appropriate each other's cultures.

And they were driven to do this out of necessity. In the complex and diverse environment of al-Andalus and the Mediterranean, the exercise of power was facilitated not by eliminating one's enemies but by co-opting them. Al-Andalus was successfully established because its Arab Muslim overlords were able to obtain the collaboration of the Visigothic nobility and the church, to give them a formally legitimate place within their new society, and to integrate them in their political project. Once they forced the natives into submission, the conquerors were able to "win their hearts and minds."

The same can be said for the Christian princes, who four hundred years later in their era of conquest subjugated and integrated Muslim minorities in their new kingdoms. This was not done out of a sense of magnanimity or solidarity, but out of necessity—the conquerors needed their subject minorities to maintain their prosperity, and the subject minorities needed to come to accommodation with their new rulers in order to survive. The principle operating here was pragmatism. Once these relationships were established, they would be periodically renegotiated, and as long as the subject communities were regarded as useful and nonthreatening, their rights would be respected. When that ceased to be the case, repression was all but inevitable.

In any case, the individuals who inhabited al-Andalus and the Spanish kingdoms that succeeded it did not see themselves only as Christians, Muslims, and Jews. They were members of ethnic communities and social classes; they were inhabitants of neighborhoods, towns, and regions; they were practitioners of crafts, trades, and vocations; they had common spiritual, intellectual, and philosophical inclinations; and they were men and women—modes of identity that crossed confessional lines. As a result, although religious identity may have framed their experience and the formal laws under which they lived, it did not determine how they saw the world in every circumstance, or who they saw as either enemies or allies. People embodied all sorts of social identities simultaneously, and the fact that many of these crossed religious lines engendered social solidarities that helped sustain diversity.

Freud conceived of the human mind as comprising three elements: the superego, the ego, and the id. The ego is the aspect of our intellect that gets things done, that observes our surroundings, assesses our options, and executes a plan of action designed to accomplish goals that we feel will give us concrete benefits. The id represents our unbridled libido and our intuitive desires, unconstrained by conscience or consideration. And the superego *is* that conscience, the policeman of our personality, which tells us what we should do and how we should understand the world around us. Formal religious identity is analogous to the superego. But, although we may aspire to follow the dictates of our conscience, we rarely do. For the most part, we are led by our ego, which inhibits our baser urges but also suppresses our higher ideals and thus enables us to obtain the practical outcomes we need to survive and prosper.

And this is how religion functioned in the social and political landscape of al-Andalus. The principalities of Islamic and Christian Spain in the Middle Ages were "kingdoms of faith" in a very real sense. Religious identity framed their institutions and provided a foundation for their laws and guidelines for policy. But this did not necessarily translate into political action. Rather, the practical demands of political survival meant that as often as not, policy ran contrary to the very precepts these formal ideologies espoused. Muslim kingdoms regularly allied with Christian kingdoms to attack fellow Muslims and vice versa on the basis of expediency, affinity, or mere circumstance. And religion functions analogously on an individual level. Even deeply pious individuals often do things that defy the moral mandates of their faith, either for some material reward or for no other reason than because it gives them pleasure. This does not necessarily diminish them or their ideology, it simply makes them human.

So, if one thing emerges out of the history of al-Andalus, it is the complexity and ambivalence of the individuals who inhabited it, the individuals who, however strong their faith, were not merely "Christians," "Muslims," and "Jews," but people. Consequently, this is a history of faith, curiosity, generosity, and creative spirit, but also of violence, pettiness, cruelty, greed, and hypocrisy. Arab al-Andalus was no Shangri-La of open-minded tolerance, nor were the Christians and Berbers who destroyed it barbarous philistines. There were no "good guys" and no "bad guys" on the civilization level, and few on the individual level. Power is ugly and violence inevitable. There are no moral lessons to be learned here.

But there is a social lesson, perhaps. And that is that differing religious ideologies and cultural orientations are not necessarily impediments to mutual respect or mutually beneficial collaboration. People of diverse origins, affiliations, and brands of conscience can not only cooperate but even embrace their differences if they do not feel threatened by one another—as long as they believe that their goals overlap and complement each other, and as long as they are willing to set aside their own moral presumptions and regard each other's beliefs as well-intentioned, even if mistaken. We have tended to look at the history of Muslim and Christian Spain as nine hundred years of unremitting conflict caused by religious difference, but in fact, it can be seen as nine hundred years of creative engagement that took place despite religious difference. And that, if nothing else, should be enough to give us all some small measure of faith.

Acknowledgments

I would not have been able to complete this book without the help and support of family, friends, and colleagues. Thanks are due first to Núria Silleras-Fernández for her love, patience, and advice; she and our children, Alexandra and Raymond, suffered along with me as I grappled, once again, with a project that turned out to be far more complex than it seemed at first blush. Thanks also to Dan Green, peerless mentor and agent extraordinaire, who suggested I take this on, and to my editor, Dan Gerstle, for advocating for the project; for suffering through delays, drafts, and dross; and for his careful reading and skillful editing. Theresa Winchell's exact and sensitive copyediting smoothed out the many bumps in my prose. A number of friends and colleagues, including Núria Silleras, Sharon Kinoshita, Thomas F. Glick, Maribel Fierro, Alejandro García Sanjuán, David Wacks, Francisco Vidal Castro, and Gerard Wiegers, carefully read through early drafts and offered suggestions and corrections, thereby greatly improving the book and saving me considerable embarrassment. Needless to say, any errors that remain are entirely my responsibility. Special gratitude is due to Roser Salicrú i Lluch, whose project "La Corona catalanoaragonesa, l'Islam i el món mediterrani" I have the honor of being a member of, and who has graciously hosted me during my annual sojourns at the Institució Milà i Fontanals in Barcelona.* In more general terms, I thank the core group and participants of the Mediterranean Seminar workshops—"Club Med"—who have continued to inspire and educate me, as well as my colleagues at the University of Colorado and the University of California, and many others too numerous to be named here. Finally, this book is a legacy of the inspiration and generosity of my dear friend and teacher, Wadjih F. al-Hamwi—of a singular Aleppo that now sadly exists only in memories.

---

*Grup de Recerca Consolidat per la Generalitat de Catalunya CAIMMed (La Corona catalanoaragonesa, l'Islam i el món mediterrani, 2014 SGR 1559).

I received the support of many institutions while working on this project, first and foremost the University of Colorado Boulder, whose capable and tireless library staff I am sure I drove to exhaustion, and the Institució Milà i Fontanals of the Consejo Superior de Investigaciones Científicas, which has generously provided me with library access and a place to work each summer. A Faculty Research Fellowship from the National Endowment for the Humanities provided me with much-needed time to carry out research. The illustrations were paid for with the generous support of a Kayden Research Grant from the University of Colorado.

Finally, these acknowledgments would not be complete without recognizing the tremendous work of the many historians upon whose work this present study is based. As scholars, we are always standing on the shoulders of giants, nowhere more so than in my case with this book.

Umayyad Amirs and Caliphs of Córdoba

Amirs of Córdoba

'Abd al-Rahman I al-Dhakil "the Falcon of the Quraysh" (756–788)

Hisham I ibn 'Abd al-Rahman (788–796)

al-Hakam I ibn Hisham (796–822)

'Abd al-Rahman II ibn al-Hakam (822–852)

Muhammad I ibn 'Abd al-Rahman II (852–886)

al-Mundhir ibn Muhammad (886–888)

'Abd Allah ibn Muhammad (888–912)

'Abd al-Rahman III ibn Muhammad ibn 'Abd Allah (912–929)

Caliphs of Córdoba

'Abd al-Rahman III ibn Muhammad ibn 'Abd Allah al-Nasir li-Din Allah (929–961)

al-Hakam II ibn 'Abd al-Rahman (961–976)
 Muhammad ibn Abi 'Amir al-Mansur (981–1002)[a]

Hisham II ibn al-Hakam (976–1009)
 'Abd al-Malik ibn Muhammad ibn Abi 'Amir al-Muzaffar (1002–1008)[a]
 'Abd al-Rahman ibn Muhammad ibn Abi 'Amir "Shanjul/ Sanchuelo" (1008–1009)[a]

---

[a] 'Amirid *hajib*.

The Post-*FITNA* Caliphs

Muhammad II ibn Hashim al-Mahdi (1009)

Hisham ibn Sulayman ibn 'Abd al-Rahman III al-Rashid (1009)[b]

Sulayman ibn al-Hakam b. Sulayman ibn 'Abd al-Rahman III
al-Musta'in (1009)

Hisham II ibn al-Hakam (1010–1113)[c]

Sulayman ibn al-Hakam b. Sulayman ibn 'Abd al-Rahman III
al-Musta'in (1013)

'Ali ibn Hammud (1016–1018)[d]

'Abd al-Rahman IV ibn Muhammad ibn 'Abd al-Malik
ibn 'Abd al-Rahman III al-Murtada (1018)[e]

al-Qasim ibn Hammud al-Nasir li-Din Allah (1018–1021)[d]

Yahya ibn 'Ali ibn Hammud (1021–1022)[d,f]

al-Qasim ibn Hammud al-Nasir li-Din Allah (1023)[d]

'Abd al-Rahman V ibn Hisham ibn 'Abd al-Jabbar al-Mustazhir
(1023–1024)

Muhammad III ibn 'Abd al-Rahman ibn 'Ubayd Allah ibn 'Abd
al-Rahman III al-Mustakfi (1024–1025)

Hisham III ibn Muhammad ibn 'Abd al-Malik ibn 'Abd al-Rahman III
al-Mu'tadd (1027–1031; d. 1036)

Pseudo-Hisham II (1035–1044/1060/1083)[g]

For lists of the rulers of the various *taifa* kingdoms, see Wasserstein,
The Rise and Fall of the Party-Kings, 83–98.

---

[b] Candidate supported by Berber mercenaries.

[c] Hisham II was said to have been killed in 1009; this Hisham may have
been Hisham II, an imposter, or pure fiction.

[d] Hammudid caliph.

[e] Candidate supported by Khayran, *Saqaliba* king of Denia.

[f] Málaga only from 1022–1035. His successors reigned here until 1057.

[g] An imposter sponsored by the 'Abbadids of Seville. In 1060, they claimed
he had, in fact, died in 1044, but his name continued to appear on coinage
in other *taifa* kingdoms until 1083.

Nasrid Sultans and Notable Figures

Names and dates in bold indicate the first reign of a sultan who ruled multiple times.

Muhammad al-Ahmar I "al-Shaykh" (1232–1273)

Muhammad II ibn Muhammad I "al-Faqih" (1273–1302)

Muhammad III ibn Muhammad II (1302–1309)
>Abu 'Abd Allah (*wazir*)

Nasr ibn Muhammad II (1309–1314)
>Shams al-Duha (*umm walad*)
>'Atiq ibn al-Mawl (*wazir*)
>Muhammad ibn al-Hajj (*wazir*)

Isma'il I ibn Abu Sa'id Faraj (1314–1325)[a]
>Fatima bint Muhammad II "Bint al-Ahmar" (queen mother)

Muhammad IV ibn Isma'il I (1325–1333)
>Muhammad ibn al-Mahruq (*wazir*)
>Abu Nu'aym Ridwan (*wazir*)
>Fatima bint Muhammad II "Bint al-Ahmar" (dowager queen mother)

Yusuf I ibn Isma'il I (1333–1354)
>Abu Nu'aym Ridwan (*hajib*)
>Fatima bint Muhammad II "Bint al-Ahmar" (dowager queen mother)

---

[a] Abu Sa'id Faraj was a paternal nephew of Muhammad I.

Muhammad V ibn Yusuf I al-Ghani bi-Llah (1354–1359)
Abu Nu'aym Ridwan (*hajib*)
Lisan al-Din Muhammad ibn al-Khatib (*wazir*)

Isma'il II ibn Yusuf I (1359–1360)
Rim (*umm walad*)

Muhammad VI ibn Isma'il al-Ghalib bi'-Llah "El Bermejo"/
"the Red Head" (1360–1362)

Muhammad V ibn Yusuf I al-Ghani bi-Llah (1362–1391)
Lisan al-Din Muhammad ibn al-Khatib (*wazir*)
Muhammad ibn Zamrak (*wazir*)

Yusuf II ibn Muhammad V (1391–1392)[b]

Muhammad VII ibn Yusuf II (1392–1408)

Yusuf III ibn Yusuf II (1408–1417)

Muhammad VIII ibn Yusuf III al-Saghir/"the Little One" (1417–1419)
'Ali al-'Amin (*wazir*/regent)

Muhammad IX ibn Nasr ibn Muhammad V al-'Aysar/"Lefty" (1419–1427)
Zahr al-Riyadh (queen)
Yusuf ibn al-Sarraj (*wazir*)

Muhammad VIII ibn Yusuf III al-Saghir/"the Little One" (1427–1430)
Ridwan Bannigash (*wazir*)

Muhammad IX ibn Nasr ibn Muhammad V al-'Aysar/"Lefty"
(1430–1431)
Yusuf ibn al-Sarraj (*wazir*)

Yusuf IV ibn Muhammad ibn al-Mawl "Abenalmao/Abenámar" (1432)[c]

Muhammad IX ibn Nasr ibn Muhammad V al-'Aysar/"Lefty"
(1432–1445)

---

[b] Yusuf II's mother was a paternal granddaughter of Isma'il I.
[c] Yusuf IV's mother was a daughter of Muhammad VI.

Yusuf V ibn Ahmad ibn Muhammad V "El Cojo"/"the Lame"
(1445–1446)[d]

Isma'il III ibn Yusuf II (1446–1447)

Muhammad IX ibn Nasr ibn Muhammad V al-'Aysar/"Lefty"
(1447–1453)

**Muhammad X ibn Muhammad VIII "El Chiquito"/"the Little
Boy" (1453–1454)**
    Umm al-Fath (wife)[e]

Sa'd ibn 'Ali ibn Yusuf II (1454–1455)
    Abu Surrur al-Mufarrij
    Yusuf ibn al-Sarraj (*wazir*)

Muhammad X ibn Muhammad VIII "El Chiquito"/"the Little Boy"
(1455)

Sa'd ibn 'Ali ibn Yusuf II (1455–1462)

Isma'il IV (1462–1463)[f]

Sa'd ibn 'Ali ibn Yusuf II (1463–1464)
    Abu 'l-Qasim ibn Bannigash (*wazir*)

Abu 'l-Hasan 'Ali ibn Sa'd "Muley Hacén" (1464–1482)
    'Aisha/Fatima (wife)
    Turaya/Isabel de Solís (wife)

Muhammad XI Abu 'l-Hasan 'Ali "Boabdil" (1482–1483)
    'Aisha/Fatima (queen mother)

Abu 'l-Hasan 'Ali ibn Sa'd "Muley Hacén" (1483–1485)

Muhammad XII ibn Sa'd al-Zaghal (1485–1487)

Muhammad XI Abu 'l-Hasan 'Ali "Boabdil" (1487–1492)
    'Aisha/Fatima (queen mother)

---

[d] His mother, Fatima, was the daughter of Muhammad V.
[e] Umm al-Fath was the daughter of Muhammad IX and Zahr al-Riyadh.
[f] Isma'il IV has not been definitely identified; it is only certain that he was a member of the Nasrid family.

Notes

1. Ibn-al-Qutiya, *Tarīkh iftitah*, 47. For the English, see James, *Early Islamic Spain*, 69.

2. Wolf, *Conquerors and Chroniclers*, 166.

3. James, *A History of Early al-Andalus*, 111.

4. Sobh, "'Abd al-Raḥmān I," 45.

5. Safran, *The Second Umayyad Caliphate*, 177.

6. López, "El conde de los Cristianos," 181.

7. Stanzas 156–176, in Brault, *The Song of Roland*, 129–147.

8. Seco de Lucena and Qalqashandī, "Un tradado árabe," 117.

9. Noble, *Charlemagne and Louis the Pious*, 30.

10. Ibid., 98–99.

11. Verlinden, "Les Radaniya," 110.

12. James, *Early Islamic Spain*, 100. This is a free adaptation.

13. Vallvé, "Abd ar-Rahmān II," 109.

14. Wilson, *Hrotsvit of Gandersheim*, 29.

15. Safran, *The Second Umayyad Caliphate*, 1.

16. Wilson, *Hrotsvit of Gandersheim*, 29.

17. Fierro Bello, *'Abd al-Rahman III*, 1.

18. Brann, "Andalusi 'Exceptionalism,'" 128–129.

19. Smith, *Christians and Moors*, vol. 1, 62–75.

20. Margoliouth, *The Irshad*, vol. 2, 67.

21. Cohen, *A Critical Edition*, 67.

22. Barton, *Conquerors, Brides, and Concubines*, 42.

23. Pérez de Úrbel, *Historia Silense*, 176.

24. Kassis, "Muslim Revival," 82.

25. Franzen, *Poems of Arab Andalusia*, 90.

26. Constable, *Medieval Iberia*, 99.

27. Tibi, *The Tibyān*, 90.

28. Ibid.

29. Dunlop, "A Christian Mission," 288.

30. Catlos, *The Victors and the Vanquished*, 60.

31. Ibn Sa'id, *al-Mughrib*, vol. 2, 436–438.

32. Dunlop, "A Christian Mission," 263.

33. Viguera Molíns, "La Taifa de Toledo," 59.

34. Gayangos, *The History*, vol. 2, 273.

35. El Allaoui, "Les échanges," 265.

36. Kennedy, *Muslim Spain and Portugal*, 158.

37. From "Until When in Exile?" in Masarwah and Tarabieh, "Longing for Granada," 314–315.

38. Nickson, "'Sovereignty Belongs to God,'" 846.

39. "The Latin Chronicle of the Kings of Castile," in Brea et al., *Crónicas hispanas*, 76.

40. Ibn Khaldun, *The Muqaddimah*, vol. 1, 315–316.

41. Huíci Miranda, *Al-bayan al-Mugrib*, vol. 2, 187.

42. Ebied and Young, "Abu 'L-Baqa' al-Rundi," 34.

43. Bennison, "Liminal States," 15.

44. Boloix Gallardo, "Mujer y poder," 288.

45. García Gómez, *Cinco poetas musulmanes*, 246.

46. Harvey, *Islamic Spain*, 221.

47. Arié, *El reino naṣrí*, 229.

48. Foster et al., eds., *Spanish Literature*, 122.

49. Szpiech, "Granada," vol. 2, 161.

50. Arié, *El reino naṣrí*, 98.

51. Perceval Verde, "Asco y asquerosidad," 23.

52. Münzer, *Viaje por España y Portugal*, 120–123.

53. After Catlos, *Muslims of Medieval Latin Christendom*, 226, 289.

54. Núñez Muley, *A Memorandum*, 81.

55. García-Arenal, *Los Moriscos*, 139.

56. Ibid., 223.

57. Acosta Montoro, *Aben Humeya*, 121–129.

58. Soyer, "'It Is Not Possible,'" 88.

59. Cervantes Saavedra, *Don Quijote*, vol. 2, 461.

GLOSSARY

The following is a list of Arabic words, names, and other non-English terms that appear in the text. A simplified form of Arabic transliteration has been employed. Plurals of Arabic words are sometimes given in Arabic, particularly when referring generically to a group, although English-style plurals (with an added *s*) are sometimes used, particularly when referring to individuals (e.g., those two *faqihs* are members of the *fuqaha'*).

'Abbadids (Ar.: Banu 'Abbad): Arab-Andalusi *taifa* dynasty that ruled Seville, 1023–1091.

'Abbasids (Ar.: Banu 'l-'Abbas): Caliphal dynasty descended from Muhammad's uncle, al-'Abbas; overthrew the Umayyad dynasty in 750 and ruled from its capital at Baghdad until 1258.

Abencerrajes (Sp.): see Sarraj, Banu 'l-.

Abi 'l-'Ula, Banu (Ar.): Family of Marinid princes, and rivals of the Banu Rahhu for control of the Nasrid *ghuzat* in the thirteenth and fourteenth centuries.

adab **(Ar.):** Refined high culture.

Aftasids (Ar.: Banu 'l-Aftas): Family of Berber origin that ruled the *taifa* of Badajoz (and briefly, Toledo), ca. 1022–1095.

Aghlabids (Ar.: Banu Aghlab): An independent dynasty that governed Ifriqiya in the ninth century in the name of the 'Abbasids.

al-Ahmar, Banu: See Nasrids.

al-Andalus: Arabic term for the Iberian Peninsula, particularly those parts under Islamic rule.

alfaquí **(Sp.; pl.: *alfaquíes,* from Ar.: *al-faqih*):** A magistrate and official of the *mudéjar* communities of the Christian kingdom of Granada.

'alim **(Ar.; pl.: *'ulama'*):** A learned person (normally in reference to knowledge of Islam).

Aljamiado (Sp.): A hybrid literary language current from the late fifteenth to the early seventeenth century in which Romance vernaculars are written using the Andalusi Arabic alphabet.

Almohads (Ar.: *al-Muwahiddun*): "Monotheists" or "Unitarians"; insurgent religio-political movement founded by Ibn Tumart in 1023 that overthrew the Almoravids and ruled most of al-Andalus, ca. 1147–1228.

Almoravids (Ar.: *al-Murabitun*): Movement of Lamtuna tribesmen (belonging to the Sanhaja nation), who conquered al-Andalus in the 1090s and ruled there until overthrown by the Almohads, beginning ca. 1147.

Alpujarras: A region on the southern slopes of the Sierra Nevada.

Amazigh: Proper name for the ethnolinguistic group commonly referred to as "Berbers."

amir **(Ar.):** "Prince," commander, or ruler.

'Amirids (Ar.: Banu 'Amir): The dynasty of *hajib*s of the Umayyad caliphs of Córdoba founded by Muhammad ibn Abi 'Amir al-Mansur. They ruled in Córdoba to 1009, and then briefly in Valencia and Denia.

'amma **(Ar.):** Common folk.

Andalusi (Ar.): An inhabitant of al-Andalus, particularly a Muslim of indigenous family origin; also the particular Islamicate culture of al-Andalus, or its attributes.

Ashqilula, Banu (Ar.): *Muwallad* family; early supporters and rivals of the Nasrids.

baladi **(Ar.; pl.: *baladiyyun*):** "Of the land"; the early Arabic settlers of al-Andalus.

Bannigash, Banu (Ar.): Powerful family in fifteenth-century Nasrid Granada, descended from Ridwan Bannigash, who was said to have been the captured son of the noble Christian Venegas family; rivals of the Banu 'l-Sarraj.

Banu (Ar.): Literally, "sons of," but refers to a clan, tribe, or lineage.

Berber: Indigenous North African ethnolinguistic group consisting of several large tribal nations, including the Sanhaja and Zanata. See Amazigh.

bint **(Ar.):** Daughter (of).

caliph: From *khalifa* (Ar.: "successor"), the head of the Islamic community.

Carolingians: Dynasty of Frankish kings and Holy Roman Emperors of the ninth and tenth centuries. Founded by Charlemagne.

Cluny: Abbey in Burgundy that, as the head abbey of the Cluniac Order, spearheaded church reform in the eleventh and twelfth centuries.

Companions (of the Prophet): Early converts to Islam who knew Muhammad personally.

converso **(Sp.):** A convert to Christianity; normally applied to former Jews and their descendants.

convivencia **(Sp.):** "Living together"; a term used to describe the more peaceful interaction of Christians, Muslims, and Jews in the Iberian peninsula.

cortes **(Sp.):** A gathering of the estates; a parliament.

dar al-harb **(Ar.):** The world or abode of war; that is, the non-Muslim world.

dar al-Islam **(Ar.):** The world or abode of Islam; that is, the Islamic world.

dhimmi **(Ar.; pl.: *dhimmiyyun*)**: A non-Muslim living under *dhimma*, the "pact of protection."

Dhu' l-Nunids (Ar.: Banu Dhi 'l-Nun): Clan of early Berber settlers who eventually ruled the *taifa* of Toledo (1032–1085), and briefly, Valencia.

dhu 'l-wizaratayn **(Ar.):** The holder of two wazirates (i.e., with civil and military authority).

dinar **(Ar.):** A gold coin modeled on the Roman *denarius*, or shilling, minted across the Islamic world.

dirham **(Ar.):** A silver coin, modeled on the Sassanian *drahm*, minted across the Islamic world.

elche **(Sp.; from Ar.: *'ilj*)**: A Christian taken captive by Muslims who converted to Islam.

fals **(Ar.; pl.: *fulus*)**: A low-value coin, analogous to the penny; usually of copper.

faqih **(Ar.; pl.: *fuqaha'*)**: An expert in *fiqh*.

Fatimids: Dynasty of Shi'i caliphs, based first in Ifriqiya, then Egypt from 909 to 1121.

fatwa **(Ar.):** A *responsum*, or legal opinion, on a real or imagined civil or religious legal dilemma, promulgated by a *mufti*.

fiqh **(Ar.):** Islamic jurisprudence.

fitna **(Ar.):** Strife, disorder, civil war.

Ghaniya, Banu (Ar.): Branch of the Banu Mu'min who briefly governed Seville, and ruled over Mallorca and, subsequently, parts of Ifriqiya.

ghuzat **(Ar.):** "Raiders"; refers to North African *mujahidun*, or "Volunteers of the Faith," in the Nasrid period.

hadith **(Ar.):** A deed or saying ascribed to Muhammad or other important early Muslims; widely regarded as one of the foundations of Islamic law.

Hafsids (Ar.: Banu Hafs): Almohad governors of Tunis who established an independent dynasty in the 1200s, maintaining Almohad *tawhid* and eventually taking the title of caliph. The dynasty survived to 1569.

hajib **(Ar.):** A royal chamberlain.

hajj **(Ar.):** The pilgrimage to Mecca.

Hakim, Banu 'l- (Ar.): Arab Andalusi family from Seville who dominated Ronda in the Nasrid period.

Hammudids (Ar.: Banu Hammud): Branch of the Idrisid family who ruled over part of the Maghrib and southern al-Andalus in the early eleventh century and briefly claimed the title of caliph.

Hapsburgs: German royal family that held the title of Holy Roman Emperor from 1438 to 1750. Ruled Castile from 1506 to 1700, the Crown of Aragon and Navarre from 1516 to 1700, and Portugal from 1581 to 1640.

hijra **(Ar.):** The migration; marks the beginning of the Islamic era.

Hudids (Ar.: Banu Hud): Family of Arab descent who displaced the Tujibids as rulers of the *taifas* of Zaragoza and Lleida from 1039 to 1110; also briefly ruled over Denia and Tortosa.

'Ibadi (Ar.: *al-'Ibadiyya*): A branch of Shi'i-inflected Kharijism popular in the Maghrib.

ibn **(Ar.):** Son (of).

'Id al-Fitr: One of the main holidays of the Islamic month of Ramadan.

Idrisids (Banu Idris): Clan descended from 'Ali ibn Abi Talib (the son-in-law and cousin of Muhammad), who ruled over parts of the Maghrib in the ninth and tenth centuries. See also Hammudids.

Ifriqiya (Ar.): The former Roman province of "Africa," corresponding to modern Tunisia, western Libya, and eastern Algeria.

imam **(Ar.):** One who leads prayers; or, the religious head of the Islamic community.

infante/infanta **(Sp.):** A prince/princess.

jihad **(Ar.):** Moral struggle, including (but not limited to) warfare in the service of Islam.

jizya **(Ar.):** A poll tax paid by *dhimmis* to the Muslim community on the rationale that non-Muslims were not required to render military service. Some held it to be emblematic of the *dhimmis'* secondary status and a means of reinforcing their humiliation.

jubba **(Ar.):** An ankle-length robe.

jund **(Ar.):** Army, particularly, the clan-based Arab forces of the early caliphal era, or in later periods, forces levied from the general populace. A *jundi* is a member of the *jund*.

katib **(Ar.; pl.: *kuttab*):** A scribe, or secretary.

Kharijites (Ar.: *al-Khawarij*): "Splitters"; a sect of scriptural literalists that originated at the Battle of Siffin in 657 by those who abandoned 'Ali's army and rejected the institution of the caliphate.

kharja **(Ar.):** The final couplet in a *muwashshah* poem, often written in Romance or colloquial Arabic.

khassa **(Ar.):** The aristocracy.

khutba **(Ar.):** In Islam, the sermon delivered at Friday prayer.

kufr **(Ar.):** "Unbelief."

madrasa **(Ar.):** A religious academy.

Maghrib (Ar.: al-Maghrib): "The West"; northwest Africa, corresponding roughly to modern Morocco and western Algeria.

al-Mahdi **(Ar.):** "The rightly-guided one"; a messianic figure expected to appear at the time of the Last Judgment, and particularly important in Shi'i traditions.

makhzan **(Ar.):** A "treasure chest," or "storehouse"; the term used by the Almohads and the Marinids for their state, as opposed to *dawla*, or "dynasty."

malik **(Ar.):** King.

Maliki (Ar.): One of the four schools of Islamic law recognized as orthodox in the Middle Ages; founded in Medina by Malik ibn Anas in the late eighth century.

maqamat **(Ar.):** A frame tale, or narrative in which stories are told from within stories.

Marinids (Ar.: Banu Marin): Zanata Berber dynasty that succeeded the Mu'minids as rulers of the Maghrib from 1255 to 1465.

Marwanids (Ar.: Banu Marwan): The branch of the Umayyad family that dominated Damascus from 684 to 750 and ruled in al-Andalus from 756 until the fall of the caliphate of Córdoba.

Mawl, Banu (Ar.): Powerful family of wazirs in Nasrid Granada, who married into the royal family and into the Banù Bannigash; rivals of the Banu 'l-Sarraj.

mawla **(Ar.; pl.: *mawali*):** A client or subordinate associate of a powerful patron.

mawlid **(Ar.):** The holiday marking the anniversary of the birth of the Prophet Muhammad.

Moor/Moorish: Antiquated and racist-tinged term for Andalusis.

Morisco (Sp.): Term referring to *mudéjares* obliged to convert to Christianity and their descendants.

Mozarab (Sp.; from Ar.: *al-musta'rab*): Term referring to Andalusi Christians who had assimilated Arabo-Islamic culture and mores, particularly those living under Christian dominion.

mudéjar **(Sp.; from Ar.: *al-mudajjan*):** A Muslim living under Christian rule.

muezzin (from the Ar.: mu'adhdhan): The person who calls Muslims to pray.

mufti **(Ar.):** A legal authority who promulgates *fatawa*, or *fatwas*.

mujahid **(Ar.; pl.: *mujahidun*):** A practitioner of *jihad*, in the military sense; a "holy warrior."

Mu'minids (Ar.: Banu Mu'min): Dynasty of caliphs (1130–1269) founded by 'Abd al-Mu'min, an Arabized Zanata Berber who succeeded Ibn Tumart as leader of the Almohad movement. See Almohads.

muwallad **(Ar.; pl.: *muwalladun*):** A convert or descendant of converted Christians of al-Andalus.

muwashshah **(Ar.):** A genre of usually secularly themed poetry that developed in al-Andalus; characterized by the use of the *kharja*.

nasab **(Ar.):** The genealogical element of Arabic names prefixed by *ibn* ("son of") or *bint* ("daughter of").

Nasrids (Ar.: Banu Nasr, or Banu 'l-Ahmar): Andalusi dynasty that ruled the sultanate of Granada from 1237 to 1492.

New Christian: In the late Middle Ages, a convert to Christianity, or descendant of converts.

Nunids: See Dhu' l-Nunids.

Old Christian: In the late Middle Ages, someone who claimed exclusively Christian ancestry.

Ottomans (Turk: Osmanlı Hanedanı): Turkic dynasty (ca. 1299–1924) of sultans and caliphs that conquered Byzantium in 1453 and ruled over much of the Mediterranean.

parias **(Sp.):** Tributary payments made by Muslim rulers to Christian rulers beginning in the *taifa* period.

People of the Book (Ar.: *ahl al-kitab*): Adherents of revealed, scriptural religions, particularly in the Abrahamic tradition (i.e., Christians and Jews).

qadi **(Ar.; pl.: *qudat*):** An Islamic magistrate.

qadi al-jama'a **(Ar.):** The chief magistrate of a kingdom or city, later known also as *qadi al-qudat*.

qasba **(Ar.):** A citadel, or fortified settlement.

Qasi, Banu (Ar.): Clan of Hispano-Roman origin that dominated the Upper March in the 800s.

qibla **(Ar.):** The direction of prayer (i.e., toward Mecca).

qiyan **(Ar.; sing.: *qayna*):** A female slave trained to sing and educated in *adab*.

qumis **(Ar.):** "Count," from the Latin *comes*. Refers to a Christian official appointed to oversee a Christian community under Andalusi rule.

Rahhu, Banu: Family of Marinid princes, and rivals of the Banu Abi 'l-'Ula for control of the Nasrid *ghuzat* in the thirteenth and fourteenth centuries; also served as mercenaries in the Crown of Aragon.

Ramadan: The Islamic holy month, marked by communal fasting.

Reconquista **(Sp.):** "Reconquest." A term referring to the Christian conquest of al-Andalus, predicated on the incorrect notion of historical continuity from Visigothic Hispania to the Christian principalities of the eighth century and later.

ribat **(Ar.):** A fortress-monastery, usually located on the fringes of the Islamic world, where Muslims could spend a period of time in contemplation and wage military jihad.

Romance: The spoken languages that evolved out of colloquial Latin and emerged as Castilian (Spanish), Catalan, Aragonese, and Galician.

sahib al-madina **(Ar.):** City overseer, or market official.

Sanhaja: One of the two major Berber nations.

Saqaliba **(Ar.; sing.:** *Saqlab***):** "Slav"; a slave of European origin, from either the north of Spain or Eastern Europe; many, but not all, male *Saqaliba* were castrated.

Sarraj, Banu 'l- (Ar.; Sp.: "Abencerrajes"): A powerful noble family of the fifteenth-century Nasrid sultanate.

sayyid **(Ar.; fem.:** *sayyida***):** "Lord," or nobleman; used as a specific designation for members of the Mu'minid dynasty.

"sciences of the ancients": Learning of the pagan classical tradition.

scriptoria **(Lat.; sing.:** *scriptorium***):** A place where manuscripts are copied.

shahada **(Ar.):** The Islamic creed, or profession of faith: "There is no god but God, and Muhammad is the Messenger of God."

Sharq al-Andalus (Ar.): The "East" of al-Andalus: Valencia, Alicante, and environs.

shaykh **(Ar.):** "Elder"; can refer to a leader or other authority.

Shi'a (Ar.): From *shi'at 'Ali*, or "Party of 'Ali"; Islamic tradition that emerged out of those who supported the claims of 'Ali and his descendants to the caliphate.

Sidi Bono, Banu (Ar.): An influential Sufi family from Sharq al-Andalus who migrated to Nasrid Granada.

sikka **(Ar.):** The caliphal prerogative to mint gold coins.

sultan **(Ar.):** "Authority"; referring to secular, typically military, authority.

Sunni (Ar.): "Orthodox"; refers to followers of the *sunna* (or "tradition"); includes the great majority of Muslims in the Middle Ages and today.

Tabi'un **(Ar.):** Companions of the Companions of the Prophet.

taifa **(Ar.):** "Sectarian"; used in reference to the *taifa* kings of the eleventh century, but also the warlords of the post-Almoravid and post-Almohad upheavals.

tawhid **(Ar.):** "Monotheism," particularly the rigorous interpretation of the Alhomads.

thaghr **(Ar.; pl.:** *thughur***):** "Frontier zone," or "March"; used to refer to the three frontier provinces of Umayyad al-Andalus: the Thaghr al-Aqsa ("Furthest"; at Zaragoza), Thaghr al-Awsat ("Middle"; at Toledo), and Thaghr al-Adna ("Lower"; at Mérida, then Badajoz).

tiraz **(Ar.):** Royal silk workshop.

Trastámaras: Castilian dynasty that ruled Castile from 1366 to 1506, and the Crown of Aragon from 1414 to 1516, as well as Navarre, Naples, Sicily, and other Mediterranean territories.

Tujibids (Ar.: Banu Tujib): Arabic clan who served as governors, then as *taifa* kings at Zaragoza from 1009 to 1039.

'ud **(Ar.):** A precursor of the lute, guitar, and other similar stringed instruments.

'ulama' **(Ar.):** See *'alim*.

Umayyads (Ar.: Banu Umayya): Caliphal dynasty descended from the Arabic clan of Umayya ibn 'Abd Shams; triumphed over the forces of 'Ali and ruled from Damascus from 660 to 750; established in al-Andalus in 756 by 'Abd al-Rahman I. See Marwanids.

umma **(Ar.):** "The people"; the collective community of Muslims.

umm walad **(Ar.):** "The mother of a son"; a slave concubine who gives birth to a male heir.

wala **(Ar.):** Clientage; the social mechanism by which powerful Muslims integrated others, particularly new converts, into their networks of patronage and kin.

wazir **(Ar.):** A government minister.

Zahiri (Ar.: *al-Zahriyya***):** A rigorously orthodox school of theology and law, which gained adherents in al-Andalus in the eleventh century.

Zanata: One of the main Berber nations.

zandaqa **(Ar.):** Heresy.

zawiya **(Ar.):** A lodge or convent for Sufis.

Zirids (Ar.: Banu Ziri): Dynasty of Sanhaja Berbers that briefly ruled over Ifriqiya and founded the eleventh-century *taifa* kingdom of Granada from 1013 to 1090. Kin of the Zirids who ruled Ifriqiya from 972 to 1148.

Works Cited

This new synthesis of the history of Islamic Spain is based on an immense amount of secondary research in a variety of fields, including politics, economics, literature, culture, and art history, as well as archaeology. On average well over one hundred articles and chapters, and many books, were reviewed for each chapter—far too many to list here. Many of the publications consulted have been written quite recently, many by scholars who are still in the relatively early stages of their career. Although important and innovative work continues to be carried out in English, the overwhelming majority of the works concerned were in Spanish, Catalan, and French. Because of this new research, much of the older historiography, important as it remains, is now regarded as less dependable and as methodologically antiquated.

For English-only readers looking to delve deeper into the history of al-Andalus and the Muslims of Spain, the works of Thomas F. Glick remain foundational, as do those of L. P. Harvey and Hugh Kennedy (the former for social, cultural, and intellectual history, the latter two for political history). Richard Fletcher has written on a number of related topics in a very accessible style. David Wasserstein is a leading historian for the *taifa* period, while Cynthia Robinson has done innovative work on art and cultural history. Amira K. Bennison's book on the Almoravids and Almohads is the best introduction to the subject written in English. Janina Safran is emerging as a leading English-language historian of the caliphal period. My own *Muslims of Medieval Latin Christendom, ca. 1050–1614* provides the most comprehensive and up-to-date overview of *mudéjar* history. Chapters on various aspects of Andalusi history can be found in *The Legacy of Muslim Spain* (edited by Salma Khadra Jayyusi) and *The Formation of al-Andalus*, Parts I and II (edited by Marín and Fierro, respectively). Standard reference works in English include volume 4 of *The New Cambridge History of Islam* and *The New Cambridge Medieval History*. Many primary sources have been translated, including an antiquated but comprehensive digest of al-Maqqari's encyclopedic *Nafh al-Tib*, edited by Pascual de Gayangos as *The History of the Mohammedan Dynasties in Spain*.

Two of the leading figures in the Spanish historiography of al-Andalus are Maribel Fierro and Mercedes García-Arenal, whose work corresponds roughly to the period up to and including the Almohad period and the period up to the expulsions, respectively. Manuela Marín has published widely on religious culture and gender. Gerard Wiegers of the Netherlands has also worked much on Morisco culture, frequently in collaboration with García-Arenal. María Jesús Viguera Molíns is an authority on the middle period, particularly the *taifa* kingdoms, while Rachid El Hour is a leading specialist on Almoravid Spain. Eduardo Manzano Moreno and Alejandro García Sanjuán have both written prolifically, mostly on the pre-Nasrid era. The French historian Rachel Arié has written the classic works on the Nasrid era, a period that has been significantly reinterpreted by Francisco Vidal Castro. Christophe Picard is an authority on Muslim Portugal and the maritime world of the caliphate. Pierre Guichard, an expert on the Sharq al-Andalus, pioneered the use of sociological and anthropological methodologies in the study of Islamic Spain. The Catalan scholar Roser Salicrú i Lluch is a leading specialist in trade and diplomatic relations, particularly from the perspective of the Crown of Aragon. Most of the above scholars have published at least some work in English. The standard reference work for the history of Spain remains the second edition of the *Historia de España de Menéndez Pidal*.

IT IS SIMPLY impossible to do justice to the multitude of historians who have transformed our understanding of the history of Islamic Spain, and the foregoing list excludes many, both well-known and as yet obscure, who have been pivotal in this process and whose contributions, although uncredited, were indispensable to the writing of this new history of al-Andalus and the Muslims of Spain. For that reason, I have only cited below a few representative works of the scholars referred to above and works that have been quoted directly in the main text. Direct quotations have been translated into English if necessary and sometimes slightly adapted.

Acosta Montoro, José. *Aben Humeya, rey de los Moriscos*. Almería: Instituto de Estudios Almerienses, 1998.

al-Qalqashandi, Aḥmad ibn ʻAli. *Subh al-Aʼsha.* Cairo: al-Muʼassasah al-Miṣriyah, 1963.

Arié, Rachel. *El reino naṣrí de Granada, 1232–1492.* Madrid: MAP-FRE, 1992.

Barton, Simon. *Conquerors, Brides, and Concubines: Interfaith Relations and Social Power in Medieval Iberia.* Philadelphia: University of Pennsylvania Press, 2015.

Bennison, Amira K. "Liminal States: Morocco and the Iberian Frontier Between the Twelfth and Nineteenth Centuries." *The Journal of North African Studies* 6 (2001): 11–28.

——. *The Almoravid and Almohad Empires.* Edinburgh: Edinburgh University Press, 2016.

Boloix Gallardo, Bárbara. "Mujer y poder en el reino nazarí de Granada: La sultana Fāṭima bint al-Aḥmar, la perla central del collar de la dinastía (siglo XIV)." *Anuario de estudios medievales,* 46 (2016): 269–300.

Brann, Ross. "Andalusi ʻExceptionalism.ʼ" In *A Sea of Languages: Rethinking the Arabic Role in Medieval Literary History,* edited by Suzanne Conklin Akbari and Karla Mallette, 128–129. Toronto: University of Toronto Press, 2013.

Brault, Gerard Joseph. *The Song of Roland: An Analytical Edition.* University Park: Pennsylvania State University Press, 1981.

Brea, L. Charlo, Juan A. Estévez Sola, and Rocio Carande Herrero. *Crónicas hispanas del siglo XIII.* Turnhout: Brepols, 2010.

Catlos, Brian A. *Infidel Kings and Unholy Warriors: Faith, Power and Violence in the Age of Crusade and Jihad.* New York: Farrar, Straus & Giroux, 2014.

——. *Muslims of Medieval Latin Christendom, ca. 1050–1614.* Cambridge: Cambridge University Press, 2014.

——. *The Victors and the Vanquished: Christians and Muslims of Catalonia and Aragon, 1050–1300.* Cambridge: Cambridge University Press, 2004.

Cervantes Saavedra, Miguel de. *Don Quijote de la Mancha.* 2 vols. Madrid: Alhambra, 1983.

Cohen, Gerson D. *A Critical Edition with a Translation and Notes of the Book of Tradition: (Sefer Ha-Qabbalah).* London: Routledge & Kegan Paul, 1969.

Constable, Olivia Remie, ed. *Medieval Iberia: Readings from Christian, Muslim, and Jewish Sources.* Philadelphia: University of Pennsylvania Press, 2012.

Dunlop, D. M. "A Christian Mission to Muslim Spain in the Eleventh Century." *Al-Andalus* 17 (1952): 259–310.

Ebied, Rifaat Y., and M. J. L. Young. "Abu 'L-Baqa' al-Rundi and His Elegy on Muslim Spain." *Muslim World* 66 (1976): 29–34.

El Allaoui, Hicham. "Les échanges diplomatiques entre Islam et monde latin." *Oriente moderno* New Series 88, (2008): 249–270.

Fierro Bello, María Isabel (Maribel). *'Abd al-Rahman III: The First Cordoban Caliph*. Oxford: Oneworld, 2005.

——. *The Almohad Revolution: Politics and Religion in the Islamic West During the Twelfth-Thirteenth Centuries*. Farnham, UK: Ashgate, 2012.

——. *The Western Islamic World: Eleventh to Eighteenth Centuries*. Cambridge: Cambridge University Press, 2010.

Fierro Bello, María Isabel, and Julio Samso, eds. *The Formation of al-Andalus, Part 2: Language, Religion, Culture and the Sciences*. Aldershot, UK: Ashgate, 1998.

Fletcher, Richard A. *The Quest for El Cid*. New York: Knopf, 1990.

Foster, David William, Daniel Altamiranda, and Carmen de Urioste, eds. *Spanish Literature: A Collection of Essays*. New York: Garland, 2001.

Franzen, Cola. *Poems of Arab Andalusia*. San Francisco: City Lights Books, 1989.

García-Arenal, Mercedes. *Almohad Revolution and the Mahdi Ibn Tumart*. London: Routledge, 2010.

——. *Los Moriscos*. Granada: Universidad de Granada, 1996.

García-Arenal, Mercedes, and Fernando Rodríguez Mediano. *The Orient in Spain: Converted Muslims, the Forged Lead Books of Granada, and the Rise of Orientalism*. Leiden: Brill, 2013.

García-Arenal, Mercedes, and Gerard Albert Wiegers, eds. *The Expulsion of the Moriscos from Spain: A Mediterranean Diaspora*. Leiden: Brill, 2014.

García Gómez, Emilio. *Cinco poetas musulmanes: Biografías y estudios*. Madrid: Espasa-Calpe, 1959.

García Sanjuán, Alejandro. *Coexistencia y conflictos: Minorías religiosas en la Península Ibérica durante la Edad Media*. Granada: Universidad de Granada, 2015.

——. "Rejecting al-Andalus, Exalting the Reconquista: Historical Memory in Contemporary Spain." *Journal of Medieval Iberian Studies* (2016): 1–19.

Gayangos, Pascual de, trans. *The History of the Mohammedan Dynasties in Spain*. 2 vols. London: Routledge, 2002.

Glick, Thomas F. *From Muslim Fortress to Christian Castle: Social and Cultural Change in Medieval Spain.* Manchester: Manchester University Press, 1995.

——. *Islamic and Christian Spain in the Early Middle Ages.* Princeton, NJ: Princeton University Press, 1979.

Guichard, Pierre. *Al-Andalus, 711–1492: Une histoire de l'Espagne musulmane.* Paris: Hachette littératures, 2001.

——. *From the Arab Conquest to the Reconquest: The Splendour and Fragility of Al-Andalus.* Granada, Spain: Fundación El Legado Andalusí, 2006.

Harvey, L. P. *Islamic Spain, 1250 to 1500.* Chicago: University of Chicago Press, 1990.

——. *Muslims in Spain, 1500 to 1614.* Chicago: University of Chicago Press, 2004.

Historia de España de Menéndez Pidal. 42 vols. Madrid: Espasa Calpe, 1975–2005.

Hourani, George F. "The Early Growth of the Secular Sciences in Andalusia." *Studia Islamica* 32 (1970): 143–156.

Huíci Miranda, Ambrosio. *Al-bayan al-Mugrib.* 2 vols. Tetuan: 1953.

Ibn-al-Qutiya, Muḥammad. *Tarīkh iftitah al-Andalus.* Cairo: Dar al-Kitab al-Misri, 1982.

Ibn Khaldun. *The Muqaddimah: An Introduction to History.* 3 vols. Translated by Franz Rosenthal. London: Routledge & Kegan Paul, 1958.

Ibn Sa'id. *Al-Mug̱hrib fi hula al-Mag̱hrib.* 2 vols. Cairo: Dar al-Ma'arif, 1953.

Irwin, Robert, ed. *The New Cambridge History of Islam.* Vol. 4, *Islamic Cultures and Societies to the End of the Eighteenth Century.* Cambridge: Cambridge University Press, 2010.

James, David. *A History of Early al-Andalus: The Akhbār Majmū'a.* New York: Routledge, 2012.

——. *Early Islamic Spain: The History of Ibn Al-Qūṭīya.* New York: Routledge, 2009.

Jayyusi, Salma Khadra, and Manuela Marín, eds. *The Legacy of Muslim Spain.* Leiden: Brill, 1992.

Kassis, Hanna E. "Muslim Revival in Spain in the Fifth/Eleventh Century: Causes and Ramifications." *Der Islam* 67 (1990): 78–110.

Kennedy, Hugh. *Muslim Spain and Portugal: A Political History of Al-Andalus.* New York: Longman, 1996.

López y López, Ángel Custodio. "El conde de los Cristianos Rabī' Ben Teodulfo, exactor y jefe de la guardia palatina del emir al-Ḥakam I." *Al-Andalus Magreb* 7 (1999): 169–184.

Mann, Vivian B., Thomas F. Glick, and Jerrilynn Denise Dodds. *Convivencia: Jews, Muslims, and Christians in Medieval Spain*. New York: Jewish Museum, 1992.

Manzano Moreno, Eduardo. *Conquistadores, emires y califas: Los Omeyas y la formación de al-Andalus*. Barcelona: Crítica, 2006.

Margoliouth, D. S., ed. *The Irshad al-arib ilā ma'rifat al-adib*. 2 vols. Leiden: Brill, 1909.

Marín, Manuela, ed. *The Formation of al-Andalus, Part 1: History and Society*. Aldershot, UK: Ashgate, 1998.

———. *Mujeres en al-Ándalus*. Madrid: Consejo Superior de Investigaciones Científicas, 2000.

Masarwah, Nader, and Abdallah Tarabieh. "Longing for Granada in Medieval Arabic and Hebrew Poetry." *Al-Masaq* 26 (2014): 299–318.

Münzer, Hieronymus. *Viaje por España y Portugal, 1494–1495*. Translated by Julio López Toro. Madrid: Almenara, 1951.

The New Cambridge Medieval History. 7 vols. Cambridge: Cambridge University Press, 1995–2005.

Nickson, Tom. "'Sovereignty Belongs to God': Text, Ornament and Magic in Islamic and Christian Seville." *Art History* 38 (2015): 838–861.

Noble, Thomas F. X. *Charlemagne and Louis the Pious: The Lives by Einhard, Notker, Ermoldus, Thegan, and the Astronomer*. University Park: Pennsylvania State University Press, 2009.

Núñez Muley, Francisco. *A Memorandum for the President of the Royal Audiencia and Chancery Court of the City and Kingdom of Granada*. Edited and translated by Vincent Barletta. Chicago: University of Chicago Press, 2007.

Perceval Verde, José María. "Asco y asquerosidad del morisco según los apologistas Cristianos del Siglo de Oro." *La Torre* 4 (1990): 21–47.

Pérez de Úrbel, Justo. *Historia Silense*. Madrid: Consejo Superior de Investigaciones Científicas, 1959.

Picard, Christophe. *Le Portugal musulman, VIIIe–XIIIe siècle: L'Occident d'al-Andalus sous domination islamique siliqua*. Paris: Maisonneuve et Larose, 2000.

———. *Sea of the Caliphs: The Mediterranean in the Medieval Islamic World*. Cambridge, MA: Belknap Press, 2018.

Robinson, Cynthia. *Medieval Andalusian Courtly Culture in the Mediterranean: Hadith Bayad wa-Riyadh.* New York: Routledge, 2007.

Safran, Janina M. *The Second Umayyad Caliphate: The Articulation of Caliphal Legitimacy in Al-Andalus.* Cambridge: Harvard University Press, 2000.

Salicrú i Lluch, Roser. "Crossing Boundaries in Late Medieval Mediterranean Iberia: Historical Glimpses of Christian-Islamic Intercultural Dialogue." *International Journal of Euro-Mediterranean Studies* 1 (2008): 33–51.

———. "The Catalano-Aragonese Commercial Presence in the Sultanate of Granada During the Reign of Alfonso the Magnanimous." *Journal of Medieval History* 27 (2001): 289–312.

Seco de Lucena Paredes, Luis, and Aḥmad ibn ʿAlī Qalqashandī. "Un tradado árabe del siglo XV sobre España extraido del 'Subh Al-aʿsá' de al Qalqasandí por Luis Seco de Lucena Paredes." *Boletín de la Universidad de Granada* 14 (1942): 87–161.

Smith, Colin. *Christians and Moors in Spain.* 3 vols. Warminster, UK: Aris & Phillips, 1988.

Sobh, Mahmud. "ʿAbd al-Raḥmān I, el Inmigrado." *Revista del Instituto Egipcio de Estudios Islámicos* 38 (2010): 31–46.

Soyer, François. "'It Is Not Possible to Be Both a Jew and a Christian': Converso Religious Identity and the Inquisitorial Trial of Custodio Nunes (1604–5)." *Mediterranean Historical Review* 26 (2011): 81–97.

Szpiech, Ryan. "Granada." In *Europe: A Literary History, 1348–1418*, edited by David Wallace, 2: 154–169. New York: Oxford University Press, 2016.

Tibi, Amin T. *The Tibyān: Memoirs of ʿAbd Allāh B. Buluggīn, Last Zīrid Amīr of Granada.* Leiden: Brill, 1986.

Vallvé Bermejo, Joaquín. "Abd ar-Rahmān II, emir de al-Andalus: Datos para una biografía." *Boletín de la Real Academia de la Historia* 188 (1991): 209–250.

———. "La primera década del reinado de al-Ḥakam I (796–806), según el Muqtabis de Ben Ḥayyān." *Anaquel de Estudios Árabes* 12 (2001): 769–78.

Verlinden, Charles. "Les Radaniya et Verdun à propos de la traite des esclaves Slaves vers l'Espagne musulmane aux 9e et 10e siècles." In *Estudios en homenaje a Don Claudio Sanchez Albornoz en sus 90 años*, edited by María del Carmen et al., 105–132. Buenos Aires: Instituto de historia de España, 1983.

Vidal Castro, Francisco. "Historia politica, en el reino Nazaríde Granada (1232–1492)." In *Historia de España Menéndez Pidal: Política, instituciones, espacio y economía*, edited by María Jesús Viguera Molíns, 3: 47–208. Madrid: Espasa-Calpe, 2000.

Viguera Molíns, María Jesús. *Los reinos de taifas y las invasiones magrebíes: al-Andalus del XI al XIII*. Madrid: Mapfre, 1992.

———. "La Taifa de Toledo." In *Entre el califato y la taifa: Mil años del Cristo de la Luz*. Toledo: Asociación de Amigos del Toledo Islámico, 2000.

Wasserstein, David. *The Rise and Fall of the Party-Kings: Politics and Society in Islamic Spain 1002–1086*. Princeton, NJ: Princeton University Press, 1985.

Wiegers, Gerard Albert. *Islamic Literature in Spanish and Aljamiado: Yça of Segovia (fl. 1450), His Antecedents and Successors*. Leiden: Brill, 1994.

Wilson, Katharina M. *Hrotsvit of Gandersheim: A Florilegium of Her Works*. Woodbridge, UK: D. S. Brewer, 1998.

Wolf, Kenneth Baxter. *Conquerors and Chroniclers of Early Medieval Spain*. Liverpool: Liverpool University Press, 1999.

INDEX

459

ABOUT THE AUTHOR

Brian A. Catlos is a professor of religious studies at the University of Colorado Boulder and research associate in humanities at the University of California Santa Cruz. He is the author of numerous books on the medieval Mediterranean, including *The Victors and the Vanquished*, winner of the Premio del Rey Award and cowinner of the John E. Fagg Prize; *The Muslims of Medieval Latin Christendom*, winner of the Albert Hourani Book Prize; and *Infidel Kings and Unholy Warriors*, which received honorable mention in the PROSE Awards. Catlos received his PhD from the University of Toronto and lives in Boulder, Colorado, and Barcelona, Spain.